Mary Shelley

COLLECTED TALES
AND STORIES

MARY SHELLEY
Miniature by Reginald Easton

Mary Shelley

COLLECTED TALES
AND STORIES

WITH ORIGINAL
ENGRAVINGS

Edited, with an Introduction and Notes, by
CHARLES E. ROBINSON

THE JOHNS HOPKINS UNIVERSITY PRESS

BALTIMORE AND LONDON

FOR MOTHER AND DAD

CONTENTS

PLATES

❧

ACKNOWLEDGMENTS

IN PREPARING this edition of Mary Shelley's stories I have been assisted in numerous ways by many colleagues, correspondents, and associates: Lord Abinger, Carolyn J. Adams, Louis A. Arena, Horst Arndt, Alistair J. Arnott, Lori Baker, George Basalla, Betty T. Bennett, Thomas W. Blanding, Kenneth G. Brooks, Sharon L. Brown, Teri Cain, Theresa A. Czajkowska, Rodney G. Dennis, Gwen Florio, Paula R. Feldman, Philip D. Flynn, Nancy Middleton Gallienne, Mrs. C. M. Gee, W. G. Harris, Hubert Heinsberg, Walter E. Houghton, William H. Lyles, William R. Maidment, J. H. Manners, Aleta A. Mason, Karen McGuire, Sam Moskowitz, Ernest J. Moyne, Dennis S. Porter, Donald H. Reiman, Frank P. Riga, Joyce Sage, William P. Sisler, Cornelia Starks, Marion Kingston Stocking, Robert H. Taylor, Robert Lee Wolff, Katherine M. Wood, and Robert Zaetta. Mary Shelley would have been gratified at being served by such a number of individuals. I am indebted to them for many particulars of this edition, from the manuscript of a story to the spelling of a word.

I especially thank Sharon L. Brown, a student who assisted me in all of the editorial labors; Professor Betty T. Bennett, a Mary Shelley editor who answered my innumerable questions and graciously provided me with her discovery of the previously unknown story, "The Smuggler and His Family"; and Professor Donald H. Reiman, a scholar committed to sharing information with his colleagues.

I am also indebted to Lord Abinger for permission to publish from manuscript "Valerius: The Reanimated Roman" and "An Eighteenth-Century Tale: A Fragment"; to Duke University Library for providing me microfilms of the Abinger papers; to Professor Kenneth G. Brooks and the Keats House, London, for permission to publish from manuscript "The Heir of Mondolfo"; to The Carl and Lily Pforzheimer Foundation, Inc., for permission to publish excerpts from the manuscripts of "The Trial of Love" and "The Dream"; to Robert H. Taylor for permission to publish excerpts from the manuscript of "Angeline"; to The Houghton Library, Harvard University, for permission to publish excerpts from the manuscripts of "The Mortal Immortal," "The Parvenue," and "Euphrasia"; to the Bodleian Library, Oxford, for permission to reproduce the miniature of Mary Shelley for the frontispiece; and to the National Portrait Gallery (London) for the use of the portrait on the jacket of this edition.

I finally thank Peggy, Clare, and John for their patience with me and with Mary Shelley during the past year.

Newark, Delaware   C. E. R.

IN AN INTRODUCTION to an edition of Mary Shelley's *Tales and Stories* in 1891, Richard Garnett observed that "in these little tales [Mary Shelley] is her perfect self, and the reader will find not only the entertainment of interesting fiction, but a fair picture of the mind . . . of a lonely, thwarted, misunderstood woman, who could seldom do herself justice, and whose precise place in the contemporary constellation of genius remains to be determined."[1] But Garnett's appeal for an understanding of and appreciation for her short fiction was in vain, and her "precise place" in literary history is still undetermined. She was born in 1797, died in 1851, and is remembered primarily as the daughter of William Godwin and Mary Wollstonecraft, the wife and widow of the poet Percy Bysshe Shelley, and the author of *Frankenstein*. But the notoriety Mary Shelley has gained because of her parents, her husband, and her science fiction novel has been at the expense of her literary reputation. Relatively few readers of *Frankenstein* realize that the author also published five other novels (*Valperga: or, The Life and Adventures of Castruccio, Prince of Lucca* in 1823; *The Last Man* in 1826; *The Fortunes of Perkin Warbeck* in 1830; *Lodore* in 1835; *Falkner* in 1837) and that she wrote one novella (*Mathilda*, first published in 1959), more than two dozen tales and stories, over half that number of reviews and essays (some not yet identified), books of travel (including the very well received *Rambles in Germany and Italy, in 1840, 1842, and 1843*), two mythological dramas (*Proserpine* and *Midas*), and five volumes of *Lives* of Italian, Spanish, Portuguese, and French writers in Lardner's *Cabinet Cyclopedia*. In addition to publishing some of her own translations and poetry, she also edited and wrote extensive notes for her husband's works.[2]

1. *Tales and Stories by Mary Wollstonecraft Shelley*—Now First Collected, with an Introduction by Richard Garnett (London: William Paterson & Co., 1891), p. xi.
2. For a detailed bibliography of these works, see Jean de Palacio, *Mary Shelley*

Despite all of this literary labor, Mary Shelley's works, with the exception of *Frankenstein*, are virtually inaccessible today. *The Last Man*, edited in 1965 by Hugh J. Luke, Jr., for the University of Nebraska Press, is still available, and a few of her short stories are occasionally reprinted in volumes of Gothic tales or science fiction. In effect, the 1891 edition of *Tales and Stories* was the first and last serious attempt to present a "collected" edition of her works. This edition is incomplete and textually imperfect, and its recent reprinting by the Gregg Press in a science fiction series (1975) has only compounded the misrepresentation of Mary Shelley. All of this neglect is the more surprising because since 1886 there have been twelve book-length biographical and critical studies on the author of *Frankenstein*.[3] In addition to the still more numerous articles and chapters on her, she often figures in books on Byron, Shelley, Leigh Hunt, Thomas Moore, Edward Trelawny, Thomas Medwin, Washington Irving, Prosper Mérimée, and other less notable literary figures.

Many of Mary Shelley's past defenders have unwittingly contributed to her current neglect. They have acknowledged her genius in writing *Frankenstein* but then embarrassingly confessed the inferiority of her other work; or, at most, selected one or two other novels, stories, or essays by which to prove that her first novel was no mere accident. In the process of their praising with not so faint damns, these Mary Shelley apologists have criticized her for lacking a sense of humor, for failing to construct plots or develop characters properly, and for writing with no nobler purpose than providing for herself and her son Percy Florence between her widowhood in 1822 and her son's coming into the Shelley estate in 1844. Each of these criticisms is false, and the last two are based on a misunderstanding of the principles and the medium of her short fiction.

Most of Mary Shelley's short stories were published in *The Keepsake*, the most enduring (1828–57) and popular of the English literary Annuals, that species of nineteenth-century gift books containing poetry and prose fiction illustrated by engraved plates. *The Keepsake*, with its rivals *The Forget-Me-Not*, *The Literary Souvenir*, *Friendship's Offering*, *Heath's*

---

dans son œuvre: Contribution aux études shelleyennes (Paris: Klincksieck, 1969), pp. 647–96; and W. H. Lyles, *Mary Shelley: An Annotated Bibliography* (New York: Garland Publishing, 1975).

3. For the best of these, see Mrs. Julian Marshall, *The Life & Letters of Mary Wollstonecraft Shelley*, 2 vols. (London: Richard Bentley & Son, 1889); R. Glynn Grylls, *Mary Shelley: A Biography* (London: Oxford University Press, 1938); Muriel Spark, *Child of Light: A Reassessment of Mary Wollstonecraft Shelley* (Hadleigh, Essex: Tower Bridge Publications, 1951); Elizabeth Nitchie, *Mary Shelley: Author of "Frankenstein"* (New Brunswick: Rutgers University Press, 1953); Palacio, *Mary Shelley* (1969); and William A. Walling, *Mary Shelley* (New York: Twayne Publishers, 1972).

Book of Beauty, and other like titles, was elaborately designed, expensively priced, and usually published in November for Christmas, New Year's, and birthday giving. Because most of the poetry and some of the stories were sentimental, contrived, and second-rate, the Annuals were frequently criticized by the reviewers. Nevertheless, *The Keepsake,* like its more respected competitors, could sell as many as fifteen thousand copies within a few months. By popularizing the short narratives of writers now long forgotten, these Annuals (both in England and in America) had no little effect on the development of the short story in the nineteenth century.[4] However, readers of Mary Shelley's fiction should not expect to discover the "short story" as it has been defined *after* these narratives were written. Some of her stories may more properly be called "tales," where a third-person narrator or first-person persona tells a story that describes character and action more than it employs dialogue in action. More interested in character than in compressed time or single action, she frequently takes the reader over a period of months or years within the space of a few pages.

At times, Mary Shelley felt the need for more space in her stories: for example, in "The Swiss Peasant," the persona is forced to "hurry over" one part of the story in "a few words"; in "The Invisible Girl," the narrator wanted "a good-sized volume to relate the causes" of the hero's grief; and in "The Trial of Love," the narrator offers two years' exposition in "the briefest possible way"—what amounts to three paragraphs. Such self-conscious expressions violate the objective point of view that has become for some a standard for modern short stories; but Mary Shelley should no more be faulted for her direct address to the reader than Percy Shelley should be for failing to write poetry according to the standards of the imagist poets of the twentieth century. As Shelley told us, "the deep truth is imageless"; his widow is merely telling us that some of her narratives required more space than her editors allowed. She made the same point in a letter to her friend Maria Gisborne, who had sent her a story in hopes that it would be published. In reply, Mary Shelley explained that it was too long for the Annuals: "When I write for them, I am worried to death to make my things shorter and shorter—till I fancy people think ideas can be

4. For more information on the phenomenon of the English Annuals, consult Chas. T. Tallent-Bateman, "The 'Forget-Me-Not,'" *Manchester Quarterly: A Journal of Literature and Art* 21 (1902): 78–98; Frederick W. Faxon, *Literary Annuals and Gift Books: A Bibliography, 1823–1903* (1912; rpt., with supplementary essays by Eleanore Jamieson and Iain Bain, Private Libraries Association, 1973); Bradford Booth's introduction to *A Cabinet of Gems: Short Stories from the English Annuals* (Berkeley, Calif.: University of California Press, 1938), pp. 1–19; Anne Renier, *Friendship's Offering: An Essay on the Annuals and Gift Books of the 19th Century* (London: Private Libraries Association, 1964); and Andrew Boyle, *An Index to the Annuals (1820–1850): The Authors* (Worcester: Andrew Boyle [Booksellers], 1967).

conveyed by intuition—and that it is a superstition to consider words necessary for their expression."[5]

Despite Mary Shelley's complaint about making her pieces shorter, the shorter stories and tales in this volume are the better ones. Even before she began to write for the Annuals, she was forced to discipline her narratives while writing essays for the *London Magazine* and the *New Monthly Magazine*. As T. O. Beachcroft has observed, the early-nineteenth-century essay contributed as much as the Annuals to the development of the modern short story. That is, the essay began "drifting away from its painstakingly expository purpose" and again began depicting character and incident in a single episode.[6] Beachcroft cites Charles Lamb and Leigh Hunt as essayists in this mode, a mode represented by two of Mary's narrative essays in this volume: "Recollections of Italy" (published in *London Magazine* in 1824) and "Roger Dodsworth: The Reanimated Englishman" (submitted to the *New Monthly Magazine* in 1826). Both offer short narratives with graphic incident, realistic dialogue, and an ironic point of view. In fact, both demonstrate a playful sense of humor that has mistakenly been overlooked in Mary Shelley's works. This sense of humor is also manifested in the gentle satire of two of her shortest stories, "The Bride of Modern Italy" (published in *London Magazine* in 1824) and "The False Rhyme" (published in *The Keepsake* for 1830). These two stories and the two narrative essays reveal that the author could effectively discipline her art to restrictions of length and, in the process, anticipate the later development of the short story.

Some of Mary Shelley's narratives, however, like "The Heir of Mondolfo" and "The Pilgrims," are longer and more diffusely plotted than the characters, incidents, and themes warrant. Others are prolonged by the author's predilection for an ornate and circumlocutious diction and syntax in her stories, especially in descriptive passages. Even in *Frankenstein*, we find the monster's studied language a little surprising: recounting his experiences with an old shepherd, the monster explained, " 'He turned on hearing a noise; and, perceiving me, shrieked loudly, and, quitting the hut, ran across the fields *with a speed of which his debilitated form hardly appeared capable.*' "[7] Such remnants of eighteenth-century formalized diction and syntax suggest that Mary Shelley should be viewed as a transitional writer in the development of the style as well as the form of the short story.

As a writer of tales and stories, Mary Shelley surpassed many of her

5. Letter of 11 June 1835, *The Letters of Mary W. Shelley*, ed. Frederick L. Jones (Norman: University of Oklahoma Press, 1944), II: 97—hereafter cited as *MSL*.
6. T. O. Beachcroft, *The Modest Art: A Survey of the Short Story in English* (London: Oxford University Press, 1968), p. 86.
7. *Frankenstein; or, The Modern Prometheus* (*The 1818 Text*), ed. James Rieger (New York: The Bobbs-Merrill Company, 1974), p. 100, my italics.

predecessors and contemporaries, because she avoided the explicit moralizing found in so many narratives in the late eighteenth and early nineteenth centuries. With the exception of "The Sisters of Albano," her short fiction successfully subordinates moral to theme and character. Like her husband, she disliked overtly didactic literature and preferred to familiarize her readers with beautiful idealisms of moral excellence (or, conversely, to teach the human heart by showing the effects of moral weakness). As she explained in a letter written shortly after her husband's death on July 8, 1822, "I shall be happy if any thing I ever produce may exalt & soften sorrow, as the writings of the divinities of our race have mine. But how can I aspire to that?"[8] She did in fact aspire to comfort her readers, and in doing so she idealized or, we might say, exaggerated the human condition. Her heroes and heroines are sometimes writ larger than life, but they never falsify the human experience. As she herself explained in "The English in Italy," one of her review essays, "a fiction must contain no glaring improbability, and yet it must never divest itself of a certain idealism, which forms its chief beauty."[9]

Mary Shelley would frequently idealize the circumstances of her narratives by a historical or Continental setting that removed her characters from the dull and sometimes painful realities of contemporary English life. Less than one-fourth of her stories are set in England; and only one of these, "The Parvenue," realistically details the social plight of a young English woman torn between responsibilities to a rich husband and to her poor family. More characteristic are tales of passionate love and hate set in medieval Italy, sixteenth-century France, or contemporary Europe. In four of these stories, Mary Shelley uses a fantastic element to idealize her narratives even further. The Roman Valerius and the seventeenth-century Roger Dodsworth were both reanimated into contemporary life; the Mortal Immortal had attained the age of 323 when he narrated his tale; and in "Transformation," the hero and a misshapen dwarf exchange bodies. Yet in each of these cases, she subordinates the science-fictional element to a study in character that is designed to "exalt & soften" human sorrow.

It is also possible to read Mary Shelley's fictions as idealizations of her own life. Many of her heroines are orphans or at least alienated from one or both parents; "The Parvenue" details a number of circumstances similar to her own; and Percy Shelley is figured as a nameless "lost friend" in "Recollections of Italy," as Horace Neville in "The Mourner," and as Marcott Alleyn in "The Bride of Modern Italy." In the last of these stories, she parodies her husband's "Platonic" relationship with Emilia Viviani in 1821. Yet here and elsewhere, she has transformed personal experience into art, in accordance with the principle she explained while reviewing her father's

8. Letter to Maria Gisborne, c. 27 August 1822 (*MSL*, I: 189).
9. *Westminster Review* 6 (October 1826): 339.

novel *Cloudesley*: "the merely copying from our own hearts will no more
form a first-rate work of art, than will the most exquisite representation of
mountains, water, wood, and glorious clouds, form a good painting, if none
of the rules of grouping or colouring are followed."[10]

Her parallel between painting and literature is somewhat ironic, in that
her narrative "rules of grouping and colouring" were sometimes violated
because of a painting that was to be engraved for the Annuals, where sixteen of her stories were published. The editors of these gift books, rather
than choosing a painting that would illustrate an already accepted story,
frequently selected the painting first and then commissioned an author to
write or rewrite a narrative to "embellish" the engraving. Such a procedure
is evident in several of her stories. In "The Dream," a structurally important scene in a gloomy setting had to be rewritten to accommodate a
painting of the heroine in a lovely bower. In "The Brother and Sister," the
name of the heroine was changed from "Angeline" to "Flora" in order to
match the title of the engraved plate. In both cases, a comparison of the
fair-copy manuscript and the printed version reveals substantial revision
that partially obscures the principles of her narrative art. A third manuscript, that of "The Parvenue," suggests that she was commissioned to
write a story that would refer to Margate, a seaside resort; and that she
incorporated a specific description of the plate into her narrative *after* the
fair-copy manuscript was completed. In some cases, the plates are only
incidentally related to the narratives, most artificially in "The Sisters of
Albano," where the narrator describes the visual details of the engraving,
suggests that " 'one might easily make out a story' " for the hunter and
contadina depicted there, but then narrates an entirely different story told
her by a companion. She probably added the description of the plate to a
narrative that she had already written. On the other hand, the narrative of
"The False Rhyme" efficiently and imaginatively complements the accompanying plate. In this case, she obviously used R. P. Bonington's painting
of "Francis the First & His Sister" as the basis for her tale.

Because these plates are essential for our understanding of the constraints
placed upon Mary Shelley's art, they are reproduced in this edition. Most of
them are from *The Keepsake*, wherein were published at least fifteen of her
stories between 1828 and 1839. Three of these plates (two entitled *Virginia
Water* for "The Mourner" and one entitled *Lake Albano* for "The Sisters
of Albano") were engraved by Robert Wallis from drawings by J. M. W.
Turner. Two other stories were also published with plates, "The Elder
Son" in another Annual, *Heath's Book of Beauty* (1835), and "The Smuggler and His Family" in *Original Compositions in Prose and Verse* (1833).
Of the remaining eight stories that were published without plates, "A Tale

10. *Blackwood's Edinburgh Magazine* 27 (May 1830): 712.

of the Passions" appeared in *The Liberal* (1823), and "Recollections of Italy" and "The Bride of Modern Italy" in *London Magazine* (1824); "The Pole," Claire Clairmont's story for which Mary Shelley wrote the conclusion, was first published in *The Court Magazine, and Belle Assemblée* (1832); "Roger Dodsworth" was submitted in 1826 to the *New Monthly Magazine* but was not printed until 1863, in a volume of Cyrus Redding's literary reminiscences; another posthumously published story, "The Heir of Mondolfo," first appeared in *Appleton's Journal* in 1877 and has been re-edited from Mary Shelley's manuscript for this edition; and "Valerius: The Reanimated Roman" and "An Eighteenth-Century Tale: A Fragment" are here published for the first time from manuscript.

Of the twenty-five stories in this volume, only seventeen were in the Garnett edition of 1891. Here collected for the first time are "Recollections of Italy," "The Bride of Modern Italy," "Roger Dodsworth: The Reanimated Englishman," "The Smuggler and His Family," "The Trial of Love," "The Heir of Mondolfo," "Valerius: The Reanimated Roman," and "An Eighteenth-Century Tale: A Fragment." For all but the last three, which have been edited from manuscript, the text for this edition is based on the first published version of each story. There are also extant fair-copy manuscripts for "The Dream," "The Brother and Sister," "The Mortal Immortal," "The Trial of Love," "The Parvenue," and "Euphrasia," but because Mary Shelley revised her stories in proof,[11] the first printed text has been preferred to the manuscript, which she viewed as a means to an end. That is, the fair-copy manuscripts, even though submitted in some cases less than four months before publication in *The Keepsake*, were deficient in spelling, tense, number, and especially punctuation—with the dash frequently used in place of comma, colon, semicolon, and period. In proof, she would not only supply or approve of the new punctuation but also revise to make her prose less wordy and more precise. She eliminated such clauses as "so that, according to the common phrase, a pin might have been heard drop"; she changed such phrases as "stuffed full of good qualities" to "overflowing with good qualities," "worn out" to "exhausted," and "being unchanged" to "constancy"; and she rewrote sentences and added or deleted modifiers to make her prose more graceful. Such alterations are not identified in the textual notes supplied for each story at the end of this volume. However, the reader may inspect passages from her manuscripts in the textual notes to "The Dream" and "The Brother and Sister," in which the substantial differences between manuscript and printed text are recorded.

Readers are also urged to inspect the notes for the following information: critical remarks on each story; location of extant manuscript; bibliographical

---

11. For evidence of this, see her letter to Frederic Mansel Reynolds, editor of *The Keepsake*, on 2 August 1832 (*MSL*, II: 62–63).

listing of the story's first and subsequent printings; identification of copy-text (the basis for the text in this edition); and textual notes recording emendations to the copy-text. This critical apparatus should interest the layman, satisfy most of the demands of the scholar, and remedy some of the injustice done to Mary Shelley, particularly by the 1891 edition of *Tales and Stories*, in which words, phrases, sentences, and even whole paragraphs were silently omitted from the original stories. In order to restore and ensure an integrity to the texts of her stories, the present editor has recorded all of his emendations to the previously printed copy-texts in the notes. And to avoid confusion with her occasional footnote to a story, he has identified his few footnotes with an (Ed.).

The present editor has enjoyed his Mary Shelley labors, particularly the literary sleuthing by which the bibliography for each story was compiled. Some entries were discovered by looking at suspicious volumes on library shelves; others by winding through fifty-eight reels of American literary Annuals on microfilm. Knowing, however, that some citations must have escaped him, he would welcome any additions to these bibliographies. He would also welcome any additions to the canon of Mary Shelley's short fiction: "Roger Dodsworth" was accidentally discovered by him less than three years ago; "The Smuggler and His Family" was more recently dis-covered by Professor Betty Bennett, with the help of Blackwell's; and other stories (and essays) still lurk between the yellowing pages of nineteenth-century journals and literary Annuals. He invites any literary sleuthing on her behalf and lists the following possible leads: "Rome in the First and Nineteenth Centuries" in the *New Monthly Magazine* (March 1824); unsigned stories in the *Forget-Me-Not* for 1827 and *The Literary Souvenir* for 1828; "The Convent of Chaillot: or, Vallière and Louis XIV" in *The Keepsake* for 1828; "The Silver Lady" in *The Keepsake* for 1838; and "The Ghost of Private Theatricals" in *The Keepsake for 1844*. The evidence by which this list is compiled is too complex to detail here, and possibly none or all of these narratives were written by Mary Shelley.[12] This editor, how-

---

12. Two of her works have never been located: "Hate," perhaps a story, which she began in September 1814 (see *Mary Shelley's Journal*, ed. Frederick L. Jones [Norman: University of Oklahoma Press, 1947], p. 14); and a "tale of 'Maurice'" which she sent to her father in 1821 (see William Godwin's letter to Mary, 10 October 1821, printed in *Shelley and Mary* [For Private Circulation Only, 1882], III: 698C–98D). This latter tale may have been the child's "story for Laurette" Mason that she wrote in August 1820 (see *Journal*, p. 136) or the same one she submitted to Leigh Hunt's *Indicator* in 1821 (see *Shelley and Mary*, III: 652). Also there may have been one or two more of her stories that were rejected by the *London Magazine*: James Hessey, writing to John Taylor on 20 October 1824, com-plained that "Mrs. Shelley's Story won't do" (quoted by Edmund Blunden, *Keats's Publisher: A Memoir of John Taylor* [London: Jonathan Cape, 1940], p. 145). This rejection may have been the one cryptically referred to in "The Lion's Head" (where the editors addressed the contributors) in the *London Magazine* 10 (December 1824): 559: "If M. S. should chance to see our present Number (and what con-

ever, has been unable to resolve his own doubts about these titles, and any
future pursuer of Mary Shelley's stories should expect the same frustrations
experienced by Victor Frankenstein while tracking his elusive monster. In
the words of that monster, who "left marks in writing on the barks of the
trees, or cut in stone" in order to keep Victor from forsaking his quest,
" 'many hard and miserable hours must you endure, until that period shall
arrive' "[13] when the pursuer meets the pursued.

---

tributor does not look at the next Number?)—she will see that we are compelled to
refuse her MS. So the one MS may be had by the other if it be desired. This mode of
reply will save us the writing to W——, and M. S. the postage." If this directive was
for Mary Shelley, the story may have been saved for later publication elsewhere.

There are also in manuscript four other fictional prose narratives that need mention
here. "Cecil," an unfinished 31-page manuscript in the Bodleian Library, is a child's
story with two chapter designations ("I—The Boy" and "II—The Youth") and
seems, therefore, to have been destined for at least a novella-length tale; but it may
have been an earlier or later version of "Maurice" or the "story for Laurette." Two
chapters ("VIII—Again Don Juan" and "IX—A step backward") of an unfinished
and untitled novel are in Lord Abinger's collection. Also in Lord Abinger's collection
is an unfinished 13-page manuscript, entitled "The Caravanserail; or, A Collection of
Eastern Stories," consisting of an introductory frame and "Tale I—Abdelazi; or, The
New Sleeper awakened." This fair-copy manuscript appears to be a transcription by
someone other than Mary Shelley, and it is therefore impossible, without other
evidence, to determine if she was the author. Finally, in the Library of Congress
is one of Percy Shelley's notebooks that contains her prose translation of Apuleius's
story of Cupid and Psyche.

13. *Frankenstein*, p. 202.

Mary Shelley

COLLECTED TALES
AND STORIES

I

❦

A Tale of the Passions

AFTER THE DEATH of Manfred, King of Naples, the Ghibellines lost their ascendency throughout Italy. The exiled Guelphs returned to their native cities; and not contented with resuming the reins of government, they prosecuted their triumph until the Ghibellines in their turn were obliged to fly, and to mourn in banishment over the violent party spirit which had before occasioned their bloody victories, and now their irretrievable defeat. After an obstinate contest the Florentine Ghibellines were forced to quit their native town; their estates were confiscated; their attempts to reinstate themselves frustrated; and receding from castle to castle, they at length took refuge in Lucca, and awaited with impatience the arrival of Corradino from Germany, through whose influence they hoped again to establish the Imperial supremacy.

The first of May was ever a day of rejoicing and festivity at Florence. The youth of both sexes, of the highest rank, paraded the streets, crowned with flowers, and singing the canzonets of the day. In the evening they assembled in the *Piazza del Duomo*, and spent the hours in dancing. The *Carroccio* was led through the principal streets, the ringing of its bell drowned in the peals that rang from every belfry in the city, and in the music of fifes and drums which made a part of the procession that followed it. The triumph of the reigning party in Florence caused them to celebrate the anniversary of the first of May, 1268, with peculiar splendour. They had indeed hoped that Charles d'Anjou, King of Naples, the head of the Guelphs in Italy, and then *Vicare* of their republic, would have been there to adorn the festival by his presence. But the expectation of Corradino had caused the greater part of his newly conquered and oppressed kingdom to revolt, and he had hastily quitted Tuscany to secure by his presence those conquests of which his avarice and cruelty endangered the loss. But although Charles somewhat feared the approaching contest with Corradino, the Florentine Guelphs, newly rein-

1

stated in their city and possessions, did not permit a fear to cloud their triumph. The principal families vied with each other in the display of their magnificence during the festival. The knights followed the *Carroccio* on horseback, and the windows were filled with ladies who leant upon gold-inwoven carpets, while their own dresses, at once simple and elegant, their only ornaments flowers, contrasted with the glittering tapestry and the brilliant colours of the flags of the various communities. The whole population of Florence poured into the principal streets, and none were left at home, except the decrepid and sick, unless it were some discontented Ghibelline, whose fear, poverty, or avarice, had caused him to conceal his party, when it had been banished from the city.

It was not the feeling of discontent which prevented Monna Gegia de' Becari from being among the first of the revellers; and she looked angrily on what she called her "Ghibelline leg," which fixed her to her chair on such a day of triumph. The sun shone in all its glory in an unclouded sky, and caused the fair Florentines to draw their *fazioles* over their dark eyes, and to bereave the youth of those beams more vivifying than the sun's rays. The same sun poured its full light into the lonely apartment of Monna Gegia, and almost extinguished the fire which was lighted in the middle of the room, over which hung the pot of *minestra*, the dinner of the dame and her husband. But she had deserted the fire and was seated by her window, holding her beads in her hand, while every now and then she peeped from her lattice (five stories high) into the narrow lane below,—but no creature passed. She looked at the opposite window; a cat slept there beside a pot of heliotrope, but no human being was heard or seen;—they had all gone to the *Piazza del Duomo*.

Monna Gegia was an old woman, and her dress of green *coloratio* shewed that she belonged to one of the *Arti Minori*. Her head was covered by a red kerchief, which, folded triangularly, hung loosely over it; her grey hairs were combed back from her high and wrinkled brow. The quickness of her eye spoke the activity of her mind, and the slight irritability that lingered about the corners of her lips might be occasioned by the continual war maintained between her bodily and mental faculties. —"Now, by St. John!" she said, "I would give my gold cross to make one of them; though by giving that I should appear on a *festa* without that which no *festa* yet ever found me wanting."—And as she spoke she looked with great complacency on a large but thin gold cross which was tied round her withered neck by a ribbon, once black, now of a rusty brown.—"Methinks this leg of mine is bewitched; and it may well be that my Ghibelline husband has used the black art to hinder me from following the *Carroccio* with the best of them."—A slight sound as of footsteps in the street far below interrupted the good woman's soliloquy.—"Perhaps it is Monna Lisabetta, or Messer Giani dei Agli, the weaver, who mounted the breach first when the castle of Pagibonzi was taken."—She looked down, but could see no one, and was about to relapse into her old train of thoughts, when her attention was again attracted by the sound of steps ascending the stairs: they were slow and heavy, but she did not doubt who her visitant was when a key was applied to the hole of the door; the latch was lifted up, and a moment after, with an unassured mien and downcast eyes, her husband entered.

He was a short stunted man, more than sixty years of age; his shoulders were broad and high; his legs short; his lank hair, though it grew now only on the back of his head, was still coal-black; his brows were overhanging and bushy; his eyes black and quick; his complexion dark and weather-beaten; his lips as it were contradicted the sternness of the upper part of his face, for their gentle curve betokened even delicacy of sentiment, and his smile was inexpressibly sweet, although a short, bushy, grey beard somewhat spoiled the expression of his countenance. His dress consisted of leather trowsers and a kind of short, coarse, cloth tunic, confined at the waist by a leathern girdle. He had on a low-crowned, red, cloth cap, which he drew over his eyes, and seating himself on a low bench by the fire, he heaved a deep sigh. He appeared disinclined to enter into any conversation, but Monna Gegia, looking on him with a smile of ineffable contempt, was resolved that he should not enjoy his melancholy mood uninterrupted.—"Have you been to mass, Cincolo?"—she asked; beginning by a question sufficiently removed from the point she longed to approach.—He shrugged his shoulders uneasily, but did not reply. —"You are too early for your dinner," continued Gegia; "Do you not go out again?"—Cincolo answered, "No!" in an accent that denoted his disinclination to further questioning. But this very impatience only served to feed the spirit of contention that was fermenting in the bosom of Gegia.—"You are not used," she said, "to pass your May days under your chimney."—No answer.—"Well," she continued, "if you will not speak, I have done!"—meaning that she intended to begin—"but by that lengthened face of thine I see that some good news is stirring abroad, and I bless the Virgin for it, whatever it may be. Come, if thou be not too curst, tell me what happy tidings make thee so woe-begone."—

Cincolo remained silent for awhile, then turning half round but not looking at his wife, he replied,—"What if old Marzio the lion be dead?" —Gegia turned pale at the idea, but a smile that lurked in the good-natured mouth of her husband reassured her. "Nay, St. John defend us!" she began;—"but that is not true. Old Marzio's death would not drive you within these four walls, except it were to triumph over your old wife. By the blessing of St. John, not one of our lions has died since the eve of the battle of Monte Aperto; and I doubt not that they were poisoned; for Mari, who fed them that night, was more than half a Ghibelline in his heart. Besides, the bells are still ringing, and the drums still beating, and all would be silent enough if old Marzio were to die. On the first of May too! Santa Reparata is too good to us to allow such ill luck;—and she has more favour, I trust, in the seventh heaven than all the Ghibelline saints in your calendar. No, good Cincolo, Marzio is not dead, nor the Holy Father, nor Messer Carlo of Naples; but I would bet my gold cross against the wealth of your banished men, that Pisa is taken—or Corradino—or—"—"And I here! No, Gegia, old as I am, and much as you need my help (and that last is why I am here at all) Pisa would not be taken while this old body could stand in the breach; or Corradino die, till this lazy blood were colder on the ground than it is in my body. Ask no more questions, and do not rouse me: there is no news, no good or ill luck, that I know. But when I saw the Neri, the Pulci, the Buondelmonti, and the rest of them, ride like kings through the streets, whose very hands are hardly dry from the blood of my kindred; when I saw their daughter crowned with flowers, and thought how the daughter of Arrigo dei Elisei was mourning for her murdered father, with ashes on her head, by the hearth of a stranger—my spirit must be more dead than it is if such a sight did not make me wish to drive among them; and methought I could scatter their pomp with my awl for a sword. But I remembered thee, and am here unstained with blood."

"That thou wilt never be!" cried Monna Gegia, the colour rising in her wrinkled cheeks:—"Since the battle of Monte Aperto, thou hast never been well washed of that shed by thee and thy confederates;—and how could ye? for the Arno has never since run clear of the blood then spilt."—"And if the sea were red with that blood, still while there is any of the Guelphs' to spill, I am ready to spill it, were it not for thee. Thou dost well to mention Monte Aperto, and thou wouldst do better to re-member over whom its grass now grows."—"Peace, Cincolo; a mother's heart has more memory in it than thou thinkest; and I well recollect who spurned me as I knelt, and dragged my only child, but sixteen years of age, to die in the cause of that misbeliever Manfred. Let us indeed speak no more. Woe was the day when I married thee! but those were happy times when there was neither Guelph nor Ghibelline;—they will never return."—"Never,—until, as thou sayest, the Arno run clear of the blood shed on its banks;—never while I can pierce the heart of a Guelph;— never till both parties are cold under one bier."—"And thou and I, Cincolo?—" "Are two old fools, and shall be more at peace under ground than above it. Rank Guelph as thou art, I married thee before I was a Ghibelline; so now I must eat from the same platter with the enemy of Manfred, and make shoes for Guelphs, instead of following the for-tunes of Corradino, and sending them, my battle-axe in my hand, to buy their shoes in Bologna."—"Hush! hush! good man, talk not so loud of thy party; hearest thou not that some one knocks?"—

Cincolo went to open the door with the air of a man who thinks himself ill used at being interrupted in his discourse, and is disposed to be angry with the intruder, however innocent he might be of any intention of breaking in upon his eloquent complaint. The appearance of his visitor calmed his indignant feelings. He was a youth whose countenance and person shewed that he could not be more than sixteen, but there was a self-possession in his demeanour and a dignity in his physiognomy that belonged to a more advanced age. His figure though not tall was slight; and his countenance though of wonderful beauty and regularity of feature, was pale as monumental marble; the thick and curling locks of his chestnut hair clustered over his brow and round his fair throat; his cap was drawn far down on his forehead. Cincolo was about to usher him with deference into his humble room, but the youth staid him with his hand, and uttered the words "Swabia, Cavalieri!" the words by which the Ghibellines were accustomed to recognize each other. He continued in a low and hurried tone: "Your wife is within?"—"She is."—"Enough; although I am a stranger to you, I come from an old friend. Harbour me until nightfall; we will then go out, and I will explain to you the motives of my intrusion. Call me Ricciardo de' Rossini of Milan, travelling to Rome. I leave Florence this evening."

Having said these words, without giving Cincolo time to reply, he motioned that they should enter the room. Monna Gegia had fixed her eyes on the door from the moment he had opened it with a look of impatient curiosity; when she saw the youth enter she could not refrain from exclaiming—"Gesu Maria!"—so different was he from any one she had expected to see.—"A friend from Milan," said Cincolo.—"More likely from Lucca," replied his wife, gazing on her visitant:—"You are doubtless one of the banished men, and you are more daring than wise to enter this town: however, if you be not a spy, you are safe with me." —Ricciardo smiled and thanked her in a low, sweet voice:—"If you do not turn me out," he said, "I shall remain under your roof nearly all the time I remain in Florence, and I leave it soon after dusk."

Gegia again gazed on her guest, nor did Cincolo scrutinize him with less curiosity. His black cloth tunic reached below his knees and was confined by a black leather girdle at the waist. He had on trowsers of coarse scarlet stuff, over which were drawn short boots, such as are now seen on the stage only: a cloak of common fox's fur, unlined, hung from his shoulder. But although his dress was thus simple, it was such as was then worn by the young Florentine nobility. At that time the Italians were simple in their private habits: the French army led by Charles d'Anjou into Italy first introduced luxury into the palaces of the Cisalpines. Manfred was a magnificent prince, but it was his saintly rival who was the author of that trifling foppery of dress and ornaments, which degrades a nation, and is a sure precursor of their downfall. But of Ricciardo—his countenance had all the regularity of a Grecian head; and his blue eyes, shaded by very long, dark eyelashes, were soft, yet full of expression: when he looked up, the heavy lids, as it were, unveiled the gentle light beneath, and then again closed over them, as shading what was too brilliant to behold. His lips expressed the deepest sensibility, and something perhaps of timidity, had not the placid confidence of his demeanour forbidden such an idea. His appearance was extraordinary, for he was young and delicate of frame, while the decision of his manner prevented the feeling of pity from arising in the spectator's mind: you might love him, but he rose above compassion.

His host and hostess were at first silent; but he asked some natural questions about the buildings of their city, and by degrees led them into discourse. When mid-day struck, Cincolo looked towards his pot of *minestra*, and Ricciardo following his look, asked if that was not the dinner. "You must entertain me," he said, "for I have not eaten to-day." A table was drawn near the window, and the *minestra* poured out into one plate was placed in the middle of it, a spoon was given to each, and a jug of wine filled from a barrel. Ricciardo looked at the two old people, and seemed somewhat to smile at the idea of eating from the same plate with them; he ate, however, though sparingly, and drank of the wine, though with still greater moderation. Cincolo, however, under pretence of serving his guest, filled his jug a second time, and was about to rise for the third measure, when Ricciardo, placing his small white hand on his arm, said, "Are you a German, my friend, that you cease not after so many draughts? I have heard that you Florentines were a sober people."

Cincolo was not much pleased with this reproof; but he felt that it was timely; so, conceding the point, he sat down again, and somewhat heated with what he had already drank, he asked his guest the news from Germany, and what hopes for the good cause? Monna Gegia bridled at these words, and Ricciardo replied, "Many reports are abroad, and high hopes entertained, especially in the North of Italy, for the success of our expedition. Corradino is arrived at Genoa, and it is hoped that, although the ranks of his army were much thinned by the desertion of his German troops, that they will be quickly filled by Italians, braver and truer than those foreigners, who, strangers to our soil, could not fight for his cause with our ardour."—"And how does he bear himself?"—"As beseems one of the house of Swabia, and the nephew of Manfred. He is inexperienced and young, even to childishness. He is not more than sixteen. His mother would hardly consent to this expedition, but wept with agony at the fear of all he might endure: for he has been bred in a palace, nursed in every luxury, and habituated to all the flattering attentions of courtiers, and the tender care of a woman, who, although she be a princess, has waited on him with the anxious solicitude of a cottager for her infant. But Corradino is of good heart; docile, but courageous; obedient to his wiser friends, gentle to his inferiors, but noble of soul. The spirit of Manfred seems to animate his unfolding mind; and surely, if that glorious prince now enjoys the reward of his surpassing virtues, he looks down with joy and approbation on him who is, I trust, destined to fill his throne."

The enthusiasm with which Ricciardo spoke suffused his pale countenance with a slight blush, while his eyes swam in the lustre of the dew that filled them. Monna Gegia was little pleased with his harangue, but curiosity kept her silent, while her husband proceeded to question his guest. "You seem to be well acquainted with Corradino?"—"I saw him at Milan, and was closely connected with his most intimate friend there. As I have said, he has arrived at Genoa, and perhaps has even now landed at Pisa: he will find many friends in that town?" "Every man there will be his friend. But during his journey southward he will have to contend with our Florentine army, commanded by the Marshals of the usurper Charles, and assisted by his troops. Charles himself has left us, and is gone to Naples to prepare for this war. But he is detested there, as a tyrant and a robber, and Corradino will be received in the Regno as a saviour: so that if he once surmount the obstacles which oppose his entrance, I do not doubt his success, and trust that he will be crowned within a month at Rome, and the week after sit on the throne of his ancestors in Naples."

"And who will crown him?" cried Gegia, unable to contain herself: "Italy contains no heretic base enough to do such a deed, unless it be a Jew; or he send to Constantinople for a Greek, or to Egypt for a Mahometan. Cursed may the race of the Frederics ever be! Thrice cursed one who has affinity to that miscreant Manfred! And little do you please me, young man, by holding such discourse in my house." Cincolo looked at Ricciardo, as if he feared that so violent a partisan for the house of Swabia would be irritated at his wife's attack; but he was looking on the aged woman with a regard of the most serene benignity; no contempt even was mingled with the gentle smile that played round his lips. "I will restrain myself," he said; and turning to Cincolo, he conversed on more general subjects, describing the various cities of Italy that he had visited; discussing their modes of government, and relating anecdotes concerning their inhabitants, with an air of experience that, contrasted with his youthful appearance, greatly impressed Cincolo, who looked on him at once with admiration and respect. Evening came on. The sound of bells died away after the *Ave Maria* had ceased to ring; but the distant sound of music was wafted to them by the night air, and its quick time indicated that the music was already begun. Ricciardo was about to address Cincolo, when a knocking at the gate interrupted him. It was Buzeccha, the Saracen, a famous chess-player, who was used to parade about under the colonnades of the Duomo, and challenge the young nobles to play; and sometimes much stress was laid on these games, and the gain and loss became the talk of Florence. Buzeccha was a tall ungainly man, with all that good-natured consequence of manner, which the fame he had acquired by his proficiency in so trifling a science, and the familiarity with which he was permitted to treat those superior to him in rank, who were pleased to measure their forces with him, might well bestow. He was beginning with, "Eh, Messere!" when perceiving Ricciardo, he cried, "Who have we here?" "A friend to good men," replied Ricciardo, smiling. "Then, by Mahomet, thou art my friend, my stripling." "Thou shouldst be a Saracen, by thy speech?" said Ricciardo. "And through the help of the Prophet, so am I. One who in Manfred's time——but no more of that. We won't talk of Manfred, eh, Monna Gegia? I am Buzeccha, the chess-player, at your service, Messer lo Forestiere."

The introduction thus made, they began to talk of the procession of the day. After a while, Buzeccha introduced his favourite subject of chess-playing; he recounted some wonderfully good strokes he had achieved, and related to Ricciardo how before the *Palagio del Popolo*, in the presence of Count Guido Novello de' Giudi, then *Vicare* of the city, he had played an hour at three chess-boards with three of the best chess-players in Florence, playing two by memory, and one by sight; and out of three games which made the board, he had won two. This account was wound up by a proposal to play with his host. "Thou art a hard-headed fellow, Cincolo, and make better play than the nobles. I would swear that thou thinkest of chess only as thou cobblest thy shoes; every hole of your awl is a square of the board, every stitch a move, and a finished pair, paid for, check-mate to your adversary; eh! Cincolo? Bring out the field of battle, man." Ricciardo interposed, "I leave Florence in two hours, and before I go, Messer Cincolo promised to conduct me to the *Piazza del Duomo*." "Plenty of time, good youth," cried Buzeccha, arranging his men; "I only claim one game, and my games never last more than a quarter of an hour; and then we will both escort you, and you shall dance a set into the bargain with a black-eyed Houri, all Nazarene as thou art. So stand out of my light, good youth, and shut the window, if you have heeding, that the torch flare not so."

Ricciardo seemed amused by the authoritative tone of the chess-player; he shut the window and trimmed the torch, which, stuck against the wall, was the only light they had, and stood by the table, over-looking the game. Monna Gegia had replaced the pot for supper, and sat somewhat uneasily, as if she were displeased that her guest did not talk with her. Cincolo and Buzeccha were deeply intent on their game, when a knock was heard at the door. Cincolo was about to rise and open it, but Ricciardo saying, "Do not disturb yourself," opened it himself, with the manner of one who does humble offices as if ennobling them, so that no one action can be more humble to them than another. The visitant was welcomed by Gegia alone, with "Ah! Messer Beppe, this is kind, on May-day night." Ricciardo glanced slightly on him, and then resumed his stand by the players. There was little in Messer Beppe to attract a favourable regard. He was short, thin, and dry; his face long-drawn and liny; his eyes deep-set and scowling; his lips straight, his nose hooked, and his head covered by a close scull-cap, his hair cut close all round. He sat down near Gegia, and began to discourse in a whining, servile voice, complimenting her on her good looks, launching forth into praise of the magnificence of certain Guelph Florentines, and concluded by declaring that he was hungry and tired.—"Hungry, Beppe?" said Gegia, "that should have been your first word, friend. Cincolo, wilt thou give thy guest to eat? Cincolo, art thou deaf? Art thou blind? Dost thou not hear? Wilt thou not see?—Here is Messer Giuseppe de' Bosticchi."

Cincolo slowly, his eyes still fixed on the board, was about to rise. But the name of the visitant seemed to have the effect of magic on Ricciardo. "Bosticchi!" he cried—"Giuseppe Bosticchi! I did not expect to find that man beneath thy roof, Cincolo, all Guelph as thy wife is—for she also has eaten of the bread of the Elisei. Farewell! thou wilt find me in the street below; follow me quickly." He was about to go, but Bosticchi placed himself before the door, saying in a tone whose whine expressed mingled rage and servility, "In what have I offended this young gentleman? Will he not tell me my offence?"—"Dare not to stop my way," cried Ricciardo, passing his hand before his eyes, "nor force me again to look on thee—Begone!" Cincolo stopped him: "Thou art too hasty, and far too passionate, my noble guest," said he: "however this man may have offended thee, thou art too violent." "Violent!" cried Ricciardo, almost suffocated by passionate emotion—"Aye, draw thy knife, and shew the blood of Arrigo dei Elisei with which it is still stained."

A dead silence followed. Bosticchi slunk out of the room; Ricciardo hid his face in his hands and wept. But soon he calmed his passion and said:—"This is indeed childish. Pardon me; that man is gone; excuse and forget my violence. Resume thy game, Cincolo, but conclude it quickly, for time gains on us—Hark! an hour of night sounds from the Campanile." "The game is already concluded," said Buzeccha, sorrowfully, "thy cloak overthrew the best check-mate this head ever planned—so God forgive thee!" "Check-mate!" cried the indignant Cincolo, "Check-mate! and my queen mowing you down, rank and file!"—"Let us begone," exclaimed Ricciardo: "Messer Buzeccha, you will play out your game with Monna Gegia. Cincolo will return ere long." So taking his host by the arm, he drew him out of the room, and descended the narrow high stairs with the air of one to whom those stairs were not unknown.

When in the street he slackened his pace, and first looking round to assure himself that none overheard their conversation, he addressed Cincolo:—"Pardon me, my dear friend; I am hasty, and the sight of that man made every drop of my blood cry aloud in my veins. But I do not come here to indulge in private sorrows or private revenge, and my design ought alone to engross me. It is necessary for me to see, speedily and secretly, Messer Guielmo Lostendardo, the Neapolitan commander. I bear a message to him from the Countess Elizabeth, the mother of Corradino, and I have some hope that its import may induce him to take at least a neutral part during the impending conflict. I have chosen you, Cincolo, to aid me in this, for not only you are of that little note in your town that you may act for me without attracting observation, but you are brave and true, and I may confide to your known worth. Lostendardo resides at the *Palagio del Governo*; when I enter its doors I am in the hands of my enemies, and its dungeons may alone know the secret of my destiny. I hope better things. But if after two hours I do not appear or let you hear of my welfare, carry this packet to Corradino at Pisa: you will then learn who I am, and if you feel any indignation at my fate, let that feeling attach you still more strongly to the cause for which I live and die."

As Ricciardo spoke he still walked on; and Cincolo observed, that without his guidance he directed his steps towards the *Palagio del Governo*. "I do not understand this," said the old man;—"by what argument, unless you bring one from the other world, do you hope to induce Messer Guielmo to aid Corradino? He is so bitter an enemy of Manfred, that although that Prince is dead, yet when he mentions his name he grasps the air as it were a dagger. I have heard him with horrible imprecations curse the whole house of Swabia." A tremor shook the frame of Ricciardo, but he replied, "Lostendardo was once the firmest support of that house and the friend of Manfred. Strange circumstances gave birth in his mind to this unnatural hatred, and he became a traitor. But perhaps now that Manfred is in Paradise, the youth, the virtues, and the inexperience of Corradino may inspire him with more generous feelings and reawaken his ancient faith. At least I must make this last trial. This cause is too holy, too sacred, to admit of common forms of reasoning or action. The nephew of Manfred must sit upon the throne of his ancestors; and to achieve that I will endure what I am about to endure."

They entered the Palace of Government. Messer Guielmo was carousing in the great hall. "Bear this ring to him, good Cincolo, and say that I wait. Be speedy, that my courage, my life, do not desert me at the moment of trial."—Cincolo, casting one more inquisitive glance on his extraordinary companion, obeyed his orders, while the youth leant against one of the pillars of the court and passionately cast up his eyes to the clear firmament. "Oh, ye stars!" he cried in a smothered voice, "ye are eternal; let my purpose, my will, be as constant as ye!" Then, more calm, he folded his arms in his cloak, and with strong inward struggle endeavoured to repress his emotion. Several servants approached him and bade him follow them. Again he looked at the sky and said, "Manfred," and then he walked on with slow but firm steps. They led him through several halls and corridors to a large apartment hung with tapestry, and well lighted by numerous torches; the marble of the floor reflected their glare, and the arched roof echoed the footsteps of one who paced the apartment as Ricciardo entered. It was Lostendardo. He made a sign that the servants should retire; the heavy door closed behind them, and Ricciardo stood alone with Messer Guielmo; his countenance pale but composed, his eyes cast down as in expectation, not in fear; and but for the convulsive motion of his lips, you would have guessed that every faculty was almost suspended by intense agitation.

Lostendardo approached. He was a man in the prime of life, tall and athletic; he seemed capable with a single exertion to crush the frail being of Ricciardo. Every feature of his countenance spoke of the struggle of passions, and the terrible egotism of one who would sacrifice even himself to the establishment of his will: his black eyebrows were scattered, his grey eyes deep set and scowling, his look at once stern and haggard. A smile seemed never to have disturbed the settled scorn which his lips expressed; his high forehead, already becoming bald, was marked by a thousand contradictory lines. His voice was studiously restrained as he said: "Wherefore do you bring that ring?"—Ricciardo looked up and met his eye, which glanced fire as he exclaimed—"Despina!" He seized her hand with a giant's grasp:—"I have prayed for this night and day, and thou art now here! Nay, do not struggle; you are mine; for by my salvation I swear that thou shalt never again escape me." Despina replied calmly—"Thou mayst well believe that in thus placing myself in thy power I do not dread any injury thou canst inflict upon me,—or I were not here. I do not fear thee, for I do not fear death. Loosen then thy hold, and listen to me. I come in the name of those virtues that were once thine; I come in the name of all noble sentiment, generosity, and ancient faith; and I trust that in listening to me your heroic nature will second my voice, and that Lostendardo will no longer rank with those whom the good and great never name but to condemn."

Lostendardo appeared to attend little to what she said. He gazed on her with triumph and malignant pride; and if he still held her, his motive appeared rather the delight he felt in displaying his power over her, than any fear that she would escape. You might read in her pale cheek and glazed eye, that if she feared, it was herself alone that she mistrusted; that her design lifted her above mortal dread, and that she was as impassive as the marble she resembled to any event that did not either advance or injure the object for which she came. They were both silent, until Lostendardo leading her to a seat, and then standing opposite to her, his arms folded, every feature dilated by triumph, and his voice sharpened by agitation, he said: "Well, speak! What wouldst thou with me?"—"I come to request, that if you cannot be induced to assist Prince Corradino in the present struggle, you will at least stand neutral, and not oppose his advance to the kingdom of his ancestors." Lostendardo laughed. The vaulted roof repeated the sound, but the harsh echo, though it resembled the sharp cry of an animal of prey whose paw is on the heart of its enemy, was not so discordant and dishuman as the laugh itself. "How," he asked, "dost thou pretend to induce me to comply? This dagger," and he touched the hilt of one, that was half concealed in his vesture, "is yet stained by the blood of Manfred; ere long it will be sheathed in the heart of that foolish boy."

Despina conquered the feeling of horror these words inspired, and replied: "Will you give me a few minutes' patient hearing?"—"I will give you a few minutes' hearing, and if I be not so patient as in the Palagio Reale, fair Despina must excuse me. Forbearance is not a virtue to which I aspire."—"Yes, it was in the Palagio Reale at Naples, the palace of Manfred, that you first saw me. You were then the bosom friend of Manfred, selected by that choice specimen of humanity as his confidant and counsellor. Why did you become a traitor? Start not at that word: if you could hear the united voice of Italy, and even of those who call themselves your friends, they would echo that name. Why did you thus degrade and belie yourself? You call me the cause, yet I am most innocent. You saw me at the court of your master, an attendant on Queen Sibilla, and one who unknown to herself had already parted with her heart, her soul, her will, her entire being, an involuntary sacrifice at the shrine of all that is noble and divine in human nature. My spirit worshipped Manfred as a saint, and my pulses ceased to beat when his eye fell upon me. I felt this, but I knew it not. You awoke me from my dream. You said that you loved me, and you reflected in too faithful a mirror my own emotions: I saw myself and shuddered. But the profound and eternal nature of my passion saved me. I loved Manfred. I loved the sun because it enlightened him; I loved the air that fed him; I deified myself for that my heart was the temple in which he resided. I devoted myself to Sibilla, for she was his wife, and never in thought or dream degraded the purity of my affection towards him. For this you hated him.

He was ignorant of my passion: my heart contained it as a treasure which you having discovered came to rifle. You could more easily deprive me of life than my devotion for your king, and therefore you were a traitor.

"Manfred died, and you thought that I had then forgotten him. But love would indeed be a mockery if death were not the most barefaced cheat. How can he die who is immortalized in my thoughts—my thoughts, that comprehend the universe, and contain eternity in their graspings? What though his earthly vesture is thrown as a despised weed beside the verde, he lives in my soul as lovely, as noble, as entire, as when his voice awoke the mute air: nay, his life is more entire, more true. For before, that small shrine that encased his spirit was all that existed of him; but now, he is a part of all things; his spirit surrounds me, interpenetrates; and divided from him during his life, his death has united me to him for ever."

The countenance of Lostendardo darkened fearfully.—When she paused, he looked black as the sea before the heavily charged thunderclouds that canopy it dissolve themselves in rain. The tempest of passion that arose in his heart seemed too mighty to admit of swift manifestation; it came slowly up from the profoundest depths of his soul, and emotion was piled upon emotion before the lightning of his anger sped to its destination. "Your arguments, eloquent Despina," he said, "are indeed unanswerable. They work well for your purpose. Corradino is I hear at Pisa: you have sharpened my dagger; and before the air of another night rust it, I may by deeds have repaid your insulting words."

"How far do you mistake me! And is praise and love of all heroic excellence insult to you? Lostendardo, when you first knew me, I was an inexperienced girl; I loved but knew not what love was, and circumscribing my passion in narrow bounds, I adored the being of Manfred as I might love an effigy of stone, which, when broken, has no longer an existence. I am now much altered. I might before have treated you with disdain or anger, but now these base feelings have expired in my heart. I am animated but by one feeling—an aspiration to another life, another state of being. All the good depart from this strange earth; and I doubt not that when I am sufficiently elevated above human weaknesses, it will also be my turn to leave this scene of woe. I prepare myself for that moment alone; and in endeavouring to fit myself for a union with all the brave, generous, and wise, that once adorned humanity, and have now passed from it, I consecrate myself to the service of this most righteous cause. You wrong me, therefore, if you think there is aught of disdain in what I say, or that any degrading feelings are mingled with my devotion of spirit when I come and voluntarily place myself in your power. You can imprison me for ever in the dungeons of this palace, as a returned Ghibelline and spy, and have me executed as a criminal. But before you do this, pause for your own sake; reflect on the choice of glory or ig-nominy that you are now about to make. Let your old sentiments of love for the house of Swabia have some sway in your heart; reflect that as you are the despised enemy, so you may become the chosen friend, of its last descendant, and receive from every heart the praise of having restored Corradino to the honours and power to which he was born.

"Compare this prince to the hypocritical, the bloody and mean-spirited Charles. When Manfred died, I went to Germany, and have resided at the court of the Countess Elizabeth; I have, therefore, been an hourly witness of the great and good qualities of Corradino. The bravery of his spirit makes him rise above the weakness of youth and inexperience: he pos-sesses all the nobility of spirit that belongs to the family of Swabia, and, in addition, a purity and gentleness that attracts the respect and love of the old and wary courtiers of Frederic and Conrad. You are brave, and would be generous, did not the fury of your passions, like a consuming fire, destroy in their violence every generous sentiment: how then can you become the tool of Charles? His scowling eyes and sneering lips betoken the selfishness of his mind. Avarice, cruelty, meanness, and artifice, are the qualities that characterise him, and render him unworthy of the majesty he usurps. Let him return to Provence, and reign with paltry despotism over the luxurious and servile French; the free-born Italians require another Lord. They are not fit to bow to one whose palace is the change-house of money-lenders, whose generals are usurers, whose courtiers are milliners or monks, and who basely vows allegiance to the enemy of freedom and virtue, Clement, the murderer of Manfred. Their king, like them, should be clothed in the armour of valour and simplicity; his ornaments, his shield and spear; his treasury, the possessions of his subjects; his army, their unshaken loves. Charles will treat you as a tool; Corradino as a friend—Charles will make you the detested tyrant of a groaning province; Corradino the governor of a prosperous and happy people.

"I cannot tell by your manner if what I have said has in any degree altered your determination. I cannot forget the scenes that passed be-tween us at Naples. I might then have been disdainful: I am not so now. Your execrations of Manfred excited every angry feeling in my mind; but, as I have said, all but the feeling of love expired in my heart when Manfred died, and methinks that where love is, excellence must be its companion. You said you loved me; and though, in other times, that love was twin-brother to hate,—though then, poor prisoner in your heart, jealousy, rage, contempt, and cruelty, were its handmaids,—yet if it were love, methinks that its divinity must have purified your heart from baser feelings; and now that I, the bride of Death, am removed from your sphere, gentler feelings may awaken in your bosom, and you may incline mildly to my voice.

"If indeed you loved me, will you not now be my friend? Shall we not hand in hand pursue the same career? Return to your ancient faith; and now that death and religion have placed the seal upon the past, let Manfred's spirit, looking down, behold his repentant friend the firm ally of his successor, the best and last scion of the house of Swabia."

She ceased; for the glare of savage triumph which, as a rising fire at night time, enlightened with growing and fearful radiance the face of Lostendardo, made her pause in her appeal. He did not reply; but when she was silent he quitted the attitude in which he had stood immoveably opposite to her, and pacing the hall with measured steps, his head declined, he seemed to ruminate on some project. Could it be that he weighed her reasonings? If he hesitated, the side of generosity and old fidelity would certainly prevail. Yet she dared not hope; her heart beat fast; she would have knelt, but she feared to move, lest any motion should disturb his thoughts, and curb the flow of good feeling which she fondly hoped had arisen within him: she looked up and prayed silently as she sat. Notwithstanding the glare of the torches, the beams of one small star struggled through the dark window pane; her eye resting on it, her thoughts were at once elevated to the eternity and space which that star symbolized: it seemed to her the spirit of Manfred, and she inwardly worshipped it, as she prayed that it would shed its benign influence on the soul of Lostendardo.

Some minutes elapsed in this fearful silence, and then he approached her. "Despina, allow me to reflect on your words; to-morrow I will answer you. You will remain in this palace until the morning, and then you shall see and judge of my repentance and returning faith."—He spoke with studious gentleness. Despina could not see his face, for the lights shone behind him. When she looked up to reply, the little star twinkled just above his head, and seemed with its gentle lustre to reassure her. Our minds, when highly wrought, are strangely given to superstition, and Despina lived in a superstitious age. She thought that the star bade her comply, and assured her of protection from heaven:—from where else could she expect it? She said therefore, "I consent. Only let me request that you acquaint the man who gave you my ring that I am safe, or he will fear for me."—"I will do as you desire."—"And I will confide myself to your care. I cannot, dare not, fear you. If you would betray me, still I trust in the heavenly saints that guard humanity."

Her countenance was so calm,—it beamed with so angelic a self-devotion and a belief in good, that Lostendardo dared not look on her. For one moment—as she, having ceased to speak, gazed upon the star—he

felt impelled to throw himself at her feet, to confess the diabolical scheme
he had forged, and to commit himself body and soul to her guidance, to
obey, to serve, to worship her. The impulse was momentary: the feeling
of revenge returned on him. From the moment she had rejected him, the
fire of rage had burned in his heart, consuming all healthy feeling, all
human sympathies and gentleness of soul. He had sworn never to sleep
on a bed, or to drink aught but water, until his first cup of wine was
mingled with the blood of Manfred. He had fulfilled this vow. A strange
alteration had worked within him from the moment he had drained that
unholy cup. The spirit, not of a man, but of a devil, seemed to live within
him, urging him to crime, from which his long protracted hope of more
complete revenge had alone deterred him. But Despina was now in his
power, and it seemed to him as if fate had preserved him so long only
that he might now wreak his full rage upon her. When she spoke of love,
he thought how from that he might extract pain. He formed his plan; and
this slight human weakness now conquered, he bent his thoughts to its
completion. Yet he feared to stay longer with her; so he quitted her,
saying that he would send attendants who would shew her an apartment
where she might repose. He left her, and several hours passed; but no one
came. The torches burnt low, and the stars of heaven could now with
twinkling beams conquer their feebler light. One by one these torches
went out, and the shadows of the high windows of the hall, before invisible, were thrown upon its marble pavement. Despina looked upon the
shade, at first unconsciously, until she found herself counting, one, two,
three, the shapes of the iron bars that lay so placidly on the stone. "Those
grates are thick," she said: "this room would be a large but secure
dungeon." As by inspiration, she now felt that she was a prisoner. No
change, no word, had intervened since she had walked fearlessly in the
room, believing herself free. But now no doubt of her situation occurred
to her mind; heavy chains seemed to fall around her; the air to feel thick
and heavy as that of a prison; and the star-beams that had before cheered
her, became the dreary messengers of fearful danger to herself, and of the
utter defeat of all the hopes she had dared nourish of success to her
beloved cause.

Cincolo waited, first with impatience, and then with anxiety, for the
return of the youthful stranger. He paced up and down before the gates of
the palace; hour after hour passed on; the stars arose and descended, and
ever and anon meteors shot along the sky. They were not more frequent
than they always are during a clear summer night in Italy; but they
appeared strangely numerous to Cincolo, and portentous of change and
calamity. Midnight struck, and at that moment a procession of monks
passed, bearing a corpse and chaunting a solemn *De Profundis*. Cincolo
felt a cold tremour shake his limbs when he reflected how ill an augury

this was for the strange adventurer he had guided to that palace. The sombre cowls of the priests, their hollow voices, and the dark burthen they carried, augmented his agitation even to terror: without confessing the cowardice to himself, he was possessed with fear lest he should be included in the evil destiny that evidently awaited his companion. Cincolo was a brave man; he had often been foremost in a perilous assault: but the most courageous among us sometimes feel our hearts fail within us at the dread of unknown and fated danger. He was struck with panic;—he looked after the disappearing lights of the procession, and listened to their fading voices: his knees shook, a cold perspiration stood on his brow: until, unable to resist the impulse, he began slowly to withdraw himself from the Palace of Government, and to quit the circle of danger which seemed to hedge him in if he remained on that spot.

He had hardly quitted his post by the gate of the palace, when he saw lights issue from it, attendant on a company of men, some of whom were armed, as appeared from the reflection their lances' heads cast; and some of them carried a litter hung with black and closely drawn. Cincolo was rooted to the spot. He could not render himself any reason for his belief, but he felt convinced that the stranger youth was there, about to be carried out to death. Impelled by curiosity and anxiety, he followed the party as they went towards the Porta Romana: they were challenged by the sentinels at the gate; they gave the word and passed. Cincolo dared not follow, but he was agitated by fear and compassion. He remembered the packet confided to his care; he dared not draw it from his bosom, lest any Guelph should be near to overlook and discover that it was addressed to Corradino; he could not read, but he wished to look at the arms of the seal, to see whether they bore the imperial ensigns. He returned back to the *Palagio del Governo*: all there was dark and silent; he walked up and down before the gates, looking up at the windows, but no sign of life appeared. He could not tell why he was thus agitated, but he felt as if all his future peace depended on the fate of this stranger youth. He thought of Gegia, her helplessness and age; but he could not resist the impulse that impelled him, and he resolved that very night to commence his journey to Pisa, to deliver the packet, to learn who the stranger was, and what hopes he might entertain for his safety.

He returned home, that he might inform Gegia of his journey. This was a painful task, but he could not leave her in doubt. He ascended his narrow stairs with trepidation. At the head of them a lamp twinkled before a picture of the Virgin. Evening after evening it burnt there, guarding through its influence his little household from all earthly or supernatural dangers. The sight of it inspired him with courage; he said an *Ave Maria* before it; and then looking around him to assure himself that no spy stood on the narrow landing place, he drew the packet from his bosom and examined the seal. All Italians in those days were conversant in heraldry, since from ensigns of the shields of the knights they learned, better than from their faces or persons, to what family and party they belonged. But it required no great knowledge for Cincolo to decypher these arms; he had known them from his childhood; they were those of the Elisei, the family to whom he had been attached as a partisan during all these civil contests. Arrigo dei Elisei had been his patron, and his wife had nursed his only daughter, in those happy days when there was neither Guelph nor Ghibelline. The sight of these arms reawakened all his anxiety. Could this youth belong to that house? The seal shewed that he really did; and this discovery confirmed his determination of making every exertion to save him, and inspired him with sufficient courage to encounter the remonstrances and fears of Monna Gegia.

He unlocked his door; the old dame was asleep in her chair, but awoke as he entered. She had slept only to refresh her curiosity, and she asked a thousand questions in a breath, to which Cincolo did not reply: he stood with his arms folded looking at the fire, irresolute how to break the subject of his departure. Monna Gegia continued to talk: "After you went, we held a consultation concerning this hot-brained youth of this morning; I, Buzeccha, Beppe de' Bosticchi who returned, and Monna Lisa from the Mercato Nuovo. We all agreed that he must be one of two persons; and be it one or the other, if he have not quitted Florence, the *Stinchi** will be his habitation by sun-rise. Eh! Cincolo, man! you do not speak; where did you part with your Prince?"—"Prince, Gegia! Are you mad?—what Prince?" "Nay, he is either a Prince or a baker; either Corradino himself, or Ricciardo the son of Messer Tommaso de' Manelli; he that lived o'th' Arno, and baked for all that Sesto, when Count Guido de' Giudi was *Vicario*. By this token, that Messer Tommaso went to Milan with Ubaldo de' Gargalandi, and Ricciardo, who went with his father, must now be sixteen. He had the fame of kneading with as light a hand as his father, but he liked better to follow arms with the Gargalandi: he was a fair, likely youth, they said; and so, to say the truth, was our youngster of this morning. But Monna Lisa will have it that it must be Corradino himself——"

Cincolo listened as if the gossip of two old women could unravel his riddle. He even began to doubt whether the last conjecture, extravagant as it was, had not hit the truth. Every circumstance forbade such an idea; but he thought of the youth and exceeding beauty of the stranger, and he began to doubt. There was none among the Elisei who answered to his appearance. The flower of their youth had fallen at Monte Aperto; the eldest of the new generation was but ten; the other males of that house

* The name of the common prison at Florence.

were of a mature age. Gegia continued to talk of the anger that Beppe de' Bosticchi evinced at being accused of the murder of Arrigo dei Elisei. "If he had done that deed," she cried, "never more should he have stood on my hearth; but he swore his innocence; and truly, poor man, it would be a sin not to believe him." Why, if the stranger were not an Elisei, should he have shewn such horror on viewing the supposed murderer of the head of that family?—Cincolo turned from the fire; he examined whether his knife hung safely in his girdle, and he exchanged his sandal-like shoes for stronger boots of common undressed fur. This last act attracted the attention of Gegia. "What are you about, good man?" she cried. "This is no hour to change your dress, but to come to bed. To-night you will not speak; but to-morrow I hope to get it all out from you. What are you about?" "I am about to leave you, my dear Gegia; and heaven bless and take care of you! I am going to Pisa." Gegia uttered a shriek, and was about to remonstrate with great volubility, while the tears rolled down her aged cheeks. Tears also filled the eyes of Cincolo, as he said, "I do not go for the cause you suspect. I do not go into the army of Corradino, though my heart will be with it. I go but to carry a letter, and will return without delay." "You will never return," cried the old woman: "the Commune will never let you enter the gates of this town again, if you set foot in that traitorous Pisa. But you shall not go; I will raise the neighbours; I will declare you mad——"—"Gegia, no more of this! Here is all the money I have: before I go, I will send your cousin 'Nunziata to you. I must go. It is not the Ghibelline cause, or Corradino, that obliges me to risk your ease and comforts; but the life of one of the Elisei is at stake; and if I can save him, would you have me rest here, and afterwards curse you and the hour when I was born?" "What! is he——? But no; there is none among the Elisei so young as he; and none so lovely, except her whom these arms carried when an infant—but she is a female. No, no; this is a tale trumped up to deceive me and gain my consent; but you shall never have it. Mind that! you will never have it; and I prophecy that if you do go, your journey will be the death of both of us." She wept bitterly. Cincolo kissed her aged cheek, and mingled his tears with hers; and then recommending her to the care of the Virgin and the saints, he quitted her, while grief choked her utterance, and the name of the Elisei had deprived her of all energy to resist his purpose.

It was four in the morning before the gates of Florence were opened and Cincolo could leave the city. At first he availed himself of the carts of the *contadini* to advance on his journey; but as he drew near Pisa, all modes of conveyance ceased, and he was obliged to take by-roads, and act cautiously, not to fall into the hands of the Florentine out-posts, or of some fierce Ghibelline, who might suspect him, and have him carried before the Podesta of a village; for if once suspected and searched, the packet addressed to Corradino would convict him, and he would pay for his temerity with his life. Having arrived at Vico Pisano, he found a troop of Pisan horse there on guard: he was known to many of the soldiers, and he obtained a conveyance for Pisa; but it was night before he arrived. He gave the Ghibelline watch-word, and was admitted within the gates. He asked for Prince Corradino: he was in the city, at the palace of the Lanfranchi. He crossed the Arno, and was admitted into the palace by the soldiers who guarded the door. Corradino had just returned from a successful skirmish in the Lucchese states, and was reposing; but when Count Gherardo Doneratico, his principal attendant, saw the seal of the packet, he immediately ushered the bearer into a small room, where the Prince lay on a fox's skin thrown upon the pavement. The mind of Cincolo had been so bewildered by the rapidity of the events of the preceding night, by fatigue and want of sleep, that he had over-wrought himself to believe that the stranger youth was indeed Corradino; and when he had heard that that Prince was in Pisa, by a strange disorder of ideas, he still imagined that he and Ricciardo were the same; that the black litter was a phantom, and his fears ungrounded. The first sight of Corradino, his fair hair and round Saxon features, destroyed this idea: it was replaced by a feeling of deep anguish, when Count Gherardo, announcing him, said, "One who brings a letter from Madonna Despina dei Elisei, waits upon your Highness."

The old man sprang forward, uncontrolled by the respect he would otherwise have felt for one of so high lineage as Corradino. "From Despina! Did you say from her? Oh! unsay your words! Not from my beloved, lost, foster-child."

Tears rolled down his cheeks. Corradino, a youth of fascinating gentleness, but, as Despina had said, "young, even to childishness," attempted to reassure him. "Oh! my gracious Lord," cried Cincolo, "open that packet, and see if it be from my blessed child—if in the disguise of Ricciardo I led her to destruction." He wrung his hands. Corradino, pale as death with fear for the destiny of his lovely and adventurous friend, broke the seal. The packet contained an inner envelope without any direction, and a letter, which Corradino read, while horror convulsed every feature. He gave it to Gherardo. "It is indeed from her. She says, that the bearer can relate all that the world will probably know of her fate. And you, old man, who weep so bitterly, you to whom my best and lovely friend refers me, tell me what you know of her." Cincolo told his story in broken accents. "May these eyes be for ever blinded!" he cried, when he had concluded, "that knew not Despina in those soft looks and heavenly smiles. Dotard that I am! When my wife railed at your family and princely self, and the sainted Manfred, why did I not read her secret in her forbearance? Would she have forgiven those words in any but her who had nursed her infancy, and been a mother to her when Madonna Pia died? And when she taxed Bosticchi with her father's death, I, blind fool, did not see the spirit of the Elisei in her eyes. My Lord, I have but one favour to ask you. Let me hear her letter, that I may judge from that what hopes remain:—but there are none—none." "Read it to him, my dear Count," said the Prince; "I will not fear as he fears. I dare not fear that one so lovely and beloved is sacrificed for my worthless cause." Gherardo read the letter.

"Cincolo de' Becari, my foster-father, will deliver this letter into your hands, my respected and dear Corradino. The Countess Elizabeth has urged me to my present undertaking; I hope nothing from it—except to labour for your cause, and perhaps through its event to quit somewhat earlier a life which is but a grievous trial to my weak mind. I go to endeavour to arouse the feelings of fidelity and generosity in the soul of the traitor Lostendardo: I go to place myself in his hands, and I do not hope to escape from them again. Corradino, my last prayer will be for your success. Mourn not for one who goes home after a long and weary exile. Burn the enclosed packet, without opening it. The Mother of God protect thee!   DESPINA."

Corradino had wept as this epistle was reading, but then starting up, he said—"To revenge or death! we may yet save her!"——

A blight had fallen on the house of Swabia, and all their enterprizes were blasted. Beloved by their subjects, noble, and with every advantage of right on their side, except those the church bestowed, they were defeated in every attempt to defend themselves against a foreigner and a tyrant, who ruled by force of arms, and those in the hands of a few only, over an extensive and warlike territory. The young and daring Corradino was also fated to perish in this contest. Having overcome the troops of his adversary in Tuscany, he advanced towards his kingdom with the highest hopes. His arch enemy, Pope Clement IV, had shut himself up in Viterbo, and was guarded by a numerous garrison. Corradino passed in triumph and hope before the town, and proudly drew out his troops before it, to display to the Holy Father his forces, and humiliate him by this show of success. The Cardinals, who beheld the lengthened line and good order of the army, hastened to the Papal palace. Clement was in his oratory, praying; the frightened monks, with pale looks, related how the excommunicated heretic dared to menace the town where the Holy Father himself resided; adding, that if the insult were carried to the pitch of an assault, it might prove dangerous warfare. The Pope smiled contemptuously. "Do not fear," he said; "the projects of these men will dissipate in smoke." He then went on the ramparts, and saw Corradino and Frederic of Austria, who defiled the line of knights in the plain below. He watched them for a time; then turning to his Cardinals, he said, "They are victims, who permit themselves to be led to sacrifice."

His words were a prophecy. Notwithstanding the first successes of Corradino, and the superior numbers of his army, he was defeated by the artifice of Charles in a pitched battle. He escaped from the field, and, with a few friends, arrived at a tower called Astura, which belonged to the family of Frangipani, of Rome. Here he hired a vessel, embarked, and put out to sea, directing his course for Sicily, which, having rebelled against Charles, would, he hoped, receive him with joy. They were already under weigh, when one of the family of the Frangipani seeing a vessel filled with Germans making all sail from shore, suspected that they were fugitives from the battle of Tagliacozzo, he followed them in other vessels, and took them all prisoners. The person of Corradino was a rich prey for him; he delivered him into the hands of his rival, and was rewarded by the donation of a fief near Benevento.

The dastardly spirit of Charles instigated him to the basest revenge; and the same tragedy was acted on those shores which has been renewed in our days. A daring and illustrious Prince was sacrificed with the mock forms of justice, at the sanguinary altar of tyranny and hypocrisy. Corradino was tried. One of his Judges alone, a Provençal, dared condemn him, and he paid with his life the forfeit of his baseness. For scarcely had he, solitary among his fellows, pronounced the sentence of death against this Prince, than Robert of Flanders, the brother-in-law of Charles himself, struck him on the breast with a staff, crying, "It behoves not thee, wretch, to condemn to death so noble and worthy a knight." The judge fell dead in the presence of the king, who dared not avenge his creature.

On the 26th of October, Corradino and his friends were led out to die in the Market-place of Naples, by the sea-side. Charles was present with all his court, and an immense multitude surrounded the triumphant king, and his more royal adversary, about to suffer an ignominious death. The funereal procession approached its destination. Corradino, agitated, but controlling his agitation, was drawn in an open car. After him came a close litter, hung with black, with no sign to tell who was within. The Duke of Austria and several other illustrious victims followed. The guard that conducted them to the scaffold was headed by Lostendardo; a malicious triumph laughed in his eyes, and he rode near the litter, looking from time to time, first at it and then at Corradino, with the dark look of a tormenting fiend. The procession stopped at the foot of the scaffold, and Corradino looked at the flashing light which every now and then arose from Vesuvius, and threw its reflection on the sea. The sun had not yet risen, but the halo if its approach illuminated the bay of Naples, its mountains, and its islands. The summits of the distant hills of Baiæ gleamed with its first beams. Corradino thought, "By the time those rays arrive here, and shadows are cast from the persons of these men,—

princes and peasants, around me, my living spirit will be shadowless."
Then he turned his eyes on the companions of his fate, and for the first
time he saw the silent and dark litter that accompanied them. At first he
thought, "It is my coffin." But then he recollected the disappearance of
Despina, and would have sprung towards it: his guards stopped him; he
looked up, and his glance met that of Lostendardo, who smiled—a smile
of dread: but the feeling of religion which had before calmed him again
descended on him; he thought that her sufferings, as well as his, would
soon be over.

They were already over. And the silence of the grave is upon those
events which had occurred since Cincolo beheld her carried out of Florence, until now that she was led by her fierce enemy to behold the death
of the nephew of Manfred. She must have endured much; for when, as
Corradino advanced to the front of the scaffold, the litter being placed
opposite to it, Lostendardo ordered the curtains to be withdrawn, the
white hand that hung inanimate from the side was thin as a winter leaf,
and her fair face, pillowed by the thick knots of her dark hair, was
sunken and ashy pale, while you could see the deep blue of her eyes
struggle through the closed eyelids. She was still in the attire in which she
had presented herself at the house of Cincolo: perhaps her tormentor
thought that her appearance as a youth would attract less compassion
than if a lovely woman were thus dragged to so unnatural a scene.

Corradino was kneeling and praying when her form was thus exposed.
He saw her, and saw that she was dead! About to die himself; about, pure
and innocent, to die ignominiously, while his base conqueror, in pomp
and glory, was spectator of his death, he did not pity those who were at
peace; his compassion belonged to the living alone, and as he rose from
his prayer he exclaimed, "My beloved mother, what profound sorrow will
the news thou art about to hear cause thee!" He looked upon the living
multitude around him, and saw that the hard-visaged partisans of the
usurper wept; he heard the sobs of his oppressed and conquered subjects;
so he drew his glove from his hand and threw it among the crowd, in
token that he still held his cause good, and submitted his head to the
axe.

During many years after those events, Lostendardo enjoyed wealth,
rank, and honour. When suddenly, while at the summit of glory and
prosperity, he withdrew from the world, took the vows of a severe order
in a convent, in one of the desolate and unhealthy plains by the sea-shore
in Calabria; and after having gained the character of a saint, through a
life of self-inflicted torture, he died murmuring the names of Corradino,
Manfred, and Despina.

II

Recollections of Italy

AFTER THREE WEEKS of incessant rain, at Midsummer, the sun shone on the town of Henley upon Thames. At first the roads were deep with mud, the grass wet, and the trees dripping; but after two unclouded days, on the second afternoon, pastoral weather commenced; that is to say, weather when it is possible to sit under a tree or lie upon the grass, and feel neither cold nor wet. Such days are too rare not to be seized upon with avidity. We English often feel like a sick man escaping into the open air after a three months' confinement within the four walls of his chamber; and if "an ounce of sweet be worth a pound of sour," we are infinitely more fortunate than the children of the south, who bask a long summer life in his rays, and rarely feel the bliss of sitting by a brook's side under the rich foliage of some well-watered tree, after having been shut up week after week in our carpeted rooms, beneath our white ceilings.

The sun shone on the town of Henley upon Thames. The inhabitants, meeting one another, exclaimed: "What enchanting weather! It has not rained these two days; and, as the moon does not change till Monday, we shall perhaps enjoy a whole week of sunshine!" Thus they congratulated themselves, and thus also I thought as, with the Eclogues of Virgil in my pocket, I walked out to enjoy one of the best gifts of heaven, a rainless, windless, cloudless day. The country around Henley is well calculated to attune to gentlest modulations the rapturous emotions to which the balmy, ambient air, gave birth in my heart. The Thames glides through grassy slopes, and its banks are sometimes shaded by beechwood, and sometimes open to the full glare of the sun. Near the spot towards which I wandered several beautiful islands are formed in the river, covered with willows, poplars, and elms. The trees of these islands unite their branches with those of the firm land, and form a green archway which numerous birds delight to frequent. I entered a park belonging to a noble mansion;

the grass was fresh and green; it had been mown a short time before; and, springing up again, was softer than the velvet on which the Princess Badroulboudour walked to Aladdin's palace. I sat down under a majestic oak by the river's side; I drew out my book and began to read the Eclogue of Silenus.

A sigh breathed near me caught my attention. How could an emotion of pain exist in a human breast at such a time. But when I looked up I perceived that it was a sigh of rapture, not of sorrow. It arose from a feeling that, finding no words by which it might express itself, clothed its burning spirit in a sigh. I well knew the person who stood beside me; it was Edmund Malville, a man young in soul, though he had passed through more than half the way allotted for man's journey. His countenance was pale; when in a quiescent state it appeared heavy; but let him smile, and Paradise seemed to open on his lips; let him talk, and his dark blue eyes brightened, the mellow tones of his voice trembled with the weight of feeling with which they were laden; and his slight, insignificant person seemed to take the aspect of an ethereal substance (if I may use the expression), and to have too little of clay about it to impede his speedy ascent to heaven. The curls of his dark hair rested upon his clear brow, yet unthinned.

Such was the appearance of Edmund Malville, a man whom I reverenced and loved beyond expression. He sat down beside me, and we entered into conversation on the weather, the river, Parry's voyage, and the Greek revolution. But our discourse dwindled into silence; the sun declined; the motion of the fleckered shadow of the oak tree, as it rose and fell, stirred by a gentle breeze; the passage of swallows, who dipt their wings into the stream as they flew over it; the spirit of love and life that seemed to pervade the atmosphere, and to cause the tall grass to tremble beneath its presence; all these objects formed the links of a chain that bound up our thoughts in silence.

Idea after idea passed through my brain; and at length I exclaimed, why or wherefore I do not remember,—"Well, at least this clear stream is better than the muddy Arno."

Malville smiled. I was sorry that I had spoken; for he loved Italy, its soil, and all that it contained, with a strange enthusiasm. But, having delivered my opinion, I was bound to support it, and I continued: "Well, my dear friend, I have also seen the Arno, so I have some right to judge. I certainly was never more disappointed with any place than with Italy— that is to say, taken all in all. The shabby villas; the yellow Arno; the bad taste of the gardens, with their cropped trees and deformed statues; the suffocating scirocco; the dusty roads; their ferries over their broad, uninteresting rivers, or their bridges crossing stones over which water never flows; that dirty Brenta (the New River Cut is an Oronooko to it); and

Venice, with its uncleaned canals and narrow lanes, where Scylla and
Charybdis meet you at every turn; and you must endure the fish and
roasted pumpkins at the stalls, or the smell—"

"Stop, blasphemer!" cried Malville, half angry, half laughing, "I give
up the Brenta; but Venice, the Queen of the sea, the city of gondolas
and romance—"

"Romance, Malville, on those ditches?—"

"Yes, indeed, romance!—genuine and soul-elevating romance! Do you
not bear in mind the first view of the majestic city from Fusina, crowning
the sea with Cybele's diadem? How well do I remember my passage over,
as with breathless eagerness I went on the self-same track which the gondolas of the fearless Desdemona, the loving Moor, the gentle Belvidera,
and brave Pierre, had traced before me; they still seemed to inhabit the
palaces that thronged on each side, and I figured them to myself gliding
near, as each dark, mysterious gondola passed by me. How deeply implanted in my memory is every circumstance of my little voyage home
from the opera each night along what you call ditches; when sitting in one
of those luxurious barks, matched only by that which bore Cleopatra to
her Antony, all combined to raise and nourish romantic feeling. The dark
canal, shaded by the black houses; the melancholy splash of the oar; the
call, or rather chaunt made by the boat-men, 'Ca Stalì!' (the words
themselves delightfully unintelligible) to challenge any other bark as we
turned a corner; the passing of another gondola, black as night and silent
as death—Is not this romantic? Then we emerged into the wide expanse
before the Place of St. Mark; the cupolas of the church of Santa Maria de
la Salute were silvered by the moonbeams; the dark tower rose in silent
majesty; the waves rippled; and the dusty line of Lido afar off was the
pledge of calm and safety. The Paladian palaces that rose from the
Canale Grande; the simple beauty of the Rialto's single arch—"

"Horrible place! I shall never forget crossing it—"

"Ay, that is the way with you of this world. But who among those who
love romance ever thinks of going on the Rialto when they have once
heard that the fish-market is held there? No place, trust an adept, equals
Venice in giving 'a local habitation and a name,'* to the restless imaginations of those who pant to quit the 'painted scene of this new world—'†
for the old world, peopled by sages who have lived in material shape, and
heroes whose existence is engendered in the mind of man alone. I have
often repeated this to myself as I passed the long hours of the silent night
watching the far lights of the distant gondolas, and listening to the chaunt
of the boatmen as they glided under my window. How quiet is Venice! no
horses; none of the hideous sounds and noises of a town. I grant that in

* Shakespeare, *A Midsummer Night's Dream* V. i. 17 (Ed.).
† Percy Shelley, *The Cenci* V. i. 78 (Ed.).

lanes—but why talk of what belongs to every town; dirty alleys, trouble-some market-women, and the mark of a maritime city, the luckless smell of fish? Why select defects, and cast from your account the peculiar excellencies of this wonderful city? The buildings rising from the waves; the silence of the watery pavement; the mysterious beauty of the black gondolas; and, not to be omitted, the dark eyes and finely-shaped brows of the women peeping from beneath their fazioles.

"You were three months in Italy?"

"Six, if you please, Malville."

"Well, six, twelve, twenty, are not sufficient to learn to appreciate Italy. We go with false notions of God knows what—of orange groves and fields of asphodel; we expect what we do not find, and are therefore disappointed with the reality; and yet to my mind the reality is not inferior to any scene of enchantment that the imagination ever conjured."

"Or rather say, my friend, that the imagination can paint objects of little worth in gaudy colours, and then become enamoured of its own work."

"Shall I tell you," continued Malville, with a smile, "how you passed your time in Italy? You traversed the country in your travelling chariot, cursing the postillions and the bad inns. You arrived at a town and went to the best hotel, at which you found many of your countrymen, mere acquaintances in England, but hailed as bosom friends in that strange land. You walked about the streets of a morning expecting to find gorgeous temples and Cyclopean ruins in every street in Florence; you came to some broken pillar, wondered what it could be, and laughed at the idea of this being one of the relics which your wise countrymen came so far to see; you lounged into a coffee-house and read Galignani; and then perhaps wandered with equal apathy into the gallery, where, if you were not transported to the seventh heaven, I can undertake your defence no further."

"My defence, Malville?"

"You dined; you went to a conversazione, where you were neither understood nor could understand; you went to the opera to hear probably the fifty-second repetition of a piece to which nobody listened; or you found yourself in Paradise at the drawing-room of the English ambassador, and fancied yourself in Grosvenor-square.

"I am a lover of nature. Towns, and the details of mixed society, are modes of life alien to my nature. I live to myself and to my affections, and nothing to that tedious routine which makes up the daily round of most men's lives. I went to Italy young, and visited with ardent curiosity and delight all of great and glorious which that country contains. I have already mentioned the charms which Venice has for me; and all Lombardy, whose aspect indeed is very different from that of the south of

Italy, is beautiful in its kind. Among the lakes of the north we meet with alpine scenery mixed with the more luxuriant vegetation of the south. The Euganean hills in gentler beauty remind one of the hills of our own country, yet painted with warmer colours. Read Ugo Foscolo's description of them in the first part of his 'Ultime lettere di Jacopo Ortis,' and you will acknowledge the romantic and even sublime sentiments which they are capable of inspiring. But Naples is the real enchantress of Italy; the scenery there is so exquisitely lovely, the remains of antiquity so perfect, wondrous, and beautiful; the climate so genial, that a festive appearance seems for ever to invest it, mingled strangely with the feeling of insecurity with which one is inspired by the sight of Vesuvius, and the marks which are every where manifest of the violent changes that have taken place in that of which in other countries we feel most certain, good Mother Earth herself. With us this same dame is a domestic wife, keeping house, and providing with earnest care and yet penurious means for her family, expecting no pleasure, and finding no amusement. At Naples my fair lady tricks herself out in rich attire, she is kept in the best humour through the perpetual attentions of her constant cavaliere servente, the sun—and she smiles so sweetly on us that we forgive her if at times she plays the coquette with us and leaves us in the lurch. Rome is still the queen of the world,—

> All that Athens ever brought forth wise,
> All that Afric ever brought forth strange,
> All that which Asia ever had of prize,
> Was here to see;—O, marvellous great change!
> Rome living was the world's sole ornament,
> And dead is now the world's sole monument.*

"If this be true, our forefathers have, in faith! a rare mausoleum for their decay, and Artemisia built a far less costly repository for her lord than widowed Time has bestowed on his dead companion, the Past; when I die may I sleep there and mingle with the glorious dust of Rome! May its radiant atmosphere enshroud these lifeless limbs, and my fading clay give birth to flowers that may inhale that brightest air.

"So I have made my voyage in that fair land, and now bring you to Tuscany. After all I have said of the delights of the south of Italy I would choose Tuscany for a residence. Its inhabitants are courteous and civilized. I confess that there is a charm for me in the manners of the common people and servants. Perhaps this is partly to be accounted for from the contrast which they form with those of my native country; and

* Spenser's *Ruins of Rome*.

all that is unusual, by divesting common life of its familiar garb, gives an air of gala to everyday concerns. These good people are courteous, and there is much *piquance* in the shades of distinction which they make between respect and servility, ease of address and impertinence. Yet this is little seen and appreciated among their English visitors. I have seen a countrywoman of some rank much shocked at being cordially embraced in a parting scene from her cook-maid; and an Englishman think himself insulted because when, on ordering his coachman to wait a few minutes for orders, the man quietly sat down: yet neither of these actions were instigated by the slightest spirit of insolence. I know not why, but there was always something heartfelt and delightful to me in the salutation that passes each evening between master and servant. On bringing the lights the servant always says, 'Felicissima sera, Signoria;' and is answered by a similar benediction. These are nothings, you will say; but such nothings have conduced more to my pleasure than other events usually accounted of more moment.

"The country of Tuscany is cultivated and fertile, although it does not bear the same stamp of excessive luxury as in the south. To continue my half-forgotten simile, the earth is here like a young affectionate wife, who loves her home, yet dresses that home in smiles. In spring, nature arises in beauty from her prison, and rains sunbeams and life upon the land. Summer comes up in its green array, giving labour and reward to the peasants. Their plenteous harvests, their Virgilian threshing floors, and looks of busy happiness, are delightful to me. The balmy air of night, Hesperus in his glowing palace of sunlight, the flower-starred earth, the glittering waters, the ripening grapes, the chestnut copses, the cuckoo, and the nightingale,—such is the assemblage which is to me what balls and parties are to others. And if a storm come, rushing like an armed band over the country, filling the torrents, bending the proud heads of the trees, causing the clouds' deafening music to resound, and the lightning to fill the air with splendour; I am still enchanted by the spectacle which diversifies what I have heard named the monotonous blue skies of Italy.

"In Tuscany the streams are fresh and full, the plains decorated with waving corn, shadowed by trees and trellised vines, and the mountains arise in woody majesty behind to give dignity to the scene. What is a land without mountains? Heaven disdains a plain; but when the beauteous earth raises her proud head to seek its high communion, then it descends to meet her, it adorns her in clouds, and invests her in radiant hues.

"On the 15th of September, 18—, I remember being one of a party of pleasure from the baths of Pisa to Vico Pisano, a little town formerly a frontier fortress between the Pisan and Florentine territories. The air inspired joy, and the pleasure I felt I saw reflected in the countenance of my beloved companions. Our course lay beneath hills hardly high enough for the name of mountains, but picturesquely shaped and covered with various wood. The cicale chirped, and the air was impregnated with the perfume of flowers. We passed the Rupe de Noce, and proceeding still at the foot of hills arrived at Vico Pisano, which is built at the extreme point of the range. The houses are old and surmounted with ancient towers; and at one end of the town there is a range of old wall, weed-grown; but never did eye behold hues more rich and strange than those with which time and the seasons have painted this relic. The lines of the cornice swept downwards, and made a shadow that served even to diversify more the colours we beheld. We returned along the same road; and not far from Vico Pisano ascended a gentle hill, at the top of which was a church dedicated to Madonna, with a grassy platform of earth before it. Here we spread and ate our rustic fare, and were waited upon by the peasant girls of the cottage attached to the church, one of whom was of extreme beauty, a beauty heightened by the grace of her motions and the simplicity of her manner. After our pic-nic we reposed under the shade of the church, on the brow of the hill. We gazed on the scene with rapture. 'Look,' cried my best, and now lost friend, 'behold the mountains that sweep into the plain like waves that meet in a chasm; the olive woods are as green as a sea, and are waving in the wind; the shadows of the clouds are spotting the bosoms of the hills; a heron comes sailing over us; a butterfly flits near; at intervals the pines give forth their sweet and prolonged response to the wind, the myrtle bushes are in bud, and the soil beneath us is carpeted with odoriferous flowers.'—My full heart could only sigh, he alone was eloquent enough to clothe his thoughts in language."

Malville's eyes glistened as he spoke, he sighed deeply; then turning away, he walked towards the avenue that led from the grounds on which we were. I followed him, but we neither of us spoke; and when at length he renewed the conversation, he did not mention Italy; he seemed to wish to turn the current of his thoughts, and by degrees he reassumed his composure.

When I took leave of him I said, smiling, "You have celebrated an Italian party of pleasure; may I propose an English one to you? Will you join some friends next Thursday in an excursion down the Thames? Perhaps the sight of its beautiful banks, and the stream itself, will inspire you with some of the delight you have felt in happier climes."

Malville consented. But dare I tell the issue of my invitation? Thursday came, and the sky was covered with clouds; it looked like rain. However, we courageously embarked, and within an hour a gentle mizzling commenced. We made an awning of sails, and wrapt ourselves up in boat-cloaks and shawls. "It is not much," cried one, with a sigh. "I do not think it will last," remarked another, in a despairing voice. A silence ensued. "Can you contrive to shelter me at this corner?" said one; "my shoulder is getting wet." In about five minutes another observed, that the water was trickling in his neck. Yet we went on. The rain ceased for a few minutes, and we tethered our boat in a small cove under dripping trees; we ate our collation, and raised our spirits with wine, so that we were able to endure with tolerable fortitude the heavy rain that accompanied us as we slowly proceeded homewards up the river.

III

The Bride of Modern Italy

My heart is fixt:
This is the sixt.—ELIA

ON A SERENE winter morning two young ladies, Clorinda and Teresa, walked up and down the garden of the convent of St. S——, at Rome. If my reader has never seen a convent, or if he has only seen the better kind, let him dismiss from his mind all he may have heard or imagined of such abodes, or he can never transport himself into the garden of St. S——. He must figure it to himself as bounded by a long, low, straggling, white-washed, weather-stained building, with grated windows, the lower ones glassless. It is a kitchen garden, but the refuse of the summer stock alone remained, except a few cabbages, which perfumed the air with their rank exhalations. The walks were neglected, yet not overgrown, but strewed with broken earthen-ware, ashes, cabbage-stalks, orange-peel, bones, and all that marks the vicinity of a much frequented, but disorderly mansion. The beds were intersected by these paths, and the whole was surrounded by a high wall. This common scene was, however, unlike what it would have been in this country. You saw the decayed and straggling boughs of the passion-flower against the walls of the convent; here and there a geranium, its luxuriant foliage starred by scarlet flowers, grew unharmed by frost among the cabbages; the lemon plants had been removed to shelter, but orange trees were nailed against the wall, the golden fruit peeping out from amidst the dark leaves; the wall itself was variegated by a thousand rich hues; and thick and pointed aloes grew beneath it. Under the highest wall, opposite the back door of the convent, a corner of ground was enclosed; this was the burial place of the nuns; and in the path that led from the door to this enclosure Clorinda and Teresa walked up and down.

"He will never come!" exclaimed Clorinda.

"I fear the dinner bell will ring and interrupt us, if he does come," observed Teresa.

"Some cruel obstacle doubtless prevents him," continued Clorinda, sighing—"and I have prayed to St. Giacomo, and vowed to give him the best flowers and a candle a foot long next Easter."

Teresa smiled: "I remember," she said, "that at Christmas you fulfilled such a vow to San Francesco,—was not that for the sake of Cieco Magni? for you change your saint as your lover changes name;—tell me, sweet Clorinda, how many saints have been benefited by your piety?"

Clorinda looked angry, and then sorrowful; the large drops gathered in her dark eyes: "You are unkind to taunt me thus, Teresina;—when did I love truly until now? believe me, never; and if heaven bestows Giacomo upon me—oh! that is his bell!—naughty Teresa, you will cause me to meet him with tears in my eyes."

Away they ran to the parlour of the convent, and were joined there by an old woman purblind and nearly deaf, who was to be present at the visit of Giacomo de' Tolomei, the brother of Teresa. He kissed the hands of the young ladies, and then they commenced a conversation, which, by the lowness of their tones, and an occasional intermixture of French, was quite incomprehensible to their Argus, who was busily employed in knitting a large green worsted shawl.

"Well?"—said Clorinda, in a tone of inquiry.

"Well, dear Clorinda, I have executed our design, though I hope little from it. I have written a proposal of marriage; if you approve of it, I will send it to your parents. Here it is."

"What is that paper?" cried the Argus.

Teresa bawled in her ear: "Only the history of the late miracle performed at Asisa" (Italians, male or female, are not great patronizers of truth), "look at it, dear Eusta." (Eusta could not read.) "I will read it to you by and bye." Eusta went on with her knitting.

The two girls looking over one another, read the proposal of marriage, which Giacomo de' Tolomei made to the parents of Clorinda Saviani. The paper was divided into two columns, one headed: "The Proposal," —the other "Observations to be made thereon"—and this latter column was left blank. The proposal itself was divided into several heads and numbered. It premised that a noble family of Sienna wishing to ally themselves to the family of the Saviani of Rome, in the persons of their eldest son and Clorinda, they presented the following considerations to the heads of that house first, that the young man was well-made, good-looking, healthy, studiously inclined, and of irreproachable morals. The circumstances of his fortune were then detailed, and the claims of dowry: it concluded by saying, that if the parents of Clorinda approved of the terms proposed, the young people might be introduced to each other, and if mutually pleased at their interview, the nuptials might be celebrated in the course of a few months. When Clorinda had finished reading, the tears that had gathered in her eyes fell drop after drop upon the paper. —"Wherefore do you weep?" asked Giacomo, "why do you distress me thus?"

"This proposal will never be accepted. You have asked twelve thousand crowns in dowry; my parents will not give more than six."

"And yet," replied Giacomo, "I have named a sum to which I am convinced my father will never agree; he will require twenty thousand at least; even if your parents accede I shall have to win his consent; but if prayers and tears can move him, I will not be chary of either."

The bell rang for dinner, old Eusta arose, and Giacomo retired. Dinner!—what dainty feast of convent-like confectionaries does the reader picture?—Let him see, in truth, a long, brick-paved floor, with long deal tables, and benches ditto; the tables covered with not white cloths; cellars of black salt; bottles of sour wine, and small loaves of bitter bread. Then came the minestra, consisting (for it was fast day) of what we call macaroni, water, oil, and cheese; then a few vegetables swimming in oil; a concluding dish of eggs fried with garlic, and the repast of one of the most highborn and loveliest girls in Rome was finished. Clorinda Saviani was indeed handsome, and all her fine features expressed the *bisogna d'amare* which ruled her heart. She was just eighteen, and had been five years in this convent, waiting until her father should find a husband of noble birth, who would be content with a slender dowry. During this time she had formed several attachments for various youths, who, under different pretexts, had visited the convent. She had written letters, prayed and wept, and then yielding to insurmountable difficulties she had changed her idol, though she had never ceased to love. The fastidious English must not be disgusted with this picture. It is, perhaps, only a coarse representation of what takes place at every ball-room with us. And if it went beyond;—the nature of the Catholic religion, which crushes the innate conscience by giving a false one in its room; the system of artifice and heartlessness that subsists in a convent; the widely spread maxim in Italy, that dishonour attaches itself to the discovered not the concealed fault—all this forms the excuse why with a tender heart and much native talent, there was neither constancy in Clorinda's love, nor dignity in her conduct.

After their repast the friends retired to Clorinda's cell; a small, though high room, floored with brick, miserably furnished, and neither clean nor orderly. A prie-dieu was beside the little bed with a crucifix over it, together with two or three prints (like our penny children's prints) of saints, among which St. Giacomo appeared with the freshest and cleanest face; beside these was a glass (resembling a bird's drinking vessel) containing holy water, rather the worse for long standing; in a closet, with the door a-jar, among tattered books and female apparel, hung a glass-case enclosing a waxen Gesù Bambino, and some flowers, gathered for this holy dedication and drooping for want of light, were placed beneath him; some mignionette, basil, and heliotrope, weeds o'ergrown, flowered in a wooden trough at the window; a broken looking glass; a leaden ink stand—such was Clorinda's boudoir.

"I despair," she exclaimed—"I see no end to my evils—and but one road open——flight——"—"Which would ruin my brother."—"How? —he is of another state."—"And your honour?"—"Honour in this dungeon!—O, let me breathe the fresh air of heaven; let me no longer see this prison room; these high walls and all the circumstances of my convent life, and I care not for the rest." "But how? You may get people into the convent—but to get out yourself is a different affair." "I have many plans:—if this proposal of your brother fail, as it will, I will disclose them to him."

A lay sister now came in to ask the young ladies if they would take coffee with the Superior. They found her alone; a little, squat, snuff-taking old woman; she was in high ill-humour: "Body of Bacchus!" she began, "you introduce strange laws in St. S——!—This coffee is detestable—Your brother, Teresina, is here every day—I detest coffee without rum—Clorinda sees him, and it begins to be talked of—when he comes to-morrow, you only must receive him, and request him to discontinue his visits."

Clorinda's tears mingled with her coffee—"The old witch!" she said, when they had retired, "she is fishing for a present."—"And must have one; what shall Giacomo bring her?"—"Let him send some rum. Did you not see the faces she made over her coffee? yet she is too niggardly to buy it herself." A note was hastily dispatched to Giacomo by Teresa, to inform him of the necessary oblation. He came the next day well provided; for the waiter of a neighbouring inn accompanied him bearing six bottles of what bore the name of *Romme*. Teresa was called and dispatched to solicit the presence of the Superior. She came; Giacomo took off his hat: "Signora," said he, "it is winter time, and I bring you a wintry gift.—Will you favour me by accepting this rum?"—"Signor, you are too courteous."—"The courtesy is yours, Signora, in honouring me by receiving my present. I hope that you will find it good."—He uncorked a bottle; Teresa ran for a glass; Giacomo filled it, and the Superior emptied it. Clorinda at the same moment tripped into the room. She started with a natural air, and after saluting Giacomo was going away, but he detained her, and they all sat down together, until the Superior was called away to give out bread for supper, and the three young people remained together.

The girls turned to Giacomo with inquiring looks: his were sorrowful. "My proposal has not been received. Your parents replied that they have proposed you to some one, and cannot break off the treaty."—"And thus I am to be sacrificed!" cried Clorinda, casting up her beautiful eyes. —"Will you consent?" said Giacomo reproachfully.—"What means have I? I have talked of flight" (Giacomo's countenance fell); "and that, although difficult, is not impossible."—"How?"—"Why, my cell adjoins that of the Superior. She is fond of sweet things; on the next holiday I will make some cakes for her, filled with sugar and a little opium. I can then steal away the keys, make an impression on wax (I have a large piece ready), and you can easily get them counterfeited."—"You would engage my brother in a dangerous enterprize," said Teresa.—"My dear, dear Clorinda, my sweet friend," said Giacomo, "you are ignorant of the world's ways. I would sacrifice my life for you; but you would thus lose your honour, I should be imprisoned, and you would be sent to some dreary convent among the mountains, till forced to marry some boor who would render you miserable for life."—"What is to be done then?" asked Clorinda, discontentedly.—"It requires thought. Something must, something shall, be done; do you be faithful to me, and refuse your parents' offer, and I do not despair. In the mean time I will set out for Sienna to-morrow and see my father."

Giacomo had formed an intimacy with a young English artist residing at Rome, and he left the cares of his love in the hands of this gentleman, while he by short days' journeys, and with a heavy heart, proceeded towards Sienna. The following day brought a letter of five pages, in a nearly illegible hand, to be delivered to Clorinda. Our Englishman had been a year in Rome, but he had never yet been within a convent. As he passed the prison-like building of St. S——, and measured with his eye the lofty walls of its garden, he had peopled it with nuns of all ages, states, and dispositions;—the solemn and demure, the ambitious, the bigoted, and those who, repenting of their vows, wetted their pallet with their midnight tears, and then, prostrate on the damp marble before the crucifix, prayed God to pardon them for being human. And then he thought of the novices fearful as brides, but not so hopeful; and of the boarders who dreamt of the world outside, as we of Paradise beyond the grave. He pictured echoing corridors, painted windows, the impenetrable grate, the religious cloister, and the garden, that most immaculate of asylums, with grassy walks, majestic trees, and veiled forms flitting under their shade. Well, thought he, I am now in for it; and if I do not lose my heart, I shall at least gain some excellent hints for my picture of the Profession of Eloisa.

He crossed the outer hall, rang at the bell, and the old tottering portress came towards the door. He asked for "the Signora Teresa de'

Tolomei." He was shown into the parlour—a vaulted room, the floor bricked, the furniture mean, without fire or chimney, though the cold east wind covered the ground with hoar frost. In a few minutes the two friends tripped into the room, followed by Eusta, who, instead of her knitting, carried a fire-pot filled with wood ashes, over which she held her withered hands and her blue nose, frost bitten. The girls were somewhat startled on seeing the stranger, who advanced, and announcing himself as Signor Marcott Alleyn, a friend of the brother of Teresa, delivered a little packet, together with a note which bade his sister confide implicitly in the Englishman.

The conversation became animated. No bashfulness intruded to prevent Clorinda from discoursing eloquently of her passion, especially when she observed the deep interest which her account excited. Alleyn was a man of infinitely pleasing manners; he had a soft tone of voice and eyes full of expression. Italian ladies are not accustomed to the English system of gallantry; since in that country either downright love is made, or the most distant coldness preserved between the sexes. Alleyn's compassion was excited in various ways. He heard that Clorinda had been imprisoned in that convent for five years; he saw the desolate garden, he felt the bitter cold, which was unalleviated by any thing except fire-pots; he had a glance at the blank corridors and squalid cells, and he saw in the victim an elegance of manners and a delicate sensitiveness that ill accorded with such dreary privations. Several visits ensued, and Alleyn became a favourite in the convent. He was only seventeen; his spirits were high; he diverted the friends, brought presents of rum and confectionary to the nuns, kissed some of the least ugly, made covert game of the Superior, and established himself with greater freedom in this seclusion in a week than Giacomo had done in a year. At first he sympathised with Clorinda, now he did more—he amused her. If she wept for the absence of Giacomo, he made her laugh at some story told *apropos*, which diverted her. If she complained of the petty tyranny of the nuns, he laid some plot of droll revenge, which she executed. He introduced a system of English jokes and hoaxes, at which the poor Italians were perfectly aghast, and to which no experience prevented their becoming victims; so utterly unable were they to comprehend the meaning of such machinations; and then, when their loud voices pealed through the arched passages in wonder and anger, they were appeased by soft words and well-timed gifts.

But this sunshine could not last for ever. Clorinda was at first more happy and gay than she had ever been. She in vain endeavoured to lament the absence of her lover. Alleyn prevented every emotion except gaiety from finding a place in her heart. She looked forward with delight for the hour of his visit, and the merriment that he excited left its traces on the rest of the day. Her step was light; and the cold of her cheerless cell was unfelt, since it had been adorned with caricatures of the Superior and nuns; their tyranny was either laid asleep or revenged, and Giacomo was, alas! forgotten. Her love-breathing letters lost their fire, and the writing them became an irksome task; her sighs were changed into smiles—but suddenly these again vanished, and Clorinda became more pensive and sad than ever. She avoided Teresa, and passed most of her time in lonely walks up and down the straight paths of the garden. She was fretful if Alleyn did not come; when he was announced, she would blush, sit silent in his presence, and, if any of his sallies provoked her laughter, it was quickly quenched by her tears. Her devotions even lost their accustomed warmth; Alleyn had no tutelar saint; no Marcott had ever been honoured with canonization, nor had any of the bones found in the catacombs been baptized with that transalpine name. "Marry, this is miching Mallecho; it means mischief,"*—the brief mischief of inconstancy, new love, and all the evils attendant on such a change. Alleyn did not suspect this turn in the tide, till, left tête-à-tête one morning, some slight attentions on his part painted her cheeks with blushes; the confession was not far behind, he heard with mingled surprise and delight, and one kiss sealed their infidelity to the absent Giacomo just as Teresa and Eusta entered.

Alleyn was only seventeen. At that age men look on women as living Edens which they dare not imagine they can ever enjoy; they love, and dream not of being loved; they seek, and their wildest fancies do not picture themselves as sought: so it was small wonder that the heart of Alleyn beat with exultation, that his step was light and his eyes sparkling as he left the convent on that day. His visits were now more frequent; Teresa was confined to her room by illness, and the lovers (though that sacred name is prophaned by such an application) were left together unwatched. Clorinda's thoughts turned wholly upon escape, and Alleyn heedlessly fostered such thoughts, until one day she said: "If I quit the convent this night, will you be under the walls to receive me?"—"My sweet Clorinda, are you serious?"—"Alas! no, I cannot. But in a few nights I trust that I shall be able to execute my project. Look, here is wax with an impression of the keys of the convent; you must get others made from it. The sisters shall sleep well that night, and before morning we will be far on our journey towards your happy country. Fear not; my disguise is ready—all will go well."

"The devil it will!" thought Alleyn, as he quitted St. S——, and carefully placing the waxen impression he had received against a sunny wall, he paced up the Corso,—"and the devil take me if ever I go within those walls again! I have sown a pretty crop, but I am not mad enough to

---

* Shakespeare, *Hamlet* III. ii. 147–48 (Ed.).

reap it; and, as the fates will have it, here is Tolomei returned to tax me with my false proceedings. I wish all convents and women——."

Tolomei now accosted him. They walked together towards the Coliseum, talking of indifferent things. They climbed to the highest part of the ruin, and then, seated amid leafy shrubs and fragrant violets and wall flowers, looking over the desert lanes and violated Forum of Rome, Giacomo asked—"What news of Clorinda?" Alleyn wished himself hanged, and, with a look that almost indicated that his wish was about to be fulfilled, replied briefly to his friend's questions, and then began a string himself, that he might escape his keen, lover-like looks—more painful than his words. Giacomo's hopes were nearly dead. His father was inexorable; and he had learnt, besides, that the person selected by her parents as a husband for Clorinda had arrived in Rome, and this accomplished his misery. He shed abundance of tears as he related this, and ended by declaring that if he still found Clorinda faithful and affectionate, the contrariety of his destiny would urge him to some desperate measure. They separated at length, having appointed to go together to St. S—— on the following day.

Alleyn broke this appointment. He sent an excuse to Giacomo, who accordingly went alone. In the evening he received a note from Clorinda. She lamented his absence; declared her utter aversion for Giacomo; bewailed her hard fate, and having acquainted him that she was to spend the following day with her parents, entreated him to call on the succeeding one. Alleyn passed the intermediate time at Tivoli, that he might avoid his injured friend, and at the appointed hour went to the convent. Teresa and Clorinda were together; they both looked disturbed and angry; when Alleyn appeared, Teresa arose, and casting a disdainful look on the conscious pair, left the parlour. Clorinda burst into tears. "Oh, my beloved friend," she cried, "I have gone through heart-breaking scenes since I last saw you. This cruel Teresa is continually upbraiding me, and Giacomo's silent looks of grief are a still greater reproach. Yet I am innocent. This heart has escaped from my control; its overwhelming sensations defy all the efforts of my reason, and I passionately love without hope, almost without a return—nor is this all." She then related, that during her visit of the day before, she had been introduced to the person on whom her parents had resolved to bestow her. "At first," she continued, "I was ignorant of the design on foot, and saw him with indifference. Presently my mother took me aside; she began with a torrent of reproaches; told me that all my artifices were discovered, and then showed me a letter of mine to Giacomo which had been intercepted by that artful monster the Superior, and concluded by telling me that I must agree instantly to marry the personage to whom I had been introduced.

'Not that you shall be forced,' she said; 'beware therefore of spreading that report; but your conduct necessitates the strongest measures. If you refuse this match, which is in every way suitable to you, you must prepare to be sent to a convent of Carthusian Nuns at Benevento, where if you do not take the veil, you will be strictly guarded, and your plots, letters, and lovers, will be of no avail.' Without permitting me to reply, this cruel mother led me back to the drawing room; this personage, whose name is Romani, came near me, and presently took an opportunity of asking whether I agreed to the arrangement of my parents. What could I say? I gave an ungracious assent, and they consider the matter settled. His estate is near Spoleto, and he is gone to prepare for my reception. The writings are drawing up; the time will soon arrive when I shall change my cage and be miserable for life. You alone, Alleyn, you, generous and brave Englishman, can aid me; take me hence; bear me away to freedom and love, and let me not be sacrificed to this unknown bridegroom, whose person I hardly know, and the idea of whom fills my heart with despair." Alleyn replied as he best might, with expressions of real sorrow, but of small consolation, and the inexorable dinner-bell rang and separated them just as he concluded his reply.

The same evening Alleyn received a note from her. "My horror of this marriage," she wrote, "increases in proportion as the period of its accomplishment approaches. I hear to-day that my parents have already given my *corrèdo* to Romani, which he is to expend in jewels and dresses for me, and thus my fate is nearly sealed. I shall be banished from Rome and my friends; I shall live with a stranger—I must be miserable. Giacomo is better than this. But as an union with him is impossible, and you refuse to aid me, and to liberate one whom you say you love, listen to a plan I have formed; some years ago I was addressed by one, who at that time gained my heart, and whom I still regard with tenderness. The smallness of my dowry caused his father to break off the treaty; this father is now dead. Go to this gentleman—find out whether he still loves me. Married to him, I should be united to one whose merits I know—I should live at Rome, and there would be some alleviation to my cruel fate. At least come to-morrow to the convent, and endeavour to console your miserable friend."

Alleyn, as may easily be supposed, did not pay the required visit to the quondam lover of Clorinda. Perhaps she expected this; for the same night she wrote to him herself. Her letter was long and eloquent. Its expressions seemed to proceed from the over-flowings of a passionate and loving heart. She referred to Alleyn as a common friend, and urged expedition in every measure that was to be pursued. This letter was intercepted and carried to her parents. On the following day Alleyn received a despairing note, entreating him not to attempt to come to the convent. "Alas!" she wrote, "how truly miserable I am! What a fate! I suffer, and am the cause of a thousand griefs to others. Oh heaven! I were better dead; then I should cease to lament, or at least to occasion wretchedness to others. Now I am hated by others, and even by myself—Oh, my incomparable friend! Angel of my heart! Can I be the cause of misery even to you? See Giacomo, my beloved friend; tell him how deeply I pity him, but counsel him in my name to desist from all further pursuit. He must permit me to obey my parents, and they will never consent. My sole aim now is to escape from this prison."

Another and another letter came; and she most earnestly begged him not to come to the convent. Thus nearly a month passed, when one morning early Alleyn was surprised by a visit from the Superior of the convent of St. S——. The old lady seemed very full of matter. She drank the rosoglio presented to her, took snuff, and opened her budget. She talked of the trouble she had ever had with poor Clorinda; inveighed against Giacomo; during her long discourse she praised her own sagacity, the tender affection of Clorinda's parents, and related how she had always opposed the entrance of young men into the convent and their free communication with Clorinda, except his own; but that his politeness and known integrity had in this particular caused her to relax her discipline; and she concluded by inviting him to visit the convent whenever it should be agreeable to him. She then took her leave.

Alleyn was much disturbed. He wished not to go to St. S——; he knew that he ought not to see Clorinda again. He resolved not to go out at all, and sat thinking of her beauty, love, and unaffected manners, until he resolved to walk that he might get rid of such thoughts. He hurried down the Corso, and before he was aware found himself before the door of the convent of St. S——. He paused, again he moved, and entered the outer hall—his hand was on the bell, when the door opened and Giacomo came out. Seeing Alleyn, he threw himself into his arms, shedding a torrent of tears. This exordium startled our Englishman; the conclusion was soon told: Clorinda had married Romani the day before, and on the same evening had quitted Rome for Spoleto.

This news sobered Alleyn at once; he shuddered almost to think of the folly he had been about to commit, feeling as one who is stayed by a friendly hand when about to place his foot beyond the brink of a high precipice. They turned from the convent door. "And yet," said Alleyn as he walked on, "are you secure of the truth of your account? The Superior called on me yesterday and invited me to visit St. S——. Why should she do this if Clorinda were gone? I have half a mind to go and fathom this mystery."

"Ay, go by all means," replied Giacomo bitterly, "you will be welcome; fill your pockets with sugar plums; dose the old lady with rosoglio, and kiss the gentle nuns, the youngest of whom bears the weight of sixty years under the fillet on her brow. They miss your good cheer, and who knows, Clorinda gone, what other nets they may weave to secure so valuable a prize. True, you are an Englishman and a heretic; words which, interpreted into pure Tuscan, mean an untired prodigal, and one, pardon me, whose conscience will no more stickle at violating yon sanctuary than at eating flesh on Fridays. Go by all means, and make the best of your good fortune among these Houris."

"Rather say, take post horses for Spoleto, friend Giacomo. And yet neither—it is all vanity and vexation of spirit. I will go paint my Profession of Eloisa."

IV

Roger Dodsworth

THE REANIMATED ENGLISHMAN

IT MAY BE REMEMBERED, that on the fourth of July last,* a paragraph
appeared in the papers importing that Dr. Hotham, of Northumberland,
returning from Italy, over Mount St. Gothard, a score or two of years
ago, had dug out from under an avalanche, in the neighbourhood of the
mountain, a human being whose animation had been suspended by the
action of the frost. Upon the application of the usual remedies, the patient was resuscitated, and discovered himself to be Mr. Dodsworth, the
son of the antiquary Dodsworth, who perished in the reign of Charles I.
He was thirty-seven years of age at the time of his inhumation, which had
taken place as he was returning from Italy, in 1654. It was added that as
soon as he was sufficiently recovered he would return to England, under
the protection of his preserver. We have since heard no more of him,
and various plans for public benefit, which have started in philanthropic
minds on reading the statement, have already returned to their pristine
nothingness. The antiquarian society had eaten their way to several votes
for medals, and had already begun, in idea, to consider what prices it
could afford to offer for Mr. Dodsworth's old clothes, and to conjecture
what treasures in the way of pamphlet, old song, or autographic letter his
pockets might contain. Poems from all quarters, of all kinds, elegiac,
congratulatory, burlesque and allegoric, were half written. Mr. Godwin had
suspended for the sake of such authentic information the history of the
Commonwealth he had just begun. It is hard not only that the world
should be baulked of these destined gifts from the talents of the country,
but also that it should be promised and then deprived of a new subject of
romantic wonder and scientific interest. A novel idea is worth much in the
commonplace routine of life, but a new fact, an astonishment, a miracle,

* 1826 (Ed.).

43

a palpable wandering from the course of things into apparent impossibili-
ties, is a circumstance to which the imagination must cling with delight,
and we say again that it is hard, very hard, that Mr. Dodsworth refuses to
appear, and that the believers in his resuscitation are forced to undergo
the sarcasms and triumphant arguments of those sceptics who always keep
on the safe side of the hedge.

Now we do not believe that any contradiction or impossibility is attached to the adventures of this youthful antique. Animation (I believe
physiologists agree) can as easily be suspended for an hundred or two
years, as for as many seconds. A body hermetically sealed up by the
frost, is of necessity preserved in its pristine entireness. That which is
totally secluded from the action of external agency, can neither have any
thing added to nor taken away from it: no decay can take place, for
something can never become nothing; under the influence of that state of
being which we call death, change but not annihilation removes from our
sight the corporeal atoma; the earth receives sustenance from them, the
air is fed by them, each element takes its own, thus seizing forcible
repayment of what it had lent. But the elements that hovered round Mr.
Dodsworth's icy shroud had no power to overcome the obstacle it presented. No zephyr could gather a hair from his head, nor could the
influence of dewy night or genial morn penetrate his more than adaman-
tine panoply. The story of the Seven Sleepers rests on a miraculous
interposition—they slept. Mr. Dodsworth did not sleep; his breast never
heaved, his pulses were stopped; death had his finger pressed on his lips
which no breath might pass. He has removed it now, the grim shadow is
vanquished, and stands wondering. His victim has cast from him the
frosty spell, and arises as perfect a man as he had lain down an hundred
and fifty years before. We have eagerly desired to be furnished with some
particulars of his first conversations, and the mode in which he has learnt
to adapt himself to his new scene of life. But since facts are denied to us,
let us be permitted to indulge in conjecture. What his first words were
may be guessed from the expressions used by people exposed to shorter
accidents of the like nature. But as his powers return, the plot thickens.
His dress had already excited Doctor Hotham's astonishment—the
peaked beard—the love locks—the frill, which, until it was thawed, stood
stiff under the mingled influence of starch and frost; his dress fashioned
like that of one of Vandyke's portraits, or (a more familiar similitude)
Mr. Sapio's costume in Winter's Opera of the Oracle, his pointed shoes—
all spoke of other times. The curiosity of his preserver was keenly awake,
that of Mr. Dodsworth was about to be roused. But to be enabled to
conjecture with any degree of likelihood the tenor of his first inquiries, we
must endeavour to make out what part he played in his former life. He
lived at the most interesting period of English History—he was lost to the

world when Oliver Cromwell had arrived at the summit of his ambition, and in the eyes of all Europe the commonwealth of England appeared so established as to endure for ever. Charles I. was dead; Charles II. was an outcast, a beggar, bankrupt even in hope. Mr. Dodsworth's father, the antiquary, received a salary from the republican general, Lord Fairfax, who was himself a great lover of antiquities, and died the very year that his son went to his long, but not unending sleep, a curious coincidence this, for it would seem that our frost-preserved friend was returning to England on his father's death, to claim probably his inheritance—how short lived are human views! Where now is Mr. Dodsworth's patrimony? Where his co-heirs, executors, and fellow legatees? His protracted absence has, we should suppose, given the present possessors to his estate—the world's chronology is an hundred and seventy years older since he seceded from the busy scene, hands after hands have tilled his acres, and then become clods beneath them; we may be permitted to doubt whether one single particle of their surface is individually the same as those which were to have been his—the youthful soil would of itself reject the antique clay of its claimant.

Mr. Dodsworth, if we may judge from the circumstance of his being abroad, was no zealous commonwealth's man, yet his having chosen Italy as the country in which to make his tour and his projected return to England on his father's death, renders it probable that he was no violent loyalist. One of those men he seems to be (or to have been) who did not follow Cato's advice as recorded in the Pharsalia; a party, if to be of no party admits of such a term, which Dante recommends us utterly to despise, and which not unseldom falls between the two stools, a seat on either of which is so carefully avoided. Still Mr. Dodsworth could hardly fail to feel anxious for the latest news from his native country at so critical a period; his absence might have put his own property in jeopardy; we may imagine therefore that after his limbs had felt the cheerful return of circulation, and after he had refreshed himself with such of earth's products as from all analogy he never could have hoped to live to eat, after he had been told from what peril he had been rescued, and said a prayer thereon which even appeared enormously long to Dr. Hotham—we may imagine, we say, that his first question would be: "If any news had arrived lately from England?"

"I had letters yesterday," Dr. Hotham may well be supposed to reply.

"Indeed," cries Mr. Dodsworth, "and pray, sir, has any change for better or worse occurred in that poor distracted country?"

Dr. Hotham suspects a Radical, and coldly replies: "Why, sir, it would be difficult to say in what its distraction consists. People talk of starving manufacturers, bankruptcies, and the fall of the Joint Stock Companies—excrescences these, excrescences which will attach themselves to a state of full health. England, in fact, was never in a more prosperous condition."

Mr. Dodsworth now more than suspects the Republican, and, with what we have supposed to be his accustomed caution, sinks for awhile his loyalty, and in a moderate tone asks: "Do our governors look with careless eyes upon the symptoms of over-health?"

"Our governors," answers his preserver, "if you mean our ministry, are only too alive to temporary embarrassment." (We beg Doctor Hotham's pardon if we wrong him in making him a high Tory; such a quality appertains to our pure anticipated cognition of a Doctor, and such is the only cognizance that we have of this gentleman.) "It were to be wished that they showed themselves more firm—the king, God bless him!"

"Sir!" exclaims Mr. Dodsworth.

Doctor Hotham continues, not aware of the excessive astonishment exhibited by his patient: "The king, God bless him, spares immense sums from his privy purse for the relief of his subjects, and his example has been imitated by all the aristocracy and wealth of England."

"The King!" ejaculates Mr. Dodsworth.

"Yes, sir," emphatically rejoins his preserver; "the king, and I am happy to say that the prejudices that so unhappily and unwarrantably possessed the English people with regard to his Majesty are now, with a few" (with added severity) "and I may say contemptible exceptions, exchanged for dutiful love and such reverence as his talents, virtues, and paternal care deserve."

"Dear sir, you delight me," replies Mr. Dodsworth, while his loyalty late a tiny bud suddenly expands into full flower; "yet I hardly understand; the change is so sudden; and the man—Charles Stuart, King Charles, I may now call him, his murder is I trust execrated as it deserves?"

Dr. Hotham put his hand on the pulse of his patient—he feared an access of delirium from such a wandering from the subject. The pulse was calm, and Mr. Dodsworth continued: "That unfortunate martyr looking down from heaven is, I trust, appeased by the reverence paid to his name and the prayers dedicated to his memory. No sentiment, I think I may venture to assert, is so general in England as the compassion and love in which the memory of that hapless monarch is held?"

"And his son, who now reigns?—"

"Surely, sir, you forget; no son; that of course is impossible. No descendant of his fills the English throne, now worthily occupied by the house of Hanover. The despicable race of the Stuarts, long outcast and wandering, is now extinct, and the last days of the last Pretender to the crown of that family justified in the eyes of the world the sentence which ejected it from the kingdom for ever."

Such must have been Mr. Dodsworth's first lesson in politics. Soon, to the wonder of the preserver and preserved, the real state of the case must have been revealed; for a time, the strange and tremendous circumstance of his long trance may have threatened the wits of Mr. Dodsworth with a total overthrow. He had, as he crossed Mount Saint Gothard, mourned a father—now every human being he had ever seen is "lapped in lead,"* is dust, each voice he had ever heard is mute. The very sound of the English tongue is changed, as his experience in conversation with Dr. Hotham assures him. Empires, religions, races of men, have probably sprung up or faded; his own patrimony (the thought is idle, yet, without it, how can he live?) is sunk into the thirsty gulph that gapes ever greedy to swallow the past; his learning, his acquirements, are probably obsolete; with a bitter smile he thinks to himself, I must take to my father's profession, and turn antiquary. The familiar objects, thoughts, and habits of my boyhood, are now antiquities. He wonders where the hundred and sixty folio volumes of MS. that his father had compiled, and which, as a lad, he had regarded with religious reverence, now are—where—ah, where? His favourite play-mate, the friend of his later years, his destined and lovely bride; tears long frozen are uncongealed, and flow down his young old cheeks.

But we do not wish to be pathetic; surely since the days of the patriarchs, no fair lady had her death mourned by her lover so many years after it had taken place. Necessity, tyrant of the world, in some degree reconciles Mr. Dodsworth to his fate. At first he is persuaded that the later generation of man is much deteriorated from his contemporaries; they are neither so tall, so handsome, nor so intelligent. Then by degrees he begins to doubt his first impression. The ideas that had taken possession of his brain before his accident, and which had been frozen up for so many years, begin to thaw and dissolve away, making room for others. He dresses himself in the modern style, and does not object much to anything except the neck-cloth and hardboarded hat. He admires the texture of his shoes and stockings, and looks with admiration on a small Genevese watch, which he often consults, as if he were not yet assured that time had made progress in its accustomed manner, and as if he should find on its dial plate occular demonstration that he had exchanged his thirty-seventh year for his two hundredth and upwards, and had left A.D. 1654 far behind to find himself suddenly a beholder of the ways of men in this enlightened nineteenth century. His curiosity is insatiable; when he reads, his eyes cannot purvey fast enough to his mind, and every now and then he lights upon some inexplicable passage, some discovery and knowledge familiar to us, but undreamed of in his days, that throws

* Shakespeare, *The Passionate Pilgrim*, l. 396 (Ed.).

him into wonder and interminable reverie. Indeed, he may be supposed to pass much of his time in that state, now and then interrupting himself with a royalist song against old Noll and the Roundheads, breaking off suddenly, and looking round fearfully to see who were his auditors, and on beholding the modern appearance of his friend the Doctor, sighing to think that it is no longer of import to any, whether he sing a cavalier catch or a puritanic psalm.

It were an endless task to develope all the philosophic ideas to which Mr. Dodsworth's resuscitation naturally gives birth. We should like much to converse with this gentleman, and still more to observe the progress of his mind, and the change of his ideas in his very novel situation. If he be a sprightly youth, fond of the shows of the world, careless of the higher human pursuits, he may proceed summarily to cast into the shade all trace of his former life, and endeavour to merge himself at once into the stream of humanity now flowing. It would be curious enough to observe the mistakes he would make, and the medley of manners which would thus be produced. He may think to enter into active life, become whig or tory as his inclinations lead, and get a seat in the, even to him, once called chapel of St. Stephens. He may content himself with turning contemplative philosopher, and find sufficient food for his mind in tracing the march of the human intellect, the changes which have been wrought in the dispositions, desires, and powers of mankind. Will he be an advocate for perfectibility or deterioration? He must admire our manufactures, the progress of science, the diffusion of knowledge, and the fresh spirit of enterprise characteristic of our countrymen. Will he find any individuals to be compared to the glorious spirits of his day? Moderate in his views as we have supposed him to be, he will probably fall at once into the temporising tone of mind now so much in vogue. He will be pleased to find a calm in politics; he will greatly admire the ministry who have succeeded in conciliating almost all parties—to find peace where he left feud. The same character which he bore a couple of hundred years ago, will influence him now; he will still be the moderate, peaceful, unenthusiastic Mr. Dodsworth that he was in 1647.

For notwithstanding education and circumstances may suffice to direct and form the rough material of the mind, it cannot create, nor give intellect, noble aspiration, and energetic constancy where dulness, wavering of purpose, and grovelling desires, are stamped by nature. Entertaining this belief we have (to forget Mr. Dodsworth for awhile) often made conjectures how such and such heroes of antiquity would act, if they were reborn in these times: and then awakened fancy has gone on to imagine that some of them are reborn; that according to the theory explained by Virgil in his sixth Æneid, every thousand years the dead return to life, and their souls endued with the same sensibilities and capacities as before, are turned naked of knowledge into this world, again to dress their skeleton powers in such habiliments as situation, education, and experience will furnish. Pythagoras, we are told, remembered many transmigrations of this sort, as having occurred to himself, though for a philosopher he made very little use of his anterior memories. It would prove an instructive school for kings and statesmen, and in fact for all human beings, called on as they are, to play their part on the stage of the world, could they remember what they had been. Thus we might obtain a glimpse of heaven and of hell, as, the secret of our former identity confined to our own bosoms, we winced or exulted in the blame or praise bestowed on our former selves. While the love of glory and posthumous reputation is as natural to man as his attachment to life itself, he must be, under such a state of things, tremblingly alive to the historic records of his honour or shame. The mild spirit of Fox would have been soothed by the recollection that he had played a worthy part as Marcus Antoninus— the former experiences of Alcibiades or even of the emasculated Steeny of James I. might have caused Sheridan to have refused to tread over again the same path of dazzling but fleeting brilliancy. The soul of our modern Corinna would have been purified and exalted by a consciousness that once it had given life to the form of Sappho. If at the present moment the witch, memory, were in a freak, to cause all the present generation to recollect that some ten centuries back they had been somebody else, would not several of our free thinking martyrs wonder to find that they had suffered as Christians under Domitian, while the judge as he passed sentence would suddenly become aware, that formerly he had condemned the saints of the early church to the torture, for not renouncing the religion he now upheld—nothing but benevolent actions and real goodness would come pure out of the ordeal. While it would be whimsical to perceive how some great men in parish affairs would strut under the consciousness that their hands had once held a sceptre, an honest artizan or pilfering domestic would find that he was little altered by being transformed into an idle noble or director of a joint stock company; in every way we may suppose that the humble would be exalted, and the noble and the proud would feel their stars and honours dwindle into baubles and child's play when they called to mind the lowly stations they had once occupied. If philosophical novels were in fashion, we conceive an excellent one might be written on the development of the same mind in various stations, in different periods of the world's history.

But to return to Mr. Dodsworth, and indeed with a few more words to bid him farewell. We entreat him no longer to bury himself in obscurity; or, if he modestly decline publicity, we beg him to make himself known personally to us. We have a thousand inquiries to make, doubts to clear up, facts to ascertain. If any fear that old habits and strangeness of appearance will make him ridiculous to those accustomed to associate with modern exquisites, we beg to assure him that we are not given to ridicule mere outward shows, and that worth and intrinsic excellence will always claim our respect.

This we say, if Mr. Dodsworth is alive. Perhaps he is again no more. Perhaps he opened his eyes only to shut them again more obstinately; perhaps his ancient clay could not thrive on the harvests of these latter days. After a little wonder; a little shuddering to find himself the dead alive—finding no affinity between himself and the present state of things —he has bidden once more an eternal farewell to the sun. Followed to his grave by his preserver and the wondering villagers, he may sleep the true death-sleep in the same valley where he so long reposed. Doctor Hotham may have erected a simple tablet over his twice-buried remains, inscribed—

To the Memory of R. Dodsworth,
An Englishman,
Born April 1, 1617; Died July 16, 1826; Aged 209.

An inscription which, if it were preserved during any terrible convulsion that caused the world to begin its life again, would occasion many learned disquisitions and ingenious theories concerning a race which authentic records showed to have secured the privilege of attaining so vast an age.

V

The Sisters of Albano

And near Albano's scarce divided waves
Shine from a sister valley;—and afar
The Tiber winds, and the broad ocean laves
The Latian coast where sprang the Epic war,
"Arms and the Man," whose re-ascending star
Rose o'er an empire; but beneath thy right
Tully reposed from Rome; and where yon bar
Of girdling mountains intercepts the sight
The Sabine farm was till'd, the weary bard's delight.*

IT WAS TO SEE this beautiful lake that I made my last excursion before quitting Rome. The spring had nearly grown into summer, the trees were all in full but fresh green foliage, the vine-dresser was singing, perched among them, training his vines; the cicala had not yet begun her song, the heats therefore had not commenced; but at evening the fireflies gleamed among the hills, and the cooing aziola assured us of what in that country needs no assurance, fine weather for the morrow. We set out early in the morning to avoid the heats, breakfasted at Albano, and till ten o'clock passed our time in visiting the Mosaic, the villa of Cicero, and other curiosities of the place. We reposed during the middle of the day in a tent elevated for us at the hill top, whence we looked on the hill-embosomed lake, and the distant eminence crowned by a town with its church. Other villages and cottages were scattered among the foldings of mountains, and beyond we saw the deep blue sea of the southern poets, which received the swift and immortal Tiber, rocking it to repose among its devouring waves. The Coliseum falls and the Pantheon decays—the very hills of Rome are perishing, but the Tiber lives for ever, flows for ever—and for ever feeds the land-encircling Mediterranean with fresh waters.

Our summer and pleasure-seeking party consisted of many: to me the most interesting person was the Countess Atanasia D——, who was as

* Byron, *Childe Harold's Pilgrimage* IV. clxxiv (Ed.).

Drawn by J. M. W. Turner

Engraved by Robert Wallis

LAKE ALBANO

beautiful as an imagination of Raphael, and good as the ideal of a poet. Two of her children accompanied her, with animated looks and gentle manners, quiet, yet enjoying. I sat near her, watching the changing shadows of the landscape before us. As the sun descended, it poured a tide of light into the valley of the lake, deluging the deep bank formed by the mountain with liquid gold. The domes and turrets of the far town flashed and gleamed, the trees were dyed in splendour; two or three slight clouds, which had drunk the radiance till it became their essence, floated golden islets in the lustrous empyrean. The waters, reflecting the brilliancy of the sky and the fire-tinted banks, beamed a second heaven, a second irradiated earth, at our feet. The Mediterranean gazing on the sun—as the eyes of a mortal bride fail and are dimmed when reflecting her lover's glance —was lost, mixed in his light, till it had become one with him.—Long (our souls, like the sea, the hills, and lake, drinking in the supreme loveliness) we gazed, till the too full cup overflowed, and we turned away with a sigh.

At our feet there was a knoll of ground, that formed the foreground of our picture; two trees lay basking against the sky, glittering with the golden light, which like dew seemed to hang amid their branches—a rock closed the prospect on the other side, twined round by creepers, and redolent with blooming myrtle—a brook crossed by huge stones gushed through the turf, and on the fragments of rock that lay about, sat two or three persons, peasants, who attracted our attention. One was a hunter, as his gun, lying on a bank not far off, demonstrated, yet he was a tiller of the soil; his rough straw hat, and his picturesque but coarse dress, belonged to that class. The other was some contadina, in the costume of her country, returning, her basket on her arm, from the village to her cottage home. They were regarding the stores of a pedlar, who with doffed hat stood near: some of these consisted of pictures and prints—views of the country, and portraits of the Madonna. Our peasants regarded these with pleased attention.

"One might easily make out a story for that pair," I said: "his gun is a help to the imagination, and we may fancy him a bandit with his contadina love, the terror of all the neighbourhood, except of her, the most defenceless being in it."

"You speak lightly of such a combination," said the lovely countess at my side, "as if it must not in its nature be the cause of dreadful tragedies. The mingling of love with crime is a dread conjunction, and lawless pursuits are never followed without bringing on the criminal, and all allied to him, ineffable misery. I speak with emotion, for your observation reminds me of an unfortunate girl, now one of the Sisters of Charity in the convent of Santa Chiara at Rome, whose unhappy passion for a man, such as you mention, spread destruction and sorrow widely around her."

I entreated my lovely friend to relate the history of the nun: for a long time she resisted my entreaties, as not willing to depress the spirit of a party of pleasure by a tale of sorrow. But I urged her, and she yielded. Her sweet Italian phraseology now rings in my ears, and her beautiful countenance is before me. As she spoke, the sun set, and the moon bent her silver horn in the ebbing tide of glory he had left. The lake changed from purple to silver, and the trees, before so splendid, now in dark masses, just reflected from their tops the mild moonlight. The fireflies flashed among the rocks; the bats circled round us: meanwhile thus commenced the Countess Atanasia:

The nun of whom I speak had a sister older than herself; I can remember them when as children they brought eggs and fruit to my father's villa. Maria and Anina were constantly together. With their large straw hats to shield them from the scorching sun, they were at work in their father's *podere* all day, and in the evening, when Maria, who was the elder by four years, went to the fountain for water, Anina ran at her side. Their cot—the folding of the hill conceals it—is at the lake side opposite; and about a quarter of a mile up the hill is the rustic fountain of which I speak. Maria was serious, gentle, and considerate; Anina was a laughing, merry little creature, with the face of a cherub. When Maria was fifteen, their mother fell ill, and was nursed at the convent of Santa Chiara at Rome. Maria attended her, never leaving her bedside day or night. The nuns thought her an angel, she deemed them saints; her mother died, and they persuaded her to make one of them; her father could not but acquiesce in her holy intention, and she became one of the Sisters of Charity, the nun-nurses of Santa Chiara. Once or twice a year she visited her home, gave sage and kind advice to Anina, and sometimes wept to part from her; but her piety and her active employments for the sick reconciled her to her fate. Anina was more sorry to lose her sister's society. The other girls of the village did not please her: she was a good child, and worked hard for her father, and her sweetest recompense was the report he made of her to Maria, and the fond praises and caresses the latter bestowed on her when they met.

It was not until she was fifteen that Anina showed any diminution of affection for her sister. Yet I cannot call it diminution, for she loved her perhaps more than ever, though her holy calling and sage lectures prevented her from reposing confidence, and made her tremble lest the nun, devoted to heaven and good works, should read in her eyes, and disapprove of the earthly passion that occupied her. Perhaps a part of her reluctance arose from the reports that were current against her lover's character, and certainly from the disapprobation and even hatred of him that her father frequently expressed. Ill-fated Anina! I know not if in the north your peasants love as ours; but the passion of Anina was entwined with the roots of her being, it was herself: she could die, but not cease to love. The dislike of her father for Domenico made their intercourse clandestine. He was always at the fountain to fill her pitcher, and lift it on her head. He attended the same mass; and when her father went to Albano, Velletri, or Rome, he seemed to learn by instinct the exact moment of his departure, and joined her in the *podere*, labouring with her and for her, till the old man was seen descending the mountain-path on his return. He said he worked for a contadino near Nemi. Anina sometimes wondered that he could spare so much time for her; but his excuses were plausible, and the result too delightful not to blind the innocent girl to its obvious cause.

Poor Domenico! the reports spread against him were too well founded: his sole excuse was that his father had been a robber before him, and he had spent his early years among these lawless men. He had better things in his nature, and yearned for the peace of the guiltless. Yet he could hardly be called guilty, for no dread crime stained him; nevertheless, he was an outlaw and a bandit, and now that he loved Anina these names were the stings of an adder to pierce his soul. He would have fled from his comrades to a far country, but Anina dwelt amid their very haunts. At this period also, the police established by the French government, which then possessed Rome, made these bands more alive to the conduct of their members, and rumours of active measures to be taken against those who occupied the hills near Albano, Nemi, and Velletri, caused them to draw together in tighter bonds. Domenico would not, if he could, desert his friends in the hour of danger.

On a *festa* at this time—it was towards the end of October—Anina strolled with her father among the villagers, who all over Italy make holiday, by congregating and walking in one place. Their talk was entirely of the *ladri* and the French, and many terrible stories were related of the extirpation of banditti in the kingdom of Naples, and the mode by which the French succeeded in their undertaking was minutely described. The troops scoured the country, visiting one haunt of the robbers after the other, and dislodging them, tracked them, as in those countries they hunt the wild beasts of the forest, till drawing the circle narrower, they enclosed them in one spot. They then drew a cordon round the place, which they guarded with the utmost vigilance, forbidding any to enter it with provisions, on pain of instant death. And as this menace was rigorously executed, in a short time the besieged bandits were starved into a surrender. The French troops were now daily expected, for they had been seen at Velletri and Nemi; at the same time it was affirmed that several outlaws had taken up their abode at Rocca Giovane, a deserted village on the summit of one of these hills, and it was supposed that they would make that place the scene of their final retreat.

The next day, as Anina worked in the *podere*, a party of French horse passed by along the road that separated her garden from the lake. Curiosity made her look at them; and her beauty was too great not to attract: their observations and address soon drove her away—for a woman in love consecrates herself to her lover, and deems the admiration of others to be profanation. She spoke to her father of the impertinence of these men, and he answered by rejoicing at their arrival, and the destruction of the lawless bands that would ensue. When, in the evening, Anina went to the fountain, she looked timidly around, and hoped that Domenico would be at his accustomed post, for the arrival of the French destroyed her feeling of security. She went rather later than usual, and a cloudy evening made it seem already dark; the wind roared among the trees, bending hither and thither even the stately cypresses; the waters of the lake were agitated into high waves, and dark masses of thunder-cloud lowered over the hill tops, giving a lurid tinge to the landscape. Anina passed quickly up the mountain-path: when she came in sight of the fountain, which was rudely hewn in the living rock, she saw Domenico leaning against a projection of the hill, his hat drawn over his eyes, his *tabarro* fallen from his shoulders, his arms folded in an attitude of dejection. He started when he saw her; his voice and phrases were broken and unconnected; yet he never gazed on her with such ardent love, nor solicited her to delay her departure with such impassioned tenderness.

"How glad I am to find you here!" she said: "I was fearful of meeting one of the French soldiers: I dread them even more than the banditti."

Domenico cast a look of eager inquiry on her, and then turned away, saying, "Sorry am I that I shall not be here to protect you. I am obliged to go to Rome for a week or two. You will be faithful, Anina mia; you will love me, though I never see you more?"

The interview, under these circumstances, was longer than usual: he led her down the path till they nearly came in sight of her cottage; still they lingered: a low whistle was heard among the myrtle underwood at the lake side; he started; it was repeated, and he answered it by a similar note: Anina, terrified, was about to ask what this meant, when, for the first time, he pressed her to his heart, kissed her roseate lips, and, with a muttered "Carissima addio," left her, springing down the bank; and as she gazed in wonder, she thought she saw a boat cross a line of light made by the opening of a cloud. She stood long absorbed in reverie, wondering and remembering with thrilling pleasure the quick embrace and impassioned farewell of her lover. She delayed so long that her father came to seek her.

Each evening after this, Anina visited the fountain at the Ave Maria; he was not there; each day seemed an age; and incomprehensible fears occupied her heart. About a fortnight after, letters arrived from Maria.

They came to say that she had been ill of the mal'aria fever, that she was now convalescent, but that change of air was necessary for her recovery, and that she had obtained leave to spend a month at home at Albano. She asked her father to come the next day to fetch her. These were pleasant tidings for Anina; she resolved to disclose every thing to her sister, and during her long visit she doubted not but that she would contrive her happiness. Old Andrea departed the following morning, and the whole day was spent by the sweet girl in dreams of future bliss. In the evening Maria arrived, weak and wan, with all the marks of that dread illness about her; yet, as she assured her sister, feeling quite well.

As they sat at their frugal supper, several villagers came in to inquire for Maria; but all their talk was of the French soldiers and the robbers, of whom a band of at least twenty was collected in Rocca Giovane, strictly watched by the military.

"We may be grateful to the French," said Andrea, "for this good deed: the country will be rid of these ruffians."

"True, friend," said another; "but it is horrible to think what these men suffer: they have, it appears, exhausted all the food they brought with them to the village, and are literally starving. They have not an ounce of maccaroni among them; and a poor fellow, who was taken and executed yesterday, was a mere anatomy; you could tell every bone in his skin."

"There was a sad story the other day," said another, "of an old man from Nemi, whose son, they say, is among them at Rocca Giovane: he was found within the lines with some baccalà under his pastrano, and shot on the spot."

"There is not a more desperate gang," observed the first speaker, "in the states and the regno put together. They have sworn never to yield but upon good terms: to secure these, their plan is to way-lay passengers and make prisoners, whom they keep as hostages for mild treatment from the government. But the French are merciless; they are better pleased that the bandits wreak their vengeance on these poor creatures than spare one of their lives."

"They have captured two persons already," said another; "and there is old Betta Tossi half frantic, for she is sure her son is taken: he has not been at home these ten days."

"I should rather guess," said an old man, "that he went there with good will: the young scape-grace kept company with Domenico Baldi of Nemi."

"No worse company could he have kept in the whole country," said Andrea: "Domenico is the bad son of a bad race. Is he in the village with the rest?"

"My own eyes assured me of that," replied the other. "When I was up

the hill with eggs and fowls to the piquette there, I saw the branches of an
ilex move; the poor fellow was weak perhaps, and could not keep his
hold; presently he dropt to the ground; every musket was levelled at him,
but he started up and was away like a hare among the rocks. Once he
turned, and then I saw Domenico as plainly, though thinner, poor lad, by
much than he was, as plainly as I now see——Santa Virgine! what is the
matter with Nina?"

She had fainted; the company broke up, and she was left to her sister's
care. When the poor child came to herself she was fully aware of her
situation, and said nothing, except expressing a wish to retire to rest.
Maria was in high spirits at the prospect of her long holiday at home, but
the illness of her sister made her refrain from talking that night, and
blessing her, as she said good night, she soon slept. Domenico starving!
—Domenico trying to escape and dying through hunger, was the vision of
horror that wholly possessed poor Anina. At another time, the discovery
that her lover was a robber might have inflicted pangs as keen as those
which she now felt; but this, at present, made a faint impression, obscured by worse wretchedness. Maria was in a deep and tranquil sleep.
Anina rose, dressed herself silently, and crept down stairs. She stored her
market basket with what food there was in the house, and, unlatching the
cottage-door, issued forth, resolved to reach Rocca Giovane, and to administer to her lover's dreadful wants. The night was dark, but this was
favourable, for she knew every path and turn of the hills; every bush and
knoll of ground between her home and the deserted village which occupies the summit of that hill: you may see the dark outline of some of its
houses about two hours' walk from her cottage. The night was dark, but
still; the libeccio brought the clouds below the mountain-tops, and veiled
the horizon in mist; not a leaf stirred; her footsteps sounded loud in her
ears, but resolution overcame fear. She had entered yon ilex grove, her
spirits rose with her success, when suddenly she was challenged by a
sentinel; no time for escape; fear chilled her blood; her basket dropped
from her arm; its contents rolled out on the ground; the soldier fired his
gun and brought several others round him; she was made prisoner.

In the morning, when Maria awoke, she missed her sister from her
side. I have overslept myself, she thought, and Nina would not disturb me.
But when she came down stairs and met her father, and Anina did not appear, they began to wonder. She was not in the *podere*; two hours passed,
and then Andrea went to seek her. Entering the near village, he saw the
contadini crowding together, and a stifled exclamation of "Ecco il padre!"
told him that some evil had betided. His first impression was that his
daughter was drowned; but the truth, that she had been taken by the
French carrying provisions within the forbidden line, was still more terrible. He returned in frantic desperation to his cottage, first to acquaint

Maria with what had happened, and then to ascend the hill to save his child from her impending fate. Maria heard his tale with horror; but an hospital is a school in which to learn self-possession and presence of mind. "Do you remain, my father," she said: "I will go. My holy character will awe these men, my tears move them: trust me; I swear that I will save my sister." Andrea yielded to her superior courage and energy.

The nuns of Santa Chiara when out of their convent do not usually wear their monastic habit, but dress simply in a black gown. Maria, however, had brought her nun's habiliments with her, and thinking thus to impress the soldiers with respect, she now put it on. She received her father's benediction, and asking that of the Virgin and the saints, she departed on her expedition. Ascending the hill, she was soon stopped by the sentinels. She asked to see their commanding officer, and being conducted to him, she announced herself as the sister of the unfortunate girl who had been captured the night before. The officer, who had received her with carelessness, now changed countenance: his serious look frightened Maria, who clasped her hands, exclaiming, "You have not injured the child! she is safe!"

"She is safe—now," he replied with hesitation; "but there is no hope of pardon."

"Holy Virgin, have mercy on her! what will be done to her?"

"I have received strict orders; in two hours she dies."

"No! no!" exclaimed Maria impetuously, "that cannot be! you cannot be so wicked as to murder a child like her."

"She is old enough, madame," said the officer, "to know that she ought not to disobey orders; mine are so strict, that were she but nine years old, she dies."

These terrible words stung Maria to fresh resolution: she entreated for mercy; she knelt; she vowed that she would not depart without her sister; she appealed to Heaven and the saints. The officer, though cold-hearted, was good-natured and courteous, and he assured her with the utmost gentleness that her supplications were of no avail; that were the criminal his own daughter he must enforce his orders. As a sole concession, he permitted her to see her sister. Despair inspired the nun with energy; she almost ran up the hill, out-speeding her guide: they crossed a folding of the hills to a little sheep-cot, where sentinels paraded before the door. There was no glass to the windows, so the shutters were shut, and when Maria first went in from the bright daylight she hardly saw the slight figure of her sister leaning against the wall, her dark hair fallen below her waist, her head sunk on her bosom, over which her arms were folded. She started wildly as the door opened, saw her sister, and sprung with a piercing shriek into her arms.

They were left alone together: Anina uttered a thousand frantic exclamations, beseeching her sister to save her, and shuddering at the near approach of her fate. Maria had felt herself, since their mother's death, the natural protectress and support of her sister, and she never deemed herself so called on to fulfil this character as now that the trembling girl clasped her neck; her tears falling on her cheeks, and her choked voice entreating her to save her. The thought—O could I suffer instead of you! was in her heart, and she was about to express it, when it suggested another idea, on which she was resolved to act. First she soothed Anina by her promises, then glanced round the cot; they were quite alone: she went to the window, and through a crevice saw the soldiers conversing at some distance. "Yes, dearest sister," she cried, "I will—I can save you— quick—we must change dresses—there is no time to be lost!—you must escape in my habit."

"And you remain to die?"

"They dare not murder the innocent, a nun! Fear not for me—I am safe."

Anina easily yielded to her sister, but her fingers trembled; every string she touched she entangled. Maria was perfectly self-possessed, pale, but calm. She tied up her sister's long hair, and adjusted her veil over it so as to conceal it; she unlaced her bodice, and arranged the folds of her own habit on her with the greatest care—then more hastily she assumed the dress of her sister, putting on, after a lapse of many years, her native contadina costume. Anina stood by, weeping and helpless, hardly hearing her sister's injunctions to return speedily to their father, and under his guidance to seek sanctuary. The guard now opened the door. Anina clung to her sister in terror, while she, in soothing tones, entreated her to calm herself.

The soldier said, they must delay no longer, for the priest had arrived to confess the prisoner.

To Anina the idea of confession associated with death was terrible; to Maria it brought hope. She whispered, in a smothered voice, "The priest will protect me—fear not—hasten to our father!"

Anina almost mechanically obeyed: weeping, with her handkerchief placed unaffectedly before her face, she passed the soldiers; they closed the door on the prisoner, who hastened to the window, and saw her sister descend the hill with tottering steps, till she was lost behind some rising ground. The nun fell on her knees—cold dew bathed her brow, instinctively she feared: the French had shown small respect for the monastic character; they destroyed the convents and desecrated the churches. Would they be merciful to her, and spare the innocent! Alas! was not Anina innocent also? Her sole crime had been disobeying an arbitrary command, and she had done the same.

"Courage!" cried Maria; "perhaps I am fitter to die than my sister is.

Gesu, pardon me my sins, but I do not believe that I shall out-live this day!"

In the meantime, Anina descended the hill slowly and tremblingly. She feared discovery—she feared for her sister—and above all at the present moment, she feared the reproaches and anger of her father. By dwelling on this last idea, it became exaggerated into excessive terror, and she determined, instead of returning to her home, to make a circuit among the hills, to find her way by herself to Albano, where she trusted to find protection from her pastor and confessor. She avoided the open paths, and following rather the direction she wished to pursue than any beaten road, she passed along nearer to Rocca Giovane than she anticipated. She looked up at its ruined houses and bell-less steeple, straining her eyes to catch a glimpse of him, the author of all her ills. A low but distinct whistle reached her ear, not far off; she started—she remembered that on the night when she last saw Domenico a note like that had called him from her side; the sound was echoed and re-echoed from other quarters; she stood aghast, her bosom heaving, her hands clasped. First she saw a dark and ragged head of hair, shadowing two fiercely gleaming eyes, rise from beneath a bush. She screamed, but before she could repeat her scream three men leapt from behind a rock, secured her arms, threw a cloth over her face, and hurried her up the acclivity. Their talk, as she went along, informed her of the horror and danger of her situation.

Pity, they said, that the holy father and some of his red stockings did not command the troops: with a nun in their hands, they might obtain any terms. Coarse jests passed as they dragged their victim towards their ruined village. The paving of the street told her when they arrived at Rocca Giovane, and the change of atmosphere that they entered a house. They unbandaged her eyes: the scene was squalid and miserable, the walls ragged and black with smoke, the floor strewn with offals and dirt; a rude table and broken bench was all the furniture; and the leaves of Indian corn, heaped high in one corner, served, it seemed, for a bed, for a man lay on it, his head buried in his folded arms. Anina looked round on her savage hosts: their countenances expressed every variety of brutal ferocity, now rendered more dreadful from gaunt famine and suffering.

"O there is none who will save me!" she cried. The voice startled the man who was lying on the floor; he leapt up—it was Domenico: Domenico, so changed, with sunk cheeks and eyes, matted hair, and looks whose wildness and desperation differed little from the dark countenances around him. Could this be her lover?

His recognition and surprise at her dress led to an explanation. When the robbers first heard that their prey was no prize, they were mortified and angry; but when she related the danger she had incurred by endeavouring to bring them food, they swore with horrid oaths that no harm should befall her, but that if she liked she might make one of them in all honour and equality. The innocent girl shuddered. "Let me go," she cried; "let me only escape and hide myself in a convent for ever!"

Domenico looked at her in agony. "Yes, poor child," he said; "go, save yourself: God grant no evil befall you; the ruin is too wide already." Then turning eagerly to his comrades, he continued—"You hear her story. She was to have been shot for bringing food to us: her sister has substituted herself in her place. We know the French; one victim is to them as good as another: Maria dies in their hands. Let us save her. Our time is up; we must fall like men, or starve like dogs: we have still ammunition, still some strength left. To arms! let us rush on the poltroons, free their prisoner, and escape or die!"

There needed but an impulse like this to urge the outlaws to desperate resolves. They prepared their arms with looks of ferocious determination. Domenico, meanwhile, led Anina out of the house, to the verge of the hill, inquiring whither she intended to go. On her saying, to Albano, he observed, "That were hardly safe; be guided by me, I entreat you: take these piastres, hire the first conveyance you find, hasten to Rome, to the convent of Santa Chiara: for pity's sake, do not linger in this neighbourhood."

"I will obey your injunctions, Domenico," she replied, "but I cannot take your money; it has cost you too dear: fear not, I shall arrive safely at Rome without that ill-fated silver."

Domenico's comrades now called loudly to him: he had no time to urge his request; he threw the despised dollars at her feet.

"Nina, adieu for ever," he said: "may you love again more happily!"

"Never!" she replied. "God has saved me in this dress; it were sacrilege to change it: I shall never quit Santa Chiara."

Domenico had led her a part of the way down the rock; his comrades appeared at the top, calling to him.

"Gesu save you!" cried he: "reach the convent—Maria shall join you there before night. Farewell!" He hastily kissed her hand, and sprang up the acclivity to rejoin his impatient friends.

The unfortunate Andrea had waited long for the return of his children. The leafless trees and bright clear atmosphere permitted every object to be visible, but he saw no trace of them on the hill side; the shadows of the dial showed noon to be passed, when, with uncontrollable impatience, he began to climb the hill, towards the spot where Anina had been taken. The path he pursued was in part the same that this unhappy girl had taken on her way to Rome. The father and daughter met: the old man saw the nun's dress, and saw her unaccompanied: she covered her face with her hands in a transport of fear and shame; but when, mistaking her for Maria, he asked in a tone of anguish for his youngest darling, her arms fell; she dared not raise her eyes, which streamed with tears.

"Unhappy girl!" exclaimed Andrea, "where is your sister?"

She pointed to the cottage prison, now discernible near the summit of a steep acclivity. "She is safe," she replied: "she saved me; but they dare not murder her."

"Heaven bless her for this good deed!" exclaimed the old man, fervently; "but you hasten on your way, and I will go in search of her."

Each proceeded on an opposite path. The old man wound up the hill, now in view, and now losing sight of the hut where his child was captive: he was aged, and the way was steep. Once, when the closing of the hill hid the point towards which he for ever strained his eyes, a single shot was fired in that direction: his staff fell from his hands, his knees trembled and failed him; several minutes of dead silence elapsed before he recovered himself sufficiently to proceed: full of fears he went on, and at the next turn saw the cot again. A party of soldiers were on the open space before it, drawn up in a line as if expecting an attack. In a few moments from above them shots were fired, which they returned, and the whole was enveloped and veiled in smoke. Still Andrea climbed the hill, eager to discover what had become of his child: the firing continued quick and hot. Now and then, in the pauses of musquetry and the answering echoes of the mountains, he heard a funereal chant; presently, before he was aware, at a turning of the hill, he met a company of priests and contadini, carrying a large cross and a bier. The miserable father rushed forward with frantic impatience; the awe-struck peasants set down their load—the face was uncovered, and the wretched man fell lifeless on the corpse of his murdered child.

The Countess Atanasia paused, overcome by the emotions inspired by the history she related. A long pause ensued: at length one of the party observed, "Maria, then, was the sacrifice to her goodness."

"The French," said the countess, "did not venerate her holy vocation; one peasant girl to them was the same as another. The immolation of any victim suited their purpose of awe-striking the peasantry. Scarcely, however, had the shot entered her heart, and her blameless spirit been received by the saints in Paradise, when Domenico and his followers rushed down the hill to avenge her and themselves. The contest was furious and bloody; twenty French soldiers fell, and not one of the banditti escaped; Domenico, the foremost of the assailants, being the first to fall."

I asked, "And where are now Anina and her father?"

"You may see them, if you will," said the countess, "on your return to Rome. She is a nun of Santa Chiara. Constant acts of benevolence and piety have inspired her with calm and resignation. Her prayers are daily put up for Domenico's soul, and she hopes, through the intercession of the Virgin, to rejoin him in the other world.

"Andrea is very old; he has outlived the memory of his sufferings; but he derives comfort from the filial attentions of his surviving daughter. But when I look at his cottage on this lake, and remember the happy laughing face of Anina among the vines, I shudder at the recollection of the passion that has made her cheeks pale, her thoughts for ever conversant with death, her only wish to find repose in the grave."

VI

Ferdinando Eboli

A TALE

DURING THIS QUIET TIME of peace, we are fast forgetting the excitements and astonishing events of the last war; and the very names of Europe's conquerors are becoming antiquated to the ears of our children. Those were more romantic days than these; for the revulsions occasioned by revolution or invasion were full of romance; and travellers in those countries in which these scenes had place hear strange and wonderful stories, whose truth so much resembles fiction, that, while interested in the narration, we never give implicit credence to the narrator. Of this kind is a tale I heard at Naples. The fortunes of war perhaps did not influence its actors; yet it appears improbable that any circumstances so out of the usual routine could have had place under the garish daylight that peace sheds upon the world.

When Murat, then called Gioacchino, king of Naples, raised his Italian regiments, several young nobles, who had before been scarcely more than vine-dressers on the soil, were inspired with a love of arms, and presented themselves as candidates for military honours. Among these was the young Count Eboli. The father of this youthful noble had followed Ferdinand to Sicily; but his estates lay principally near Salerno, and he was naturally desirous of preserving them; while the hopes that the French government held out of glory and prosperity to his country made him often regret that he had followed his legitimate but imbecil king to exile. When he died, therefore, he recommended his son to return to Naples, to present himself to his old and tried friend, the Marchese Spina, who held a high office in Murat's government, and through his means to reconcile himself to the new king. All this was easily achieved. The young and gallant Count was permitted to possess his patrimony; and, as a further pledge of good fortune, he was betrothed to the only child of the Mar-

65

chese Spina. The nuptials were deferred till the end of the ensuing campaign.

Meanwhile the army was put in motion, and Count Eboli only obtained such short leave of absence as permitted him to visit for a few hours the villa of his future father-in-law, there to take leave of him and his affianced bride. The villa was situated on one of the Apennines to the north of Salerno, and looked down, over the plain of Calabria, in which Pæstum is situated, on to the blue Mediterranean. A precipice on one side, a brawling mountain torrent, and a thick grove of ilex, added beauty to the sublimity of its site. Count Eboli ascended the mountain path in all the joy of youth and hope. His stay was brief. An exhortation and a blessing from the Marchese, a tender farewell, graced by gentle tears, from the fair Adalinda, were the recollections he was to bear with him, to inspire him with courage and hope in danger and absence. The sun had just sunk behind the distant isle of Istria, when, kissing his lady's hand, he said at last "Addio," and with slower steps, and more melancholy mien, rode down the mountain on his road to Naples.

That same night Adalinda retired early to her apartment, dismissing her attendants; and then, restless from mingled fear and hope, she threw open the glass door that led to a balcony looking over the edge of the hill upon the torrent, whose loud rushing often lulled her to sleep; but whose waters were concealed from sight by the ilex trees, which lifted their topmost branches above the guarding parapet of the balcony.

Leaning her cheek upon her hand, she thought of the dangers her lover would encounter, of her loneliness the while, of his letters, and of his return. A rustling sound now caught her ear: was it the breeze among the ilex trees? her own veil was unwaved by every wind, her tresses even, heavy in their own rich beauty only, were not lifted from her cheek. Again those sounds. Her blood retreated to her heart, and her limbs trembled. What could it mean? Suddenly the upper branches of the nearest tree were disturbed; they opened, and the faint starlight showed a man's figure among them. He prepared to spring from his hold, on to the wall. It was a feat of peril. First the soft voice of her lover bade her "Fear not," and on the next instant he was at her side, calming her terrors, and recalling her spirits, that almost left her gentle frame, from mingled surprise, dread, and joy. He encircled her waist with his arm, and pouring forth a thousand passionate expressions of love, she leant on his shoulder, and wept from agitation; while he covered her hands with kisses, and gazed on her with ardent adoration.

Then in calmer mood they sat together; triumph and joy lighted up his eyes, and a modest blush glowed on her cheek; for never before had she sat alone with him, nor heard unrestrained his impassioned assurances of affection. It was indeed Love's own hour. The stars trembled on the roof of his eternal temple; the dashing of the torrent, the mild summer atmosphere, and the mysterious aspect of the darkened scenery, were all in unison, to inspire security and voluptuous hope. They talked of how their hearts, through the medium of divine nature, might hold commune during absence; of the joys of re-union, and of their prospect of perfect happiness.

The moment at last arrived when he must depart. "One tress of this silken hair," said he, raising one of the many curls that clustered on her neck. "I will place it on my heart, a shield to protect me against the swords and balls of the enemy." He drew his keen-edged dagger from its sheath. "Ill weapon for so gentle a deed," he said, severing the lock, and at the same moment many drops of blood fell fast on the fair arm of the lady. He answered her fearful inquiries by showing a gash he had awkwardly inflicted on his left hand. First he insisted on securing his prize, and then he permitted her to bind his wound, which she did half laughing, half in sorrow, winding round his hand a riband loosened from her own arm. "Now farewell," he cried; "I must ride twenty miles ere dawn, and the descending Bear shows that midnight is past." His descent was difficult, but he achieved it happily, and the stave of a song, whose soft sounds rose like the smoke of incense from an altar, from the dell below, to her impatient ear, assured her of his safety.

As is always the case when an account is gathered from eye-witnesses, I never could ascertain the exact date of these events. They occurred however while Murat was king of Naples, and when he raised his Italian regiments, Count Eboli, as aforesaid, became a junior officer in them, and served with much distinction; though I cannot name either the country, or the battle in which he acted so conspicuous a part, that he was on the spot promoted to a troop.

Not long after this event, and while he was stationed in the north of Italy, Gioacchino, sending for him to head-quarters late one evening, intrusted him with a confidential mission, across a country occupied by the enemy's troops, to a town possessed by the French. It was necessary to undertake the expedition during the night, and he was expected to return on that, succeeding the following, day. The king himself gave him his despatches and the word; and the noble youth, with modest firmness, protested that he would succeed, or die, in the fulfilment of his trust.

It was already night, and the crescent moon was low in the west, when Count Ferdinando Eboli mounting his favourite horse, at a quick gallop, cleared the streets of the town; and then, following the directions given him, crossed the country among the fields planted with vines, carefully avoiding the main road. It was a beauteous and still night; calm, and sleep, occupied the earth; war, the bloodhound, slumbered; the spirit of love alone had life at that silent hour. Exulting in the hope of glory, our young hero commenced his journey, and visions of aggrandizement and love formed his reveries. A distant sound roused him; he checked his horse and listened; voices approached; when recognising the speech of a German, he turned from the path he was following, to a still straighter way. But again the tone of an enemy was heard, and the trampling of horses. Eboli did not hesitate; he dismounted, tied his steed to a tree, and, skirting along the enclosure of the field, trusted to escape thus unobserved. He succeeded after an hour's painful progress, and arrived on the borders of a stream, which, as the boundary between two states, was the mark of his having finally escaped danger. Descending the steep bank of the river, which, with his horse, he might perhaps have forded, he now prepared to swim. He held his despatch in one hand, threw away his cloak, and was about to plunge into the water, when from under the dark shade of the *argine*, which had concealed them, he was suddenly arrested by unseen hands, cast on the ground, bound, gagged and blinded, and then placed in a little boat, which was sculled with infinite rapidity down the stream.

There seemed so much of premeditation in the act that it baffled conjecture, yet he must believe himself a prisoner to the Austrian. While, however, he still vainly reflected, the boat was moored, he was lifted out, and the change of atmosphere made him aware that they entered some house. With extreme care and celerity, yet in the utmost silence, he was stripped of his clothes, and two rings he wore, drawn from his fingers; other habiliments were thrown over him; and then no departing footstep was audible: but soon he heard the splash of a single oar, and he felt himself alone. He lay perfectly unable to move; the only relief his captor or captors had afforded him being the exchange of the gag for a tightly bound handkerchief. For hours he thus remained, with a tortured mind, bursting with rage, impatience, and disappointment; now writhing, as well as he could, in his endeavours to free himself, now still, in despair. His despatches were taken away, and the period was swiftly passing when he could by his presence have remedied in some degree this evil. The morning dawned; and though the full glare of the sun could not visit his eyes, he felt it play upon his limbs. As the day advanced, hunger preyed on him, and though amidst the visitation of mightier, he at first disdained this minor, evil; towards evening, it became, in spite of himself, the predominant sensation. Night approached, and the fear that he should remain, and even starve, in this unvisited solitude had more than once thrilled through his frame, when feminine voices and a child's gay laugh met his ear. He heard persons enter the apartment, and he was asked in his native language, while the ligature was taken from his mouth, the cause of his present situation. He attributed it to banditti: his bonds were quickly cut, and his banded eyes restored to sight. It was long before he recovered himself. Water brought from the stream, however, was some refreshment, and by degrees he resumed the use of his senses, and saw that he was in a dilapidated shepherd's cot; with no one near him save the peasant girl and a child who had liberated him. They rubbed his ankles and wrists, and the little fellow offered him some bread, and eggs; after which refreshment, and an hour's repose, Ferdinand felt himself sufficiently restored to revolve his adventure in his mind, and to determine on the conduct he was to pursue.

He looked at the dress which had been given him in exchange for that which he had worn. It was of the plainest and meanest description. Still no time was to be lost; and he felt assured that the only step he could take was to return with all speed to the head-quarters of the Neapolitan army, and inform the king of his disasters and his loss.

It were long to follow his backward steps, and to tell all of indignation and disappointment that swelled his heart. He walked painfully but resolutely all night, and by three in the morning entered the town where Gioacchino then was. He was challenged by the sentinels; he gave the word confided to him by Murat, and was instantly made prisoner by the soldiers. He declared to them his name and rank, and the necessity he was under of immediately seeing the king. He was taken to the guard-house, and the officer on duty there listened with contempt to his representations, telling him that Count Ferdinando Eboli had returned three hours before, ordering him to be confined for further examination as a spy. Eboli loudly insisted that some impostor had taken his name; and while he related the story of his capture, another officer came in, who recognised his person; other individuals acquainted with him joined the party; and as the impostor had been seen by none but the officer of the night, his tale gained ground.

A young Frenchman of superior rank, who had orders to attend the king early in the morning, carried a report of what was going forward to Murat himself. The tale was so strange that the king sent for the young Count; and then, in spite of having seen and believed in his counterfeit a few hours before, and having received from him an account of his mission, which had been faithfully executed, the appearance of the youth staggered him, and he commanded the presence of him who, as Count Eboli, had appeared before him a few hours previously. As Ferdinand stood beside the king, his eye glanced at a large and splendid mirror. His matted hair, his blood-shot eyes, his haggard looks, and torn and mean dress, derogated from the nobility of his appearance; and still less did he appear like the magnificent Count Eboli, when, to his utter confusion and astonishment, his counterfeit stood beside him.

He was perfect in all the outward signs that denoted high birth; and so like him whom he represented, that it would have been impossible to discern one from the other apart. The same chestnut hair clustered on his brow; the sweet and animated hazel eyes were the same; the one voice was the echo of the other. The composure and dignity of the pretender gained the suffrages of those around. When he was told of the strange appearance of another Count Eboli, he laughed in a frank good humoured manner, and turned to Ferdinand, said, "You honour me much, in selecting me for your personation; but there are two or three things I like about myself so well, that you must excuse my unwillingness to exchange myself for you." Ferdinand would have answered, but the false Count, with greater haughtiness, turned to the king, said, "Will your majesty decide between us? I cannot bandy words with a fellow of this sort." Irritated by scorn, Ferdinand demanded leave to challenge the pretender; who said, that if the king and his brother officers did not think that he should degrade himself and disgrace the army by going out with a common vagabond, he was willing to chastise him, even at the peril of his own life. But the king, after a few more questions, feeling assured that the unhappy noble was an impostor, in severe and menacing terms reprehended him for his insolence, telling him that he owed it to his mercy alone that he was not executed as a spy, ordering him instantly to be conducted without the walls of the town, with threats of weighty punishment if he ever dared to subject his impostures to further trial.

It requires a strong imagination, and the experience of much misery, fully to enter into Ferdinand's feelings. From high rank, glory, hope, and love, he was hurled to utter beggary and disgrace. The insulting words of his triumphant rival, and the degrading menaces of his so lately gracious sovereign, rang in his ears; every nerve in his frame writhed with agony. But, fortunately for the endurance of human life, the worst misery in early youth is often but a painful dream, which we cast off when slumber quits our eyes. After a struggle with intolerable anguish, hope and courage revived in his heart. His resolution was quickly made. He would return to Naples, relate his story to the Marchese Spina, and through his influence obtain at least an impartial hearing from the king. It was not, however, in his peculiar situation, an easy task to put his determination into effect. He was pennyless; his dress bespoke poverty; he had neither friend nor kinsman near, but such as would behold in him the most impudent of swindlers. Still his courage did not fail him. The kind Italian soil, in the autumnal season now advanced, furnished him with chestnuts, arbutus berries, and grapes. He took the most direct road over the hills, avoiding towns, and indeed every habitation; travelling principally in the night, when, except in cities, the officers of government had retired from their stations. How he succeeded in getting from one end of Italy to the other it is difficult to say; but certain it is, that, after the interval of a few weeks, he presented himself at the Villa Spina.

With considerable difficulty he obtained admission to the presence of the Marchese, who received him standing, with an inquiring look, not at all recognising the noble youth. Ferdinand requested a private interview, for there were several visitors present. His voice startled the Marchese, who complied, taking him into another apartment. Here Ferdinand disclosed himself, and, with rapid and agitated utterance, was relating the history of his misfortunes, when the tramp of horses was heard, the great bell rang, and a domestic announced "Count Ferdinando Eboli." "It is himself," cried the youth, turning pale. The words were strange, and they appeared still more so, when the person announced entered; the perfect semblance of the young noble, whose name he assumed, as he had appeared, when last, at his departure, he trod the pavement of the hall. He inclined his head gracefully to the baron, turning with a glance of some surprise, but more disdain, towards Ferdinand, exclaiming, "Thou here!"

Ferdinand drew himself up to his full height. In spite of fatigue, ill fare, and coarse garments, his manner was full of dignity. The Marchese looked at him fixedly, and started as he marked his proud mien, and saw in his expressive features the very face of Eboli. But again he was perplexed when he turned and discerned, as in a mirror, the same countenance reflected by the new comer, who underwent this scrutiny somewhat impatiently. In brief and scornful words, he told the Marchese that this was a second attempt in the intruder to impose himself as Count Eboli; that the trick had failed before, and would again; adding, laughing, that it was hard to be brought to prove himself to be himself, against the assertion of a *briccone*, whose likeness to him, and matchless impudence, were his whole stock in trade.

"Why, my good fellow," continued he, sneeringly, "you put me out of conceit with myself, to think that one, apparently so like me, should get on no better in the world."

The blood mounted into Ferdinand's cheeks on his enemy's bitter taunts; with difficulty he restrained himself from closing with his foe, while the words "traitorous impostor!" burst from his lips. The baron commanded the fierce youth to be silent, and, moved by a look that he remembered to be Ferdinand's, he said, gently, "By your respect for me, I adjure you to be patient; fear not but that I will deal impartially." Then turning to the pretended Eboli, he added that he could not doubt but that he was the true Count, and asked excuse for his previous indecision. At first the latter appeared angry, but at length he burst into a laugh, and then, apologizing for his ill breeding, continued laughing heartily at the perplexity of the Marchese. It is certain, his gayety gained more credit with his auditor than the indignant glances of poor Ferdinand. The false Count then said that, after the king's menaces, he had entertained no expectation that the farce was to be played over again. He had obtained leave of absence, of which he profited to visit his future father-in-law, after having spent a few days in his own palazzo at Naples. Until now, Ferdinand had listened silently with a feeling of curiosity, anxious to learn all he could of the actions and motives of his rival; but at these last words he could no longer contain himself. "What!" cried he, "hast thou usurped my place in my own father's house, and dared assume my power in my ancestral halls?" A gush of tears overpowered the youth; he hid his face in his hands. Fierceness and pride lit up the countenance of the pretender. "By the eternal God and the sacred cross, I swear," he exclaimed, "that palace is my father's palace; those halls the halls of my ancestors!" Ferdinand looked up with surprise. "And the earth opens not," he said, "to swallow the perjured man." He then, at the call of the Marchese, related his adventures, while scorn mantled on the features of his rival. The Marchese, looking at both, could not free himself from doubt. He turned from one to the other: in spite of the wild and disordered appearance of poor Ferdinand, there was something in him that forbade his friend to condemn him as the impostor; but then it was utterly impossible to pronounce such the gallant and noble-looking youth, who could only be acknowledged as the real Count by the disbelief of the other's tale. The Marchese, calling an attendant, sent for his fair daughter. "This decision," said he, "shall be made over to the subtle judgment of a woman, and the keen penetration of one who loves." Both the youths now smiled—the same smile; the same expression—that, of anticipated triumph. The baron was more perplexed than ever.

Adalinda had heard of the arrival of Count Eboli, and entered, resplendent in youth and happiness. She turned quickly towards him who resembled most the person she expected to see; when a well-known voice pronounced her name, and she gazed aghast on the double appearance of the lover. Her father, taking her hand, briefly explained the mystery, and bade her assure herself which was her affianced husband.

"Signorina," said Ferdinand, "disdain me not because I appear before you thus in disgrace and misery. Your love, your goodness will restore me to prosperity and happiness."

"I know not by what means," said the wondering girl, "but surely you are Count Eboli."

"Adalinda," said the rival youth, "waste not your words on a villain. Lovely and deceived one, I trust, trembling I say it, that I can with one word assure you that I am Eboli."

"Adalinda," said Ferdinand, "I placed the nuptial ring on your finger; before God your vows were given to me."

The false Count approached the lady, and bending one knee, took from his heart a locket, enclosing hair tied with a green riband, which she recognised to have worn, and pointed to a slight scar on his left hand.

Adalinda blushed deeply, and turning to her father, said, motioning towards the kneeling youth,

"He is Ferdinand."

All protestations now from the unhappy Eboli were vain. The Marchese would have cast him into a dungeon; but, at the earnest request of his rival, he was not detained, but thrust ignominiously from the villa. The rage of a wild beast newly chained was less than the tempest of indignation that now filled the heart of Ferdinand. Physical suffering, from fatigue and fasting, was added to his internal anguish; for some hours madness, if that were madness which never forgets its ill, possessed him. In a tumult of feelings there was one predominant idea: it was, to take possession of his father's house, and to try, by ameliorating the fortuitous circumstances of his lot, to gain the upper hand of his adversary. He expended his remaining strength in reaching Naples, entered his family palace, and was received and acknowledged by his astonished domestics.

One of his first acts was to take from a cabinet a miniature of his father encircled with jewels, and to invoke the aid of the paternal spirit. Refreshment and a bath restored him to some of his usual strength; and he looked forward with almost childish delight to one night to be spent in peace under the roof of his father's house. This was not permitted. Ere midnight the great bell sounded: his rival entered as master, with the Marchese Spina. The result may be divined. The Marchese appeared more indignant than the false Eboli. He insisted that the unfortunate youth should be imprisoned. The portrait, whose setting was costly, found on him, proved him guilty of robbery. He was given into the hands of the police, and thrown into a dungeon. I will not dwell on the subsequent scenes. He was tried by the tribunal, condemned as guilty, and sentenced to the galleys for life.

On the eve of the day when he was to be removed from the Neapolitan prison to work on the roads in Calabria, his rival visited him in his dungeon. For some moments both looked at the other in silence. The impostor gazed on the prisoner with mingled pride and compassion: there was evidently a struggle in his heart. The answering glance of Ferdinand was calm, free, and dignified. He was not resigned to his hard fate, but he disdained to make an exhibition of despair to his cruel and successful foe. A spasm of pain seemed to wrench the bosom of the false one; and he turned aside, striving to recover the hardness of heart which had hitherto supported him in the prosecution of his guilty enterprise. Ferdinand spoke first.

"What would the triumphant criminal with his innocent victim?"

His visitant replied haughtily, "Do not address such epithets to me, or I leave you to your fate: I am that which I say I am."

"To me this boast," cried Ferdinand, scornfully; "but perhaps these walls have ears."

"Heaven, at least, is not deaf," said the deceiver; "favouring Heaven, which knows and admits my claim. But a truce to this idle discussion. Compassion—a distaste to see one so very like myself in such ill condition—a foolish whim, perhaps, on which you may congratulate yourself —has led me hither. The bolts of your dungeon are drawn; here is a purse of gold; fulfil one easy condition, and you are free."

"And that condition?"

"Sign this paper."

He gave to Ferdinand a writing, containing a confession of his imputed crimes. The hand of the guilty youth trembled as he gave it; there was confusion in his mien, and a restless uneasy rolling of his eye. Ferdinand wished in one mighty word, potent as lightning, loud as thunder, to convey his burning disdain of this proposal: but expression is weak, and calm is more full of power than storm. Without a word, he tore the paper in two pieces, and threw them at the feet of his enemy.

With a sudden change of manner, his visitant conjured him, in voluble and impetuous terms, to comply. Ferdinand answered only by requesting to be left alone. Now and then a half word broke uncontrollably from his lips; but he curbed himself. Yet he could not hide his agitation when, as an argument to make him yield, the false Count assured him that he was already married to Adalinda. Bitter agony thrilled poor Ferdinand's frame; but he preserved a calm mien, and an unaltered resolution. Having exhausted every menace and every persuasion, his rival left him, the purpose for which he came unaccomplished. On the morrow, with many others, the refuse of mankind, Count Ferdinando Eboli was led in chains to the unwholesome plains of Calabria, to work there at the roads.

I must hurry over some of the subsequent events; for a detailed account of them would fill volumes. The assertion of the usurper of Ferdinand's right, that he was already married to Adalinda, was, like all else he said, false. The day was, however, fixed for their union, when the illness and the subsequent death of the Marchese Spina delayed its celebration. Adalinda retired, during the first months of mourning, to a castle belonging to her father not far from Arpino, a town of the kingdom of Naples, in the midst of the Apennines, about fifty miles from the capital. Before she went, the deceiver tried to persuade her to consent to a private marriage. He was probably afraid that, in the long interval that was about to ensue before he could secure her, she would discover his imposture. Besides, a rumour had gone abroad that one of the fellow-prisoners of Ferdinand, a noted bandit, had escaped, and that the young Count was his companion in flight. Adalinda, however, refused to comply with her lover's entreaties, and retired to her seclusion with an old aunt, who was blind and deaf, but an excellent duenna.

The false Eboli seldom visited his mistress; but he was a master in his art, and subsequent events showed that he must have spent all his time disguised in the vicinity of the castle. He contrived by various means, unsuspected at the moment, to have all Adalinda's servants changed for creatures of his own; so that, without her being aware of the restraint, she was, in fact, a prisoner in her own house. It is impossible to say what first awakened her suspicions concerning the deception put upon her. She was an Italian, with all the habitual quiescence and lassitude of her country-women in the ordinary routine of life, and with all their energy and passion when roused. The moment the doubt darted into her mind, she resolved to be assured; a few questions relative to scenes that had passed between poor Ferdinand and herself sufficed for this. They were asked so suddenly and pointedly that the pretender was thrown off his guard; he looked confused, and stammered in his replies. Their eyes met, he felt that he was detected, and she saw that he perceived her now confirmed suspicions. A look such as is peculiar to an impostor, a glance that deformed his beauty, and filled his usually noble countenance with the hideous lines of cunning and cruel triumph, completed her faith in her own discernment. "How," she thought, "could I have mistaken this man for my own gentle Eboli?" Again their eyes met: the peculiar expression of his terrified her, and she hastily quitted the apartment.

Her resolution was quickly formed. It was of no use to attempt to explain her situation to her old aunt. She determined to depart immediately for Naples, throw herself at the feet of Gioacchino, and to relate and obtain credit for her strange history. But the time was already lost when she could have executed this design. The contrivances of the deceiver were complete—she found herself a prisoner. Excess of fear gave her boldness, if not courage. She sought her jailor. A few minutes before, she had been a young and thoughtless girl, docile as a child, and as unsuspecting. Now she felt as if she had suddenly grown old in wisdom, and that the experience of years had been gained in that of a few seconds.

During their interview, she was wary and firm; while the instinctive power of innocence over guilt gave majesty to her demeanour. The contriver of her ills for a moment cowered beneath her eye. At first he would by no means allow that he was not the person he pretended to be: but the energy and eloquence of truth bore down his artifice, so that, at length driven into a corner, he turned—a stag at bay. Then it was her turn to quail; for the superior energy of a man gave him the mastery. He declared the truth. He was the elder brother of Ferdinand, a natural son of the old Count Eboli. His mother, who had been wronged, never forgave her injuror, and bred her son in deadly hate for his parent, and a belief that the advantages enjoyed by his more fortunate brother were rightfully his own. His education was rude; but he had an Italian's subtle talents, swiftness of perception, and guileful arts.

"It would blanch your cheek," he said to his trembling auditress, "could I describe all that I have suffered to achieve my purpose. I would trust to none—I executed all myself. It was a glorious triumph, but due to my perseverance and my fortitude, when I and my usurping brother stood, I, the noble, he, the degraded outcast, before our sovereign."

Having rapidly detailed his history, he now sought to win the favourable ear of Adalinda, who stood with averted and angry looks. He tried by the varied shows of passion and tenderness to move her heart. Was he not, in truth, the object of her love? Was it not he who scaled her balcony at Villa Spina? He recalled scenes of mutual overflow of feeling to her mind, thus urging arguments the most potent with a delicate woman: pure blushes tinged her cheek, but horror of the deceiver predominated over every other sentiment. He swore that as soon as they should be united he would free Ferdinand, and bestow competency, nay, if so she willed it, half his possessions, on him. She coldly replied, that she would rather share the chains of the innocent and misery, than link herself with imposture and crime. She demanded her liberty, but the untamed and even ferocious nature that had borne the deceiver through his career of crime now broke forth, and he invoked fearful imprecations on his head, if she ever quitted the castle except as his wife. His look of conscious power and unbridled wickedness terrified her; her flashing eyes spoke abhorrence: it would have been far easier for her to have died than have yielded the smallest point to a man who made her feel for one moment his irresistible power, arising from her being an unprotected woman, wholly in his hands. She left him, feeling as if she had just escaped from the impending sword of an assassin.

One hour's deliberation suggested to her a method of escape from her terrible situation. In a wardrobe at the castle lay in their pristine gloss the habiliments of a page of her mother, who had died suddenly, leaving these unworn relics of his station. Dressing herself in these, she tied up her dark shining hair, and even, with a somewhat bitter feeling, girded on the slight sword that appertained to the costume. Then, through a private passage leading from her own apartment to the chapel of the castle, she glided with noiseless steps, long after the Ave Maria sounded at twenty-four o'clock, had, on a November night, given token that half an hour had passed since the setting of the sun. She possessed the key of the chapel door—it opened at her touch; she closed it behind her, and she was free. The pathless hills were around her, the starry heavens above, and a cold wintry breeze murmured around the castle walls; but fear of

Drawn by Alfred E. Chalon   *Engraved by Charles Heath*

ADALINDA

her enemy conquered every other fear, and she tripped lightly on, in a kind of ecstasy, for many a long hour over the stony mountain-path— she, who had never before walked more than a mile or two at any time in her life,—till her feet were blistered, her slight shoes cut through, her way utterly lost. At morning's dawn she found herself in the midst of the wild ilex-covered Apennines, and neither habitation nor human being apparent.

She was hungry and weary. She had brought gold and jewels with her, but here were no means of exchanging these for food. She remembered stories of banditti; but none could be so ruffian-like and cruel as him from whom she fled. This thought, a little rest, and a draught of water from a pure mountain-spring, restored her to some portion of courage, and she continued her journey. Noonday approached; and, in the south of Italy, the noonday sun, when unclouded, even in November, is oppressively warm, especially to an Italian woman, who never exposes herself to its beams. Faintness came over her. There appeared recesses in the mountain-side along which she was travelling, grown over with bay and arbutus: she entered one of these, there to repose. It was deep, and led to another that opened into a spacious cavern lighted from above: there were cates, grapes, and a flagon of wine, on a rough hewn table. She looked fearfully around, but no inhabitant appeared. She placed herself at the table, and, half in dread, ate of the food presented to her, and then sat, her elbow on the table, her head resting on her little snow-white hand; her dark hair shading her brow and clustering round her throat. An appearance of languor and fatigue diffused through her attitude, while her soft black eyes filled at intervals with large tears, as pitying herself, she recurred to the cruel circumstances of her lot. Her fanciful but elegant dress, her feminine form, her beauty and her grace, as she sat pensive and alone in the rough unhewn cavern, formed a picture a poet would describe with delight, an artist love to paint.

"She seemed a being of another world; a seraph, all light and beauty; a Ganymede, escaped from his thrall above to his natal Ida. It was long before I recognised, looking down on her from the opening hill, my lost Adalinda." Thus spoke the young Count Eboli, when he related this story; for its end was as romantic as its commencement.

When Ferdinand had arrived a galley-slave in Calabria, he found himself coupled with a bandit, a brave fellow, who abhorred his chains, from love of freedom, as much as his fellow-prisoner did, from all the combination of disgrace and misery they brought upon him. Together they devised a plan of escape, and succeeded in effecting it. On their road, Ferdinand related his story to the outlaw, who encouraged him to hope a favourable turn of fate; and meanwhile invited and persuaded the desperate man to share his fortunes as a robber among the wild hills of Calabria.

The cavern where Adalinda had taken refuge was one of their fastnesses, whither they betook themselves at periods of imminent danger for safety only, as no booty could be collected in that unpeopled solitude; and there, one afternoon, returning from the chase, they found the wandering, fearful, solitary, fugitive girl; and never was lighthouse more welcome to tempest-tost sailor than was her own Ferdinand to his lady-love.

Fortune, now tired of persecuting the young noble, favoured him still further. The story of the lovers interested the bandit chief, and promise of reward secured him. Ferdinand persuaded Adalinda to remain one night in the cave, and on the following morning they prepared to proceed to Naples; but at the moment of their departure they were surprised by an unexpected visitant: the robbers brought in a prisoner—it was the impostor. Missing on the morrow her who was the pledge of his safety and success, but assured that she could not have wandered far, he despatched emissaries in all directions to seek her; and himself, joining in the pursuit, followed the road she had taken, and was captured by these lawless men, who expected rich ransom from one whose appearance denoted rank and wealth. When they discovered who their prisoner was, they generously delivered him up into his brother's hands.

Ferdinand and Adalinda proceeded to Naples. On their arrival, she presented herself to Queen Caroline; and, through her, Murat heard with astonishment the device that had been practised on him. The young Count was restored to his honours and possessions, and within a few months afterwards was united to his betrothed bride.

The compassionate nature of the Count and Countess led them to interest themselves warmly in the fate of Ludovico, whose subsequent career was more honourable but less fortunate. At the intercession of his relative, Gioacchino permitted him to enter the army, where he distinguished himself, and obtained promotion. The brothers were at Moscow together, and mutually assisted each other during the horrors of the retreat. At one time overcome by drowsiness, the mortal symptom resulting from excessive cold, Ferdinand lingered behind his comrades; but Ludovico refusing to leave him, dragged him on in spite of himself, till, entering a village, food and fire restored him, and his life was saved. On another evening, when wind and sleet added to the horror of their situation, Ludovico, after many ineffective struggles, slid from his horse lifeless; Ferdinand was at his side, and, dismounting, endeavoured by every means in his power to bring back pulsation to his stagnant blood. His comrades went forward, and the young Count was left alone with his dying brother in the white boundless waste. Once Ludovico opened his eyes and recognised him; he pressed his hand, and his lips moved to utter a blessing as he died. At that moment the welcome sounds of the enemy's approach roused Ferdinand from the despair into which his dreadful situation plunged him. He was taken prisoner, and his life was thus saved. When Napoleon went to Elba, he, with many others of his countrymen, was liberated, and returned to Naples.

VII

The Mourner

One fatal remembrance, one sorrow that throws
Its bleak shade alike o'er our joys and our woes,
To which life nothing darker or brighter can bring,
For which joy has no balm, and affliction no sting!—MOORE.

A GORGEOUS SCENE OF kingly pride is the prospect now before us!—the offspring of art, the nursling of nature—where can the eye rest on a landscape more deliciously lovely than the fair expanse of Virginia Water, now an open mirror to the sky, now shaded by umbrageous banks, which wind into dark recesses, or are rounded into soft promontories? Looking down on it, now that the sun is low in the west, the eye is dazzled, the soul oppressed, by excess of beauty. Earth, water, air, drink to overflowing, the radiance that streams from yonder well of light: the foliage of the trees seems dripping with the golden flood; while the lake, filled with no earthly dew, appears but an imbasining of the sun-tinctured atmosphere; and trees and gay pavilion float in its depth, more clear, more distinct, than their twins in the upper air. Nor is the scene silent: strains more sweet than those that lull Venus to her balmy rest, more inspiring than the song of Tiresias which awoke Alexander to the deed of ruin, more solemn than the chantings of St. Cecilia, float along the waves and mingle with the lagging breeze, which ruffles not the lake. Strange, that a few dark scores should be the key to this fountain of sound; the unconscious link between unregarded noise, and harmonies which unclose paradise to our entranced senses!

The sun touches the extreme boundary, and a softer, milder light mingles a roseate tinge with the fiery glow. Our boat has floated long on the broad expanse; now let it approach the umbrageous bank. The green tresses of the graceful willow dip into the waters, which are checked by them into a ripple. The startled teal dart from their recess, skimming the waves with splashing wing. The stately swans float onward; while in-

Drawn by J. M. W. Turner

Engraved by Robert Wallis

VIRGINIA WATER

numerable water fowl cluster together out of the way of the oars. The twilight is blotted by no dark shades; it is one subdued, equal receding of the great tide of day, which leaves the shingles bare, but not deformed. We may disembark and wander yet amid the glades, long before the thickening shadows speak of night. The plantations are formed of every English tree, with an old oak or two standing out in the walks. There the glancing foliage obscures heaven, as the silken texture of a veil a woman's lovely features: beneath such fretwork we may indulge in light-hearted thoughts; or, if sadder meditations lead us to seek darker shades, we may pass the cascade towards the large groves of pine, with their vast under-growth of laurel, reaching up to the Belvidere; or, on the opposite side of the water, sit under the shadow of the silver-stemmed birch, or beneath the leafy pavilions of those fine old beeches, whose high fantastic roots seem formed in nature's sport; and the near jungle of sweet-smelling myrica leaves no sense unvisited by pleasant ministration.

Now this splendid scene is reserved for the royal possessor; but in past years, while the lodge was called the Regent's Cottage, or before, when the under ranger inhabited it, the mazy paths of Chapel Wood were open, and the iron gates enclosing the plantations and Virginia Water were guarded by no Cerberus untamable by sops. It was here, on a summer's evening, that Horace Neville and his two fair cousins floated idly on the placid lake,

> "In that sweet mood when pleasant thoughts
> Bring sad thoughts to the mind."*

Neville had been eloquent in praise of English scenery. "In distant climes," he said, "we may find landscapes grand in barbaric wildness, or rich in the luxuriant vegetation of the south, or sublime in Alpine mag-nificence. We may lament, though it is ungrateful to say so on such a night as this, the want of a more genial sky; but where find scenery to be compared to the verdant, well-wooded, well-watered groves of our native land; the clustering cottages, shadowed by fine old elms; each garden blooming with early flowers, each lattice gay with geraniums and roses; the blue-eyed child devouring his white bread, while he drives a cow to graze; the hedge redolent with summer blooms; the enclosed cornfields, seas of golden grain, weltering in the breeze; the stile, the track across the meadow, leading through the copse, under which the path winds, and the meeting branches overhead, which give, by their dimming tracery, a ca-thedral-like solemnity to the scene; the river, winding 'with sweet inland murmur;'† and, as additional graces, spots like these—Oases of taste—

---

* Wordsworth, "Lines Written in Early Spring" (Ed.).
† Wordsworth, "Tintern Abbey," 1. 4 (Ed.).

Drawn by J. M. W. Turner

Engraved by Robert Wallis

VIRGINIA WATER

gardens of Eden—the works of wealth, which evince at once the greatest power and the greatest will to create beauty?

"And yet," continued Neville, "it was with difficulty that I persuaded myself to reap the best fruits of my uncle's will, and to inhabit this spot, familiar to my boyhood, associated with unavailing regrets and recollected pain."

Horace Neville was a man of birth—of wealth; but he could hardly be termed a man of the world. There was in his nature a gentleness, a sweetness, a winning sensibility, allied to talent and personal distinction, that gave weight to his simplest expressions, and excited sympathy for all his emotions. His younger cousin, his junior by several years, was attached to him by the tenderest sentiments—secret long—but they were now betrothed to each other—a lovely, happy pair. She looked inquiringly; but he turned away. "No more of this," he said; and giving a swifter impulse to their boat, they speedily reached the shore, landed, and walked through the long extent of Chapel Wood. It was dark night before they met their carriage at Bishopsgate.

A week or two after, Horace received letters to call him to a distant part of the country: it even seemed possible that he might be obliged to visit an estate in the north of Ireland. A few days before his departure, he requested his cousin to walk with him. They bent their steps across several meadows to Old Windsor churchyard. At first he did not deviate from the usual path; and as they went they talked cheerfully—gaily: the beauteous sunny day might well exhilarate them; the dancing waves sped onwards at their feet, the country church lifted its rustic spire into the bright pure sky. There was nothing in their conversation that could induce his cousin to think that Neville had led her hither for any saddening purpose; but when they were about to quit the churchyard, Horace, as if he had suddenly recollected himself, turned from the path, crossed the greensward, and paused beside a grave near the river. No stone was there to commemorate the being who reposed beneath—it was thickly grown with rich grass, starred by a luxuriant growth of humble daisies: a few dead leaves, a broken bramble twig, defaced its neatness; Neville removed these, and then said, "Juliet, I commit this sacred spot to your keeping while I am away.—

"There is no monument," he continued; "for her commands were implicitly obeyed by the two beings to whom she addressed them. One day another may lie near, and his name will be her epitaph.—I do not mean myself," he said, half smiling at the terror his cousin's countenance expressed; "but promise me, Juliet, to preserve this grave from every violation. I do not wish to sadden you by the story; yet, if I have excited your curiosity—your interest, I should say—I will satisfy it; but not now—not here."

Leaving the churchyard, they found their horses in attendance, and they prolonged their ride across Bishopsgate Heath. Neville's mind was full of the events to which he had alluded: he began the tale, and then abruptly broke off. It was not till the following day, when, in company with her sister, they again visited Virginia Water, that, seated under the shadow of its pines, whose melodious swinging in the wind breathed unearthly harmony, and looking down upon the water, association of place, and its extreme beauty, reviving, yet soothing, the recollections of the past, unasked by his companions, Neville at once commenced his story.

"I was sent to Eton at eleven years of age. I will not dwell upon my sufferings there; I would hardly refer to them, did they not make a part of my present narration. I was a fag to a hard taskmaster; every labour he could invent—and the youthful tyrant was ingenious—he devised for my annoyance; early and late, I was forced to be in attendance, to the neglect of my school duties, so incurring punishment. There were worse things to bear than these: it was his delight to put me to shame, and,—finding that I had too much of my mother in my blood,—to endeavour to compel me to acts of cruelty from which my nature revolted—I refused to obey. Speak of West Indian slavery! I hope things may be better now; in my days, the tender years of aristocratic childhood were yielded up to a capricious, unrelenting, cruel bondage, far beyond the measured despotism of Jamaica.

"One day—I had been two years at school, and was nearly thirteen—my tyrant, I will give him no other name, issued a command, in the wantonness of power, for me to destroy a poor little bullfinch I had tamed and caged. In a hapless hour he found it in my room, and was indignant that I should dare to appropriate a single pleasure. I refused, stubbornly, dauntlessly, though the consequence of my disobedience was immediate and terrible. At this moment a message came from my tormentor's tutor—his father had arrived. 'Well, old lad,' he cried, 'I shall pay you off some day!' Seizing my pet at the same time, he wrung its neck, threw it at my feet, and, with a laugh of derision, quitted the room.

"Never before—never may I again feel the same swelling, boiling fury in my bursting heart;—the sight of my nursling expiring at my feet—my desire of vengeance—my impotence, created a Vesuvius within me, that no tears flowed to quench. Could I have uttered—acted—my passion, it would have been less torturous: it was so when I burst into a torrent of abuse and imprecation. My vocabulary—it must have been a choice collection—was supplied by him against whom it was levelled. But words were air—I desired to give more substantial proof of my resentment—I destroyed every thing in the room belonging to him; I tore them to pieces, I stamped on them, crushed them with more than childish strength. My last act was to seize a timepiece, on which my tyrant infinitely prided himself, and to dash it to the ground. The sight of this, as it lay shattered at my feet, recalled me to my senses, and something like an emotion of fear allayed the tumult in my heart. I began to meditate an escape: I got out of the house, ran down a lane, and across some meadows, far out of bounds, above Eton. I was seen by an elder boy, a friend of my tormentor. He called to me, thinking at first that I was performing some errand for him; but seeing that I *shirked*, he repeated his 'Come up!' in an authoritative voice. It put wings to my heels; he did not deem it necessary to pursue.—But I grow tedious, my dear Juliet; enough that fears the most intense, of punishment both from my masters and the upper boys, made me resolve to run away. I reached the banks of the Thames, tied my clothes over my head, swam across, and, traversing several fields, entered Windsor Forest, with a vague childish feeling of being able to hide myself for ever in the unexplored obscurity of its immeasurable wilds. It was early autumn; the weather was mild, even warm; the forest oaks yet showed no sign of winter change, though the fern beneath wore a yellowy tinge. I got within Chapel Wood; I fed upon chestnuts and beechnuts; I continued to hide myself from the gamekeepers and woodmen. I lived thus two days.

"But chestnuts and beechnuts were sorry fare to a growing lad of thirteen years old. A day's rain occurred, and I began to think myself the most unfortunate boy on record. I had a distant, obscure idea of starvation: I thought of the Children in the Wood, of their leafy shroud, gift of the pious robin; this brought my poor bullfinch to my mind, and tears streamed in torrents down my cheeks. I thought of my father and mother; of you, then my little baby cousin and playmate; and I cried with renewed fervour, till, quite exhausted, I curled myself up under a huge oak among some dry leaves, the relics of a hundred summers, and fell asleep.

"I ramble on in my narration as if I had a story to tell; yet I have little except a portrait—a sketch—to present, for your amusement or interest. When I awoke, the first object that met my opening eyes was a little foot, delicately clad in silk and soft kid. I looked up in dismay, expecting to behold some gaily dressed appendage to this indication of high-bred elegance; but I saw a girl, perhaps seventeen, simply clad in a dark cotton dress, her face shaded by a large very coarse straw hat; she was pale even to marmoreal whiteness; her chestnut-coloured hair was parted in plain tresses across a brow which wore traces of extreme suffering; her eyes were blue, full, large, melancholy, often even suffused with tears; but her mouth had an infantine sweetness and innocence in its expression, that softened the otherwise sad expression of her countenance.

"She spoke to me. I was too hungry, too exhausted, too unhappy, to resist her kindness, and gladly permitted her to lead me to her home. We passed out of the wood by some broken palings on to Bishopsgate Heath, and after no long walk arrived at her habitation. It was a solitary, dreary-looking cottage; the palings were in disrepair, the garden waste, the lattices unadorned by flowers or creepers; within, all was neat, but sombre, and even mean. The diminutiveness of a cottage requires an appearance of cheerfulness and elegance to make it pleasing; the bare floor—clean, it is true—the rush chairs, deal table, checked curtains of this cot, were beneath even a peasant's rusticity; yet it was the dwelling of my lovely guide, whose little white hand, delicately gloved, contrasted with her unadorned attire, as did her gentle self with the clumsy appurtenances of her too humble dwelling.

"Poor child! she had meant entirely to hide her origin, to degrade herself to a peasant's state, and little thought that she for ever betrayed herself by the strangest incongruities. Thus, the arrangements of her table were mean, her fare meagre for a hermit; but the linen was matchlessly fine, and wax lights stood in candlesticks which a beggar would almost have disdained to own. But I talk of circumstances I observed afterwards; then I was chiefly aware of the plentiful breakfast she caused her single attendant, a young girl, to place before me, and of the sweet soothing voice of my hostess, which spoke a kindness with which lately I had been little conversant. When my hunger was appeased, she drew my story from me, encouraged me to write to my father, and kept me at her abode till, after a few days, I returned to school pardoned. No long time elapsed before I got into the upper forms, and my woeful slavery ended.

"Whenever I was able, I visited my disguised nymph. I no longer associated with my schoolfellows; their diversions, their pursuits, appeared vulgar and stupid to me; I had but one object in view—to accomplish my lessons, and to steal to the cottage of Ellen Burnet.

"Do not look grave, love! true, others as young as I then was have loved, and I might also; but not Ellen. Her profound, her intense melancholy, sister to despair—her serious, sad discourse—her mind, estranged from all worldly concerns, forbade that; but there was an enchantment in her sorrow, a fascination in her converse, that lifted me above commonplace existence; she created a magic circle, which I entered as holy ground: it was not akin to heaven, for grief was the presiding spirit; but there was an exaltation of sentiment, an enthusiasm, a view beyond the grave, which made it unearthly, singular, wild, enthralling. You have often observed that I strangely differ from all other men; I mingle with them, make one in their occupations and diversions, but I have a portion of my being sacred from them:—a living well, sealed up from their contamination, lies deep in my heart—it is of little use, but there it is; Ellen opened the spring, and it has flowed ever since.

"Of what did she talk? She recited no past adventures, alluded to no past intercourse with friend or relative; she spoke of the various woes that wait on humanity, on the intricate mazes of life, on the miseries of passion, of love, remorse, and death, and that which we may hope or fear beyond the tomb; she spoke of the sensation of wretchedness alive in her own broken heart, and then she grew fearfully eloquent, till, suddenly pausing, she reproached herself for making me familiar with such wordless misery. 'I do you harm,' she often said; 'I unfit you for society; I have tried, seeing you thrown upon yonder distorted miniature of a bad world, to estrange you from its evil contagion; I fear that I shall be the cause of greater harm to you than could spring from association with your fellow-creatures in the ordinary course of things. This is not well—avoid the stricken deer.'

"There were darker shades in the picture than those which I have already developed. Ellen was more miserable than the imagination of one like you, dear girl, unacquainted with woe, can portray. Sometimes she gave words to her despair—it was so great as to confuse the boundary between physical and mental sensation—and every pulsation of her heart was a throb of pain. She has suddenly broken off in talking of her sorrows, with a cry of agony—bidding me leave her—hiding her face on her arms, shivering with the anguish some thought awoke. The idea that chiefly haunted her, though she earnestly endeavoured to put it aside, was self-destruction—to snap the silver cord that bound together so much grace, wisdom, and sweetness—to rob the world of a creation made to be its ornament. Sometimes her piety checked her; oftener a sense of unendurable suffering made her brood with pleasure over the dread resolve. She spoke of it to me as being wicked; yet I often fancied this was done rather to prevent her example from being of ill effect to me, than from any conviction that the Father of all, would regard angrily the last act of his miserable child. Once she had prepared the mortal beverage; it was on the table before her when I entered; she did not deny its nature, she did not attempt to justify herself; she only besought me not to hate her and to sooth by my kindness her last moments.—'I cannot live!' was all her explanation, all her excuse; and it was spoken with such fervent wretchedness that it seemed wrong to attempt to persuade her to prolong the sense of pain. I did not act like a boy; I wonder I did not; I made one simple request, to which she instantly acceded, that she should walk with me to this Belvidere. It was a glorious sunset; beauty and the spirit of love breathed in the wind, and hovered over the softened hues of the landscape. 'Look, Ellen,' I cried, 'if only such loveliness of nature existed, it were worth living for!'

" 'True, if a latent feeling did not blot this glorious scene with murky shadows. Beauty is as we see it—my eyes view all things deformed and evil.' She closed them as she said this; but, young and sensitive, the visitings of the soft breeze already began to minister consolation. 'Dearest Ellen,' I continued, 'what do I not owe to you? I am your boy, your pupil; I might have gone on blindly as others do, but you opened my eyes; you have given me a sense of the just, the good, the beautiful—and have you done this merely for my misfortune? If you leave me, what can become of me?' The last words came from my heart, and tears gushed from my eyes. 'Do not leave me, Ellen,' I said; 'I cannot live without you—and I cannot die, for I have a mother—a father.' She turned quickly round, saying, 'You are blessed sufficiently.' Her voice struck me as unnatural; she grew deadly pale as she spoke, and was obliged to sit down. Still I clung to her, prayed, cried; till she—I had never seen her shed a tear before—burst into passionate weeping. After this she seemed to forget her resolve. We returned by moonlight, and our talk was even more calm and cheerful than usual. When in her cottage, I poured away the fatal draught. Her 'good night' bore with it no traces of her late agitation; and the next day she said, 'I have thoughtlessly, even wickedly, created a new duty to myself, even at a time when I had forsworn all; but I will be true to it. Pardon me for making you familiar with emotions and scenes so dire; I will behave better—I will preserve myself, if I can, till the link between us is loosened, or broken, and I am free again.'

"One little incident alone occurred during our intercourse that appeared at all to connect her with the world. Sometimes I brought her a newspaper, for those were stirring times; and though, before I knew her, she had forgotten all except the world her own heart enclosed, yet, to please me, she would talk of Napoleon—Russia, from whence the emperor now returned overthrown—and the prospect of his final defeat. The paper lay one day on her table; some words caught her eye; she bent eagerly down to read them, and her bosom heaved with violent palpitation; but she subdued herself, and after a few moments told me to take the paper away. Then, indeed, I did feel an emotion of even impertinent inquisitiveness; I found nothing to satisfy it—though afterwards I became aware that it contained a singular advertisement, saying, 'If these lines meet the eye of any one of the passengers who were on board the St. Mary, bound for Liverpool from Barbadoes, which sailed on the third of May last, and was destroyed by fire in the high seas, a part of the crew only having been saved by his majesty's frigate the Bellerophon, they are entreated to communicate with the advertiser: and if any one be acquainted with the particulars of the Hon. Miss Eversham's fate and present abode, they are earnestly requested to disclose them, directing to L. E., Stratton-street, Park-lane.'

"It was after this event, as winter came on, that symptoms of decided ill health declared themselves in the delicate frame of my poor Ellen. I have often suspected that, without positively attempting her life, she did many things that tended to abridge it and to produce mortal disease. Now, when really ill, she refused all medical attendance; but she got better again, and I thought her nearly well when I saw her for the last time, before going home for the Christmas holidays. Her manner was full of affection: she relied, she said, on the continuation of my friendship; she made me promise never to forget her, though she refused to write to me, and forbade any letters from me.

"Even now I see her standing at her humble door-way. If an appearance of illness and suffering can ever be termed lovely, it was in her. Still she was to be viewed as the wreck of beauty. What must she not have been in happier days, with her angel expression of face, her nymph-like figure, her voice, whose tones were music? 'So young—so lost!' was the sentiment that burst even from me, a young lad, as I waved my hand to her as a last adieu. She hardly looked more than fifteen, but none could doubt that her very soul was impressed by the sad lines of sorrow that rested so unceasingly on her fair brow. Away from her, her figure for ever floated before my eyes;—I put my hands before them, still she was there: my day, my night, dreams were filled by my recollections of her.

"During the winter holidays, on a fine soft day, I went out to hunt: you, dear Juliet, will remember the sad catastrophe; I fell and broke my leg. The only person who saw me fall was a young man who rode one of the most beautiful horses I ever saw, and I believe it was by watching him as he took a leap, that I incurred my disaster: he dismounted, and was at my side in a minute. My own animal had fled; he called his; it obeyed his voice; with ease he lifted my light figure on to the saddle, contriving to support my leg, and so conducted me a short distance to a lodge situated in the woody recesses of Elmore-park, the seat of the Earl of D——, whose second son my preserver was. He was my sole nurse for a day or two, and during the whole of my illness passed many hours of each day by my bedside. As I lay gazing on him, while he read to me, or talked, narrating a thousand strange adventures which had occurred during his service in the Peninsula, I thought—is it for ever to be my fate to fall in with the highly gifted and excessively unhappy?

"The immediate neighbour of Lewis' family was Lord Eversham. He had married in very early youth, and became a widower young. After this misfortune, which passed like a deadly blight over his prospects and possessions, leaving the gay view utterly sterile and bare, he left his surviving infant daughter under the care of Lewis' mother, and travelled for many years in far distant lands. He returned when Clarice was about ten, a lovely sweet child, the pride and delight of all connected with her. Lord Eversham, on his return—he was then hardly more than thirty—devoted himself to her education. They were never separate: he was a good musician, and she became a proficient under his tutoring. They rode—walked—read together. When a father is all that a father may be, the sentiments of filial piety, entire dependence, and perfect confidence being united, the love of a daughter is one of the deepest and strongest, as it is the purest passion of which our natures are capable. Clarice worshipped her parent, who came, during the transition from mere childhood to the period when reflection and observation awaken, to adorn a common-place existence with all the brilliant adjuncts which enlightened and devoted affection can bestow. He appeared to her like an especial gift of Providence, a guardian angel—but far dearer, as being akin to her own nature. She grew, under his eye, in loveliness and refinement both of intellect and heart. These feelings were not divided—almost strengthened, by the engagement that had place between her and Lewis:—Lewis was destined for the army, and, after a few years' service, they were to be united.

"It is hard, when all is fair and tranquil, when the world, opening before the ardent gaze of youth, looks like a well-kept demesne, unincumbered by let or hinderance for the annoyance of the young traveller, that we should voluntarily stray into desert wilds and tempest-visited districts. Lewis Elmore was ordered to Spain; and, at the same time, Lord Eversham found it necessary to visit some estates he possessed in Barbadoes. He was not sorry to revisit a scene, which had dwelt in his memory as an earthly paradise, nor to show to his daughter a new and strange world, so to form her understanding and enlarge her mind. They were to return in three months, and departed as on a summer tour. Clarice was glad that, while her lover gathered experience and knowledge in a distant land, she should not remain in idleness—she was glad that there would be some diversion for her anxiety during his perilous absence; and in every way she enjoyed the idea of travelling with her beloved father, who would fill every hour, and adorn every new scene, with pleasure and delight. They sailed.—Clarice wrote home, with enthusiastic expressions of rapture and delight, from Madeira:—yet, without her father, she said, the fair scene had been blank to her. More than half her letter was filled by the expressions of her gratitude and affection for her adored and revered parent. While he, in his, with fewer words, perhaps, but with no less energy, spoke of his satisfaction in her improvement, his pride in her beauty, and his grateful sense of her love and kindness.

"Such were they, a matchless example of happiness in the dearest connexion in life, as resulting from the exercise of their reciprocal duties and affections. A father and daughter; the one all care, gentleness, and sympathy, consecrating his life for her happiness; the other, fond, duteous, grateful:—such had they been,—and where were they now—the noble, kind, respected parent, and the beloved and loving child? They had departed from England as on a pleasure voyage down an inland stream; but the ruthless car of destiny had overtaken them on their unsuspecting way, crushing them under its heavy wheels—scattering love, hope, and joy, as the bellowing avalanche overwhelms and grinds to mere spray the streamlet of the valley. They were gone: but whither? Mystery hung over the fate of the most helpless victim; and my friend's anxiety was, to penetrate the clouds that hid poor Clarice from his sight.

"After an absence of a few months, they had written, fixing their departure in the St. Mary, to sail from Barbadoes in a few days. Lewis, at the same time, returned from Spain: he was invalided, in his very first action, by a bad wound in his side. He arrived, and each day expected to hear of the landing of his friends; when that common messenger, the newspaper, brought him tidings to fill him with more than anxiety—with fear and agonizing doubt. The St. Mary had caught fire and had burned in the open sea. A frigate, the Bellerophon, had saved a part of the crew. In spite of illness and a physician's commands, Lewis set out the same day for London, to ascertain as speedily as possible the fate of her he loved. There he heard that the frigate was expected in the Downs. Without alighting from his travelling chaise, he posted thither, arriving in a burning fever. He went on board, saw the commander, and spoke with the crew. They could give him few particulars as to whom they had saved: they had touched at Liverpool, and left there most of the persons, including all the passengers rescued from the St. Mary. Physical suffering for awhile disabled Mr. Elmore; he was confined by his wound and consequent fever, and only recovered to give himself up to his exertions to discover the fate of his friends;—they did not appear nor write; and all Lewis' inquiries only tended to confirm his worst fears; yet still he hoped, and still continued indefatigable in his perquisitions. He visited Liverpool, and Ireland, whither some of the passengers had gone, and learnt only scattered, incongruous details of the fearful tragedy, that told nothing of Miss Eversham's present abode; though much, that confirmed his suspicion that she still lived.

"The fire on board the St. Mary had raged long and fearfully before the Bellerophon hove in sight, and boats came off for the rescue of the crew. The women were to be first embarked; but Clarice clung to her father, and refused to go till he should accompany her. Some fearful presentiment that, if she were saved, he would remain and die, gave such energy to her resolve, that not the entreaties of her father, nor the angry expostulations of the captain, could shake it. Lewis saw this man, after the lapse of two or three months, and he threw most light on the dark scene. He well remembered that, transported with anger by her woman's obstinacy, he had said to her, 'You will cause your father's death—and be as much a parricide as if you put poison into his cup—you are not the first girl who has murdered her father in her wilful mood.' Still Clarice passionately refused to go—there was no time for long parley—the point was yielded, and she remained pale, but firm, near her parent, whose arm was around her, supporting her during the awful interval. It was no period for regular action and calm order: a tempest was rising, the scorching flames blew this way and that, making a fearful day of the night which veiled all except the burning ship. The boats returned with difficulty, and one only could contrive to approach; it was nearly full: Lord Eversham and his daughter advanced to the deck's edge, to get in. 'We can only take one of you,' vociferated the sailors: 'keep back on your life! throw the girl to us—we will come back for you if we can.' Lord Eversham cast with a strong arm his daughter, who had now entirely lost her self-possession, into the boat; she was alive again in a minute, she called to her father, held out her arms to him, and would have thrown herself into the sea, but was held back by the sailors. Meanwhile Lord Eversham feeling that no boat could again approach the lost vessel, contrived to heave a spar overboard, and threw himself into the sea, clinging to it. The boat, tossed by the huge waves, with difficulty made its way to the frigate; and as it rose from the trough of the sea, Clarice saw her father struggling with his fate—battling with the death that at last became the victor—the spar floated by, his arms had fallen from it—were those his pallid features? She neither wept nor fainted, but her limbs grew rigid, her face colourless, and she was lifted as a log on to the deck of the frigate.

"The captain allowed that on her homeward voyage, the people had rather a horror of her, as having caused her father's death; her own servants had perished, few people remembered who she was; but they talked together with no careful voices as they passed her, and a hundred times she must have heard herself accused of having destroyed her parent. She spoke to no one, or only in brief reply when addressed; to avoid the rough remonstrances of those around, she appeared at table, ate as well as she could; but there was a settled wretchedness in her face that never changed. When they landed at Liverpool, the captain conducted her to an hotel; he left her, meaning to return, but an opportunity of sailing that night for the Downs occurred, of which he availed himself, without again visiting her. He knew, he said, and truly, that she was in her native country, where she had but to write a letter to gather crowds of friends about her; and where can greater civility be found than at an English hotel, if it is known that you are perfectly able to pay your bill?

"This was all that Mr. Elmore could learn, and it took many months to gather together these few particulars. He went to the hotel at Liverpool. It seemed that as soon as there appeared some hope of rescue from the frigate, Lord Eversham had given his pocket-book to his daughter's care, containing bills on a banking-house at Liverpool to the amount of a few hundred pounds. On the second day after Clarice's arrival there, she had sent for the master of the hotel, and showed him these. He got the cash for her; and the next day, she quitted Liverpool in a little coasting vessel. In vain Lewis endeavoured to trace her. Apparently she had crossed to Ireland; but whatever she had done, wherever she had gone, she had taken infinite pains to conceal, and all clue was speedily lost.

"Lewis had not yet despaired; he was even now perpetually making journeys, sending emissaries, employing every possible means for her discovery. From the moment he told me this story, we talked of nothing else. I became deeply interested, and we ceaselessly discussed the prob- abilities of the case, and where she might be concealed: that she did not meditate suicide was evident from her having possessed herself of money; yet, unused to the world, young, lovely, and inexperienced; what could be her plan? What might not have been her fate?

"Meanwhile I continued for nearly three months confined by the frac- ture of my limb; before the lapse of that time, I had begun to crawl about the ground, and now I considered myself as nearly recovered. It had been settled that I should not return to Eton, but be entered at Oxford; and this leap from boyhood to man's estate elated me considerably. Yet still I thought of my poor Ellen, and was angry at her obstinate silence. Once or twice I had, disobeying her command, written to her, mentioning my accident, and the kind attentions of Mr. Elmore: still she wrote not; and I began to fear that her illness might have had a fatal termination. She had made me vow so solemnly never to mention her name, never to inquire about her during my absence, that, considering obedience the first duty of a young inexperienced boy to one older than himself, I resisted each suggestion of my affection or my fears, to transgress her orders.

"And now spring came; with its gift of opening buds, odoriferous flowers, and sunny genial days. I returned home, and found my family on the eve of their departure for London; my long confinement had weak- ened me—it was deemed inadvisable for me to encounter the bad air and fatigues of the metropolis, and I remained to rusticate. I rode and hunted, and thought of Ellen; missing the excitement of her conversation, and feeling a vacancy in my heart which she had filled. I began to think of riding across the country from Shropshire to Berks for the purpose of seeing her. The whole landscape haunted my imagination—the fields round Eton—the silver Thames—the majestic forest—this lovely scene of Virginia Water—the heath and her desolate cottage—she herself pale, slightly bending from weakness of health, awakening from dark abstraction to bestow on me a kind smile of welcome. It grew into a passionate desire of my heart to behold her, to cheer her as I might by my affectionate attentions, to hear her, and to hang upon her accents of inconsolable despair, as if it had been celestial harmony. As I meditated on these things, a voice seemed for ever to repeat, Now go, or it will be too late; while another yet more mournful tone responded, You can never see her more!

"I was occupied by these thoughts, as, on a summer moonlight night, I loitered in the shrubbery, unable to quit a scene of entrancing beauty, when I was startled at hearing myself called by Mr. Elmore. He came on his way to the coast; he had received a letter from Ireland, which made him think that Miss Eversham was residing near Enniscorthy; a strange place for her to select, but as concealment was evidently her object, not an improbable one. Yet his hopes were not high; on the contrary, he performed this journey more from the resolve to leave nothing undone, than in expectation of a happy result. He asked me if I would accompany him; I was delighted with the offer, and we departed together on the following morning.

"We arrived at Milford Haven, where we were to take our passage. The packet was to sail early in the morning—we walked on the beach, and beguiled the time by talk. I had never mentioned Ellen to Lewis; I felt now strongly inclined to break my vow, and to relate my whole adventure with her; but restrained myself, and we spoke only of the unhappy Clarice—of the despair that must have been hers, of her remorse and unavailing regret.

"We retired to rest, and early in the morning I was called to prepare for going on board. I got ready, and then knocked at Lewis' door; he admitted me, for he was dressed, though a few of his things were still unpacked, and scattered about the room. The morocco case of a miniature was on his table; I took it up—'Did I never show you that?' said Elmore; 'poor dear Clarice! she was very happy when that was painted!'

"I opened it;—rich luxuriant curls clustered on her brow and the snow-white throat; there was a light zephyr appearance in the figure; an expression of unalloyed exuberant happiness in the countenance; but those large dove's eyes, the innocence that dwelt on her mouth, could not be mistaken, and the name of Ellen Burnet burst from my lips.

"There was no doubt: why had I ever doubted? the thing was so plain! who but the survivor of such a parent, and she the apparent cause of his death, could be so miserable as Ellen? A torrent of explanation followed, and a thousand minute circumstances, forgotten before, now assured us that my sad hermitess was the beloved of Elmore. No more sea voyage—not a second of delay—our chaise, the horses' heads turned to the east, rolled on with lightning rapidity, yet far too slowly to satisfy our impatience. It was not until we arrived at Worcester that the tide of expectation, flowing all one way, ebbed. Suddenly, even while I was telling Elmore some anecdote to prove that, in spite of all, she would be accessible to consolation, I remembered her ill health and my fears. Lewis saw the change my countenance underwent; for some time I could not command my voice; and when at last I spoke, my gloomy anticipations passed like an electric shock into my friend's soul.

"When we arrived at Oxford, we halted for an hour or two, unable to proceed; yet we did not converse on the subject so near our hearts, nor until we arrived in sight of Windsor did a word pass between us; then Elmore said, 'To-morrow morning, dear Neville, you shall visit Clarice; we must not be too precipitate.'

"The morrow came. I arose with that intolerable weight at my breast, which it is grief's worst heritage to feel. A sunny day it was; yet the atmosphere looked black to me; my heart was dead within me. We sat at the breakfast table, but neither ate, and after some restless indecision, we left our inn, and (to protract the interval) walked to Bishopsgate. Our conversation belied our feelings; we spoke as if we expected all to be well, we felt that there was no hope. We crossed the heath along the accustomed path. On one side was the luxuriant foliage of the forest; on the other, the wide-spread moor: her cottage was situated at one extremity, and could hardly be distinguished, until we should arrive close to it. When we drew near, Lewis bade me go on alone, he would wait my return; I obeyed, and reluctantly approached the confirmation of my fears. At length it stood before me, the lonely cot and desolate garden; the unfastened wicket swung in the breeze; every shutter was closed.

"To stand motionless and gaze on these symbols of my worst forebodings, was all that I could do. My heart seemed to me to call aloud for Ellen—for such was she to me—her other name might be a fiction—but silent as her own life-deserted lips were mine. Lewis grew impatient, and advanced—my stay had occasioned a transient ray of hope to enter his mind—it vanished when he saw me, and *her* deserted dwelling. Slowly we turned away, and were directing our steps back again, when my name was called by a child. A little girl came running across some fields towards us, whom at last I recognised as having seen before with Ellen. 'Mr. Neville, there is a letter for you!' cried the child. 'A letter—where?—who?' 'The lady left a letter for you. You must go to Old Windsor, to Mr. Cooke's; he has got it for you.'

"She had left a letter:—was she then departed on an earthly journey? 'I will go for it immediately. Mr. Cooke! Old Windsor! where shall I find him? who is he?'

"'Oh, Sir, every body knows him,' said the child; 'he lives close to the churchyard, he is the sexton. After the burial, Nancy gave him the letter to take care of.'

"Had we hoped? had we for a moment indulged the expectation of ever again seeing our miserable friend? Never! O never! Our hearts had told us that the sufferer was at peace—the unhappy orphan with her father in the abode of spirits! Why then were we here? Why had a smile dwelt on our lips, now wreathed into the expression of anguish? Our full hearts demanded one consolation—to weep upon her grave; her sole link now with us, her mourners. There at last my boy's grief found vent in tears, in lamentation. You saw the spot; the grassy mound rests lightly on the bosom of fair Clarice, of my own poor Ellen. Stretched upon this, kissing the scarcely springing turf; for many hours no thought visited me, but the wretched one—that she had lived—and was lost to me forever!

"If Lewis had ever doubted the identity of my friend with her he loved, the letter put into our hands undeceived him; the handwriting was Miss Eversham's, it was directed to me, and contained words like these:—

"'April 11.

"'I have vowed never to mention certain beloved names, never to communicate with beings who cherished me once, to whom my deepest gratitude is due; and, as well as poor bankrupt can, is paid. Perhaps it is a mere prevarication to write to you, dear Horace, concerning them; but, Heaven pardon me! my disrobed spirit would not repose, I fear, if I did not thus imperfectly bid them a last farewell.

"'You know him, Neville; and know that he for ever laments her whom he has lost. Describe your poor Ellen to him, and he will speedily see that *she* died on the waves of the murderous Atlantic. Ellen had nothing in common with *her*, save love for, and interest in him. Tell him, it had been well for him, perhaps, to have united himself to the child of prosperity, the nursling of deep love; but it had been destruction, even could he have meditated such an act, to wed the parrici——.

"'I will not write that word. Sickness and near death have taken the sting from my despair. The agony of woe which you witnessed, is melted into tender affliction and pious hope. I am not miserable now. Now! When you read these words, the hand that writes, the eye that sees, will be a little dust, becoming one with the earth around it. You, perhaps he, will visit my quiet retreat, bestow a few tears on my fate, but let them be secret; they may make green my grave, but do not let a misplaced feeling adorn it with any other tribute. It is my last request; let no stone, no name, mark that spot.

"'Farewell, dear Horace! Farewell, to one other whom I may not name. May the God to whom I am about to resign my spirit in confidence and hope, bless your earthly career! Blindly, perhaps, you will regret me for your own sakes; but for mine, you will be grateful to the Providence which has snapt the heavy chain binding me to unutterable sorrow, and which permits me from my lowly grass-grown tomb to say to you, I am at peace.

" 'ELLEN.' "

VIII

❦

The Evil Eye

The wild Albanian kirtled to his knee,
  With shawl-girt head, and ornamented gun,
  And gold-embroider'd garments, fair to see;
  The crimson-scarfed man of Macedon.—LORD BYRON.*

THE MOREOT, Katusthius Ziani, travelled wearily, and in fear of its robber-inhabitants, through the pashalik of Yannina; yet he had no cause for dread. Did he arrive, tired and hungry, in a solitary village—did he find himself in the uninhabited wilds suddenly surrounded by a band of Klephts—or in the larger towns did he shrink at finding himself sole of his race among the savage mountaineers and despotic Turk—as soon as he announced himself the Pobratimo† of Dmitri of the Evil Eye, every hand was held out, every voice spoke welcome.

The Albanian, Dmitri, was a native of the village of Korvo. Among the savage mountains of the district between Yannina and Tepellenè, the deep broad stream of Argyro-Castro flows; bastioned to the west by abrupt wood-covered precipices, shadowed to the east by elevated mountains. The highest among these is Mount Trebucci; and in a romantic folding of that hill, distinct with minarets, crowned by a dome rising from out a group of pyramidal cypresses, is the picturesque village of Korvo. Sheep and goats form the apparent treasure of its inhabitants; their guns and yataghans, their warlike habits, and, with them, the noble profession of robbery, are sources of still greater wealth. Among a race renowned for dauntless courage and sanguinary enterprise, Dmitri was distinguished.

It was said that in his youth, this Klepht was remarkable for a gentler disposition and more refined taste than is usual with his countrymen. He

---

* *Childe Harold* II. lviii (Ed.).

† In Greece, especially in Illyria and Epirus, it is no uncommon thing for persons of the same sex to swear friendship; the church contains a ritual to consecrate this vow. Two men thus united are called *pobratimi*, the women *posestrime*.

100

had been a wanderer, and had learned European arts, of which he was not a little proud. He could read and write Greek, and a book was often stowed beside his pistols in his girdle. He had spent several years in Scio, the most civilized of the Greek islands, and had married a Sciote girl. The Albanians are characterized as despisers of women; but Dmitri, in becoming the husband of Helena, inlisted under a more chivalrous rule, and became the proselyte of a better creed. Often he returned to his native hills, and fought under the banner of the renowned Ali, and then came back to his island home. The love of the tamed barbarian was concentrated, burning, and something beyond this—it was a portion of his living, beating heart—the nobler part of himself—the diviner mould in which his rugged nature had been recast.

On his return from one of his Albanian expeditions, he found his home ravaged by the Mainotes. Helena—they pointed to her tomb, nor dared tell him how she died; his only child, his lovely infant daughter, was stolen; his treasure-house of love and happiness was rifled; its gold-excelling wealth changed to blank desolation. Dmitri spent three years in endeavours to recover his lost offspring. He was exposed to a thousand dangers—underwent incredible hardships: he dared the wild beast in his lair, the Mainote in his port of refuge; he attacked, and was attacked by them. He wore the badge of his daring in a deep gash across his eyebrow and cheek. On this occasion he had died, but that Katusthius, seeing a scuffle on shore and a man left for dead, disembarked from a Moreot sacoleva, carried him away, tended and cured him. They exchanged vows of friendship, and for some time the Albanian shared his brother's toils; but they were too pacific to suit his taste, and he returned to Korvo.

Who in the mutilated savage could recognise the handsomest amongst the Arnaoots? His habits kept pace with his change of physiognomy—he grew ferocious and hard-hearted—he only smiled when engaged in dangerous enterprise; he had arrived at that worst state of ruffian feeling, the taking delight in blood. He grew old in these occupations; his mind became reckless, his countenance more dark; men trembled before his glance, women and children exclaimed in terror, "The Evil Eye!" The opinion became prevalent—he shared it himself—he gloried in the dread privilege; and when his victim shivered and withered beneath the mortal influence, the fiendish laugh with which he hailed this demonstration of his power, struck with worse dismay the failing heart of the fascinated person. But Dmitri could command the arrows of his sight; and his comrades respected him the more for his supernatural attribute, since they did not fear the exercise of it on themselves.

Dmitri had just returned from an expedition beyond Prevesa. He and his comrades were laden with spoil. They killed and roasted a goat whole for their repast; they drank dry several wine skins; then, round the fire in the court, they abandoned themselves to the delights of the kerchief dance, roaring out the chorus, as they dropped upon and then rebounded from their knees, and whirled round and round with an activity all their own. The heart of Dmitri was heavy; he refused to dance, and sat apart, at first joining in the song with his voice and lute, till the air changed to one that reminded him of better days; his voice died away—his instrument dropped from his hands—and his head sank upon his breast.

At the sound of stranger footsteps he started up; in the form before him he surely recognised a friend—he was not mistaken. With a joyful exclamation he welcomed Katusthius Ziani, clasping his hand, and kissing him on his cheek. The traveller was weary, so they retired to Dmitri's own home; a neatly plastered, white-washed cottage, whose earthen floor was perfectly dry and clean, and the walls hung with arms, some richly ornamented, and other trophies of his Klephtic triumphs. A fire was kindled by his aged female attendant; the friends reposed on mats of white rushes, while she prepared the pilaf and seethed flesh of kid. She placed a bright tin tray on a block of wood before them, and heaped upon it cakes of Indian corn, goat's milk cheese, eggs, and olives: a jar of water from their purest spring, and skin of wine, served to refresh and cheer the thirsty traveller.

After supper, the guest spoke of the object of his visit. "I come to my Pobratimo," he said, "to claim the performance of his vow. When I rescued you from the savage Kakovougnis of Boularias, you pledged to me your gratitude and faith; do you disclaim the debt?"

Dmitri's brow darkened. "My brother," he cried, "need not remind me of what I owe. Command my life—in what can the mountain Klepht aid the son of the wealthy Ziani?"

"The son of Ziani is a beggar," rejoined Katusthius, "and must perish, if his brother deny his assistance."

The Moreot then told his tale. He had been brought up as the only son of a rich merchant of Corinth. He had often sailed as caravokeiri* of his father's vessels to Stamboul, and even to Calabria. Some years before, he had been boarded and taken by a Barbary corsair. His life since then had been adventurous, he said; in truth, it had been a guilty one—he had become a renegade—and won regard from his new allies, not by his superior courage, for he was cowardly, but by the frauds that make men wealthy. In the midst of this career some superstition had influenced him, and he had returned to his ancient religion. He escaped from Africa, wandered through Syria, crossed to Europe, found occupation in Constantinople; and thus years passed. At last, as he was on the point of marriage with a Fanariote beauty, he fell again into poverty, and he returned to Corinth to see if his father's fortunes had prospered during his long wanderings. He found

---

* Master of a merchant ship.

that while these had improved to a wonder, they were lost to him for ever. His father, during his protracted absence, acknowledged another son as his; and dying a year before, had left all to him. Katusthius found this unknown kinsman, with his wife and child, in possession of his expected inheritance. Cyril divided with him, it is true, their parent's property; but Katusthius grasped at all, and resolved to obtain it. He brooded over a thousand schemes of murder and revenge; yet the blood of a brother was sacred to him; and Cyril, beloved and respected at Corinth, could only be attacked with considerable risk. Then his child was a fresh obstacle. As the best plan that presented itself, he hastily embarked for Butrinto, and came to claim the advice and assistance of the Arnaoot whose life he had saved, whose Pobratimo he was. Not thus barely, did he tell his tale, but glossed it over; so that had Dmitri needed the incitement of justice, which was not at all a desideratum with him, he would have been satisfied that Cyril was a base interloper, and that the whole transaction was one of imposture and villany.

All night these men discussed a variety of projects, whose aim was, that the deceased Ziani's wealth should pass undivided into his elder son's hands. At morning's dawn Katusthius departed, and two days afterwards Dmitri quitted his mountain-home. His first care had been to purchase a horse, long coveted by him on account of its beauty and fleetness; he provided cartridges, and replenished his powder-horn. His accoutrements were rich, his dress gay; his arms glittered in the sun. His long hair fell straight from under the shawl twisted round his cap, even to his waist; a shaggy white capote hung from his shoulder; his face wrinkled and puckered by exposure to the seasons; his brow furrowed with care; his mustachios long and jet black; his scarred face; his wild, savage eyes; his whole appearance, not deficient in barbaric grace, but stamped chiefly with ferocity and bandit pride, inspired, and we need not wonder, the superstitious Greek with a belief that a supernatural spirit of evil dwelt in his aspect, blasting and destroying. Now prepared for his journey, he departed from Korvo, crossing the woods of Acarnania, on his way to the Morea.

"Wherefore does Zella tremble, and press her boy to her bosom, as if fearful of evil?" Thus asked Cyril Ziani, returning from the city of Corinth to his own rural abode. It was a home of beauty. The abruptly broken hills covered with olives, or brighter plantations of orange-trees, overlooked the blue waves of the Gulf of Aegina. A myrtle underwood spread sweet scent around, and dipped its dark shining leaves into the sea itself. The low-roofed house was shaded by two enormous fig-trees: while vineyards and corn-land stretched along the gentle upland to the north. When Zella saw her husband, she smiled, though her cheek was still pale and her lips quivering—"Now you are near to guard us," she said, "I dismiss fear; but danger threatens our Constans, and I shudder to remember that an Evil Eye has been upon him."

Cyril caught up his child—"By my head!" he cried, "thou speakest of an ill thing. The Franks call this superstition; but let us beware. His cheek is still rosy; his tresses flowing gold—Speak, Constans, hail thy father, my brave fellow!"

It was but a short-lived fear; no ill ensued, and they soon forgot an incident which had causelessly made their hearts to quail. A week afterwards Cyril returned, as he was wont, from shipping a cargo of currants, to his retreat on the coast. It was a beautiful summer evening; the creaking water-wheel, which produced the irrigation of the land, chimed in with the last song of the noisy cicala; the rippling waves spent themselves almost silently among the shingles. This was his home; but where its lovely flower? Zella did not come forth to welcome him. A domestic pointed to a chapel on a neighbouring acclivity, and there he found her; his child (nearly three years of age) was in his nurse's arms; his wife was praying fervently, while the tears streamed down her cheeks. Cyril demanded anxiously the meaning of this scene; but the nurse sobbed; Zella continued to pray and weep; and the boy, from sympathy, began to cry. This was too much for man to endure. Cyril left the chapel; he leant against a walnut-tree: his first exclamation was a customary Greek one—"Welcome this misfortune, so that it come single!" But what was the ill that had occurred? Unapparent was it yet; but the spirit of evil is most fatal when unseen. He was happy—a lovely wife, a blooming child, a peaceful home, competence, and the prospect of wealth; these blessings were his: yet how often does Fortune use such as her decoys? He was a slave in an enslaved land, a mortal subject to the high destinies, and ten thousand were the envenomed darts which might be hurled at his devoted head. Now timid and trembling, Zella came from the chapel: her explanation did not calm his fears. Again the Evil Eye had been on his child, and deep malignity lurked surely under this second visitation. The same man, an Arnaoot, with glittering arms, gay attire, mounted on a black steed, came from the neighbouring ilex grove, and, riding furiously up to the door, suddenly checked and reined in his horse at the very threshold. The child ran towards him: the Arnaoot bent his sinister eyes upon him:— "Lovely art thou, bright infant," he cried; "thy blue eyes are beaming, thy golden tresses fair to see; but thou art a vision fleeting as beautiful; —look at me!" The innocent looked up, uttered a shriek, and fell gasping on the ground. The women rushed forward to seize him; the Albanian put spurs to his horse, and galloping swiftly across the little plain, up the wooded hill-side, he was soon lost to sight. Zella and the nurse bore the child to the chapel, they sprinkled him with holy water, and, as he revived, besought the Panagia with earnest prayers to save him from the menaced ill.

Several weeks elapsed; little Constans grew in intelligence and beauty; no blight had visited the flower of love, and its parents dismissed fear. Sometimes Cyril indulged in a joke at the expense of the Evil Eye; but Zella thought it unlucky to laugh, and crossed herself whenever the event was alluded to. At this time Katusthius visited their abode. "He was on his way," he said, "to Stamboul, and he came to know whether he could serve his brother in any of his transactions in the capital." Cyril and Zella received him with cordial affection: they rejoiced to perceive that fraternal love was beginning to warm his heart. He seemed full of ambition and hope: the brothers discussed his prospects, the politics of Europe, and the intrigues of the Fanar: the petty affairs of Corinth even were made subjects of discourse; and the probability that in a short time, young as he was, Cyril would be named Codja-Bashee of the province. On the morrow, Katusthius prepared to depart—"One favour does the voluntary exile ask; will my brother and sister accompany me some hours on my way to Napoli, whence I embark?"

Zella was unwilling to quit her home, even for a short interval; but she suffered herself to be persuaded, and they proceeded altogether for several miles towards the capital of the Morea. At noontide they made a repast under the shadow of a grove of oaks, and then separated. Returning homeward, the wedded pair congratulated themselves on their tranquil life and peaceful happiness, contrasted with the wanderer's lonely and homeless pleasures. These feelings increased in intensity as they drew nearer their dwelling, and anticipated the lisped welcome of their idolized child. From an eminence they looked upon the fertile vale which was their home: it was situated on the southern side of the isthmus, and looked upon the Gulf of Aegina: all was verdant, tranquil, and beautiful. They descended into the plain; there a singular appearance attracted their attention. A plough with its yoke of oxen had been deserted midway in the furrow; the animals had dragged it to the side of the field, and endeavoured to repose as well as their conjunction permitted. The sun already touched its western bourne, and the summits of the trees were gilded by its parting beams. All was silent; even the eternal water-wheel was still; no menials appeared at their usual rustic labours. From the house the voice of wailing was too plainly heard.—"My child!" Zella exclaimed. Cyril began to reassure her; but another lament arose, and he hurried on. She dismounted, and would have followed him, but sank on the road's side. Her husband returned—"Courage, my beloved," he cried; "I will not repose night or day until Constans is restored to us—trust to me—farewell!" With these words he rode swiftly on. Her worst fears

were thus confirmed; her maternal heart, late so joyous, became the
abode of despair, while the nurse's narration of the sad occurrence tended
but to add worse fear to fear. Thus it was: the same stranger of the Evil
Eye had appeared, not as before, bearing down on them with eagle speed,
but as if from a long journey; his horse lame and with drooping head; the
Arnaoot himself covered with dust, apparently scarcely able to keep his
seat. "By the life of your child," he said, "give a cup of water to one who
faints with thirst." The nurse, with Constans in her arms, got a bowl of
the desired liquid, and presented it. Ere the parched lips of the stranger
touched the wave, the vessel fell from his hands. The women started
back, while he, at the same moment darting forward, tore with strong arm
the child from her embrace. Already both were gone—with arrowy speed
they traversed the plain, while her shrieks, and cries for assistance, called
together all the domestics. They followed on the track of the ravisher,
and none had yet returned. Now, as night closed in, one by one they came
back; they had nothing to relate; they had scoured the woods, crossed the
hills—they could not even discover the route which the Albanian had
taken.

On the following day Cyril returned, jaded, haggard, miserable; he had
obtained no tidings of his son. On the morrow he again departed on his
quest, nor came back for several days. Zella passed her time wearily—
now sitting in hopeless despondency, now climbing the near hill to see
whether she could perceive the approach of her husband. She was not
allowed to remain long thus tranquil; the trembling domestics, left in
guard, warned her that the savage forms of several Arnaoots had been
seen prowling about: she herself saw a tall figure, clad in a shaggy white
capote, steal round the promontory, and on seeing her, shrink back: once
at night the snorting and trampling of a horse roused her, not from
slumber, but from her sense of security. Wretched as the bereft mother
was, she felt personally almost reckless of danger; but she was not her
own, she belonged to one beyond expression dear; and duty, as well as
affection for him, enjoined self-preservation. He, Cyril, again returned:
he was gloomier, sadder than before; but there was more resolution on
his brow, more energy in his motions; he had obtained a clue, yet it might
only lead him to the depths of despair.

He discovered that Katusthius had not embarked at Napoli. He had
joined a band of Arnaoots lurking about Vasilico, and had proceeded to
Patras with the Protoklepht; thence they put off together in a monoxylon
for the northern shores of the gulf of Lepanto: nor were they alone; they
bore a child with them wrapt in a heavy torpid sleep. Poor Cyril's blood
ran cold when he thought of the spells and witchcraft which had probably
been put in practice on his boy. He would have followed close upon the
robbers, but for the report that reached him, that the remainder of the

Albanians had proceeded southward towards Corinth. He could not enter upon a long wandering search among the pathless wilds of Epirus, leaving Zella exposed to the attacks of these bandits. He returned to consult with her, to devise some plan of action which at once ensured her safety, and promised success to his endeavours.

After some hesitation and discussion, it was decided that he should first conduct her to her native home, consult with her father as to his present enterprise, and be guided by his warlike experience before he rushed into the very focus of danger. The seizure of his child might only be a lure, and it were not well for him, sole protector of that child and its mother, to rush unadvisedly into the toils.

Zella, strange to say, for her blue eyes and brilliant complexion belied her birth, was the daughter of a Mainote: yet dreaded and abhorred by the rest of the world as are the inhabitants of Cape Tænarus, they are celebrated for their domestic virtues and the strength of their private attachments. Zella loved her father, and the memory of her rugged rocky home, from which she had been torn in an adverse hour. Near neighbours of the Mainotes, dwelling in the ruder and most incult portion of Maina, are the Kakovougnis, a dark suspicious race, of squat and stunted form, strongly contrasted with the tranquil cast of countenance characteristic of the Mainote. The two tribes are embroiled in perpetual quarrels; the narrow sea-girt abode which they share affords at once a secure place of refuge from the foreign enemy, and all the facilities of internal mountain warfare. Cyril had once, during a coasting voyage, been driven by stress of weather into the little bay on whose shores is placed the small town of Kardamyla. The crew at first dreaded to be captured by the pirates; but they were reassured on finding them fully occupied by their domestic dissensions. A band of Kakovougnis were besieging the castellated rock overlooking Kardamyla, blockading the fortress in which the Mainote Capitano and his family had taken refuge. Two days passed thus, while furious contrary winds detained Cyril in the bay. On the third evening the western gale subsided, and a land breeze promised to emancipate them from their perilous condition; when in the night, as they were about to put off in a boat from shore, they were hailed by a party of Mainotes, and one, an old man of commanding figure, demanded a parley. He was the Capitano of Kardamyla, the chief of the fortress, now attacked by his implacable enemies: he saw no escape—he must fall—and his chief desire was to save his treasure and his family from the hands of his enemies. Cyril consented to receive them on board: the latter consisted of an old mother, a paramana, and a young and beautiful girl, his daughter. Cyril conducted them in safety to Napoli. Soon after, the Capitano's mother and paramana returned to their native town, while, with her father's consent, fair Zella became the wife of her preserver. The fortunes of the

Mainote had prospered since then, and he stood first in rank, the chief of a large tribe, the Capitano of Kardamyla.

Thither then the hapless parents repaired; they embarked on board a small sacoleva, which dropt down the Gulf of Aegina, weathered the islands of Skyllo and Cerigo, and the extreme point of Tænarus: favoured by prosperous gales, they made the desired port, and arrived at the hospitable mansion of old Camaraz. He heard their tale with indignation; swore by his beard to dip his poniard in the best blood of Katusthius, and insisted upon accompanying his son-in-law on his expedition to Albania. No time was lost—the gray-headed mariner, still full of energy, hastened every preparation. Cyril and Zella parted; a thousand fears, a thousand hours of misery rose between the pair, late sharers in perfect happiness. The boisterous sea and distant lands were the smallest of the obstacles that divided them; they would not fear the worst; yet hope, a sickly plant, faded in their hearts as they tore themselves asunder after a last embrace.

Zella returned from the fertile district of Corinth to her barren native rocks. She felt all joy expire as she viewed from the rugged shore the lessening sails of the sacoleva. Days and weeks passed, and still she remained in solitary and sad expectation: she never joined in the dance, nor made one in the assemblies of her country-women, who met together at evening-tide to sing, tell stories, and wile away the time in dance and gaiety. She secluded herself in the most lonely part of her father's house, and gazed unceasingly from the lattice upon the sea beneath, or wandered on the rocky beach; and when tempest darkened the sky, and each precipitous promontory grew purple under the shadows of the wide-winged clouds, when the roar of the surges was on the shore, and the white crests of the waves, seen afar upon the ocean-plain, showed like flocks of new-shorn sheep scattered along wide-extended downs, she felt neither gale nor inclement cold, nor returned home till recalled by her attendants. In obedience to them she sought the shelter of her abode, not to remain long; for the wild winds spoke to her, and the stormy ocean reproached her tranquillity. Unable to control the impulse, she would rush from her habitation on the cliff, nor remember, till she reached the shore, that her papooshes were left midway on the mountain path, and that her forgotten veil and disordered dress were unmeet for such a scene. Often the un-numbered hours sped on, while this orphaned child of happiness leant on a cold dark rock; the low-browed crags beetled over her, the surges broke at her feet, her fair limbs were stained by spray, her tresses dishevelled by the gale. Hopelessly she wept until a sail appeared on the horizon; and then she dried her fast flowing tears, fixing her large eyes upon the nearing hull or fading topsail. Meanwhile the storm tossed the clouds into a thousand gigantic shapes, and the tumultuous sea grew blacker and more

Drawn by Henry Corbould   Engraved by Charles Heath

ZELLA

wild; her natural gloom was heightened by superstitious horror; the Moirae, the old Fates of her native Grecian soil, howled in the breezes; apparitions, which told of her child pining under the influence of the Evil Eye, and of her husband, the prey of some Thracian witchcraft, such as still is practised in the dread neighbourhood of Larissa, haunted her broken slumbers, and stalked like dire shadows across her waking thoughts. Her bloom was gone, her eyes lost their lustre, her limbs their round full beauty; her strength failed her, as she tottered to the accustomed spot to watch—vainly, yet for ever to watch.

What is there so fearful as the expectation of evil tidings delayed? Sometimes in the midst of tears, or worse, amidst the convulsive gaspings of despair, we reproach ourselves for influencing the eternal fates by our gloomy anticipations: then, if a smile wreathe the mourner's quivering lip, it is arrested by a throb of agony. Alas! are not the dark tresses of the young, painted gray; the full cheek of beauty, delved with sad lines by the spirits of such hours? Misery is a more welcome visitant, when she comes in her darkest guise, and wraps us in perpetual black, for then the heart no longer sickens with disappointed hope.

Cyril and old Camaraz had found great difficulty in doubling the many capes of the Morea as they made a coasting expedition from Kardamyla to the gulf of Arta, north of Cefalonia and St. Mauro. During their voyage they had time to arrange their plans. As a number of Moreots travelling together might attract too much attention, they resolved to land their comrades at different points, and travel separately into the interior of Albania: Yannina was their first place of rendezvous. Cyril and his father-in-law disembarked in one of the most secluded of the many creeks which diversify the winding and precipitous shores of the gulf. Six others, chosen from the crew, would, by other routes, join them at the capital. They did not fear for themselves; alone, but well armed, and secure in the courage of despair, they penetrated the fastnesses of Epirus. No success cheered them: they arrived at Yannina without having made the slightest discovery. There they were joined by their comrades, whom they directed to remain three days in the town, and then separately to proceed to Tepellenè, whither they immediately directed their steps. At the first village on their way thither, at "monastic Zitza,"* they obtained some information, not to direct, but to encourage their endeavours. They sought refreshment and hospitality in the monastery which is situated on a green eminence, crowned by a grove of oak-trees, immediately behind the village. Perhaps there is not in the world a more beautiful or more romantic spot, sheltered itself by clustering trees, looking out on one widespread landscape of hill and dale, enriched by vineyards, dotted with

* Byron, *Childe Harold's Pilgrimage* II. xlviii (Ed.).

frequent flocks; while the Calamas in the depth of the vale gives life to the scene, and the far blue mountains of Zoumerkas, Sagori, Sulli, and Acroceraunia, to the east, west, north, and south, close in the various prospects. Cyril half envied the Caloyers their inert tranquillity. They received the travellers gladly, and were cordial though simple in their manners. When questioned concerning the object of their journey, they warmly sympathised with the father's anxiety, and eagerly told all they knew. Two weeks before, an Arnaoot, well known to them as Dmitri of the Evil Eye, a famous Klepht of Korvo, and a Moreot, arrived, bringing with them a child, a bold, spirited, beautiful boy, who, with firmness beyond his years, claimed the protection of the Caloyers, and accused his companions of having carried him off by force from his parents.—"By my head!" cried the Albanian, "a brave Palikar: he keeps his word, brother; he swore by the Panagia, in spite of our threats of throwing him down a precipice, food for the vulture, to accuse us to the first good men he saw: he neither pines under the Evil Eye, nor quails beneath our menaces." Katusthius frowned at these praises, and it became evident during their stay at the monastery, that the Albanian and the Moreot quarrelled as to the disposal of the child. The rugged mountaineer threw off all his sternness as he gazed upon the boy. When little Constans slept, he hung over him, fanning away, with woman's care, the flies and gnats. When he spoke, he answered with expressions of fondness, winning him with gifts, teaching him, all baby as he was, a mimicry of warlike exercises. When the boy knelt and besought the Panagia to restore him to his parents, his infant voice quivering, and tears running down his cheeks, the eyes of Dmitri overflowed; he cast his cloak over his face; his heart whispered to him—"Thus, perhaps, my child prayed. Heaven was deaf— alas! where is she now?"—Encouraged by such signs of compassion, which children are quick to perceive, Constans twined his arms round his neck, telling him that he loved him, and that he would fight for him when a man, if he would take him back to Corinth. At such words Dmitri would rush forth, seek Katusthius, remonstrate with him, till the unrelenting man checked him by reminding him of his vow. Still he swore that no hair of the child's head should be injured; while the uncle, unvisited by compunction, meditated his destruction. The quarrels which thence arose were frequent and violent, till Katusthius, weary of opposition, had recourse to craft to obtain his purpose. One night he secretly left the monastery, bearing the child with him. When Dmitri heard of his evasion, it was a fearful thing to the good Caloyers only to look upon him; they instinctively clutched hold of every bit of iron on which they could lay their hands, so to avert the Evil Eye which glared with native and untamed fierceness. In their panic a whole score of them had rushed to the iron-plated door which led out of their abode: with the strength of a lion,

Dmitri tore them away, threw back the portal, and, with the swiftness of a torrent fed by the thawing of the snows in spring, he dashed down the steep hill: the flight of an eagle not more rapid; the course of a wild beast not more resolved.

Such was the clue afforded to Cyril. It were too long to follow him in his subsequent search; he, with old Camaraz, wandered through the vale of Argyro-Castro, and climbed Mount Trebucci to Korvo. Dmitri had returned; he had gathered together a score of faithful comrades, and sallied forth again; various were the reports of his destination, and the enterprise which he meditated. One of these led our adventurers to Tepel-lenè, and hence back towards Yannina: and now chance again favoured them. They rested one night in the habitation of a priest at the little village of Mosme, about three leagues to the north of Zitza; and here they found an Arnaoot who had been disabled by a fall from his horse; this man was to have made one of Dmitri's band: they learned from him that the Arnaoot had tracked Katusthius, following him close, and forcing him to take refuge in the monastery of the Prophet Elias, which stands on an elevated peak of the mountains of Sagori, eight leagues from Yannina. Dmitri had followed him, and demanded the child. The Caloyers refused to give it up, and the Klepht, roused to mad indignation, was now besieging and battering the monastery, to obtain by force this object of his newly-awakened affections.

At Yannina, Camaraz and Cyril collected their comrades, and departed to join their unconscious ally. He, more impetuous than a mountain-stream or ocean's fiercest waves, struck terror into the hearts of the recluses by his ceaseless and dauntless attacks. To encourage them to further resistance, Katusthius, leaving the child behind in the monastery, departed for the nearest town of Sagori, to entreat its Belouk-Bashee to come to their aid. The Sagorians are a mild, amiable, social people; they are gay, frank, clever; their bravery is universally acknowledged, even by the more uncivilized mountaineers of Zoumerkas; yet robbery, murder, and other acts of violence, are unknown among them. These good people were not a little indignant when they heard that a band of Arnaoots was besieging and battering the sacred retreat of their favourite Caloyers. They assembled in a gallant troop, and taking Katusthius with them, hastened to drive the insolent Klephts back to their ruder fastnesses. They came too late. At midnight, while the monks prayed fervently to be delivered from their enemies, Dmitri and his followers tore down their iron-plated door, and entered the holy precincts. The Protoklepht strode up to the gates of the sanctuary, and placing his hands upon it, swore that he came to save, not to destroy. Constans saw him. With a cry of delight he disengaged himself from the Caloyer who held him, and rushed into his arms: this was sufficient triumph. With assurances of sincere regret for having disturbed them, the Klepht quitted the chapel with his followers, taking his prize with him.

Katusthius returned some hours after, and so well did the traitor plead his cause with the kind Sagorians, bewailing the fate of his little nephew among these evil men, that they offered to follow, and, superior as their numbers were, to rescue the boy from their destructive hands. Katusthius, delighted with the proposition, urged their immediate departure. At dawn they began to climb the mountain summits, already trodden by the Zoumerkians.

Delighted with repossessing his little favourite, Dmitri placed him before him on his horse, and, followed by his comrades, made his way over the elevated mountains, clothed with old Dodona's oaks, or, in higher summits, by dark gigantic pines. They proceeded for some hours, and at length dismounted to repose. The spot they chose was the depth of a dark ravine, whose gloom was increased by the broad shadows of dark ilexes; an entangled underwood, and a sprinkling of craggy isolated rocks, made it difficult for the horses to keep their footing. They dismounted, and sat by the little stream. Their simple fare was spread, and Dmitri enticed the boy to eat by a thousand caresses. Suddenly one of his men, set as a guard, brought intelligence that a troop of Sagorians, with Katusthius as their guide, was advancing from the monastery of St. Elias; while another man gave the alarm of the approach of six or eight well-armed Moreots, who were advancing on the road from Yannina; in a moment every sign of encampment had disappeared. The Arnaoots began to climb the hills, getting under cover of the rocks, and behind the large trunks of the forest-trees, keeping concealed till their invaders should be in the very midst of them. Soon the Moreots appeared, turning round the defile, in a path that only allowed them to proceed two by two; they were unaware of danger, and walked carelessly, until a shot that whizzed over the head of one, striking the bough of a tree, recalled them from their security. The Greeks, accustomed to the same mode of warfare, betook themselves also to the safeguards of the rocks, firing from behind them, striving with their adversaries which should get to the most elevated station; jumping from crag to crag, and dropping down and firing as quickly as they could load: one old man alone remained on the pathway. The mariner, Camaraz, had often encountered the enemy on the deck of his caick, and would still have rushed foremost at a boarding, but this warfare required too much activity. Cyril called on him to shelter himself beneath a low, broad stone: the Mainote waved his hand. "Fear not for me," he cried; "I know how to die!"—The brave love the brave. Dmitri saw the old man stand, unflinching, a mark for all the balls, and he started from behind his rocky screen, calling on his men to cease. Then addressing his enemy, he cried, "Who art thou? wherefore art thou here? If ye come in peace, proceed on your way. Answer, and fear not!"

The old man drew himself up, saying, "I am a Mainote, and cannot fear. All Hellas trembles before the pirates of Cape Matapan, and I am one of these! I do not come in peace! Behold! you have in your arms the cause of our dissension! I am the grandsire of that child—give him to me!"

Dmitri, had he held a snake, which he felt awakening in his bosom, could not so suddenly have changed his cheer:—"the offspring of a Mainote!"—he relaxed his grasp;—Constans would have fallen had he not clung to his neck. Meanwhile each party had descended from their rocky station, and were grouped together in the pathway below. Dmitri tore the child from his neck; he felt as if he could, with savage delight, dash him down the precipice—when, as he paused and trembled from excess of passion, Katusthius, and the foremost Sagorians, came down upon them.

"Stand!" cried the infuriated Arnaoot. "Behold Katusthius! behold, friend, whom I, driven by the resistless fates, madly and wickedly forswore! I now perform thy wish—the Mainote child dies! the son of the accursed race shall be the victim of my just revenge!"

Cyril, in a transport of fear, rushed up the rock; he levelled his musket, but he feared to sacrifice his child. The old Mainote, less timid and more desperate, took a steady aim; Dmitri saw the act, and hurled the dagger, already raised against the child, at him—it entered his side—while Constans, feeling his late protector's grasp relax, sprung from it into his father's arms.

Camaraz had fallen, yet his wound was slight. He saw the Arnaoots and Sagorians close round him; he saw his own followers made prisoners. Dmitri and Katusthius had both thrown themselves upon Cyril, struggling to repossess themselves of the screaming boy. The Mainote raised himself —he was feeble of limb, but his heart was strong; he threw himself before the father and child; he caught the upraised arm of Dmitri. "On me," he cried, "fall all thy vengeance! I of the evil race! for the child, he is innocent of such parentage! Maina cannot boast him for a son!"

"Man of lies!" commenced the infuriated Arnaoot, "this falsehood shall not stead thee!"

"Nay, by the souls of those you have loved, listen!" continued Camaraz, "and if I make not good my words, may I and my children die! The boy's father is a Corinthian, his mother, a Sciote girl!"

"Scio!" the very word made the blood recede to Dmitri's heart. "Villain!" he cried, dashing aside Katusthius's arm, which was raised against poor Constans, "I guard this child—dare not to injure him! Speak, old man, and fear not, so that thou speakest the truth."

"Fifteen years ago," said Camaraz, "I hovered with my caick, in search of prey, on the coast of Scio. A cottage stood on the borders of a chestnut wood, it was the habitation of the widow of a wealthy islander— she dwelt in it with her only daughter, married to an Albanian, then absent;—the good woman was reported to have a concealed treasure in her house—the girl herself would be rich spoil—it was an adventure worth the risk. We ran our vessel up a shady creek, and, on the going down of the moon, landed; stealing under the covert of night towards the lonely abode of these women."—

Dmitri grasped at his dagger's hilt—it was no longer there; he half drew a pistol from his girdle—little Constans, again confiding in his former friend, stretched out his infant hands and clung to his arm; the Klepht looked on him, half yielded to his desire to embrace him, half feared to be deceived; so he turned away, throwing his capote over his face, veiling his anguish, controlling his emotions, till all should be told. Camaraz continued:

"It became a worse tragedy than I had contemplated. The girl had a child—she feared for its life, and struggled with the men like a tigress defending her young. I was in another room seeking for the hidden store, when a piercing shriek rent the air—I never knew what compassion was before—this cry went to my heart—but it was too late, the poor girl had sunk to the ground, the life-tide oozing from her bosom. I know not why, but I turned woman in my regret for the slain beauty. I meant to have carried her and her child on board, to see if aught could be done to save her, but she died ere we left the shore. I thought she would like her island grave best, and truly feared that she might turn vampire to haunt me, did I carry her away; so we left her corse for the priests to bury, and carried off the child, then about two years old. She could say few words except her own name, that was Zella, and she is the mother of this boy!"

A succession of arrivals in the bay of Kardamyla had kept poor Zella watching for many nights. Her attendant had, in despair of ever seeing her sleep again, drugged with opium the few cates she persuaded her to eat, but the poor woman did not calculate on the power of mind over body, of love over every enemy, physical or moral, arrayed against it. Zella lay on her couch, her spirit somewhat subdued, but her heart alive, her eyes unclosed. In the night, led by some unexplained impulse, she crawled to her lattice, and saw a little sacoleva enter the bay; it ran in swiftly, under favour of the wind, and was lost to her sight under a jutting crag. Lightly she trod the marble floor of her chamber; she drew a large shawl close round her; she descended the rocky pathway, and reached, with swift steps, the beach—still the vessel was invisible, and she was half inclined to think that it was the offspring of her excited imagination—yet she lingered. She felt a sickness at her very heart whenever she attempted to move, and her eyelids weighed down in spite of herself. The desire of sleep at last became irresistible; she lay down on the shingles, reposed her head on the cold, hard pillow, folded her shawl still closer, and gave herself up to forgetfulness.

So profoundly did she slumber under the influence of the opiate, that for many hours she was insensible of any change in her situation. By degrees only she awoke, by degrees only became aware of the objects around her; the breeze felt fresh and free—so was it ever on the wave-beaten coast; the waters rippled near, their dash had been in her ears as she yielded to repose; but this was not her stony couch, that canopy, not the dark overhanging cliff. Suddenly she lifted up her head—she was on the deck of a small vessel, which was skimming swiftly over the ocean-waves—a cloak of sables pillowed her head; the shores of Cape Matapan were to her left, and they steered right towards the noonday sun. Wonder rather than fear possessed her: with a quick hand she drew aside the sail that veiled her from the crew—the dreaded Albanian was sitting close at her side, her Constans cradled in his arms—she uttered a cry—Cyril turned at the sound, and in a moment she was folded in his embrace.

IX

The False Rhyme

Come, tell me where the maid is found
Whose heart can love without deceit,
And I will range the world around
To sigh one moment at her feet.—THOMAS MOORE

ON A FINE July day, the fair Margaret, Queen of Navarre, then on a visit to her royal brother, had arranged a rural feast for the morning following, which Francis declined attending. He was melancholy; and the cause was said to be some lover's quarrel with a favourite dame. The morrow came, and dark rain and murky clouds destroyed at once the schemes of the courtly throng. Margaret was angry, and she grew weary: her only hope for amusement was in Francis, and he had shut himself up—an excellent reason why she should the more desire to see him. She entered his apartment: he was standing at the casement, against which the noisy shower beat, writing with a diamond on the glass. Two beautiful dogs were his sole companions. As Queen Margaret entered, he hastily let down the silken curtain before the window, and looked a little confused.

"What treason is this, my liege," said the queen, "which crimsons your cheek? I must see the same."

"It is treason," replied the king, "and therefore, sweet sister, thou mayest not see it."

This the more excited Margaret's curiosity, and a playful contest ensued: Francis at last yielded: he threw himself on a huge high-backed settee; and as the lady drew back the curtain with an arch smile, he grew grave and sentimental, as he reflected on the cause which had inspired his libel against all womankind.

"What have we here?" cried Margaret: "nay, this is lèse majesté—

'Souvent femme varie,
Bien fou qui s'y fie!'

117

Painted by Richard Parkes Bonington   *Engraved by Charles Heath*

FRANCIS THE FIRST & HIS SISTER

Very little change would greatly amend your couplet:—would it not run better thus—

> 'Souvent homme varie,
> Bien folle qui s'y fie'?

I could tell you twenty stories of man's inconstancy."

"I will be content with one true tale of woman's fidelity," said Francis, drily; "but do not provoke me. I would fain be at peace with the soft Mutabilities, for thy dear sake."

"I defy your grace," replied Margaret, rashly, "to instance the falsehood of one noble and well reputed dame."

"Not even Emilie de Lagny?" asked the king.

This was a sore subject for the queen. Emilie had been brought up in her own household, the most beautiful and the most virtuous of her maids of honour. She had long loved the Sire de Lagny, and their nuptials were celebrated with rejoicings but little ominous of the result. De Lagny was accused but a year after of traitorously yielding to the emperor a fortress under his command, and he was condemned to perpetual imprisonment. For some time Emilie seemed inconsolable, often visiting the miserable dungeon of her husband, and suffering on her return, from witnessing his wretchedness, such paroxysms of grief as threatened her life. Suddenly, in the midst of her sorrow, she disappeared; and inquiry only divulged the disgraceful fact, that she had escaped from France, bearing her jewels with her, and accompanied by her page, Robinet Leroux. It was whispered that, during their journey, the lady and the stripling often occupied one chamber; and Margaret, enraged at these discoveries, commanded that no further quest should be made for her lost favourite.

Taunted now by her brother, she defended Emilie, declaring that she believed her to be guiltless, even going so far as to boast that within a month she would bring proof of her innocence.

"Robinet was a pretty boy," said Francis, laughing.

"Let us make a bet," cried Margaret: "if I lose, I will bear this vile rhyme of thine as a motto to my shame to my grave; if I win——"

"I will break my window, and grant thee whatever boon thou askest."

The result of this bet was long sung by troubadour and minstrel. The queen employed a hundred emissaries—published rewards for any intelligence of Emilie—all in vain. The month was expiring, and Margaret would have given many bright jewels to redeem her word. On the eve of the fatal day, the jailor of the prison in which the Sire de Lagny was confined sought an audience of the queen; he brought her a message from the knight to say, that if the Lady Margaret would ask his pardon as her boon, and obtain from her royal brother that he might be brought before him, her bet was won. Fair Margaret was very joyful, and readily made the desired promise. Francis was unwilling to see his false servant, but he was in high good humour, for a cavalier had that morning brought intelligence of a victory over the Imperialists. The messenger himself was lauded in the despatches as the most fearless and bravest knight in France. The king loaded him with presents, only regretting that a vow prevented the soldier from raising his visor or declaring his name.

That same evening as the setting sun shone on the lattice on which the ungallant rhyme was traced, Francis reposed on the same settee, and the beautiful Queen of Navarre, with triumph in her bright eyes, sat beside him. Attended by guards, the prisoner was brought in: his frame was attenuated by privation, and he walked with tottering steps. He knelt at the feet of Francis, and uncovered his head; a quantity of rich golden hair then escaping, fell over the sunken cheeks and pallid brow of the suppliant. "We have treason here!" cried the king: "sir jailor, where is your prisoner?"

"Sire, blame him not," said the soft faltering voice of Emilie; "wiser men than he have been deceived by woman. My dear lord was guiltless of the crime for which he suffered. There was but one mode to save him:—I assumed his chains—he escaped with poor Robinet Leroux in my attire —he joined your army: the young and gallant cavalier who delivered the despatches to your grace, whom you overwhelmed with honours and reward, is my own Enguerrard de Lagny. I waited but for his arrival with testimonials of his innocence, to declare myself to my lady, the queen. Has she not won her bet? And the boon she asks——"

"Is de Lagny's pardon," said Margaret, as she also knelt to the king: "spare your faithful vassal, sire, and reward this lady's truth."

Francis first broke the false-speaking window, then he raised the ladies from their supplicatory posture.

In the tournament given to celebrate this "Triumph of Ladies," the Sire de Lagny bore off every prize; and surely there was more loveliness in Emilie's faded cheek—more grace in her emaciated form, type as they were of truest affection—than in the prouder bearing and fresher complexion of the most brilliant beauty in attendance on the courtly festival.

X

Transformation

Forthwith this frame of mine was wrench'd
  With a woful agony,
Which forced me to begin my tale,
  And then it set me free.
Since then, at an uncertain hour,
  That agony returns;
And till my ghastly tale is told
  This heart within me burns.—COLERIDGE'S ANCIENT MARINER.

I HAVE HEARD it said, that, when any strange, supernatural, and necro-
mantic adventure has occurred to a human being, that being, however
desirous he may be to conceal the same, feels at certain periods torn up
as it were by an intellectual earthquake, and is forced to bare the inner
depths of his spirit to another. I am a witness of the truth of this. I have
dearly sworn to myself never to reveal to human ears the horrors to
which I once, in excess of fiendly pride, delivered myself over. The holy
man who heard my confession, and reconciled me to the church, is dead.
None knows that once——

Why should it not be thus? Why tell a tale of impious tempting of
Providence, and soul-subduing humiliation? Why? answer me, ye who are
wise in the secrets of human nature! I only know that so it is; and in spite
of strong resolve—of a pride that too much masters me—of shame, and
even of fear, so to render myself odious to my species—I must speak.

Genoa! my birth-place—proud city! looking upon the blue waves of
the Mediterranean sea—dost thou remember me in my boyhood, when
thy cliffs and promontories, thy bright sky and gay vineyards, were my
world? Happy time! when to the young heart the narrow-bounded universe, which leaves, by its very limitation, free scope to the imagination,
enchains our physical energies, and, sole period in our lives, innocence
and enjoyment are united. Yet, who can look back to childhood, and not
remember its sorrows and its harrowing fears? I was born with the most

imperious, haughty, tameless spirit, with which ever mortal was gifted. I quailed before my father only; and he, generous and noble, but capricious and tyrannical, at once fostered and checked the wild impetuosity of my character, making obedience necessary, but inspiring no respect for the motives which guided his commands. To be a man, free, independent; or, in better words, insolent and domineering, was the hope and prayer of my rebel heart.

My father had one friend, a wealthy Genoese noble, who in a political tumult was suddenly sentenced to banishment, and his property confiscated. The Marchese Torella went into exile alone. Like my father, he was a widower: he had one child, the almost infant Juliet, who was left under my father's guardianship. I should certainly have been an unkind master to the lovely girl, but that I was forced by my position to become her protector. A variety of childish incidents all tended to one point,—to make Juliet see in me a rock of refuge; I in her, one, who must perish through the soft sensibility of her nature too rudely visited, but for my guardian care. We grew up together. The opening rose in May was not more sweet than this dear girl. An irradiation of beauty was spread over her face. Her form, her step, her voice—my heart weeps even now, to think of all of relying, gentle, loving, and pure, that was enshrined in that celestial tenement. When I was eleven and Juliet eight years of age, a cousin of mine, much older than either—he seemed to us a man—took great notice of my playmate; he called her his bride, and asked her to marry him. She refused, and he insisted, drawing her unwillingly towards him. With the countenance and emotions of a maniac I threw myself on him—I strove to draw his sword—I clung to his neck with the ferocious resolve to strangle him: he was obliged to call for assistance to disengage himself from me. On that night I led Juliet to the chapel of our house: I made her touch the sacred relics—I harrowed her child's heart, and profaned her child's lips with an oath, that she would be mine, and mine only.

Well, those days passed away. Torella returned in a few years, and became wealthier and more prosperous than ever. When I was seventeen, my father died; he had been magnificent to prodigality; Torella rejoiced that my minority would afford an opportunity for repairing my fortunes. Juliet and I had been affianced beside my father's deathbed—Torella was to be a second parent to me.

I desired to see the world, and I was indulged. I went to Florence, to Rome, to Naples; thence I passed to Toulon, and at length reached what had long been the bourne of my wishes, Paris. There was wild work in Paris then. The poor king, Charles the Sixth, now sane, now mad, now a monarch, now an abject slave, was the very mockery of humanity. The queen, the dauphin, the Duke of Burgundy, alternately friends and foes—

now meeting in prodigal feasts, now shedding blood in rivalry—were blind to the miserable state of their country, and the dangers that impended over it, and gave themselves wholly up to dissolute enjoyment or savage strife. My character still followed me. I was arrogant and self-willed; I loved display, and above all, I threw all control far from me. Who could control me in Paris? My young friends were eager to foster passions which furnished them with pleasures. I was deemed handsome—I was master of every knightly accomplishment. I was disconnected with any political party. I grew a favourite with all: my presumption and arrogance were pardoned in one so young: I became a spoiled child. Who could control me? not the letters and advice of Torella—only strong necessity visiting me in the abhorred shape of an empty purse. But there were means to refill this void. Acre after acre, estate after estate, I sold. My dress, my jewels, my horses and their caparisons, were almost unrivalled in gorgeous Paris, while the lands of my inheritance passed into possession of others.

The Duke of Orleans was waylaid and murdered by the Duke of Burgundy. Fear and terror possessed all Paris. The dauphin and the queen shut themselves up; every pleasure was suspended. I grew weary of this state of things, and my heart yearned for my boyhood's haunts. I was nearly a beggar, yet still I would go there, claim my bride, and rebuild my fortunes. A few happy ventures as a merchant would make me rich again. Nevertheless, I would not return in humble guise. My last act was to dispose of my remaining estate near Albaro for half its worth, for ready money. Then I despatched all kinds of artificers, arras, furniture of regal splendour, to fit up the last relic of my inheritance, my palace in Genoa. I lingered a little longer yet, ashamed at the part of the prodigal returned, which I feared I should play. I sent my horses. One matchless Spanish jennet I despatched to my promised bride; its caparisons flamed with jewels and cloth of gold. In every part I caused to be entwined the initials of Juliet and her Guido. My present found favour in hers and in her father's eyes.

Still to return a proclaimed spendthrift, the mark of impertinent wonder, perhaps of scorn, and to encounter singly the reproaches or taunts of my fellow-citizens, was no alluring prospect. As a shield between me and censure, I invited some few of the most reckless of my comrades to accompany me: thus I went armed against the world, hiding a rankling feeling, half fear and half penitence, by bravado and an insolent display of satisfied vanity.

I arrived in Genoa. I trod the pavement of my ancestral palace. My proud step was no interpreter of my heart, for I deeply felt that, though surrounded by every luxury, I was a beggar. The first step I took in claiming Juliet must widely declare me such. I read contempt or pity in the looks of all. I fancied, so apt is conscience to imagine what it deserves, that rich and poor, young and old, all regarded me with derision. Torella came not near me. No wonder that my second father should expect a son's deference from me in waiting first on him. But, galled and stung by a sense of my follies and demerit, I strove to throw the blame on others. We kept nightly orgies in Palazzo Carega. To sleepless, riotous nights, followed listless, supine mornings. At the Ave Maria we showed our dainty persons in the streets, scoffing at the sober citizens, casting insolent glances on the shrinking women. Juliet was not among them—no, no; if she had been there, shame would have driven me away, if love had not brought me to her feet.

I grew tired of this. Suddenly I paid the Marchese a visit. He was at his villa, one among the many which deck the suburb of San Pietro d'Arena. It was the month of May—a month of May in that garden of the world —the blossoms of the fruit trees were fading among thick, green foliage; the vines were shooting forth; the ground strewed with the fallen olive blooms; the fire-fly was in the myrtle hedge; heaven and earth wore a mantle of surpassing beauty. Torella welcomed me kindly, though seriously; and even his shade of displeasure soon wore away. Some resemblance to my father—some look and tone of youthful ingenuousness, lurking still in spite of my misdeeds, softened the good old man's heart. He sent for his daughter—he presented me to her as her betrothed. The chamber became hallowed by a holy light as she entered. Hers was that cherub look, those large, soft eyes, full dimpled cheeks, and mouth of infantine sweetness, that expresses the rare union of happiness and love. Admiration first possessed me; she is mine! was the second proud emotion, and my lips curled with haughty triumph. I had not been the *enfant gâté* of the beauties of France not to have learnt the art of pleasing the soft heart of woman. If towards men I was overbearing, the deference I paid to them was the more in contrast. I commenced my courtship by the display of a thousand gallantries to Juliet, who, vowed to me from infancy, had never admitted the devotion of others; and who, though accustomed to expressions of admiration, was uninitiated in the language of lovers.

For a few days all went well. Torella never alluded to my extravagance; he treated me as a favourite son. But the time came, as we discussed the preliminaries to my union with his daughter, when this fair face of things should be overcast. A contract had been drawn up in my father's lifetime. I had rendered this, in fact, void, by having squandered the whole of the wealth which was to have been shared by Juliet and myself. Torella, in consequence, chose to consider this bond as cancelled, and proposed another, in which, though the wealth he bestowed was immeasurably increased, there were so many restrictions as to the mode of spending it, that I, who saw independence only in free career being given to my own imperious will, taunted him as taking advantage of my situation, and refused utterly to subscribe to his conditions. The old man mildly strove to recall me to reason. Roused pride became the tyrant of my thought: I listened with indignation—I repelled him with disdain.

"Juliet, thou art mine! Did we not interchange vows in our innocent childhood? are we not one in the sight of God? and shall thy cold-hearted, cold-blooded father divide us? Be generous, my love, be just; take not away a gift, last treasure of thy Guido—retract not thy vows—let us defy the world, and setting at nought the calculations of age, find in our mutual affection a refuge from every ill."

Fiend I must have been, with such sophistry to endeavour to poison that sanctuary of holy thought and tender love. Juliet shrank from me affrighted. Her father was the best and kindest of men, and she strove to show me how, in obeying him, every good would follow. He would receive my tardy submission with warm affection; and generous pardon would follow my repentance. Profitless words for a young and gentle daughter to use to a man accustomed to make his will, law; and to feel in his own heart a despot so terrible and stern, that he could yield obedience to nought save his own imperious desires! My resentment grew with resistance; my wild companions were ready to add fuel to the flame. We laid a plan to carry off Juliet. At first it appeared to be crowned with success. Midway, on our return, we were overtaken by the agonized father and his attendants. A conflict ensued. Before the city guard came to decide the victory in favour of our antagonists, two of Torella's servitors were dangerously wounded.

This portion of my history weighs most heavily with me. Changed man as I am, I abhor myself in the recollection. May none who hear this tale ever have felt as I. A horse driven to fury by a rider armed with barbed spurs, was not more a slave than I, to the violent tyranny of my temper. A fiend possessed my soul, irritating it to madness. I felt the voice of conscience within me; but if I yielded to it for a brief interval, it was only to be a moment after torn, as by a whirlwind, away—borne along on the stream of desperate rage—the plaything of the storms engendered by pride. I was imprisoned, and, at the instance of Torella, set free. Again I returned to carry off both him and his child to France; which hapless country, then preyed on by freebooters and gangs of lawless soldiery, offered a grateful refuge to a criminal like me. Our plots were discovered. I was sentenced to banishment; and, as my debts were already enormous, my remaining property was put in the hands of commissioners for their payment. Torella again offered his mediation, requiring only my promise not to renew my abortive attempts on himself and his daughter. I spurned his offers, and fancied that I triumphed when I was thrust out from

Genoa, a solitary and penniless exile. My companions were gone: they had been dismissed the city some weeks before, and were already in France. I was alone—friendless; with nor sword at my side, nor ducat in my purse.

I wandered along the sea-shore, a whirlwind of passion possessing and tearing my soul. It was as if a live coal had been set burning in my breast. At first I meditated on what *I should do.* I would join a band of freebooters. Revenge!—the word seemed balm to me:—I hugged it—caressed it—till, like a serpent, it stung me. Then again I would abjure and despise Genoa, that little corner of the world. I would return to Paris, where so many of my friends swarmed; where my services would be eagerly accepted; where I would carve out fortune with my sword, and might, through success, make my paltry birth-place, and the false Torella, rue the day when they drove me, a new Coriolanus, from her walls. I would return to Paris—thus, on foot—a beggar—and present myself in my poverty to those I had formerly entertained sumptuously? There was gall in the mere thought of it.

The reality of things began to dawn upon my mind, bringing despair in its train. For several months I had been a prisoner: the evils of my dungeon had whipped my soul to madness, but they had subdued my corporeal frame. I was weak and wan. Torella had used a thousand artifices to administer to my comfort; I had detected and scorned them all—and I reaped the harvest of my obduracy. What was to be done? —Should I crouch before my foe, and sue for forgiveness?—Die rather ten thousand deaths!—Never should they obtain that victory! Hate—I swore eternal hate! Hate from whom?—to whom?—From a wandering outcast—to a mighty noble. I and my feelings were nothing to them: already had they forgotten one so unworthy. And Juliet!—her angel-face and sylph-like form gleamed among the clouds of my despair with vain beauty; for I had lost her—the glory and flower of the world! Another will call her his!—that smile of paradise will bless another!

Even now my heart fails within me when I recur to this rout of grim-visaged ideas. Now subdued almost to tears, now raving in my agony, still I wandered along the rocky shore, which grew at each step wilder and more desolate. Hanging rocks and hoar precipices overlooked the tideless ocean; black caverns yawned; and for ever, among the seaworn recesses, murmured and dashed the unfruitful waters. Now my way was almost barred by an abrupt promontory, now rendered nearly impracticable by fragments fallen from the cliff. Evening was at hand, when, seaward, arose, as if on the waving of a wizard's wand, a murky web of clouds, blotting the late azure sky, and darkening and disturbing the till now placid deep. The clouds had strange fantastic shapes; and they changed, and mingled, and seemed to be driven about by a mighty spell. The waves raised their white crests; the thunder first muttered, then roared from across the waste of waters, which took a deep purple dye, flecked with foam. The spot where I stood, looked, on one side, to the wide-spread ocean; on the other, it was barred by a rugged promontory. Round this cape suddenly came, driven by the wind, a vessel. In vain the mariners tried to force a path for her to the open sea—the gale drove her on the rocks. It will perish!—all on board will perish!—Would I were among them! And to my young heart the idea of death came for the first time blended with that of joy. It was an awful sight to behold that vessel struggling with her fate. Hardly could I discern the sailors, but I heard them. It was soon all over!—A rock, just covered by the tossing waves, and so unperceived, lay in wait for its prey. A crash of thunder broke over my head at the moment that, with a frightful shock, the skiff dashed upon her unseen enemy. In a brief space of time she went to pieces. There I stood in safety; and there were my fellow-creatures, battling, how hopelessly, with annihilation. Methought I saw them struggling—too truly did I hear their shrieks, conquering the barking surges in their shrill agony. The dark breakers threw hither and thither the fragments of the wreck: soon it disappeared. I had been fascinated to gaze till the end: at last I sank on my knees—I covered my face with my hands: I again looked up; something was floating on the billows towards the shore. It neared and neared. Was that a human form?—It grew more distinct; and at last a mighty wave, lifting the whole freight, lodged it upon a rock. A human being bestriding a sea-chest!—A human being!—Yet was it one? Surely never such had existed before—a misshapen dwarf, with squinting eyes, distorted features, and body deformed, till it became a horror to behold. My blood, lately warming towards a fellow-being so snatched from a watery tomb, froze in my heart. The dwarf got off his chest; he tossed his straight, straggling hair from his odious visage:

"By St. Beelzebub!" he exclaimed, "I have been well bested." He looked round and saw me. "Oh, by the fiend! here is another ally of the mighty one. To what saint did you offer prayers, friend—if not to mine? Yet I remember you not on board."

I shrank from the monster and his blasphemy. Again he questioned me, and I muttered some inaudible reply. He continued:—

"Your voice is drowned by this dissonant roar. What a noise the big ocean makes! Schoolboys bursting from their prison are not louder than these waves set free to play. They disturb me. I will no more of their ill-timed brawling.—Silence, hoary One!—Winds, avaunt!—to your homes! —Clouds, fly to the antipodes, and leave our heaven clear!"

As he spoke, he stretched out his two long lank arms, that looked like spider's claws, and seemed to embrace with them the expanse before him. Was it a miracle? The clouds became broken, and fled; the azure sky first peeped out, and then was spread a calm field of blue above us; the stormy gale was exchanged to the softly breathing west; the sea grew calm; the waves dwindled to riplets.

"I like obedience even in these stupid elements," said the dwarf. "How much more in the tameless mind of man! It was a well got up storm, you must allow—and all of my own making."

It was tempting Providence to interchange talk with this magician. But *Power*, in all its shapes, is venerable to man. Awe, curiosity, a clinging fascination, drew me towards him.

"Come, don't be frightened, friend," said the wretch: "I am good-humoured when pleased; and something does please me in your well-proportioned body and handsome face, though you look a little woe-begone. You have suffered a land—I, a sea wreck. Perhaps I can allay the tempest of your fortunes as I did my own. Shall we be friends?" —And he held out his hand; I could not touch it. "Well, then, companions—that will do as well. And now, while I rest after the buffeting I underwent just now, tell me why, young and gallant as you seem, you wander thus alone and downcast on this wild sea-shore."

The voice of the wretch was screeching and horrid, and his contortions as he spoke were frightful to behold. Yet he did gain a kind of influence over me, which I could not master, and I told him my tale. When it was ended, he laughed long and loud: the rocks echoed back the sound: hell seemed yelling around me.

"Oh, thou cousin of Lucifer!" said he; "so thou too hast fallen through thy pride; and, though bright as the son of Morning, thou art ready to give up thy good looks, thy bride, and thy well-being, rather than submit thee to the tyranny of good. I honour thy choice, by my soul!—So thou hast fled, and yield the day; and mean to starve on these rocks, and to let the birds peck out thy dead eyes, while thy enemy and thy betrothed rejoice in thy ruin. Thy pride is strangely akin to humility, methinks."

As he spoke, a thousand fanged thoughts stung me to the heart.

"What would you that I should do?" I cried.

"I!—Oh, nothing, but lie down and say your prayers before you die. But, were I you, I know the deed that should be done."

I drew near him. His supernatural powers made him an oracle in my eyes; yet a strange unearthly thrill quivered through my frame as I said— "Speak!—teach me—what act do you advise?"

"Revenge thyself, man!—humble thy enemies!—set thy foot on the old man's neck, and possess thyself of his daughter!"

"To the east and west I turn," cried I, "and see no means! Had I gold, much could I achieve; but, poor and single, I am powerless."

The dwarf had been seated on his chest as he listened to my story. Now he got off; he touched a spring; it flew open!—What a mine of wealth—of blazing jewels, beaming gold, and pale silver—was displayed therein. A mad desire to possess this treasure was born within me.

"Doubtless," I said, "one so powerful as you could do all things."

"Nay," said the monster, humbly, "I am less omnipotent than I seem. Some things I possess which you may covet; but I would give them all for a small share, or even for a loan of what is yours."

"My possessions are at your service," I replied, bitterly—"my poverty, my exile, my disgrace—I make a free gift of them all."

"Good! I thank you. Add one other thing to your gift, and my treasure is yours."

"As nothing is my sole inheritance, what besides nothing would you have?"

"Your comely face and well-made limbs."

I shivered. Would this all-powerful monster murder me? I had no dagger. I forgot to pray—but I grew pale.

"I ask for a loan, not a gift," said the frightful thing: "lend me your body for three days—you shall have mine to cage your soul the while, and, in payment, my chest. What say you to the bargain?—Three short days."

We are told that it is dangerous to hold unlawful talk; and well do I prove the same. Tamely written down, it may seem incredible that I should lend any ear to this proposition; but, in spite of his unnatural ugliness, there was something fascinating in a being whose voice could govern earth, air, and sea. I felt a keen desire to comply; for with that chest I could command the world. My only hesitation resulted from a fear that he would not be true to his bargain. Then, I thought, I shall soon die here on these lonely sands, and the limbs he covets will be mine no more:—it is worth the chance. And, besides, I knew that, by all the rules of art-magic, there were formula and oaths which none of its practisers dared break. I hesitated to reply; and he went on, now displaying his wealth, now speaking of the petty price he demanded, till it seemed madness to refuse. Thus is it: place our bark in the current of the stream, and down, over fall and cataract it is hurried; give up our conduct to the wild torrent of passion, and we are away, we know not whither.

He swore many an oath, and I adjured him by many a sacred name; till I saw this wonder of power, this ruler of the elements, shiver like an autumn leaf before my words; and as if the spirit spake unwillingly and per force within him, at last, he, with broken voice, revealed the spell whereby he might be obliged, did he wish to play me false, to render up the unlawful spoil. Our warm life-blood must mingle to make and to mar the charm.

Enough of this unholy theme. I was persuaded—the thing was done. The morrow dawned upon me as I lay upon the shingles, and I knew not my own shadow as it fell from me. I felt myself changed to a shape of horror, and cursed my easy faith and blind credulity. The chest was there—there the gold and precious stones for which I had sold the frame of flesh which nature had given me. The sight a little stilled my emotions: three days would soon be gone.

They did pass. The dwarf had supplied me with a plenteous store of food. At first I could hardly walk, so strange and out of joint were all my limbs; and my voice—it was that of the fiend. But I kept silent, and turned my face to the sun, that I might not see my shadow, and counted the hours, and ruminated on my future conduct. To bring Torella to my feet—to possess my Juliet in spite of him—all this my wealth could easily achieve. During dark night I slept, and dreamt of the accomplishment of my desires. Two suns had set—the third dawned. I was agitated, fearful. Oh expectation, what a frightful thing art thou, when kindled more by fear than hope! How dost thou twist thyself round the heart, torturing its pulsations! How dost thou dart unknown pangs all through our feeble mechanism, now seeming to shiver us like broken glass, to nothingness— now giving us a fresh strength, which can *do* nothing, and so torments us by a sensation, such as the strong man must feel who cannot break his fetters, though they bend in his grasp. Slowly paced the bright, bright orb up the eastern sky; long it lingered in the zenith, and still more slowly wandered down the west: it touched the horizon's verge—it was lost! Its glories were on the summits of the cliff—they grew dun and gray. The evening star shone bright. He will soon be here.

He came not!—By the living heavens, he came not!—and night dragged out its weary length, and, in its decaying age, "day began to grizzle its dark hair;"* and the sun rose again on the most miserable wretch that ever upbraided its light. Three days thus I passed. The jewels and the gold—oh, how I abhorred them!

Well, well—I will not blacken these pages with demoniac ravings. All too terrible were the thoughts, the raging tumult of ideas that filled my soul. At the end of that time I slept; I had not before since the third sunset; and I dreamt that I was at Juliet's feet, and she smiled, and then she shrieked—for she saw my transformation—and again she smiled, for still her beautiful lover knelt before her. But it was not I—it was he, the fiend, arrayed in my limbs, speaking with my voice, winning her with my looks of love. I strove to warn her, but my tongue refused its office; I strove to tear him from her, but I was rooted to the ground—I awoke with the agony. There were the solitary hoar precipices—there the plashing sea, the quiet strand, and the blue sky over all. What did it mean? was my dream but a mirror of the truth? was he wooing and winning my

* Byron, *Werner* III. iv. 152-3 (Ed.).

betrothed? I would on the instant back to Genoa—but I was banished. I laughed—the dwarf's yell burst from my lips—*I* banished! O, no! they had not exiled the foul limbs I wore; I might with these enter, without fear of incurring the threatened penalty of death, my own, my native city.

I began to walk towards Genoa. I was somewhat accustomed to my distorted limbs; none were ever so ill adapted for a straight-forward movement; it was with infinite difficulty that I proceeded. Then, too, I desired to avoid all the hamlets strewed here and there on the sea-beach, for I was unwilling to make a display of my hideousness. I was not quite sure that, if seen, the mere boys would not stone me to death as I passed, for a monster: some ungentle salutations I did receive from the few peasants or fishermen I chanced to meet. But it was dark night before I approached Genoa. The weather was so balmy and sweet that it struck me that the Marchese and his daughter would very probably have quitted the city for their country retreat. It was from Villa Torella that I had attempted to carry off Juliet; I had spent many an hour reconnoitring the spot, and knew each inch of ground in its vicinity. It was beautifully situated, embosomed in trees, on the margin of a stream. As I drew near, it became evident that my conjecture was right; nay, moreover, that the hours were being then devoted to feasting and merriment. For the house was lighted up; strains of soft and gay music were wafted towards me by the breeze. My heart sank within me. Such was the generous kindness of Torella's heart that I felt sure that he would not have indulged in public manifestations of rejoicing just after my unfortunate banishment, but for a cause I dared not dwell upon.

The country people were all alive and flocking about; it became necessary that I should study to conceal myself; and yet I longed to address some one, or to hear others discourse, or in any way to gain intelligence of what was really going on. At length, entering the walks that were in immediate vicinity to the mansion, I found one dark enough to veil my excessive frightfulness; and yet others as well as I were loitering in its shade. I soon gathered all I wanted to know—all that first made my very heart die with horror, and then boil with indignation. To-morrow Juliet was to be given to the penitent, reformed, beloved Guido—to-morrow my bride was to pledge her vows to a fiend from hell! And I did this!—my accursed pride—my demoniac violence and wicked self-idolatry had caused this act. For if I had acted as the wretch who had stolen my form had acted—if, with a mien at once yielding and dignified, I had presented myself to Torella, saying, I have done wrong, forgive me; I am unworthy of your angel-child, but permit me to claim her hereafter, when my altered conduct shall manifest that I abjure my vices, and endeavour to become in some sort worthy of her. I go to serve against the infidels; and when my zeal for religion and my true penitence for the past shall appear to you to cancel my crimes, permit me again to call myself your son. Thus had he spoken; and the penitent was welcomed even as the prodigal son of scripture: the fatted calf was killed for him; and he, still pursuing the same path, displayed such open-hearted regret for his follies, so humble a concession of all his rights, and so ardent a resolve to reacquire them by a life of contrition and virtue, that he quickly conquered the kind, old man; and full pardon, and the gift of his lovely child, followed in swift succession.

O! had an angel from Paradise whispered to me to act thus! But now, what would be the innocent Juliet's fate? Would God permit the foul union—or, some prodigy destroying it, link the dishonoured name of Carega with the worst of crimes? To-morrow at dawn they were to be married: there was but one way to prevent this—to meet mine enemy, and to enforce the ratification of our agreement. I felt that this could only be done by a mortal struggle. I had no sword—if indeed my distorted arms could wield a soldier's weapon—but I had a dagger, and in that lay my every hope. There was no time for pondering or balancing nicely the question: I might die in the attempt; but besides the burning jealousy and despair of my own heart, honour, mere humanity, demanded that I should fall rather than not destroy the machinations of the fiend.

The guests departed—the lights began to disappear; it was evident that the inhabitants of the villa were seeking repose. I hid myself among the trees—the garden grew desert—the gates were closed—I wandered round and came under a window—ah! well did I know the same!—a soft twilight glimmered in the room—the curtains were half withdrawn. It was the temple of innocence and beauty. Its magnificence was tempered, as it were, by the slight disarrangements occasioned by its being dwelt in, and all the objects scattered around displayed the taste of her who hallowed it by her presence. I saw her enter with a quick light step—I saw her approach the window—she drew back the curtain yet further, and looked out into the night. Its breezy freshness played among her ringlets, and wafted them from the transparent marble of her brow. She clasped her hands, she raised her eyes to Heaven. I heard her voice. Guido! she softly murmured, Mine own Guido! and then, as if overcome by the fulness of her own heart, she sank on her knees:—her upraised eyes—her negligent but graceful attitude—the beaming thankfulness that lighted up her face —oh, these are tame words! Heart of mine, thou imagest ever, though thou canst not pourtray, the celestial beauty of that child of light and love.

I heard a step—a quick firm step along the shady avenue. Soon I saw a cavalier, richly dressed, young and, methought, graceful to look on, advance.—I hid myself yet closer.—The youth approached; he paused

Painted by Miss Sharpe   *Engraved by J. C. Edwards*

JULIET

beneath the window. She arose, and again looking out she saw him, and said—I cannot, no, at this distant time I cannot record her terms of soft silver tenderness; to me they were spoken, but they were replied to by him.

"I will not go," he cried: "here where you have been, where your memory glides like some Heaven-visiting ghost, I will pass the long hours till we meet, never, my Juliet, again, day or night, to part. But do thou, my love, retire; the cold morn and fitful breeze will make thy cheek pale, and fill with languor thy love-lighted eyes. Ah, sweetest! could I press one kiss upon them, I could, methinks, repose."

And then he approached still nearer, and methought he was about to clamber into her chamber. I had hesitated, not to terrify her; now I was no longer master of myself. I rushed forward—I threw myself on him—I tore him away—I cried, "O loathsome and foul-shaped wretch!"

I need not repeat epithets, all tending, as it appeared, to rail at a person I at present feel some partiality for. A shriek rose from Juliet's lips. I neither heard nor saw—I *felt* only mine enemy, whose throat I grasped, and my dagger's hilt; he struggled, but could not escape: at length hoarsely he breathed these words: "Do!—strike home! destroy this body—you will still live: may your life be long and merry!"

The descending dagger was arrested at the word, and he, feeling my hold relax, extricated himself and drew his sword, while the uproar in the house, and flying of torches from one room to the other, showed that soon we should be separated—and I—oh! far better die: so that he did not survive, I cared not. In the midst of my frenzy there was much calculation:—fall I might, and so that he did not survive, I cared not for the death-blow I might deal against myself. While still, therefore, he thought I paused, and while I saw the villanous resolve to take advantage of my hesitation, in the sudden thrust he made at me, I threw myself on his sword, and at the same moment plunged my dagger, with a true desperate aim, in his side. We fell together, rolling over each other, and the tide of blood that flowed from the gaping wound of each mingled on the grass. More I know not—I fainted.

Again I returned to life: weak almost to death, I found myself stretched upon a bed—Juliet was kneeling beside it. Strange! my first broken request was for a mirror. I was so wan and ghastly, that my poor girl hesitated, as she told me afterwards; but, by the mass! I thought myself a right proper youth when I saw the dear reflection of my own well-known features. I confess it is a weakness, but I avow it, I do entertain a considerable affection for the countenance and limbs I behold, whenever I look at a glass; and have more mirrors in my house, and consult them oftener than any beauty in Venice. Before you too much condemn me, permit me to say that no one better knows than I the value of his own body; no one, probably, except myself, ever having had it stolen from him.

Incoherently I at first talked of the dwarf and his crimes, and reproached Juliet for her too easy admission of his love. She thought me raving, as well she might, and yet it was some time before I could prevail on myself to admit that the Guido whose penitence had won her back for me was myself; and while I cursed bitterly the monstrous dwarf, and blest the well-directed blow that had deprived him of life, I suddenly checked myself when I heard her say—Amen! knowing that him whom she reviled was my very self. A little reflection taught me silence—a little practice enabled me to speak of that frightful night without any very excessive blunder. The wound I had given myself was no mockery of one—it was long before I recovered—and as the benevolent and generous Torella sat beside me, talking such wisdom as might win friends to repentance, and mine own dear Juliet hovered near me, administering to my wants, and cheering me by her smiles, the work of my bodily cure and mental reform went on together. I have never, indeed, wholly recovered my strength—my cheek is paler since—my person a little bent. Juliet sometimes ventures to allude bitterly to the malice that caused this change, but I kiss her on the moment, and tell her all is for the best. I am a fonder and more faithful husband—and true is this—but for that wound, never had I called her mine.

I did not revisit the sea-shore, nor seek for the fiend's treasure; yet, while I ponder on the past, I often think, and my confessor was not backward in favouring the idea, that it might be a good rather than an evil spirit, sent by my guardian angel, to show me the folly and misery of pride. So well at least did I learn this lesson, roughly taught as I was, that I am known now by all my friends and fellow-citizens by the name of Guido il Cortese.

The Swiss Peasant

WHY IS THE MIND of man so apt to be swayed by contraries? why does the imagination for ever paint the impossible in glittering tints, and the hearts of wayward mortals cling, with the greatest tenacity, to what, eel-like, is bent on escaping from their grasp? Why—to bring the matter home—is solitude abhorrent to me, now that I enjoy it in perfection? I have apostrophised the coy nymph in ball-rooms, when the bright lamps of heaven were shamed by brighter earth-stars, and lamented her absence at a pic-nic party, where the nightingale was silenced by the fiddle, and the flowery turf was strewed with the impertinent finery of ugly old women, and the greenwood shade made redolent with the fumes of roasted fowls.

And now, O solitude! I abjure thee, in thy fitting temple—in Switzerland—among cloud-piercing mountains, by the resounding waves of the isle-surrounding lake. I am beside the waters of Uri—where Tell lived—in Brunnen, where the Swiss patriots swore to die for freedom. It rains—magic word to destroy the spell to which these words give rise—the clouds envelop the hills—the white mists veil the ravines—there is a roar and a splash in my ears—and now, and then, the vapours break and scatter themselves, and I see something dark between, which is the hoar side of a dark precipice, but which might as well be the turf stack or old wall that bounded Cumberland's view as he wrote the "Wheel of Fortune."

The sole book that I possess is the Prisoner of Chillon. I have read it through three times within an hour.—Its noble author composed it to beguile weary hours like these when he remained rain-bound for three days in a little inn on the shores of the Lake of Geneva; and cannot I, following with unequal steps, so cheat the minutes in this dim spot? I never, by the by, could invent the commonest incident. As a man of honour, of course I never lie; but, as a nursery child and schoolboy, I never did; simply, as I remember, because I never could concoct one—

but a true tale was lately narrated to me by its very heroine, the incidents of which haunt my memory, adorned as they were, by her animated looks and soft silvery accent. Let me try to record them, stripped though they must be of their greatest charm.

I was, but a week ago, travelling with my friend Ashburn in a coupée, in the district of Subiaco, in the ecclesiastical territory. We were jolted along a rough ravine, through which the river Anio sped, and beetling mountains and shady trees, a distant convent and a picturesque cell on a hill, formed a view which so awoke the pictorial propensities of my friend, that he stopped the coupée (though we were assured that we should never reach our inn by nightfall, and that the road was dangerous in the dark), took out his portfolio, and began to sketch. As he drew I continued to speak in support of an argument we had entered upon before. I had been complaining of the commonplace and ennui of life. Ashburn insisted that our existence was only too full of variety and change—tragic variety and wondrous incredible change.—"Even," said the painter, "as sky, and earth, and water seem for ever the same to the vulgar eye, and yet to the gifted one assume a thousand various guises and hues—now robed in purple—now shrouded in black—now resplendent with living gold—and anon sinking into sober and unobtrusive gray, so do our mortal lives change and vary. No living being among us but could tell a tale of soul-subduing joys and heart-consuming woes, worthy, had they their poet, of the imagination of Shakspeare or Goethe. The veriest weather-worn cabin is a study for colouring, and the meanest peasant will offer all the acts of a drama in the apparently dull routine of his humble life."

"This is pure romance," I replied; "put it to the test. Let us take, for example, yonder woman descending the mountain-path."

"What a figure!" cried Ashburn; "oh that she would stay thus but one quarter of an hour!—she has come down to bathe her child—her upturned face—her dark hair—her picturesque costume—the little plump fellow bestriding her—the rude scenery around——"

"And the romantic tale she has to tell."

"I would wager a louis that hers has been no common fate. She steps a goddess—her attitude—her looks, are all filled with majesty."

I laughed at his enthusiasm, and accepted his bet. We hurried to join our fair peasantess, and thus formed acquaintance with Fanny Chaumont. A sudden storm, as we were engaged conversing with her, came, driven down from the tempest-bearing hills, and she gave us a cordial invitation to her cottage.

It was situated on a sunny slope, yet sheltered from the winds. There was a look of cheerfulness and *aisance* about it, beyond what is usually met in that part of Switzerland, reminding me of the cottages of the inhabitants of the free states. There, also, we found her husband. I always feel curious to know on whom a woman, who bears the stamp of superior intellect; who is beautiful and refined—for peasant as she was, Fanny was both—has been induced to bestow herself.

Louis Chaumont was considerably older than his wife; he was handsome, with brown lively eyes, curly chesnut hair, a visage embrowned by the sun, bearing every mark of having led an active, even an adventurous life; there was, besides, an expression which, if it were not ferocity, resembled it nearly, in his vivacious glances, and in the sternness of his deeply-lined forehead; while she, in spite of her finely-formed brow, her majestic person, and her large expressive eyes, looked softness and patience itself. There was something incongruous in the pair, and more strangely matched they seemed when we heard their story. It lost me my louis, but proved Fanny at once to be a fitting heroine for romance, and was a lesson, moreover, to teach the strange pranks love can play with us, mingling fire and water, blending in one harmonious concord the harsh base, and melodious tenor of two differently stringed instruments. Though their child was five years old, Fanny and her husband were attached to each other with the tenderness and passion of early love; they were happy—his faults were tempered by her angel disposition, and her too melancholy and feeling-fraught spirit was enlivened and made plastic to the purposes of this world by his energy and activity.

Fanny was a Bernese by birth: she was the child of humble cottagers, one among a large family. They lived on the brow of one summit and at the foot of another. The snowy mountains were piled about them; thaw-fed torrents brawled around; during the night a sound like thunder, a crash among the tempest-beaten pines would tell of an avalanche; or the snow-drift, whirring past the lattice, threatened to bury the little fabric. Winter was the season of peace in the deep vales, not so in the higher district. The peasant was often kept waking by the soft-falling snow which threatened insidiously to encroach on, and to overwhelm his habitation; or a straying cow would lead him far into the depths of the stormy hills, and his fearful family would count in agony the hours of his absence. Perpetual hardship and danger, however, rather brutify than exalt the soul of man; and those of the Swiss who are most deeply planted among the rocky wilds are often stultified and sullen.

Fanny opened her youthful eyes and observation on this scene. She was one of those lovely children only to be seen in Switzerland, whose beauty is heartfelt but indescribable: hers was the smooth candid brow, the large hazel eyes, half soft, half wild; the round dimpled cheek, the full sensitive mouth, the pointed chin, and (as framework to the picture) the luxuriant curly chesnut hair, and voice which is sweetest music. The exceeding beauty of little Fanny gained her the observation of the wife of

Painted by Henry Howard   Engraved by Charles Heath

THE SWISS PEASANT

the governor of the chateau which overlooked and commanded the district, and at ten years of age she became a frequent visitor there. Fanny's little soul was love, so she soon twined herself round the kind lady's heart, became a pet with the governor, and the favourite playmate of their only son.

One fête day Fanny had dined at the chateau. It had been fine warm spring weather, but wind and storm came on with the setting sun; the snow began to fall thickly, and it was decided that Fanny must pass the night in the chateau. She had been unusually eager to return home; and when the tempest came on, she crept near her protectress, and begged to be sent to her mother. *C'est impossible*—Fanny pressed no further, but she clambered to a window, and looked out wistfully to where, hidden by the hills, her parents' cottage stood. It was a fatal night for her: the thunders of frequent avalanches, the roaring of torrents, the crash of trees, spoke of devastation, and her home was its chief prey. Father, mother, brothers, and sisters, not one survived. Where, the day before, cottage and outhouse and flower-adorned garden had stood, the little lawn where she played, and the grove that sheltered her, there was now a monumental pile of snow, and the rocky path of a torrent; no trace remained, not one survivor to tell the tale. From that night Fanny became a constant inmate of the chateau.

It was Madame de Marville's project to give her a bourgeois education, which would raise her from the hardships of a peasant's life, and yet not elevate her above her natural position in society. She was brought up kindly, but humbly; it was the virtues of her disposition which raised her in the eyes of all around her, not any ill-judged favour of her benefactress. The night of the destruction of her family never passed away from her memory; it set a seal of untimely seriousness on her childish brow, awoke deep thoughts in her infant heart, and a strong resolve that while she lived, her beloved friends should find her, as far as her humble powers admitted, a source of good alone—a reason to rejoice that they had saved her from the destruction that had overwhelmed her family.

Thus Fanny grew up in beauty and in virtue. Her smiles were as the rainbows of her native torrents: her voice, her caresses, her light step, her unalterable sweetness and ceaseless devotion to the wishes of others, made her the idol of the family. Henry, the only child of her protectors, was of her own age, or but a few months her senior. Every time Henry returned from school to visit his parents, he found Fanny more beautiful, more kind, more attractive than before; and the first passion his youthful heart knew was for the lovely peasant girl, whose virtues sanctified his home. A look, a gesture betrayed his secret to his mother; she turned a hasty glance on Fanny, and saw on her countenance innocence and confidence alone. Half reassured, yet still fearful, Madame de Marville began to reflect on some cure for the threatened evil. She could not bear to send away Fanny; she was solicitous that her son should for the present reside in his home. The lovely girl was perfectly unconscious of the sentiments of the young seigneur; but would she always continue so? and was the burning heart that warmed her gentle bosom to be for ever insensible to the despotic and absorbing emotions of love?

It was with wonder, and a curious mixture of disappointed maternal pride and real gladness, that the lady, at length, discovered a passion dawning in fair Fanny's heart for Louis Chaumont, a peasant some ten years older than herself. It was natural that one with such high wrought feelings as our heroine should love one to whom she could look up, and on whom to depend, rather than her childhood's playmate—the gay thoughtless Henry. Louis's family had been the victim of a moral ruin, as hers of a physical one. They had been oppressed, reduced to poverty, driven from their homes by some feudal tyrant, and had come poor and forlorn from a distant district. His mother, accustomed to a bourgeois' life, died broken-hearted: his father, a man of violent passions, nourished in his own and in his son's heart, sentiments of hatred and revenge against the "proud oppressors of the land." They were obliged to labour hard, yet in the intervals of work, father and son would read or discourse concerning the ills attendant on humanity, and they traced all to the social system, which made the few, the tyrants of the many.

Louis was handsome, bold, and active; he excelled his compeers in every hardy exercise; his resolution, his eloquence, his daring, made him, in spite of his poverty, a kind of leader among them. He had many faults: he was too full of passion, of the spirit of resistance and revenge; but his heart was kind; his understanding, when not thwarted, strong; and the very depth of his feelings made him keenly susceptible to love. Fanny, in her simple but majestic beauty, in her soft kindness of manner, mingled with the profoundest sensibility, made a deep impression on the young man's heart. His converse, so different and so superior to those of his fellows, won her attention.

Hitherto Fanny had never given utterance to the secrets of her soul. Habitual respect held her silent with Madame, and Henry, as spirited and as heedless as a chamois, could ill understand her; but Louis became the depositary of the many feelings which, piled up in secresy and silence, were half awful to herself; he brought reason, or what he deemed such, to direct her heart-born conclusions. To have heard them talk of life and death, and all its shows, you would have wondered by what freak, philosophy had dressed herself in youth and a peasant's garb, and wandered from the schools to these untaught wilds.

Madame de Marville saw and encouraged this attachment. Louis was not exactly the person she would have selected for Fanny; but he was the only being for whom she had ever evinced a predilection; and, besides, the danger of a misalliance which threatened her own son, rendered her eager to build an insurmountable wall between him and the object of his affections. Thus Fanny enjoyed the heart-gladdening pride of hearing her choice applauded and praised by the person she most respected and loved in the world. As yet, however, love had been covert; the soul but not the apparent body of their intercourse. Louis was kept in awe by this high-minded girl, and Fanny had not yet learned her own secret. It was Henry who made the discovery for them;—Henry, who, with all the impetuosity of his vivacious character, contrived a thousand ways to come between them; who, stung by jealousy to injustice, reviled Louis for his ruin, his poverty, his opinions, and brought the spirit of dissension to disquiet a mind entirely bent, as she imagined, on holy and pure thoughts.

Under this clash of passion, the action of the drama rapidly developed itself, and, for nearly a year, a variety of scenes were acted among these secluded mountains of no interest save to the parties themselves, but to them fateful and engrossing. Louis and Fanny exchanged vows; but that sufficed not. Fanny insisted on the right of treating with uniform kindness the son of her best friend, in spite of his injustice and insolence. The young men were often, during the rural festivals, brought into angry collision. Fanny was the peace-maker: but a woman is the worst possible mediator between her rival lovers. Henry was sometimes irritated to complain to his father of Louis's presumption. The spirit of the French revolution then awakening, rendered a peasant's assumptions peculiarly grating; and it required Madame de Marville's impartial gentleness to prevent Fanny's betrothed, as now he was almost considered, from being farther oppressed.

At length it was decided that Henry should absent himself for a time, and visit Paris. He was enraged in the extreme by what he called his banishment. Noble and generous as he naturally was, love was the tyrant of his soul, and drove him almost to crime. He entered into a fierce quarrel with his rival on the very eve of his departure: it ended in a scene of violence and bloodshed. No great real harm was done; but Monsieur de Marville, hitherto scarcely kept back from such a measure by his wife, suddenly obtained an order for Louis (his father had died a year before) to quit the territory within twelve hours. Fanny was commanded, as she valued the favour of her friends, to give him up. The young men were both gone before any intercession could avail; and that kind of peace which resembles desolation took possession of the chateau.

Aware of the part she had taken in encouraging Fanny's attachment to her peasant-lover, Madame de Marville did not make herself a party to the tyranny of her husband; she requested only of her protégée to defer any decisive step, and not to quit her guardianship until the return of her son, which was to take place the following year. Fanny consented to such a delay, although in doing so, she had to resist the angry representations of her lover, who exacted that she should quit the roof of his oppressors. It was galling to his proud spirit that she should continue to receive benefits from them, and injurious to his love that she should remain where his rival's name was the constant theme of discourse and the object of interest. Fanny in vain represented her debt of gratitude, the absence of Henry, the impossibility that she could feel any undue sentiment towards the young seigneur; not to hate him was a crime in Louis's eyes; yet how, in spite of his ill conduct, could Fanny hate her childhood's playmate—her brother? His violent passions excited to their utmost height—jealousy and the sense of impotent indignation raging in his heart —Louis swore to revenge himself on the Marvilles—to forget and to abhor his mistress!—his last words were a malediction on them, and a violent denunciation of scorn upon her.

"It will all be well yet," thought Fanny, as she strove to calm the tumultuous and painful emotions to which his intemperate passion gave rise. "Not only are storms the birth of the wild elements, but of the heart of man, and we can oppose patience and fortitude alone to their destructive violence. A year will pass—I shall quit the chateau; Louis will acknowledge my truth, and retract his frightful words."

She continued, therefore, to fulfil her duties cheerfully, not permitting her thoughts to dwell on the idea, that, in spite of her struggles, too painfully occupied her—the probability that Louis would in the end renounce or forget her; but committing her cause to the spirit of good, she trusted that its influence would in the end prevail.

She had, however, much to endure; four months passed, and no tidings reached her of Louis. Often she felt sick at heart; often she became the prey of the darkest despair; above all, her tender heart missed the fond attentions of love, the bliss of knowing that she bestowed happiness, and the unrestrained intercourse to which mutual affection had given rise. She cherished hope as a duty, and faith in love, rather than in her unjust and cruelly neglectful lover. It was a hard task, for she had nowhere to turn for consolation or encouragement. Madame de Marville marked with gladness the total separation between them. Now that the danger that threatened her son was averted, she repented having been influential in producing an attachment between Fanny and one whom she deemed unworthy of her. She redoubled her kindness, and, in the true continental fashion, tried to get up a match between her and some one among her many and more prosperous admirers. She failed, but did not despair, till she saw the poor girl's cheek grow pale and her vivacity desert her, as month after month passed away, and the very name of Louis appeared to be forgotten by all except herself.

The stirring and terrible events that took place at this time in France added to Fanny's distress of mind. She had been familiarized to the discussion of the theories, now attempted to be put in practice, by the conversations of Chaumont. As each fresh account brought information of the guilty and sanguinary acts of men whose opinions were the same as those of her lover, her fears on his account increased. In a few words I shall hurry over this part of her story. Switzerland became agitated by the same commotions as tore the near kingdom. The peasantry rose in tumult; acts of violence and blood were committed; at first at a distance from her retired valley, but gradually approaching its precincts, until at last the tree of liberty was set up in the neighbouring village. Monsieur de Marville was an aristocrat of the most bigoted species. In vain was the danger represented to him, and the unwarlike state of his retinue. He armed them—he hurried down—he came unawares on the crowd who were proclaiming the triumph of liberty, rather by feasting than force. On the first attack, they were dispersed, and one or two among them were wounded; the pole they had gathered round was uprooted, the emblematic cap trampled to the earth. The governor returned victorious to his chateau.

This act of violence on his part seemed the match to fire a train of organized resistance to his authority, of which none had dreamt before. Strangers from other cantons thronged into the valley; rustic labours were cast aside; popular assemblies were held, and the peasants exercised in the use of arms. One was coming to place himself at their head, it was said, who had been a party in the tumults at Geneva. Louis Chaumont was coming—the champion of liberty, the sworn enemy of M. de Marville. The influence of his presence soon became manifest. The inhabitants of the chateau were, as it were, besieged. If one ventured beyond a certain limit he was assailed by stones and knives. It was the resolve of Louis that all within its walls should surrender themselves to his mercy. What that might be, the proud curl of his lip and the fire that glanced from his dark eyes rendered scarcely problematic. Fanny would not believe the worst of her lover, but Monsieur and Madame de Marville, no longer restrained by any delicacy, spoke of the leveller in unmeasured terms of abhorrence, comparing him to the monsters who then reigned in France, while the danger they incurred through him added a bitter sting to their words. The peril grew each day; famine began to make its appearance in the chateau; while the intelligence which some of the more friendly peasants brought was indicative of preparations for a regular attack of the most formidable nature. A summons at last came from the insurgents. They were resolved to destroy the emblem of their slavery—the feudal halls of their tyrants. They declared their intention of firing the chateau the next day, and called on all within to deliver themselves up, if they would not be buried in its ruins. They offered their lives and free leave to depart to all, save the governor himself, who must place himself unconditionally at the mercy of their leader—"The wretch," exclaimed his lady, "who thirsts for your blood! Fly! if there is yet time for flight; we, you see, are safe. Fly! nor suffer these cruel dastards to boast of having murdered you."

M. de Marville yielded to these entreaties and representations. He had sent for a military force to aid him—it had been denied; he saw that he himself, as the detested person, was the cause of danger to his family. It was therefore agreed that he should seek a chalet situated on a mountain ten leagues distant, where he might lie concealed till his family joined him. Accordingly, in a base disguise, he quitted at midnight the walls he was unable to defend; a miserable night for the unfortunate beings left behind. The coming day was to witness the destruction of their home; and they, beggars in the world, were to wander through the inhospitable mountains, till, with caution and terror, they could unobserved reach the remote and miserable chalet, and learn the fate of the unhappy fugitive. It was a sleepless night for all. To add to Madame's agony, she knew that her son's life was in danger in Paris—that he had been denounced—and though yet untaken, his escape was still uncertain. From the turret of the castle, that, situated high on a rock, commanded the valley below, she sat the livelong night watching for every sound—fearful of some shout, some report of fire-arms, which would announce the capture of her husband. It was September; the nights were chill; pale and trembling, she saw day break over the hills. Fanny had busied herself during these anxious hours by preparing for their departure; the terrified domestics had already fled; she, the lady, and the old lame gardener were all that remained. At dawn she brought forth the mule, and harnessed him to the rude vehicle which was to convey them to their place of refuge. Whatever was most valuable in the chateau had already been sent away long before, or was secreted; a few necessaries alone she provided. And now she ascended the turret stairs, and stood before her protectress, announcing that all was ready, and that they must depart. At this last moment, Madame de Marville appeared deprived of strength; she strove to rise—she sank to the ground in a fit. Forgetful of her deserted state, Fanny called aloud for help, and then her heart beat wildly, as a quick, youthful step was heard on the stairs. Who could he be? would *he* come to insult their wretchedness—he, the author of their wo? The first glance changed the object of her terror. Henry flew to his mother's side, and, with broken exclamations and agitated questions, demanded an explanation of what he saw. He had fled for safety to the habitation of his parents—he found it deserted; the first voice he heard was that of Fanny crying for help—the first sight that presented itself was his mother, to all appearance dead, lying on the floor of the turret. Her recovery was followed by brief explanations, and a consultation of how his safety was to be provided for. The name of Chaumont excited his bitterest execrations. With a soldier's haughty resolve, he was darting from the castle, to meet and to wreak vengeance on his rival. His mother threw herself at his feet, clasping his knees, calling wildly on him not to desert her. Fanny's gentle, sweet voice was of more avail to calm his passion. "Chevalier," she said, "it is not thus that you must display your courage or protect the helpless. To encounter yonder infuriated mob would be to run on certain death; you must preserve yourself for your family—you must have pity on your mother, who cannot survive you. Be guided by me, I beseech you."

Henry yielded to her voice, and a more reasonable arrangement took place. The departure of Madame de Marville and Fanny was expected at the village, and a pledge had been given that they should proceed unmolested. But deeply had the insurgents sworn, that if the governor or his son (whose arrival in the chateau had been suspected) attempted to escape with them, they should be immediately sacrificed to *justice*. No disguise would suffice—the active observation of their enemies was known. Every inhabitant of the castle had been numbered—the fate of each ascertained, save that of the two most detested—the governor, whose flight had not been discovered, and his son, whose arrival was so unexpected and ill-timed. As still they consulted, a beat to arms was heard in the valley below: it was the signal that the attack on the empty castle walls would soon begin. There was no time for delay or hesitation; Henry placed himself at the bottom of the charrette; straw and a variety of articles were heaped upon him; the two women ascended in trepidation; and the old gardener sat in front and held the reins.

In consequence of the disturbed state of the districts through which they were to pass,—where the appearance of one of the upper classes excited the fiercest enmity, and frightful insult, if not death, was their sure welcome,—Madame and her friend assumed a peasant's garb. And thus they wound their way down the steep; the unhappy lady weeping bitterly —Fanny, with tearless eyes, but with pale cheek and compressed lips, gazing for the last time on the abode which had been her refuge when, in helpless infancy, she was left an orphan—where kindness and benevolence had waited on her, and where her days had passed in innocence and peace. "And he drives us away!—him, whom I loved—whom I love!—O misery!"

They reached the foot of the eminence on which the chateau was placed, and proceeded along the road which led directly through the village. With the approach of danger, vain regrets were exchanged for a lively sense of fear in the bosom of the hapless mother, and for the exertion of her courage and forethought in Fanny's more energetic mind.

They passed a peasant or two, who uttered a malediction or imprecation on them as they went; then groups of two or three, who were even more violent in gesture and menace; when suddenly the sound of many steps came on their ears, and, at a turn of the road, they met Chaumont with a band of about twenty disciplined men.

"Fear not," he said to Madame de Marville; "I will protect you from danger till you are beyond the village."

With a shriek, the lady, in answer, threw herself in Fanny's arms, crying, "He is here!—save me!—he will murder us."

"Fear not, Madame—he dares not injure you. Begone, Louis! insult us not by your presence. Begone! I say."

Fanny spoke angrily. She had not adopted this tone, but that the lady's terror, and the knowledge that even then the young soldier crouched at their feet, burnt to spring up and confront his enemy, made her use an authority which a woman always imagines that a lover dare not resist.

"I do not insult you," repeated Chaumont—"I save you. I have no quarrel with the lady; tyrants alone need fear me. You are not safe without my escort. Do not you, false girl, irritate me. I have ensured her escape; but yours—you are in my power."

A violent movement at the bottom of the charrette called forth all Fanny's terrors.

"Take me!" she cried; "do with me what you please; but you dare not, you cannot raise a finger against the innocent. Begone, I say! let me never see you more!"

"You are obeyed. On you fall the consequences."

Thus, after many months of separation, did Fanny and her lover meet. She had purposed when she should see him to make an appeal to his better nature—his reason; she had meant to use her all-persuasive voice to recall him from the dangerous path he was treading. Several times, indeed, since his arrival in the valley, she had endeavoured to obtain an interview with him, but he dreaded her influence: he had resolved on revenge, and he feared to be turned back. But now the unexpected presence of his rival robbed her of her self-possession, and forced her to change her plans. She saw frightful danger in their meeting, and all her endeavours were directed to the getting rid of her lover.

Louis and his companions proceeded towards the chateau, while the charrette of the fugitives moved on in the opposite direction. They met many a ferocious group, who were rushing forward to aid in the destruction of their home; and glad they were, in that awful hour, that any object had power to divert the minds of their enemies from attention to themselves. The road they pursued wound through the valley; the precipitous mountain on one side, a brawling stream on the other. Now they ascended higher and now again descended in their route, while the road, broken by the fall of rocks, intersected by torrents, which tore their way athwart it, made their progress slow. To get beyond the village was the aim of their desires; when, lo! just as they came upon it, and were in the very midst of its population, which was pouring towards the castle, suddenly the charrette sank in a deep rut; it half upset, and every spoke in the wheel giving way rendered the vehicle wholly useless.

"Mais, descendez donc, mesdames," said a peasant; "il faut bien marcher."

Fanny had indeed already sprung to the ground to examine what hope remained: there was none. "Grand Dieu! nous sommes perdues!" were the first words that escaped her, while her friend stood aghast, trembling, almost insensible, knowing that the hope of her life, the existence of her son, depended on these miserable moments.

A peasant who owed Fanny some kindness now advanced, and in a kind of cavalier way, as if to blemish as much as he could the matter of his offer by its manner, told them, that, for the pleasure of getting rid of the aristocrats, he would lend his car—there it was, let them quickly bestow their lading in it and pursue their way. As he spoke, he caught up a box, and began the transfer from one car to the other.

"No, no!" cried Madame de Marville, as, with a scream, she sprang forward and grasped the arm of the man as he was in the very act of discovering her son's hiding-place. "We will accept nothing from our base enemies!—Begone with your offers! we will die here, rather than accept any thing from such *canaille*."

The word was electric. The fierce passions of the mob, excited by the mischief they were about to perpetrate, now burst like a stream into this new channel. With violent execrations they rushed upon the unfortunate woman: they would have torn her from the car, but already her son had sprung from his hiding-place, and striking a violent blow at the foremost assailant, checked for a moment their brutal outrages. Then again, with a yell, such as the savage Indians alone could emulate, they rushed on their prey. Mother and son were torn asunder, and cries of "A bas les aristocrats!"—"A la lanterne!" declared too truly their sanguinary designs.

At this moment, Louis appeared—Louis, whose fears for Fanny had overcome his indignation, and who returned to guard her; while she, perceiving him, with a burst of joy, called on him to rescue her friends. His cry of "Arretez-vous!" was loud and distinct amidst the uproar. It was obeyed; and then first he beheld his rival, his oppressor, his enemy in his power. At first, rage inflamed every feature, to be replaced by an expression of triumph and implacable hatred. Fanny caught the fierce glance of his eye, and grew pale. She trembled as, trying to be calm, she said, "Yes, you behold he is here.—And you must save him—and your own soul. Rescue him from death, and be blest that your evil career enables you at least to perform this one good action."

For a moment Louis seemed seeking for a word, as a man, meaning to stab, may fumble for his dagger's hilt, unable in his agitation to grasp his weapon.

"My friends," at length he said, "let the women depart—we have promised it. Ye may deal with the young aristocrat according to his merits."

"A la lanterne!" burst in response from a hundred voices.

"Let his mother first depart!"

Could it be Louis that spoke these words, and had she loved this man? To appeal to him was to rouse a tiger from his lair. Another thought darted into Fanny's mind; she scarcely knew what she said or did: but already knives were drawn; already, with a thrill of horror, she thought she saw the blood of her childhood's playmate spilt like water on the earth. She rushed forward—she caught the upraised arm of one—"He is no aristocrat!" she cried; "he is my husband!—Will you murder one who, forgetting his birth, his duty, his honour, has married a peasant girl—one of yourselves?"

Even this appeal had little effect upon the mob; but it strangely affected her cruel lover. Grasping her arm with iron fingers, he cried, "Is this tale true? Art thou married to that man—his wife?"

"Even so!"—the words died on her lips as she strove to form them, terrified by their purport, and the effect they might produce. An inexplicable expression passed over Chaumont's face; the fierceness that jealousy had engendered for a moment was exalted almost to madness, and then faded wholly away. The stony heart within him softened at once. A tide of warm, human, and overpowering emotion flowed into his soul: he looked on her he had loved even to guilt and crime, on her whom he had lost for ever; and tears rushed into his eyes, as he saw her gasping, trembling before him—at his mercy.

"Fear not," at last he said; "fear neither for him nor yourself.—Poor girl! so young, you shall not lose all—so young, you shall not become a widow.—He shall be saved!"

Yet it was no easy task, even for him, to stem the awakened passions of the blood-thirsty mob. He had spent many an hour in exciting them against their seigneurs, and now at once to control the violence to which he had given rise seemed impossible. Yet his energy, his strong will overcame all opposition. They should pierce the chevalier's heart, he swore, through his alone. He prevailed—the fugitives were again seated in their car. He took the rein of their mule, and saying to his comrades "Attendez-moi," he led them out of the village. All were silent; Fanny knew not what to say, and surprise held the others mute. Louis went with them until a turn in the road hid them from the view of the village. What his thoughts were, none could guess: he looked calm, as resigning the rein into the chevalier's hands, he gently wished them "Bon voyage," touching his hat in reply to their salutations. They moved on, and Fanny looked back to catch a last view of her lover: he was standing where they left him, when suddenly, instead of returning on his steps into the village, she saw him with rapid strides ascend the mountain side, taking a well-known path that conducted him away from the scene of his late exploits. His pace was that of a man flying from pursuers—soon he was lost to sight.

Astonishment still kept the fugitives silent, as they pursued their way; and when at last joy broke forth, and Madame de Marville, rejoicing in their escape, embraced again and again her son, he with the softest tenderness thanked Fanny for his life: she answered not, but withdrawing to the furthest part of the charrette, wept bitterly.

Late that night, they reached the destined chalet, and found Monsieur de Marville arrived. It was a half-ruined miserable habitation perched among the snows, cold and bare; food was ill to be obtained, and danger breathed around them. Fanny attended on them with assiduous care, but she never spoke of the scene in the village; and though she strove to look the same, Henry never addressed her but her cheeks grew white, and her voice trembled. She could not divine her distant lover's thoughts, but she knew that he believed her married to another; and that other, earnestly though she strove to rule her feelings, became an object of abhorrence to her.

Three weeks they passed in this wretched abode; three weeks replete with alarm, for the district around was in arms, and the life of Monsieur de Marville loudly threatened. They never slept but they dreaded the approach of the murderers; food they had little, and the inclement season visited them roughly. Fanny seemed to feel no inconvenience; her voice was cheerful: to console, encourage, and assist her friends appeared to occupy her whole heart. At length one night they were roused by a violent knocking at the door of their hut: Monsieur de Marville and Henry were on their feet in a moment, seizing their weapons as they rose. It was a domestic of their own, come to communicate the intelligence that the troubles were over, that the legal government had reasserted its authority, and invited the governor to return to Berne.

They descended from their mountain refuge, and the name of Louis hovered on Fanny's lips, but she spoke it not. He seemed everywhere forgotten. It was not until some time afterwards that she ascertained the fact, that he had never been seen or heard of, since he had parted from her on the morning of their escape. The villagers had waited for him in vain; they suspended their designs, for they all depended upon him; but he came not.

Monsieur and Madame de Marville returned to their chateau with their son, but Fanny remained behind. She would not inhabit the same roof as Henry; she recoiled even from receiving further benefits from his parents. What could she do? Louis would doubtless discover the falsehood of her marriage, but he dared not return; and even if he communicated with her, even though yet she loved him, could she unite herself with one accused too truly of the most frightful crimes? At first, these doubts agitated her, but by degrees they faded as oblivion closed over Chaumont's name—and he came not and she heard not of him, and he was as dead to her. Then the memory of the past revived in her heart; her love awoke with her despair; his mysterious flight became the sole occupation of her thoughts: time rolled on and brought its changes. Madame de Marville died— Henry was united to another—Fanny remained, to her own thoughts, alone in the world. A relation, who lived at Subiaco, sent for her, and there she went to take up her abode. In vain she strove to wean herself from the memory of Louis—her love for him haunted her soul.

There was war in Europe, and every man was converted into a soldier; the country was thinned of its inhabitants, and each victory or defeat brought a new conscription. At length peace came again, and its return was celebrated with rejoicing. Many a soldier returned to his home—and one came back who had no home. A man, evidently suffering from recent wounds, way-worn, and sick, asked for hospitality at Fanny's cottage; it was readily afforded, and he sat at her cottage fire, and removed his cap from his brows. His person was bent—his cheeks fallen in—yet those eyes of fire, that quick animated look, which almost brought the bright expression of youth back into his face, could never be forgotten. Fanny gazed almost in alarm, and then in joy, and at last, in her own sweet voice, she said, "Et toi, Louis—tu aussi es de retour."

Louis had endured many a sorrow and many a hardship, and, most of all, he had been called on to wage battle with his own fierce spirit. The rage and hate which he had sedulously nourished suddenly became his tormentors and his tyrants—at the moment that love, before too closely allied to them, emancipated itself from their control. Love, which is the source of all that is most generous and noble in our nature, of self-devotion and of high intent, separated from the alloy he had blended with it, asserted its undivided power over him—strange that it should be so, at the moment that he believed that he had lost her he loved for ever!

All his plans had been built for revenge. He would destroy the family that oppressed him—unbuild, stone by stone, the proud abode of their inheritance—he would be the sole refuge and support of his mistress in exile and in poverty. He had entered upon his criminal career with this design alone, and with the anticipation of ending all by heaping benefits and the gifts of fortune upon Fanny. The very steps he had taken, he now believed to be those that occasioned his defeat. He had lost her—the lovely and the good—he had lost her by proving unworthy—yet not so unworthy was he as to make her the victim of his crimes. The family he had vowed to ruin was now hers, and every injury that befel them visited her; to save her he must unweave his pernicious webs—to keep her scatheless, his dearest designs must fall to the ground.

A veil seemed rent before his eyes—he had fled, for he would not assist in the destruction of her fortunes—he had not returned, for it was torture to him to know that she lived, the wife of another. He entered the French army—but in every change his altered feelings pursued him, and to prove himself worthy of her he had lost, was the constant aim of his ambition. His excellent conduct led to his promotion, and yet mishap still waited on him. He was wounded, even dangerously, and became so incapable of service as to be forced to solicit his dismission. This had occurred at the end of a hard campaign in Germany, and his intention was to pass into Italy, where a friend, with whom he had formed an intimacy in the army, promised to procure him some employment under government. He passed through Subiaco in his way, and, ignorant of its occupiers, had asked for hospitality in his mistress's cottage.

If guilt can be expiated by repentance and reform, as is the best lesson of religion, Louis had expiated his. If constancy in love deserve reward, these lovers deserved that, which they reaped, in the happiness consequent on their union. Her image, side by side with all that is good in our nature, had dwelt in his heart; which thus became a shrine at which he sacrificed every evil passion. It was a greater bliss than he had ever dared to anticipate, to find, that in so doing, he had at the same time been conducing to the welfare of her he loved, and that the lost and idolized being whom he worshipped founded the happiness of her life upon his return to virtue, and the constancy of his affection.

XII

❦

The Dream

Chi dice mal d'amore
Dice una falsità!—ITALIAN SONG

THE TIME of the occurrence of the little legend about to be narrated, was that of the commencement of the reign of Henry IV. of France, whose accession and conversion, while they brought peace to the kingdom whose throne he ascended, were inadequate to heal the deep wounds mutually inflicted by the inimical parties. Private feuds, and the memory of mortal injuries, existed between those now apparently united; and often did the hands that had clasped each other in seeming friendly greeting, involuntarily, as the grasp was released, clasp the dagger's hilt, as fitter spokesman to their passions than the words of courtesy that had just fallen from their lips. Many of the fiercer Catholics retreated to their distant provinces; and while they concealed in solitude their rankling discontent, not less keenly did they long for the day when they might show it openly.

In a large and fortified chateau built on a rugged steep overlooking the Loire, not far from the town of Nantes, dwelt the last of her race and the heiress of their fortunes, the young and beautiful Countess de Villeneuve. She had spent the preceding year in complete solitude in her secluded abode; and the mourning she wore for a father and two brothers, the victims of the civil wars, was a graceful and good reason why she did not appear at court, and mingle with its festivities. But the orphan countess inherited a high name and broad lands; and it was soon signified to her that the king, her guardian, desired that she should bestow them, together with her hand, upon some noble whose birth and accomplishments should entitle him to the gift. Constance, in reply, expressed her intention of taking vows, and retiring to a convent. The king earnestly and resolutely forbade this act, believing such an idea to be the result of sensibility overwrought by sorrow, and relying on the hope that, after a time, the genial spirit of youth would break through this cloud.

153

Painted by Miss Louisa Sharpe   *Engraved by Charles Heath*

CONSTANCE

A year passed, and still the countess persisted; and at last Henry, unwilling to exercise compulsion—desirous, too, of judging for himself of the motives that led one so beautiful, young, and gifted with fortune's favours, to desire to bury herself in a cloister—announced his intention, now that the period of her mourning was expired, of visiting her chateau; and if he brought not with him, the monarch said, inducement sufficient to change her design, he would yield his consent to its fulfillment.

Many a sad hour had Constance passed—many a day of tears, and many a night of restless misery. She had closed her gates against every visitant; and, like the Lady Olivia in "Twelfth Night," vowed herself to loneliness and weeping. Mistress of herself, she easily silenced the entreaties and remonstrances of underlings, and nursed her grief as it had been the thing she loved. Yet it was too keen, too bitter, too burning, to be a favoured guest. In fact, Constance, young, ardent, and vivacious, battled with it, struggled, and longed to cast it off; but all that was joyful in itself, or fair in outward show, only served to renew it; and she could best support the burthen of her sorrow with patience, when, yielding to it, it oppressed but did not torture her.

Constance had left the castle to wander in the neighbouring grounds. Lofty and extensive as were the apartments of her abode, she felt pent up within their walls, beneath their fretted roofs. The clear sky, the spreading uplands, the antique wood, associated to her with every dear recollection of her past life, enticed her to spend hours and days beneath their leafy coverts. The motion and change eternally working, as the wind stirred among the boughs, or the journeying sun rained its beams through them, soothed and called her out of that dull sorrow which clutched her heart with so unrelenting a pang beneath her castle roof.

There was one spot on the verge of the well-wooded park, one nook of ground, whence she could discern the country extended beyond, yet which was in itself thick set with tall umbrageous trees—a spot which she had forsworn, yet whither unconsciously her steps for ever tended, and where now again, for the twentieth time that day, she had unaware found herself. She sat upon a grassy mound, and looked wistfully on the flowers she had herself planted to adorn the verdurous recess—to her the temple of memory and love. She held the letter from the king which was the parent to her of so much despair. Dejection sat upon her features, and her gentle heart asked fate why, so young, unprotected, and forsaken, she should have to struggle with this new form of wretchedness.

"I but ask," she thought, "to live in my father's halls—in the spot familiar to my infancy—to water with my frequent tears the graves of those I loved; and here in these woods, where such a mad dream of happiness was mine, to celebrate for ever the obsequies of Hope!"

A rustling among the boughs now met her ear—her heart beat quick—

all again was still. "Foolish girl!" she half muttered: "dupe of thine own passionate fancy: because here we met; because seated here I have expected, and sounds like these have announced, his dear approach; so now every coney as it stirs, and every bird as it awakens silence, speaks of him. O Gaspar!—mine once—never again will this beloved spot be made glad by thee—never more!"

Again the bushes were stirred, and footsteps were heard in the brake. She rose; her heart beat high: it must be that silly Manon, with her impertinent entreaties for her to return. But the steps were firmer and slower than would be those of her waiting-woman; and now emerging from the shade, she too plainly discerned the intruder. Her first impulse was to fly:—but once again to see him—to hear his voice:—once again before she placed eternal vows between them, to stand together, and find the wide chasm filled which absence had made, could not injure the dead, and would soften the fatal sorrow that made her cheek so pale.

And now he was before her the same beloved one with whom she had exchanged vows of constancy. He, like her, seemed sad, nor could she resist the imploring glance that entreated her for one moment to remain.

"I come, lady," said the young knight, "without a hope to bend your inflexible will. I come but once again to see you, and to bid you farewell before I depart for the Holy Land. I come to beseech you not to immure yourself in the dark cloister to avoid one as hateful as myself:—one you will never see more. Whether I die or live in Palestine, France and I are parted for ever!"

"Palestine!" said Constance; "that were fearful, were it true; but King Henry will never so lose his favourite cavalier. The throne you helped to build, you still will guard. Nay, as I ever had power over thought of thine, go not to Palestine."

"One word of yours could detain me—one smile—Constance——" and the youthful lover knelt before her; but her harsher purpose was recalled by the image once so dear and familiar, now so strange and so forbidden.

"Linger no longer here!" she cried. "No smile, no word of mine will ever again be yours. Why are you here—here, where the spirits of the dead wander, and, claiming these shades as their own, curse the false girl who permits their murderer to disturb their sacred repose?"

"When love was young and you were kind," replied the knight, "you taught me to thread the intricacies of these woods—you welcomed me to this dear spot, where once you vowed to be my own—even beneath these ancient trees."

"A wicked sin it was," said Constance, "to unbar my father's doors to the son of his enemy, and dearly is it punished!"

The young knight gained courage as she spoke; yet he dared not move, lest she, who, every instant, appeared ready to take flight, should be startled from her momentary tranquillity; but he slowly replied:—"Those were happy days, Constance, full of terror and deep joy, when evening brought me to your feet; and while hate and vengeance were as its atmosphere to yonder frowning castle, this leafy, star-lit bower was the shrine of love."

"*Happy?*—miserable days!" echoed Constance; "when I imagined good could arise from failing in my duty, and that disobedience would be rewarded of God. Speak not of love, Gaspar!—a sea of blood divides us for ever! Approach me not! The dead and the beloved stand even now between us: their pale shadows warn me of my fault, and menace me for listening to their murderer."

"That am not I!" exclaimed the youth. "Behold, Constance, we are each the last of our race. Death has dealt cruelly with us, and we are alone. It was not so when first we loved—when parent, kinsman, brother, nay, my own mother breathed curses on the house of Villeneuve; and in spite of all I bless'd it. I saw thee, my lovely one, and bless'd it. The God of peace planted love in our hearts, and with mystery and secrecy we met during many a summer night in the moon-lit dells; and when daylight was abroad, in this sweet recess we fled to avoid its scrutiny, and here, even here, where now I kneel in supplication, we both knelt and made our vows.—Shall they be broken?"

Constance wept as her lover recalled the images of happy hours. "Never," she exclaimed, "O never! Thou knowest, or wilt soon know, Gaspar, the faith and resolves of one who dare not be yours. Was it for us to talk of love and happiness, when war, and hate, and blood were raging around? The fleeting flowers our young hands strewed were trampled by the deadly encounter of mortal foes. By your father's hand mine died; and little boots it to know whether, as my brother swore, and you deny, your hand did or did not deal the blow that destroyed him. You fought among those by whom he died. Say no more—no other word: it is impiety towards the unreposing dead to hear you. Go, Gaspar; forget me. Under the chivalrous and gallant Henry your career may be glorious; and many a fair girl will listen, as once I did, to your vows, and be made happy by them. Farewell! May the Virgin bless you! In my cell and cloister-home I will not forget the best Christian lesson—to pray for our enemies. Gaspar, farewell!"

She glided hastily from the bower: with swift steps she threaded the glade and sought the castle. Once within the seclusion of her own apartment she gave way to the burst of grief that tore her gentle bosom like a tempest; for hers was that worst sorrow which taints past joys, making remorse wait upon the memory of bliss, and linking love and fancied guilt in such fearful society as that of the tyrant when he bound a living body to a corpse. Suddenly a thought darted into her mind. At first she rejected it as puerile and superstitious; but it would not be driven away. She called hastily for her attendant. "Manon," she said, "didst thou ever sleep on St. Catherine's couch?"

Manon crossed herself. "Heaven forefend! None ever did, since I was born, but two: one fell into the Loire and was drowned; the other only looked upon the narrow bed, and returned to her own home without a word. It is an awful place; and if the votary have not led a pious and good life, woe betide the hour when she rests her head on the holy stone!"

Constance crossed herself also. "As for our lives, it is only through our Lord and the blessed saints that we can any of us hope for righteousness. I will sleep on that couch to-morrow night!"

"Dear, my lady! and the king arrives to-morrow."

"The more need that I resolve. It cannot be that misery so intense should dwell in any heart, and no cure be found. I had hoped to be the bringer of peace to our houses; and is the good work to be for me a crown of thorns? Heaven shall direct me. I will rest to-morrow night on St. Catherine's bed: and if, as I have heard, the saint deigns to direct her votaries in dreams, I will be guided by her; and believing that I act according to the dictates of Heaven, I shall feel resigned even to the worst."

The king was on his way to Nantes from Paris, and he slept on this night at a castle but a few miles distant. Before dawn a young cavalier was introduced into his chamber. The knight had a serious, nay, a sad aspect; and all beautiful as he was in feature and limb, looked way-worn and haggard. He stood silent in Henry's presence, who, alert and gay, turned his lively blue eyes upon his guest, saying gently, "So thou foundest her obdurate, Gaspar?"

"I found her resolved on our mutual misery. Alas! my liege, it is not, credit me, the least of my grief, that Constance sacrifices her own happiness when she destroys mine."

"And thou believest that she will say nay to the gaillard chevalier whom we ourselves present to her?"

"Oh! my liege, think not that thought! it cannot be. My heart deeply, most deeply, thanks you for your generous condescension. But she whom her lover's voice in solitude—whose entreaties, when memory and seclusion aided the spell—could not persuade, will resist even your majesty's commands. She is bent upon entering a cloister; and I, so please you, will now take my leave:—I am henceforth a soldier of the cross, and will die in Palestine."

"Gaspar," said the monarch, "I know woman better than thou. It is not by submission nor tearful plaints she is to be won. The death of her relatives naturally sits heavy at the young countess' heart; and nourishing in solitude her regret and her repentance, she fancies that Heaven itself forbids your union. Let the voice of the world reach her—the voice of earthly power and earthly kindness—the one commanding, the other pleading, and both finding response in her own heart—and by my fay and the Holy Cross, she will be yours. Let our plan still hold. And now to horse: the morning wears, and the sun is risen."

The king arrived at the bishop's palace, and proceeded forthwith to mass in the cathedral. A sumptuous dinner succeeded, and it was after-noon before the monarch proceeded through the town beside the Loire to where, a little above Nantes, the Chateau Villeneuve was situated. The young countess received him at the gate. Henry looked in vain for the cheek blanched by misery, the aspect of downcast despair which he had been taught to expect. Her cheek was flushed, her manner animated, her voice scarce tremulous. "She loves him not," thought Henry, "or already her heart has consented."

A collation was prepared for the monarch; and after some little hesita-tion, arising even from the cheerfulness of her mien, he mentioned the name of Gaspar. Constance blushed instead of turning pale, and replied very quickly, "To-morrow, good my liege; I ask for a respite but until to-morrow;—all will then be decided;—to-morrow I am vowed to God—or—"

She looked confused, and the king, at once surprised and pleased, said, "Then you hate not young De Vaudemont;—you forgive him for the inimical blood that warms his veins."

"We are taught that we should forgive, that we should love our en-emies," the countess replied with some trepidation.

"Now by Saint Denis that is a right welcome answer for the nonce," said the king, laughing. "What ho! my faithful serving-man, Dan Apollo in disguise! come forward, and thank your lady for her love."

In such disguise as had concealed him from all, the cavalier had hung behind, and viewed with infinite surprise the demeanour and calm coun-tenance of the lady. He could not hear her words: but was this even she whom he had seen trembling and weeping the evening before?—this she whose very heart was torn by conflicting passion?—who saw the pale ghosts of parent and kinsman stand between her and the lover whom more than her life she adored? It was a riddle hard to solve. The king's call was in unison with his impatience, and he sprang forward. He was at her feet; while she, still passion-driven, overwrought by the very calmness she had assumed, uttered one cry as she recognised him, and sank sense-less on the floor.

All this was very unintelligible. Even when her attendants had brought her to life, another fit succeeded, and then passionate floods of tears; while the monarch, waiting in the hall, eyeing the half-eaten collation, and humming some romance in commemoration of woman's wayward-ness, knew not how to reply to Vaudemont's look of bitter disappoint-ment and anxiety. At length the countess' chief attendant came with an apology: "her lady was ill, very ill. The next day she would throw herself at the king's feet, at once to solicit his excuse, and to disclose her pur-pose."

"To-morrow—again to-morrow!—Does to-morrow bear some charm, maiden?" said the king. "Can you read us the riddle, pretty one? What strange tale belongs to to-morrow, that all rests on its advent?"

Manon coloured, looked down, and hesitated. But Henry was no tyro in the art of enticing ladies' attendants to disclose their ladies' counsel. Manon was besides frightened by the countess' scheme, on which she was still obstinately bent, so she was the more readily induced to betray it. To sleep in St. Catherine's bed, to rest on a narrow ledge overhanging the deep rapid Loire, and if, as was most probable, the luckless dreamer escaped from falling into it, to take the disturbed visions that such uneasy slumber might produce for the dictate of Heaven, was a madness of which even Henry himself could scarcely deem any woman capable. But could Constance, her whose beauty was so highly intellectual, and whom he had heard perpetually praised for her strength of mind and talents, could *she* be so strangely infatuated! And can passion play such freaks with us?—like death, levelling even the aristocracy of the soul, and bring-ing noble and peasant, the wise and foolish, under one thraldom? It was strange—yet she must have her way. That she hesitated in her decision was much; and it was to be hoped that St. Catherine would play no ill-natured part. Should it be otherwise, a purpose to be swayed by a dream might be influenced by other waking thoughts. To the more material kind of danger some safeguard should be brought.

There is no feeling more awful than that which invades a weak human heart bent upon gratifying its ungovernable impulses in contradiction to the dictates of conscience. Forbidden pleasures are said to be the most agreeable:—it may be so to rude natures, to those who love to struggle, combat, and contend; who find happiness in a fray, and joy in the conflict of passion. But softer and sweeter was the gentle spirit of Constance; and love and duty contending crushed and tortured her poor heart. To com-mit her conduct to the inspirations of religion, or, if it was so to be named, of superstition, was a blessed relief. The very perils that threat-ened her undertaking gave a zest to it;—to dare for his sake was happi-ness;—the very difficulty of the way that led to the completion of her wishes, at once gratified her love and distracted her thoughts from her despair. Or if it was decreed that she must sacrifice all, the risk of danger and of death were of trifling import in comparison with the anguish which would then be her portion for ever.

The night threatened to be stormy—the raging wind shook the casements—and the trees waved their huge shadowy arms, as giants might in fantastic dance and mortal broil. Constance and Manon, unattended, quitted the chateau by a postern, and began to descend the hill side. The moon had not yet risen; and though the way was familiar to both, Manon tottered and trembled; while the countess, drawing her silken cloak round her, walked with a firm step down the steep. They came to the river's side, where a small boat was moored, and one man was in waiting. Constance stepped lightly in, and then aided her fearful companion. In a few moments they were in the middle of the stream. The warm, tempestuous, animating, equinoctial wind swept over them. For the first time since her mourning, a thrill of pleasure swelled the bosom of Constance. She hailed the emotion with double joy. It cannot be, she thought, that Heaven will forbid me to love one so brave, so generous, and so good as the noble Gaspar. Another I can never love; I shall die if divided from him: and this heart, these limbs, so alive with glowing sensation, are they already predestined to an early grave? Oh, no! life speaks aloud within them. I shall live to love. Do not all things love?—the winds as they whisper to the rushing waters? the waters they kiss the flowery banks, and speed to mingle with the sea? Heaven and earth are sustained by, live through, love; and shall Constance alone, whose heart has ever been a deep, gushing, overflowing well of true affection, be compelled to set a stone upon the fount to lock it up for ever?

These thoughts bid fair for pleasant dreams; and perhaps the countess, an adept in the blind god's lore, therefore indulged them the more readily. But as thus she was engrossed by soft emotions, Manon caught her arm:—"Lady, look," she cried; "it comes—yet the oars have no sound. Now the Virgin shield us! Would we were at home!"

A dark boat glided by them. Four rowers, habited in black cloaks, pulled at oars which, as Manon said, gave no sound; another sat at the helm: like the rest, his person was veiled in a dark mantle, but he wore no cap; and though his face was turned from them, Constance recognised her lover. "Gaspar," she cried aloud, "dost thou live?"—but the figure in the boat neither turned its head nor replied, and quickly it was lost in the shadowy waters.

How changed now was the fair countess' reverie! Already Heaven had begun its spell, and unearthly forms were around, as she strained her eyes through the gloom. Now she saw and now she lost view of the bark that

occasioned her terror; and now it seemed that another was there, which
held the spirits of the dead; and her father waved to her from shore, and
her brothers frowned on her.

Meanwhile they neared the landing. Her bark was moored in a little
cove, and Constance stood upon the bank. Now she trembled, and half
yielded to Manon's entreaty to return; till the unwise *suivante* mentioned
the king's and De Vaudemont's name, and spoke of the answer to be
given to-morrow. What answer, if she turned back from her intent?

She now hurried forward up the broken ground of the bank, and then
along its edge, till they came to a hill which abruptly hung over the tide.
A small chapel stood near. With trembling fingers the countess drew forth
the key and unlocked its door. They entered. It was dark—save that a
little lamp, flickering in the wind, showed an uncertain light from before
the figure of Saint Catherine. The two women knelt; they prayed; and
then rising, with a cheerful accent the countess bade her attendant good
night. She unlocked a little low iron door. It opened on a narrow cavern.
The roar of waters was heard beyond. "Thou mayest not follow, my poor
Manon," said Constance,—"nor dost thou much desire:—this adventure
is for me alone."

It was hardly fair to leave the trembling servant in the chapel alone,
who had neither hope nor fear, nor love nor grief, to beguile her; but, in
those days, esquires and waiting-women often played the part of sub-
alterns in the army, gaining knocks and no fame. Besides, Manon was
safe in holy ground. The countess meanwhile pursued her way groping in
the dark through the narrow tortuous passage. At length what seemed
light to her long-darkened sense gleamed on her. She reached an open
cavern in the overhanging hill's side, looking over the rushing tide beneath. She looked out upon the night. The waters of the Loire were
speeding, as since that day have they ever sped—changeful, yet the same;
the heavens were thickly veiled with clouds, and the wind in the trees was
as mournful and ill-omened as if it rushed round a murderer's tomb.
Constance shuddered a little, and looked upon her bed—a narrow ledge
of earth and a moss-grown stone bordering on the very verge of the
precipice. She doffed her mantle—such was one of the conditions of the
spell;—she bowed her head, and loosened the tresses of her dark hair—
she bared her feet—and thus, fully prepared for suffering to the utmost
the chill influence of the cold night, she stretched herself on the narrow
couch that scarce afforded room for her repose, and whence, if she moved
in sleep, she must be precipitated into the cold waters below.

At first it seemed to her as if she never should sleep again. No great
wonder that exposure to the blast and her perilous position should forbid
her eyelids to close. At length she fell into a reverie so soft and soothing
that she wished even to watch—and then by degrees her senses became

confused—and now she was on St. Catherine's bed—the Loire rushing beneath, and the wild wind sweeping by—and now—O whither?—and what dreams did the saint send, to drive her to despair, or to bid her be blest for ever?

Beneath the rugged hill, upon the dark tide, another watched, who feared a thousand things, and scarce dared hope. He had meant to precede the lady on her way, but when he found that he had outstaid his time, with muffled oars and breathless haste he had shot by the bark that contained his Constance, nor even turned at her voice, fearful to incur her blame, and her commands to return. He had seen her emerge from the passage, and shuddered as she leant over the cliff. He saw her step forth, clad as she was in white, and could mark her as she lay on the ledge beetling above. What a vigil did the lovers keep!—she given up to visionary thoughts, he knowing—and the consciousness thrilled his bosom with strange emotion—that love, and love for him, had led her to that perilous couch; and that while dangers surrounded her in every shape, she was alive only to the small still voice that whispered to her heart the dream which was to decide their destinies. She slept perhaps—but he waked and watched; and night wore away, as, now praying, now entranced by alternating hope and fear, he sat in his boat, his eyes fixed on the white garb of the slumberer above.

Morning—was it morning that struggled in the clouds? Would morning ever come to waken her? And had she slept? and what dreams of weal or woe had peopled her sleep? Gaspar grew impatient. He commanded his boatmen still to wait, and he sprang forward, intent on clambering the precipice. In vain they urged the danger, nay, the impossibility of the attempt; he clung to the rugged face of the hill, and found footing where it would seem no footing was. The acclivity, indeed, was not high; the dangers of St. Catherine's bed arising from the likelihood that any one who slept on so narrow a couch would be precipitated into the waters beneath. Up the steep ascent Gaspar continued to toil, and at last reached the roots of a tree that grew near the summit. Aided by its branches, he made good his stand at the very extremity of the ledge, near the pillow on which lay the uncovered head of his beloved. Her hands were folded on her bosom; her dark hair fell round her throat and pillowed her cheek; her face was serene: sleep was there in all its innocence and in all its helplessness; every wilder emotion was hushed, and her bosom heaved in regular breathing. He could see her heart beat as it lifted her fair hands crossed above. No statue hewn of marble in monumental effigy was ever half so fair; and within that surpassing form dwelt a soul true, tender, self-devoted, and affectionate as ever warmed a human breast.

With what deep passion did Gaspar gaze, gathering hope from the placidity of her angel countenance! A smile wreathed her lips; and he too involuntarily smiled, as he hailed the happy omen; when suddenly her cheek was flushed, her bosom heaved, a tear stole from her dark lashes, and then a whole shower fell, as starting up she cried, "No!—he shall not die!—I will unloose his chains!—I will save him!" Gaspar's hand was there. He caught her light form ready to fall from the perilous couch. She opened her eyes and beheld her lover, who had watched over her dream of fate, and who had saved her.

Manon also had slept well, dreaming or not, and was startled in the morning to find that she waked surrounded by a crowd. The little desolate chapel was hung with tapestry—the altar adorned with golden chalices— the priest was chanting mass to a goodly array of kneeling knights. Manon saw that King Henry was there; and she looked for another whom she found not, when the iron door of the cavern passage opened, and Gaspar de Vaudemont entered from it, leading the fair form of Constance; who, in her white robes and dark dishevelled hair, with a face in which smiles and blushes contended with deeper emotion, approached the altar, and kneeling with her lover, pronounced the vows that united them for ever.

It was long before the happy Gaspar could win from his lady the secret of her dream. In spite of the happiness she now enjoyed, she had suffered too much not to look back even with terror to those days when she thought love a crime, and every event connected with them wore an awful aspect. Many a vision, she said, she had that fearful night. She had seen the spirits of her father and brothers in Paradise; she had beheld Gaspar victoriously combating among the infidels; she had beheld him in King Henry's court, favoured and beloved, and she herself—now pining in a cloister, now a bride—now grateful to Heaven for the full measure of bliss presented to her, now weeping away her sad days—till suddenly she thought herself in Paynim land; and the saint herself, Saint Catherine, guiding her unseen through the city of the infidels. She entered a palace and beheld the miscreants rejoicing in victory; and then descending to the dungeons beneath, they groped their way through damp vaults, and low mildewed passages, to one cell, darker and more frightful than the rest. On the floor lay one with soiled and tattered garments, with unkempt locks and wild matted beard. His cheek was worn and thin; his eyes had lost their fire; his form was a mere skeleton; the chains hung loosely on the fleshless bones.

"And was it my appearance in that attractive state and winning costume that softened the hard heart of Constance?" asked Gaspar, smiling at this painting of what would never be.

"Even so," replied Constance; "for my heart whispered me that this was my doing: and who could recall the life that waned in your pulses— who restore, save the destroyer? My heart never warmed to my living happy knight as then it did to his wasted image, as it lay, in the visions of night, at my feet. A veil fell from my eyes; a darkness was dispelled from before me. Methought I then knew for the first time what life and what death was. I was bid believe that to make the living happy was not to injure the dead; and I felt how wicked and how vain was that false philosophy which placed virtue and good in hatred and unkindness. You should not die: I would loosen your chains and save you, and bid you live for love. I sprung forward, and the death I deprecated for you would, in my presumption, have been mine—then, when first I felt the real value of life—but that your arm was there to save me, your dear voice to bid me be blest for evermore."

XIII

The Brother and Sister

AN ITALIAN STORY

IT IS WELL KNOWN that the hatred borne by one family against another, and the strife of parties, which often led to bloodshed in the Italian cities during the middle ages, so vividly described by Shakespeare in Romeo and Juliet, was not confined to the Montecchi and Capelletti of Verona, but existed with equal animosity in almost every other town of that beautiful peninsula. The greatest men among them were the victims; and crowds of exiles—families who but the day before were in the full enjoyment of the luxuries of life and the endearing associations of home—were every now and then seen issuing from the gates of their native cities, deprived of every possession, and with melancholy and slow steps, dragging their wearied limbs to the nearest asylum offered them, thence to commence a new career of dependence and poverty, to endure to the end of their lives, or until some lucky accident should enable them to change places with their enemies, making those the sufferers who were late the tyrants. In that country, where each town formed an independent state, to change one for the other was to depart from the spot cherished as a country and a home for distant banishment—or worse—for as each city entertained either hatred or contempt for its neighbour, it often happened that the mourning exile was obliged to take up his abode among a people whom he had injured or scoffed. Foreign service offered a resource to the young and bold among the men. But lovely Italy was to be left, the ties of young hearts severed, and all the endearing associations of kin and country broken and scattered for ever. The Italians were always peculiarly susceptible to these misfortunes. They loved their native walls, the abodes of their ancestors, the famliar scenes of youth, with all the passionate fervour characteristic of that clime.

It was therefore no uncommon thing for any one among them, like Foscari of Venice, to prefer destitution and danger in their own city, to a

precarious subsistence among strangers in distant lands; or, if compelled
to quit the beloved precincts of their native walls, still to hover near, ready
to avail themselves of the first occasion that should present itself for
reversing the decree that condemned them to misery.

For three days and nights there had been warfare in the streets of
Sienna—blood flowed in torrents—yet the cries and groans of the fallen
but excited their friends to avenge them—not their foes to spare. On the
fourth morning, Ugo Mancini, with a scanty band of followers, was
driven from the town: succours from Florence had arrived for his enemies, and he was forced to yield. Burning with rage, writhing with an
impotent thirst for vengeance, Ugo went round to the neighbouring villages
to rouse them, not against his native town, but the victorious Tolomei.
Unsuccessful in these endeavours, he next took the more equivocal step
of seeking warlike aid from the Pisans. But Florence kept Pisa in check,
and Ugo found only an inglorious refuge where he had hoped to acquire
active allies. He had been wounded in these struggles; but, animated by a
superhuman spirit, he had forgotten his pain and surmounted his weakness; nor was it until a cold refusal was returned to his energetic representations that he sank beneath his physical sufferings. He was stretched on a
bed of torture when he received intelligence that an edict of perpetual
banishment and confiscation of property was passed against him. His two
children, beggars now, were sent to him. His wife was dead, and these
were all of near relations that he possessed. His bitter feelings were still
too paramount for him to receive comfort from their presence; yet these
agitated and burning emotions appeared in after-times a remnant of happiness compared to the total loss of every hope—the wasting inaction of
sickness and of poverty.

For five years Ugo Mancini lay stretched on his couch, alternating
between states of intense pain and overpowering weakness; and then he
died. During this interval, the wreck of his fortunes, consisting of the rent
of a small farm, and the use of some money lent, scantily supported him.
His few relatives and followers were obliged to seek their subsistence
elsewhere, and he remained alone to his pain, and to his two children,
who yet clung to the paternal side.

Hatred to his foes, and love for his native town, were the sentiments
that possessed his soul, and which he imparted in their full force to the
plastic mind of his son, which received like molten metal the stamp he
desired to impress. Lorenzo was scarcely twelve years old at the period of
his father's exile, and he naturally turned with fondness towards the spot
where he had enjoyed every happiness, where each hour had been spent
in light-hearted hilarity, and the kindness and observance of many attended on his steps. Now, how sad the contrast!—dim penury—a solitude

cheered by no encouraging smiles or sunny flatteries—perpetual attendance on his father, and untimely cares, cast their dark shadows over his
altered lot.

Lorenzo was many years older than his sister. Friendless and destitute
as was the exile's family, it was he who overlooked its moderate disburse-
ments, who was at once his father's nurse and his sister's guardian, and
acted as the head of the family during the incapacity of his parent. But
instead of being narrowed or broken in spirit by these burthens, his
ardent soul rose to meet them, and grew enlarged and lofty from the very
calls made upon it. His look was serious, not care-worn—his manner
calm, not humble—his voice had all the tenderness of a woman—his eye
all the pride and fire of a hero.

Still his unhappy father wasted away, and Lorenzo's hours were entirely spent beside his bed. He was indefatigable in his attentions—weariness never seemed to come near him. His limbs were always alert—his
speech inspiriting and kind. His only pastime was during any interval in
his parent's sufferings, to listen to his eulogiums on his native town, and
to the history of the wrongs which, from time immemorial, the Mancini
had endured from the Tolomei. Lorenzo, though replete with noble qualities, was still an Italian; and fervent love for his birthplace, and violent
hatred towards the foes of his house, were the darling passions of his
heart. Nursed in loneliness, they acquired vigour; and the nights he spent
in watching his father were varied by musing on the career he should
hereafter follow—his return to his beloved Sienna, and the vengeance he
would take on his enemies.

Ugo often said, I die because I am an exile:—at length these words
were fulfilled, and the unhappy man sank beneath the ills of fortune.
Lorenzo saw his beloved father expire—his father, whom he loved as a
mother loves a sickly infant which she has led from its birth to an early
five years' old tomb. He seemed to deposit in his obscure grave all that
best deserved reverence and honour in the world; and turning away his
steps, he lamented the sad occupation of so many years, and regretted the
exchange he made from his father's sick bed to a lonely and unprized
freedom.

The first use he made of the liberty he had thus acquired was to return
to Sienna with his little sister. He entered his native town as it if were a
paradise, and he found it a desert in all save the hues of beauty and
delight with which his imagination loved to invest it. There was no one to
whom he could draw near in friendship within the whole circuit of its
walls. According to the barbarous usage of the times, his father's palace
had been razed, and the mournful ruins stood as a tomb to commemorate
the fall of his fortunes. Not as such did Lorenzo view them—he often

stole out at nightfall, when the stars alone beheld his enthusiasm, and, clambering to the highest part of the massy fragments, spent long hours in mentally rebuilding the desolate walls, and in consecrating once again the weed-grown hearth to family love and hospitable festivity. It seemed to him that the air was more balmy and light, breathed amidst these memorials of the past; and his heart warmed with rapture over the tale they told of what his progenitors had been—what he again would be.

Yet, had he viewed his position sanely, he would have found it full of mortification and pain; and he would have become aware that his native town was perhaps the only place in the world where his ambition would fail in the attainment of its aim. The Tolomei reigned over it. They had led its citizens to conquest, and enriched them with spoils. They were adored; and to flatter them, the populace were prone to revile and scoff at the name of Mancini. Lorenzo did not possess one friend within its walls: he heard the murmur of hatred as he passed along, and beheld his enemies raised to the pinnacle of power and honour; and yet, so strangely framed is the human heart, that he continued to love Sienna, and would not have exchanged his obscure and penurious abode within its walls to become the favoured follower of the German emperor. Such a place, through education and the natural prejudices of man, did Sienna hold in his imagination, that a lowly condition there, seemed a nobler destiny than to be great in any other spot.

To win back the friendship of its citizens and humble his enemies was the dream that shed so sweet an influence over his darkened hours. He dedicated his whole being to this work, and he did not doubt but that he should succeed. The house of Tolomei had for its chief, a youth but a year or two older than himself—with him, when an opportunity should present itself, he would enter the lists. It seemed the bounty of Providence that gave him one so nearly equal with whom to contend; and during the interval that must elapse before they could clash, he was busy in educating himself for the struggle. Count Fabian de' Tolomei bore the reputation of being a youth full of promise and talent; and Lorenzo was glad to anticipate a worthy antagonist. He occupied himself in the practice of arms, and applied with perseverance to the study of the few books that fell in his way. He appeared in the market-place on public occasions modestly attired; yet his height, his dignified carriage, and the thoughtful cast of his noble countenance, drew the observation of the bystanders;—though, such was the prejudice against his name, and the flattery of the triumphant party, that taunts and maledictions followed him. His nobility of appearance was called pride; his affability, meanness; his aspiring views, faction;—and it was declared that it would be a happy day when he should no longer blot their sunshine with his shadow. Lorenzo smiled

—he disdained to resent, or even to feel, the mistaken insults of the crowd, who, if fortune changed, would the next day throw up their caps for him. It was only when loftier foes approached that his brow grew dark, that he drew himself up to his full height, repaying their scorn with glances of defiance and hate.

But although he was ready in his own person to encounter the contumely of his townsmen, and walked on with placid mien, regardless of their sneers, he carefully guarded his little sister from such scenes. She was led by him each morning, closely veiled, to hear mass in an obscure church. And when, on feast-days, the public walks were crowded with cavaliers and dames in splendid attire, and with citizens and peasants in their holiday garb, this gentle pair might be seen in some solitary and shady spot, he bending down and smiling on the lovely child, who looked up to him with eyes expressive of unutterable affection. In the whole world, Flora knew none to love except her brother—she was his junior by nearly seven years—she had grown under his eyes from infancy; and while he attended on the sick bed of their father, he was father, brother, tutor, guardian to Flora—the fondest mother could not have been more indulgent; and yet there was mingled a something beyond, pertaining to their difference of sex. Uniformly observant and kind, he treated her as if she had been a high-born damsel, nurtured in her gayest bower.

Her attire was simple—but thus, she was instructed, it befitted every damsel to dress; her needle-works were such as a princess might have emulated; and while she learnt under her brother's tutelage to be reserved, studious of obscurity, and always occupied, she was taught that such were the virtues becoming her sex, and no idea of dependence or penury was raised in her mind. Had he been the sole human being that approached her, she might have believed herself to be on a level with the highest in the land; but coming in contact with dependants and various females in the humble class of life, Flora became acquainted with her true position; and learnt, at the same time, to understand and appreciate the unequalled kindness of her brother, and to regard his virtues as superhuman.

Two years passed while this brother and sister continued, in obscurity and poverty, to cherish the dearest blessings of life, hope, honour, and mutual love. If an anxious thought ever crossed Lorenzo, it was for the future destiny of Flora, whose beauty as a child gave promise of perfect loveliness hereafter. For her sake he was anxious to begin the career he had marked out for himself, and resolved no longer to delay his endeavours to revive his party in Sienna, and to seek rather than avoid any contest with the young Count Fabian, on whose overthrow he would rise—Count Fabian, the darling of the citizens, vaunted as a model for a youthful cavalier, overflowing with good qualities, and so adorned by gallantry, subtle wit, and gay, winning manners, that he stepped by right of nature, as well as birth, on the pedestal which exalted him the idol of all around.

It was on a day of public feasting that Lorenzo first presented himself in rivalship with Fabian. His person was unknown to the Count, who, in all the pride of rich dress and splendid accoutrements, looked down with a smile of patronage on the poorly mounted and plainly attired youth, who presented himself to a run a tilt with him. But before the challenge was accepted, the name of his antagonist was whispered to Fabian; then, all the bitterness engendered by family feuds; all the spirit of vengeance, which had been taught as a religion, arose at once in the young noble's heart; he wheeled round his steed, and riding rudely up to his competitor, ordered him instantly to retire from the course, nor dare to disturb the revels of the citizens by the hated presence of a Mancini. Lorenzo answered with equal scorn; and Fabian, governed by uncontrollable passion, called together his followers to drive the youth with ignominy from the lists. A fearful array was mustered against the hateful intruder; but had their number been trebled, the towering spirit of Lorenzo had met them all. One fell—another was disabled by his weapon before he was disarmed and made prisoner; but his bravery did not avail to extract admiration from his prejudiced foes: they rather poured execrations on him for its disastrous effects, as they hurried him to a dungeon, and called loudly for his punishment and death.

Far from this scene of turmoil and bloodshed, in her poor but quiet chamber, in a remote and obscure part of the town, sat Flora, occupied by her embroidery, musing, as she worked, on her brother's project, and anticipating his success. Hours passed, and Lorenzo did not return,—the day declined, and still he tarried. Flora's busy fancy forged a thousand causes for the delay. Her brother's prowess had awaked the chilly zeal of the partisans of their family;—he was doubtless feasting among them, and the first stone was laid for the rebuilding of their house. At last, a rush of steps upon the staircase, and a confused clamour of female voices calling loudly for admittance, made her rise and open the door;—in rushed several of the women of the house—dismay was painted on their faces—their words flowed in torrents—their eager gestures helped them to a meaning, and, though not without difficulty, amidst the confusion, Flora heard of the disaster and imprisonment of her brother—of the blood shed by his hand, and the fatal issue that such a deed ensured. Flora grew pale as marble. Her young heart was filled with speechless terror; she could form no image of the thing she dreaded, but its indistinct idea was full of fear. Lorenzo was in prison—Count Fabian had placed him there—he was to die! Overwhelmed by such tidings, yet in a moment she rose above their benumbing power, and without proffering a word, or listening to the questions and remonstrances of the women, she rushed past them, down the high staircase, into the street; and then with swift pace to where the public prison was situated. She knew the spot she wished to reach, but she had so seldom quitted her home that she soon got entangled among the streets, and proceeded onwards at random. Breathless, at length, she paused before the lofty portal of a large palace —no one was near—the fast fading twilight of an Italian evening had deepened into absolute darkness. At this moment the glare of flambeaux was thrown upon the street, and a party of horsemen rode up; they were talking and laughing gaily. She heard one addressed as Count Fabian: she involuntarily drew back with instinctive hate; and then rushed forward and threw herself at his horse's feet, exclaiming, "Save my brother!" The young cavalier reined up shortly his prancing steed, angrily reproving her for her heedlessness, and, without deigning another word, entered the court-yard. He had not, perhaps, heard her prayer;—he could not see the suppliant, he spoke but in the impatience of the moment;—but the poor child, deeply wounded by what had the appearance of a personal insult, turned proudly from the door, repressing the bitter tears that filled her eyes. Still she walked on; but night took from her every chance of finding her way to the prison, and she resolved to return home, to engage one of the women of the house, of which she occupied a part, to accompany her. But even to find her way back became matter of difficulty; and she wandered on, discovering no clue to guide her, and far too timid to address any one she might chance to meet. Fatigue and personal fear were added to her other griefs, and tears streamed plentifully down her cheeks as she continued her hopeless journey. At length, at the corner of a street, she recognized an image of the Madonna in a niche, with a lamp burning over it, familiar to her recollection as being near her home. With characteristic piety she knelt before it in thankfulness, and was offering a prayer for Lorenzo, when the sound of steps made her start up, and her brother's voice hailed, and her brother's arms encircled her; it seemed a miracle, but he was there, and all her fears were ended.

Lorenzo anxiously asked whither she had been straying; her explanation was soon given; and he in return related the misfortunes of the morning—the fate that impended over him, averted by the generous intercession of young Fabian himself; and yet—he hesitated to unfold the bitter truth—he was not freely pardoned—he stood there a banished man, condemned to die if the morrow's sun found him within the walls of Sienna.

They had arrived, meanwhile, at their home; and with feminine care, Flora placed a simple repast before her brother, and then employed herself very busily in making various packages. Lorenzo paced the room, absorbed in thought; at length he stopped, and kissing the fair girl, said,

"Where can I place thee in safety? how preserve thee, my flower of beauty, while we are divided?"

Flora looked up fearfully. "Do I not go with you?" she asked; "I was making preparations for our journey."

"Impossible, dearest; I go to privation and hardship."

"And I would share them with thee."

"It may not be, sweet sister," replied Lorenzo, "fate divides us, and we must submit. I go to camps—to the society of rude men; to struggle with such fortune as cannot harm me, but which for thee would be fraught with peril and despair. No, my Flora, I must provide safe and honourable guardianship for thee, even in this town." And again Lorenzo meditated deeply on the part he should take, till suddenly a lightning thought flashed on his mind. "It is hazardous," he murmured, "and yet I do him wrong to call it so. Were our fates reversed, should I not think myself highly honoured by such a trust?" And then he told his sister to don hastily her best attire; to wrap her veil round her, and to come with him. She obeyed —for obedience to her brother was the first and dearest of her duties. But she wept bitterly while her trembling fingers braided her long hair, and she hastily changed her dress.

At length they walked forth again, and proceeded slowly, as Lorenzo employed the precious minutes in consoling and counselling his sister. He promised as speedy a return as he could accomplish; but if he failed to appear as soon as he could wish, yet he vowed solemnly that, if alive and free, she should see him within five years from the moment of parting. Should he not come before, he besought her earnestly to take patience, and to hope for the best till the expiration of that period; and made her promise not to bind herself by any vestal or matrimonial vow in the interim. They had arrived at their destination, and entered the court-yard of a spacious palace. They met no servants; so crossed the court, and ascended the ample stairs. Flora had endeavoured to listen to her brother. He had bade her be of good cheer, and he was about to leave her; he told her to hope; and he spoke of an absence to endure five years—an endless term to her childish anticipations. She promised obedience, but her voice was choked by sobs, and her tottering limbs would not have supported her without his aid. She now perceived that they were entering the light and inhabited rooms of a noble dwelling, and tried to restrain her tears, as she drew her veil closely around her. They passed from room to room, in which preparations for festivity were making; the servants ushered them on, as if they had been invited guests, and conducted them into a hall filled with all the nobility and beauty of Sienna. Each eye turned with curiosity and wonder on the pair. Lorenzo's tall person, and the lofty yet sweet expression of his handsome countenance put the ladies in good-humour with him, while the cavaliers tried to peep under Flora's veil.

"It is a mere child," they said, "and a sorrowing one—what can this mean?"

The youthful master of the house, however, instantly recognized his uninvited and unexpected guest; but before he could ask the meaning of his coming, Lorenzo had advanced with his sister to the spot where he stood, and addressed him.

"I never thought, Count Fabian, to stand beneath your roof, and much less to approach you as a suitor. But that Supreme Power, to whose decrees we must all bend, has reduced me to such adversity as, if it be his will, may also visit you, notwithstanding the many friends that now surround you, and the sunshine of prosperity in which you bask. I stand here a banished man and a beggar. Nor do I repine at this my fate. Most willing am I that my right arm alone should create my fortunes; and, with the blessing of God, I hope so to direct my course, that we may yet meet upon more equal terms. In this hope, I turn my steps, not unwillingly, from this city; dear as its name is to my heart—and dear the associations which link its proud towers with the memory of my forefathers. I leave it a soldier of fortune; how I may return is written in the page where your unread destiny is traced as well as mine. But my care ends not with myself. My dying father bequeathed to me this child, my orphan sister, whom I have, until now, watched over with a parent's love. I should ill perform the part intrusted to me, were I to drag this tender blossom from its native bower into the rude highways of life. Lord Fabian, I can count no man my friend; for it would seem that your smiles have won the hearts of my fellow-citizens from me; and death and exile have so dealt with my house, through the intervention of yours, that not one of my name exists within the walls of Sienna. To you alone can I intrust this precious charge. Will you accept it until called upon to render it back to me, her brother, or to the juster hands of our Creator, pure and untarnished as I now deliver her to you? I ask you to protect her helplessness, to guard her honour; will you—dare you accept a treasure, with the assurance of restoring it unsoiled, unhurt?"

The deep expressive voice of the noble youth and his earnest eloquence enchained the ears of the whole assembly; and when he ceased, Fabian, proud of the appeal, and nothing loth in the buoyant spirit of youth to undertake a charge which, thus proffered before his assembled kinsmen and friends, became an honour, answered readily—"I agree, and solemnly before Heaven accept your offer. I declare myself the guardian and protector of your sister; she shall dwell in safety beneath my kind mother's care, and if the saints permit your return, she shall be delivered back to you as spotless as she now is."

Lorenzo bowed his head; something choked his utterance as he thought that he was about to part for ever from his Flora; but he disdained to betray this weakness before his enemies. He took his sister's hand and gazed upon her slight girlish form with a look of earnest fondness, then murmuring a blessing over her, and kissing her brow, he again saluted Count Fabian, and turning away with measured steps and lofty mien, left the hall. Flora, scarcely understanding what had passed, stood trembling and weeping under her veil. She yielded her passive hand to Fabian, who leading her to his mother, said: "Madam, I ask of your goodness, and the maternal indulgence you have ever shown, to assist me in fulfilling my promise to yonder stripling, by taking under your gracious charge this young orphan."

"You command here, my son," said the countess, "and your will shall be obeyed." Then making a sign to one of her attendants, Flora was conducted from the hall, to where, in solitude and silence, she wept over her brother's departure, and her own strange and humiliating position.

Flora thus became an inmate of the dwelling of her ancestral foes, and the ward of her most bitter enemy. Lorenzo was gone she knew not wither, and her only pleasure consisted in reflecting that she was obeying his behests. Her life was uniform and tranquil. Her occupation was working tapestry, in which she displayed taste and skill. Sometimes she had the more mortifying task imposed on her of waiting on the Countess de' Tolomei, who having lost two brothers in the last contest with the Mancini, nourished a deep hatred towards the whole race, and never smiled on the luckless orphan. Flora submitted to every command imposed upon her. She was buoyed up by the reflection that her sufferings were imposed on her by Lorenzo; schooling herself in any moment of impatience by the idea that thus she shared his adversity. No murmur escaped her, though the pride and independence of her nature were often cruelly offended by the taunts and supercilious airs of her patroness or mistress, who was not a bad woman, but who thought it virtue to ill-treat a Mancini. Often, indeed, she neither heard nor heeded these things. Her thoughts were far away, and grief for the loss of her brother's society weighed too heavily on her to allow her to spend more than a passing sigh on her personal injuries.

The countess was unkind and disdainful, but it was not thus with Flora's companions. They were amiable and affectionate girls, either of the bourgeois class, or daughters of dependants of the house of Tolomei. The length of time which had elapsed since the overthrow of the Mancini, had erased from their young minds the bitter duty of hatred, and it was impossible for them to live on terms of daily intercourse with the orphan daughter of this ill-fated race, and not to become strongly attached to her. She was wholly devoid of selfishness, and content to perform her daily tasks in inoffensive silence. She had no envy, no wish to shine, no desire of pleasure. She was nevertheless ever ready to sympathise with her companions, and glad to have it in her power to administer to their happiness. To help them in the manufacture of some piece of finery; to assist them in their work; and, perfectly prudent and reserved herself, to listen to all their sentimental adventures; to give her best advice, and to aid them in any difficulty, were the simple means she used to win their unsophisticated hearts. They called her an angel; they looked up to her as to a saint, and in their hearts respected her more than the countess herself.

One only subject ever disturbed Flora's serene melancholy. The praises she perpetually heard lavished on Count Fabian, her brother's too successful rival and oppressor, was an unendurable addition to her many griefs. Content with her own obscurity, her ambition, her pride, her aspiring thoughts were spent upon her brother. She hated Count Fabian as Lorenzo's destroyer, and the cause of his unhappy and hazardous exile. His accomplishments she despised as painted vanities; his person she contemned as the opposite of his prototype. His blue eyes, clear and open as day; his fair complexion and light brown hair; his slight elegant person; his voice, whose tones in song won each listener's heart to tenderness and love; his wit, his perpetual flow of spirits, and unalterable good-humour, were impertinences and frivolities to her who cherished with such dear worship the recollection of her serious, ardent, noble-hearted brother, whose soul was ever set on high thoughts, and devoted to acts of virtue and self-sacrifice; whose fortitude and affectionate courtesy seemed to her the crown and glory of manhood; how different from the trifling flippancy of the butterfly, Fabian: "Name an eagle," she would say, "and we raise our eyes to Heaven, there to behold a creature fashioned in Nature's bounty; but it is a degradation to waste one thought on the insect of a day." Some speech similar to this had been kindly reported to the young count's lady mother, who idolised her son as the ornament and delight of his age and country. She severely reprimanded the incautious Flora, who, for the first time, listened proudly and unyieldingly. From this period her situation grew more irksome; all she could do was to endeavour to withdraw herself entirely from observation, and to brood in deeper secresy over the perfections, while she lamented yet more feelingly the absence, of her brother.

Two or three years thus flew away, and Flora grew from a childish-looking girl of twelve into the bewitching beauty of fifteen. She unclosed like a flower, whose fairest petals are yet shut, but whose half-veiled loveliness is yet more attractive. It was at this time that on occasion of doing honour to a prince of France, who was passing on to Naples, the Countess Tolomei and her son, with a bevy of friends and followers, went out to meet and to escort the royal traveller on his way. Assembled in the hall of the palace, and waiting for the arrival of some of their number, Count Fabian went round his mother's circle, saying agreeable and merry things to all. Wherever his cheerful blue eyes lighted, there smiles were awakened and each young heart beat with vanity at his harmless flatteries. After a gallant speech or two he espied Flora, retired behind her companions.

"What flower is this," he said, "playing at hide and seek with her beauty?" And then, struck by the modest sweetness of her aspect, her eyes cast down, and a rosy blush mantling over her cheek, he added, "What fair angel makes one of your company?"

"An angel indeed, my lord," exclaimed one of the younger girls, who dearly loved her best friend; "she is Flora Mancini."

"Mancini!" exclaimed Fabian, while his manner became at once respectful and kind: "are you the orphan daughter of Ugo—the sister of Lorenzo, committed by him to my care?" For since then, through her careful avoidance, Fabian had never even seen his fair ward. She bowed an assent to his questions, while her swelling heart denied her speech; and Fabian, going up to his mother, said, "Madam, I hope for our honour's sake that this has not before happened. The adverse fortune of this young lady may render retirement and obscurity befitting; but it is not for us to turn into a menial one sprung from the best blood in Italy. Let me entreat you not to permit this to occur again. How shall I redeem my pledged honour, or answer to her brother for this unworthy degradation?"

"Would you have me make a friend and a companion of a Mancini?" asked the countess, with raised colour.

"I ask you not, mother, to do aught displeasing to you," replied the young noble; "but Flora is my ward, not our servant:—permit her to retire; she will probably prefer the privacy of home, to making one among the festive crowd of her house's enemies. If not, let the choice be hers. —Say, gentle one, will you go with us or retire?"

She did not speak, but raising her soft eyes, curtsied to him and to his mother, and quitted the room; so tacitly making her selection.

From this time Flora never quitted the more secluded apartments of the palace, nor again saw Fabian. She was unaware that he had been profuse in his eulogium on her beauty; but that while frequently expressing his interest in his ward, he rather avoided the dangerous power of her loveliness. She led rather a prison life, walking only in the palace garden when it was else deserted, but otherwise her time was at her own disposal, and no commands interfered with her freedom. Her labours were all spontaneous. The countess seldom even saw her, and she lived among this lady's attendants like a free boarder in a convent, who cannot quit the walls, but who is not subservient to the rules of the asylum. She was more busy than ever at her tapestry frame, because the countess prized her work; and thus she could in some degree repay the protection afforded her. She never mentioned Fabian, and always imposed silence on her companions when they spoke of him. But she did this in no disrespectful terms. "He is a generous enemy, I acknowledge," she would say, "but still he is my enemy, and while through him my brother is an exile and a wanderer upon earth, it is painful to me to hear his name."

After the lapse of many months spent in entire seclusion and tranquillity, a change occurred in the tenor of her life. The countess suddenly resolved to pass the Easter festival at Rome. Flora's companions were wild with joy at the prospect of the journey, the novelty, and the entertainment they promised themselves from this visit, and pitied the dignity of their friend, which prevented her from making one in their mistress's train; for it was soon understood that Flora was to be left behind; and she was informed that the interval of the lady's absence was to be passed by her in a villa belonging to the family situated in a sequestered nook among the neighbouring Apennines.

The countess departed in pomp and pride on her so called pilgrimage to the sacred city, and at the same time Flora was conveyed to her rural retreat. The villa was inhabited only by the peasant and his family who cultivated the farm, or podere, attached to it, and the old cassiere or housekeeper. The cheerfulness and freedom of the country were delightful, and the entire solitude consonant to the habits of the meditative girl, accustomed to the confinement of the city, and the intrusive prattle of her associates. Spring was opening with all the beauty which that season showers upon favoured Italy; while blights and chilling rain usually characterise it in these northern lands. The almond and peach-trees were in blossom; and the vine-dresser sang at his work, perched with his pruning-knife among the trees. Blossoms and flowers, in laughing plenty, graced the soil; and the trees, swelling with buds ready to expand into leaves, seemed to feel the life that animated their dark old boughs. Flora was enchanted; the country labours interested her, and the hoarded experience of old Sandra was a treasure-house of wisdom and amusement. Her attention had hitherto been directed to giving the most vivid hues and truest imitation to her transcript with her needle of some picture given her as a model; but here was a novel occupation.—She learned the history of the bees, watched the habits of the birds, and inquired into the culture of plants. Sandra was delighted with her new companion; and, though notorious for being cross, yet could wriggle her antique lips into smiles for Flora.

To repay the kindness of her guardian and his mother, she still devoted much time to her needle. This occupation but engaged half her attentions; and while she pursued it, she could give herself up to endless reverie on the subject of Lorenzo's fortunes. Three years had flown since he had left her; and, except a little gold cross brought to her by a pilgrim from Milan, but one month after his departure, she had received no tidings of him. Whether from Milan he had proceeded to France, Germany, or the Holy Land, she did not know; by turns her fancy led him to either of these places, and fashioned the course of events that might have befallen him. She figured to herself his toilsome journeys—his life in the camp—his achievements, and the honours showered on him by kings and nobles: her cheek glowed at the praises he received, and her eye kindled with delight as it imaged him standing with modest pride and an erect but gentle mien before them. Then the fair enthusiast paused; it crossed her recollection like a shadow, that if all had gone prosperously, he had returned to share his prosperity with her, and her faltering heart turned to sadder scenes to account for his protracted absence.

Sometimes, while thus employed, she brought her work into the trellised arbour of the garden, or, when it was too warm for the open air, she had a favourite shady window, which looked down a deep ravine into a majestic wood, whence the sound of falling water met her ears. One day, while she employed her fingers upon the spirited likeness of a hound which made a part of the hunting-piece she was working for the countess, a sharp, wailing cry suddenly broke on her ear, followed by trampling of horses and the hurried steps and loud vociferations of men. They entered the villa on the opposite side from that which her window commanded; but the noise continuing, she rose to ask the reason, when Sandra burst into the room, crying, "O Madonna! he is dead! come and help him;—he has been thrown from his horse, and he will never speak more." Flora, for an instant, could only think of her brother, as if expecting to see him stretched on his bier. She rushed past the old woman, down into the great hall, in which, lying on a rude litter of boughs, she beheld the inanimate body of Count Fabian. He was surrounded by servitors and peasants, who were all clasping their hands and tearing their hair as, with frightful shrieks, they pressed round their lord, not one of them endeavouring to restore him to life. Flora's first impulse was to retire; but, casting a second glance on the livid brow of the young count, she saw his eyelids move, and the blood falling in quick drops from his hair on the pavement; she exclaimed, "He is not dead—he bleeds! hasten some of you for a leech!" And meanwhile she hurried to get some water, sprinkled it on his face, and, dispersing the group that hung over him and impeded the free air, the soft breeze playing on his forehead revived him, and he gave manifest tokens of life; so that when the physician arrived, he found that, though he was seriously and even dangerously hurt, every hope might be entertained of his recovery.

Flora undertook the office of his nurse, and fulfilled its duties with unwearied attention. She watched him by night and waited on him by day with that spirit of Christian humility and benevolence which animates a Sister of Charity as she tends the sick. For several days Fabian's soul seemed on the wing to quit its earthly abode; and the state of weakness that followed his insensibility was scarcely less alarming. At length, he recognized and acknowledged the care of Flora, but she alone possessed any power to calm and guide him during the state of irritability and fever that then ensued. Nothing except her presence controlled his impatience; before her he was so lamb-like, that she could scarcely have credited the accounts that others gave her of his violence, but that, whenever she returned, after leaving him for any time, she heard his voice far off in anger, and found him with flushed cheeks and flashing eyes, all which demonstrations subsided into meek acquiescence when she drew near.

In a few weeks he was able to quit his room; but the motion of his horse was forbidden him, and any noise or sudden sound drove him almost insane. So loud is an Italian's quietest movements, that Flora was obliged to prevent the approach of any except herself; and her soft voice and noiseless footfall were the sweetest medicine she could administer to her patient. It was painful to her to be in perpetual attendance on Loren-zo's rival and foe, but she subdued her heart to her duty, and custom helped to reconcile her. As he grew better, she could not help remarking the intelligence of his countenance, and the kindness and cordiality of his manners. There was an unobtrusive and delicate attention and care in his intercourse with her that won her to be pleased. When he conversed, his discourse was full of entertainment and variety. His memory was well-stored with numerous *fabliaux, novelle,* and romances, which he quickly discovered to be highly interesting to her, and so contrived to have one always ready from the exhaustless stock he possessed. These romantic stories reminded her of the imaginary adventures she had invented, in solitude and silence, for her brother; and each tale of foreign countries had a peculiar charm, which animated her face as she listened, so that Fabian could have gone on for ever, only to mark the varying expression of her countenance as he proceeded. Yet she acknowledged these attrac-tions in him as a Catholic nun may the specious virtues of a heretic; and, while he contrived each day to increase the pleasure she derived from his society, she satisfied her conscience with regard to her brother by cherish-ing in secret a little quiet stock of family hate, and by throwing over her manners, whenever she could recollect so to do, a cold and ceremonious tone, which she had the pleasure of seeing vexed him heartily.

Nearly two months had passed, and he was so well recovered, that Flora began to wonder that he did not return to Sienna, and of course to fulfil her duty by wishing that he should; and yet, while his cheek was sunk through past sickness, and his elastic step grown slow, she, as a nurse desirous of completing her good work, felt averse to his entering too soon on the scene of the busy town and its noisy pleasures. At length, two or three of his friends having come over to see him, he agreed to return with them to the city. A significant glance which they cast on his young nurse probably determined him. He parted from her with a grave courtesy and a profusion of thanks, unlike his usual manner, and rode off without alluding to any probability of their meeting again.

She fancied that she was relieved from a burthen when he went, and was surprised to find the days grow tedious, and mortified to perceive that her thoughts no longer spent themselves so spontaneously on her brother, and to feel that the occupation of a few weeks could unhinge her mind and dissipate her cherished reveries;—thus, while she felt annoyance from the absence of Fabian, she hated him the more for having, in addition to his other misdeeds, invaded the sanctuary of her dearest thoughts. She was beginning to conquer this listlessness, and to return with renewed zest to her usual occupations, when, in about a week after his departure, Fabian suddenly returned. He came upon her as she was gathering flowers for the shrine of the Madonna; and, on seeing him, she blushed as rosy red as the roses she held. He looked infinitely worse in health than when he went: his wan cheeks and sunk eyes excited her concern; and her earnest and kind questions somewhat revived him. He kissed her hand, and continued to stand beside her as she finished her nosegay. Had any one seen the glad, fond look with which he regarded her as she busied herself among the flowers, even old Sandra might have prognosticated his entire recovery under her care.

Flora was totally unaware of the feelings that were excited in Fabian's heart, and the struggle he made to overcome a passion too sweet and too seductive, when awakened by so lovely a being, ever to be subdued. He had been struck with her some time ago, and avoided her. It was through his suggestion that she passed the period of the countess's pilgrimage in this secluded villa; nor had he thought of visiting her there; but, riding over one day to inquire concerning a foal rearing for him, his horse had thrown him, and caused him that injury which had made him so long the inmate of the same abode. Already prepared to admire her—her kindness, her gentleness, and her unwearied patience during his illness, easily conquered a heart most ready and yet most unwilling to yield. He had returned to Sienna resolved to forget her; but he came back assured that his life and death were in her hands.

At first Count Fabian had forgot that he had any but his own feelings and prejudices, and those of his mother and kindred, to overcome; but when the tyranny of love vanquished these, he began to fear a more insurmountable impediment in Flora. The first whisper of love fell like mortal sin upon her ear; and disturbed, and even angry, she replied:

"Methinks you wholly forget who I am, and what you are. I speak not of ancient feuds, though there were enough to divide us for ever. Know that I hate you as my brother's murderer. Restore Lorenzo to me—recall him from banishment—erase the memory of all that he has suffered through you—win his love and approbation; and when all this is fulfilled, which never can be, speak a language which now it is as the bitterness of death for me to hear!"

And saying this, she hastily retired, to conceal the floods of tears which this, as she termed it, insult had caused to flow; to lament yet more deeply her brother's absence and her own dependence.

Fabian was not so easily silenced; and Flora had no wish to renew scenes and expressions of violence so foreign to her nature. She imposed a rule on herself, never swerving from which she hoped to destroy the ill-omened love of her protector. She absented herself from him as much as possible; and when with him assumed such chilling indifference of manner, and made apparent in her silence so absolute and cold a rejection of all his persuasions, that had not love with its unvanquishable hopes reigned absolutely in young Fabian's heart, he must have despaired. He ceased to speak of his affection, so to win back her ancient kindness. This was at first difficult; for she was timid as a young bird, whose feet have touched the limed twigs. But naturally credulous, and quite inexperienced, she soon began to believe that her alarm was exaggerated, and to resume those habits of intimacy which had heretofore subsisted between them. By degrees Fabian contrived to insinuate the existence of his attachment—he could not help it. He asked no return—he would wait for Lorenzo's arrival, which he was sure could not be far distant. Her displeasure could not change, nor silence destroy, a sentiment which survived in spite of both. Intrenched in her coldness and her indifference, she could not quarrel with each word he spoke; and hoping to weary him out by her defensive warfare, she fancied that he would soon cease his pursuit in disgust.

The countess had been long away; she had proceeded on to view the feast of San Gennaro at Naples, and had not received tidings of her son's illness. She was now expected back; and Fabian, still lingering at the villa, resolved to return to Sienna in time to receive her. Both he and Flora were therefore surprised one day, when she suddenly entered the apartment where they both were. Flora had long peremptorily insisted that he should not intrude while she was employed on her embroidery frame; but this day he had made so good a pretext, that for the first time he was admitted, and then suffered to stay a few minutes—they now neither of them knew how long; she was busy at her work; and he sitting near, gazing unreproved on her unconscious face and graceful figure, felt himself happier than he had ever been before.

The countess was sufficiently surprised, and not a little angry; but before she could do more than utter one exclamation, Fabian interrupted, by entreating her not to spoil all. He drew her away—he made his own explanations, and urged his wishes with resistless persuasion. The countess had been used to indulge him in every wish; it was impossible for her to deny any strongly urged request; his pertinacity—his agitation—his entreaties half won her; and the account of his illness, and his assurances, seconded by those of all the family, that Flora had saved his life, completed the conquest, and she became in her turn a suitor for her son, to the orphan daughter of Mancini.

Flora, educated till the age of twelve by one who never consulted his own pleasures and gratifications, but went right on in the path of duty, regardless of pain or disappointment, had no idea of doing aught merely because she or others might wish it. Since that time she had been thrown on her own resources; and jealously cherishing her individuality in the midst of her enemies, every feeling of her heart had been strengthened by solitude and by a sense of mental independence. She was the least likely of any one to go with the stream, or to yield to the mere influence of circumstances. She felt, she knew, what it became her to do, and that must be done in spite of every argument.

The countess's expostulations and entreaties were of no avail. The promise she had made to her brother of engaging herself by no vow for five years must be observed under every event; it was asked her at the sad and solemn hour of their parting, and was thus rendered doubly sacred. So constituted, indeed, were her feelings, that the slightest wish ever remembered by her having been expressed by Lorenzo, had more weight with her than the most urgent prayers of another. He was a part of her religion; reverence and love for him had been moulded into the substance of her soul from infancy; their very separation had tended to render these impressions irradicable. She brooded over them for years; and when no sympathy or generous kindness was afforded her—when the countess treated her like an inferior and a dependant, and Fabian had forgotten her existence, she had lived from month to month, and from year to year, cherishing the image of her brother, and only able to tolerate the annoyances that beset her existence, by considering that her patience, her fortitude, and her obedience, were all offerings at the shrine of her beloved Lorenzo's desires.

It is true that the generous and kindly disposition of Fabian won her to regard him with a feeling nearly approaching tenderness, though this emotion was feeble, the mere ripple of the waves, compared to the mighty tide of affection that set her will all one way, and made her deem every thing trivial except Lorenzo's return—Lorenzo's existence—obedience to Lorenzo. She listened to her lover's persuasions so unyieldingly that the countess was provoked by her inflexibility; but she bore her reproaches with such mildness, and smiled so sweetly, that Fabian was the more charmed. She admitted that she owed him a certain submission as the

guardian set over her by her brother; Fabian would have gladly exchanged this authority for the pleasure of being commanded by her; but
this was an honour he could not attain, so in playful spite he enforced
concessions from her. At his desire she appeared in society, dressed as
became her rank, and filled in his house the station a sister of his own
would have held. She preferred seclusion, but she was averse to contention, and it was little that she yielded, while the purpose of her soul was
as fixed as ever.

The fifth year of Lorenzo's exile was now drawing to a close, but he
did not return, nor had any intelligence been received of him. The decree
of his banishment had been repealed, the fortunes of his house restored,
and his palace, under Fabian's generous care, rebuilt. These were acts
that demanded and excited Flora's gratitude; yet they were performed in
an unpretending manner, as if the citizens of Sienna had suddenly become
just and wise, without his interference. But these things dwindled into
trifles while the continuation of Lorenzo's absence seemed the pledge of
her eternal misery; and the tacit appeal made to her kindness, while she
had no thought but for her brother, drove her to desperation. She could
no longer tolerate the painful anomaly of her situation;—she could not
endure her suspense for her brother's fate, nor the reproachful glances of
Fabian's mother and his friends. He himself was more generous,—he
read her heart, and, as the termination of the fifth year drew nigh, ceased
to allude to his own feelings, and appeared as wrapt as herself in doubt
concerning the fate of the noble youth, whom they could scarcely entertain a hope of ever seeing more. This was small comfort to Flora. She had
resolved that when the completion of the fifth year assured her that her
brother was for ever lost, she would never see Fabian again. At first she
had resolved to take refuge in a convent, and in the sanctity of religious
vows. But she remembered how averse Lorenzo had always shown himself to this vocation, and that he had preferred to place her beneath the
roof of his foe, than within the walls of a nunnery. Besides, young as she
was, and despite herself, full of hope, she recoiled from shutting the gates
of life upon herself for ever. Notwithstanding her fears and sorrow, she
clung to the belief that Lorenzo lived; and this led her to another plan.
When she had received her little cross from Milan, it was accompanied by
a message, that he believed he had found a good friend in the archbishop
of that place. This prelate, therefore, would know whither Lorenzo had
first bent his steps, and to him she resolved to apply. Her scheme was
easily formed. She possessed herself of the garb of a pilgrim, and resolved
on the day following the completion of the fifth year to depart from
Sienna, and bend her steps towards Lombardy, buoyed up by the hope
that she should gain some tidings of the object of all her care.

Meanwhile Fabian had formed a similar resolve. He had learnt the fact from Flora, of Lorenzo having first resorted to Milan, and he determined to visit that city, and not to return without certain information. He acquainted his mother with his plan, but begged her not to inform Flora, that she might not be tortured by double doubt during his absence.

The anniversary of the fifth year was come, and with it the eve of these several and separate journeys. Flora had retired to spend the day at the villa before mentioned. She had chosen to retire thither for various reasons. Her escape was more practicable thence than in the town; and she was anxious to avoid seeing both Fabian and his mother, now that she was on the point of inflicting severe pain on them. She spent the day at the villa and in its gardens, musing on her plans, regretting the quiet of her past life—saddened on Fabian's account—grieving bitterly for Lorenzo. She was not alone, for she had been obliged to confide in one of her former companions, and to obtain her assistance. Poor little Angeline was dreadfully frightened with the trust reposed in her, but did not dare expostulate with or betray her friend; and she continued near her during this last day, by turns trying to console and weeping with her. Towards evening they wandered together into the wood contiguous to the villa. Flora had taken her harp with her, but her trembling fingers refused to strike its chords; she left it, she left her companion, and strayed on alone to take leave of a spot consecrated by many a former visit. Here the umbrageous trees gathered about her, and shaded her with their thick and drooping foliage;—a torrent dashed down from a neighbouring rock, and fell from a height into a rustic basin, hollowed to receive it; then, overflowing the margin at one spot, it continued falling over successive declivities, till it reached the bottom of a little ravine, when it stole on in a placid and silent course. This had ever been a favourite resort of Flora. The twilight of the wood and the perpetual flow, the thunder, the hurry, and the turmoil of the waters, the varied sameness of the eternal elements, accorded with the melancholy of her ideas, and the endless succession of her reveries. She came to it now; she gazed on the limpid cascade —for the last time; a soft sadness glistened in her eyes, and her attitude denoted the tender regret that filled her bosom;—her long bright tresses streaming in elegant disorder, her light veil and simple, yet rich, attire, were fitfully mirrored in the smooth face of the rushing waters. At this moment the sound of steps more firm and manly than those of Angeline struck her ear, and Fabian himself stood before her; he was unable to bring himself to depart on his journey without seeing her once again. He had ridden over to the villa, and, finding that she had quitted it, sought and found her in the lone recess where they had often spent hours together which had been full of bliss to him. Flora was sorry to see him, for her secret was on her lips, and yet she resolved not to give it utterance. He was ruled by the same feeling. Their interview was therefore short, and neither alluded to what sat nearest the heart of each. They parted with a simple "Good night," as if certain of meeting the following morning: each deceived the other, and each was in turn deceived. There was more of tenderness in Flora's manner than there had ever been; it cheered his faltering soul, about to quit her, while the anticipation of the blow he was about to receive from her made her regard as venial this momentary softening towards her brother's enemy.

Fabian passed the night at the villa, and early the next morning he departed for Milan. He was impatient to arrive at the end of his journey, and often he thrust his spurs into his horse's sides, and put him to his speed, which even then appeared slow. Yet he was aware that his arrival at Milan might advance him not a jot towards the ultimate object of his journey; and he called Flora cruel and unkind, until the recollection of her kind farewell came across to console and cheer him.

He stopped the first night at Empoli, and, crossing the Arno, began to ascend the Apennines on the northern side. Soon he penetrated their fastnesses, and entered deep into the ilex woods. He journeyed on perseveringly, and yet the obstructions he met with were many, and borne with impatience. At length, on the afternoon of the third day, he arrived at a little rustic inn, hid deep in a wood, which shewed signs of seldom being visited by travellers. The burning sun made it a welcome shelter for Fabian; and he deposited his steed in the stable, which he found already partly occupied by a handsome black horse, and then entered the inn to seek refreshment for himself. There seemed some difficulty in obtaining this. The landlady was the sole domestic, and it was long before she made her appearance, and then she was full of trouble and dismay; a sick traveller had arrived—a gentleman to all appearance dying of a malignant fever. His horse, his well-stored purse, and rich dress shewed that he was a cavalier of consequence:—the more the pity. There was no help, nor any means of carrying him forward; yet half his pain seemed to arise from his regret at being detained—he was so eager to proceed to Sienna. The name of his own town excited the interest of Count Fabian, and he went up to visit the stranger, while the hostess prepared his repast.

Meanwhile Flora awoke with the lark, and with the assistance of Angeline attired herself in her pilgrim's garb. From the stir below, she was surprised to find that Count Fabian had passed the night at the villa, and she lingered till he should have departed, as she believed, on his return to Sienna. Then she embraced her young friend, and taking leave of her with many blessings and thanks, alone, with heaven, as she trusted, for her guide, she quitted Fabian's sheltering roof, and with a heart that maintained its purpose in spite of her feminine timidity, began her pilgrimage.

Drawn by Miss Louisa Sharpe   *Engraved by Francis Engleheart*

FLORA

Her journey performed on foot was slow, so that there was no likelihood that she could overtake her lover, already many miles in the advance. Now that she had begun it, her undertaking appeared to her gigantic, and her heart almost failed her. The burning sun scorched her; never having before found herself alone in a highway, a thousand fears assailed her, and she grew so weary, that soon she was unable to support herself. By the advice of a landlady at an inn, where she stopped, she purchased a mule to help her on in her long drawn way. Yet with this help, it was the third night before she arrived at Empoli, and then crossing the Arno, as her lover had done before, her disasters seemed to begin to unfold themselves, and to grow gigantic, as she entered the dark woods of the Apennines, and found herself amidst the solitude of its vast forests. Her pilgrim's garb inspired some respect, and she rested at convents by the way. The pious sisters held up their hands in admiration of her courage; while her heart beat faintly with the knowledge that she possessed absolutely none. Yet, again and again, she repeated to herself, that the Apennines once passed, the worst would be over. So she toiled on, now weary, now frightened—very slowly, and yet very anxious to get on with speed.

On the evening of the seventh day after her quitting Sienna, she was still entangled in the mazes of these savage hills. She was to sleep at a convent on their summit that night, and the next day arrive at Bologna. This hope had cheered her through the day; but evening approached, the way grew more intricate, and no convent appeared. The sun had set, and she listened anxiously for the bell of the Ave Maria, which would give her hope that the goal she sought was nigh; but all was silent, save the swinging boughs of the vast trees, and the timid beating of her own heart; darkness closed around her, and despair came with the increased obscurity, till a twinkling light, revealing itself among the trees, afforded her some relief. She followed this beamy guide till it led her to a little inn, where the sight of a kind-looking woman and the assurance of safe shelter, dispelled her terrors, and filled her with grateful pleasure.

Seeing her so weary, the considerate hostess hastened to place food before her, and then conducted her to a little low room where her bed was prepared. "I am sorry, lady," said the landlady, in a whisper, "not to be able to accommodate you better; but a sick cavalier occupies my best room—it is next to this—and he sleeps now, and I would not disturb him. Poor gentleman! I never thought he would rise more; and under Heaven he owes his life to one who, whether he is related to him or not, I cannot tell, for he did not accompany him. Four days ago he stopped here, and I told him my sorrow—how I had a dying guest, and he charitably saw him, and has since then nursed him more like a twin brother than a stranger."

The good woman whispered on. Flora heard but little of what she said;

and overcome by weariness and sleep, paid no attention to her tale. But having performed her orisons, placed her head on the pillow, and was quickly lapped in the balmy slumber she so much needed.

Early in the morning she was awoke by a murmur of voices in the next room. She started up, and recalling her scattered thoughts, tried to remember the account the hostess had given her the preceding evening. The sick man spoke, but his accent was low, and the words did not reach her;—he was answered—could Flora believe her senses? did she not know the voice that spoke these words?—"Fear nothing, a sweet sleep has done you infinite good; and I rejoice in the belief that you will speedily recover. I have sent to Sienna for your sister, and do indeed expect that Flora will arrive this very day."

More was said, but Flora heard no more: she had risen, and was hastily dressing herself; in a few minutes she was by her brother's, her Lorenzo's bedside, kissing his wan hand, and assuring him that she was indeed Flora.

"These are indeed wonders," he at last said, "and if you are mine own Flora, you perhaps can tell me who this noble gentleman is, who day and night has watched beside me, as a mother may by her only child, giving no time to repose, but exhausting himself for me."

"How, dearest brother," said Flora, "can I truly answer your question? to mention the name of our benefactor were to speak of a mask and a disguise, not a true thing. He is my protector and guardian, who has watched over and preserved me, while you wandered far; his is the most generous heart in Italy, offering past enmity and family pride as sacrifices at the altar of nobleness and truth. He is the restorer of your fortunes in your native town——"

"And the lover of my sweet sister.—I have heard of these things, and was on my way to confirm his happiness and to find my own, when sickness laid me thus low, and would have destroyed us both for ever, but for Fabian Tolomei——"

"Who now exerts his expiring authority to put an end to this scene," interrupted the young count: "not till this day has Lorenzo been sufficiently composed to hear any of these explanations, and we risk his returning health by too long a conversation. The history of these things and of his long wanderings, now so happily ended, must be reserved for a future hour; when assembled in our beloved Sienna, exiles and foes no longer, we shall long enjoy the happiness which Providence, after so many trials, has bounteously reserved for us."

XIV

The Invisible Girl

THIS SLENDER NARRATIVE has no pretensions to the regularity of a story, or the development of situations and feelings; it is but a slight sketch, delivered nearly as it was narrated to me by one of the humblest of the actors concerned: nor will I spin out a circumstance interesting principally from its singularity and truth, but narrate, as concisely as I can, how I was surprised on visiting what seemed a ruined tower, crowning a bleak promontory overhanging the sea, that flows between Wales and Ireland, to find that though the exterior preserved all the savage rudeness that betokened many a war with the elements, the interior was fitted up somewhat in the guise of a summer-house, for it was too small to deserve any other name. It consisted but of the ground-floor, which served as an entrance, and one room above, which was reached by a staircase made out of the thickness of the wall. This chamber was floored and carpeted, decorated with elegant furniture; and, above all, to attract the attention and excite curiosity, there hung over the chimney-piece—for to preserve the apartment from damp a fire-place had been built evidently since it had assumed a guise so dissimilar to the object of its construction—a picture simply painted in water-colours, which seemed more than any part of the adornments of the room to be at war with the rudeness of the building, the solitude in which it was placed, and the desolation of the surrounding scenery. This drawing represented a lovely girl in the very pride and bloom of youth; her dress was simple, in the fashion of the day—(remember, reader, I write at the beginning of the eighteenth century), her countenance was embellished by a look of mingled innocence and intelligence, to which was added the imprint of serenity of soul and natural cheerfulness. She was reading one of those folio romances which have so long been the delight of the enthusiastic and young; her mandoline was at her feet—her parroquet perched on a huge mirror near her; the arrangement of furniture and hangings gave token of a luxurious

190

Painted by William Boxall   *Engraved by J. C. Edwards*

ROSINA

dwelling, and her attire also evidently that of home and privacy, yet bore with it an appearance of ease and girlish ornament, as if she wished to please. Beneath this picture was inscribed in golden letters, "The Invisible Girl."

Rambling about a country nearly uninhabited, having lost my way, and being overtaken by a shower, I had lighted on this dreary looking tenement, which seemed to rock in the blast, and to be hung up there as the very symbol of desolation. I was gazing wistfully and cursing inwardly my stars which led me to a ruin that could afford no shelter, though the storm began to pelt more seriously than before, when I saw an old woman's head popped out from a kind of loophole, and as suddenly withdrawn:— a minute after a feminine voice called to me from within, and penetrating a little brambly maze that skreened a door, which I had not before observed, so skilfully had the planter succeeded in concealing art with nature, I found the good dame standing on the threshold and inviting me to take refuge within. "I had just come up from our cot hard by," she said, "to look after the things, as I do every day, when the rain came on—will ye walk up till it is over?" I was about to observe that the cot hard by, at the venture of a few rain drops, was better than a ruined tower, and to ask my kind hostess whether "the things" were pigeons or crows that she was come to look after, when the matting of the floor and the carpeting of the staircase struck my eye. I was still more surprised when I saw the room above; and beyond all, the picture and its singular inscription, naming her invisible, whom the painter had coloured forth into very agreeable visibility, awakened my most lively curiosity: the result of this, of my exceeding politeness towards the old woman, and her own natural garrulity, was a kind of garbled narrative which my imagination eked out, and future inquiries rectified, till it assumed the following form.

Some years before in the afternoon of a September day, which, though tolerably fair, gave many tokens of a tempestuous evening, a gentleman arrived at a little coast town about ten miles from this place; he expressed his desire to hire a boat to carry him to the town of —— about fifteen miles further on the coast. The menaces which the sky held forth made the fishermen loathe to venture, till at length two, one the father of a numerous family, bribed by the bountiful reward the stranger promised— the other, the son of my hostess, induced by youthful daring, agreed to undertake the voyage. The wind was fair, and they hoped to make good way before nightfall, and to get into port ere the rising of the storm. They pushed off with good cheer, at least the fishermen did; as for the stranger, the deep mourning which he wore was not half so black as the melancholy that wrapt his mind. He looked as if he had never smiled—as if some unutterable thought, dark as night and bitter as death, had built its nest within his bosom, and brooded therein eternally; he did not mention his name; but one of the villagers recognised him as Henry Vernon, the son of a baronet who possessed a mansion about three miles distant from the town for which he was bound. This mansion was almost abandoned by the family; but Henry had, in a romantic fit, visited it about three years before, and Sir Peter had been down there during the previous spring for about a couple of months.

The boat did not make so much way as was expected; the breeze failed them as they got out to sea, and they were fain with oar as well as sail, to try to weather the promontory that jutted out between them and the spot they desired to reach. They were yet far distant when the shifting wind began to exert its strength, and to blow with violent though unequal puffs. Night came on pitchy dark, and the howling waves rose and broke with frightful violence, menacing to overwhelm the tiny bark that dared resist their fury. They were forced to lower every sail, and take to their oars; one man was obliged to bale out the water, and Vernon himself took an oar, and rowing with desperate energy, equalled the force of the more practised boatmen. There had been much talk between the sailors before the tempest came on; now, except a brief command, all were silent. One thought of his wife and children, and silently cursed the caprice of the stranger that endangered in its effects, not only his life, but their welfare; the other feared less, for he was a daring lad, but he worked hard, and had no time for speech; while Vernon bitterly regretting the thoughtlessness which had made him cause others to share a peril, unimportant as far as he himself was concerned, now tried to cheer them with a voice full of animation and courage, and now pulled yet more strongly at the oar he held. The only person who did not seem wholly intent on the work he was about, was the man who baled; every now and then he gazed intently round, as if the sea held afar off, on its tumultuous waste, some object that he strained his eyes to discern. But all was blank, except as the crests of the high waves showed themselves, or far out on the verge of the horizon, a kind of lifting of the clouds betokened greater violence for the blast. At length he exclaimed—"Yes, I see it!—the larboard oar!—now! if we can make yonder light, we are saved!" Both the rowers instinctively turned their heads,—but cheerless darkness answered their gaze.

"You cannot see it," cried their companion, "but we are nearing it; and, please God, we shall outlive this night." Soon he took the oar from Vernon's hand, who, quite exhausted, was failing in his strokes. He rose and looked for the beacon which promised them safety;—it glimmered with so faint a ray, that now he said, "I see it;" and again, "it is nothing:" still, as they made way, it dawned upon his sight, growing more steady and distinct as it beamed across the lurid waters, which themselves became smoother, so that safety seemed to arise from the bosom of the ocean under the influence of that flickering gleam.

"What beacon is it that helps us at our need?" asked Vernon, as the men, now able to manage their oars with greater ease, found breath to answer his question.

"A fairy one, I believe," replied the elder sailor, "yet no less a true: it burns in an old tumble-down tower, built on the top of a rock which looks over the sea. We never saw it before this summer; and now each night it is to be seen,—at least when it is looked for, for we cannot see it from our village;—and it is such an out of the way place that no one has need to go near it, except through a chance like this. Some say it is burnt by witches, some say by smugglers; but this I know, two parties have been to search, and found nothing but the bare walls of the tower. All is deserted by day, and dark by night; for no light was to be seen while we were there, though it burned sprightly enough when we were out at sea."

"I have heard say," observed the younger sailor, "it is burnt by the ghost of a maiden who lost her sweetheart in these parts; he being wrecked, and his body found at the foot of the tower: she goes by the name among us of the 'Invisible Girl.'"

The voyagers had now reached the landing-place at the foot of the tower. Vernon cast a glance upward,—the light was still burning. With some difficulty, struggling with the breakers, and blinded by night, they contrived to get their little bark to shore, and to draw her up on the beach: they then scrambled up the precipitous pathway, overgrown by weeds and underwood, and, guided by the more experienced fishermen, they found the entrance to the tower, door or gate there was none, and all was dark as the tomb, and silent and almost as cold as death.

"This will never do," said Vernon; "surely our hostess will show her light, if not herself, and guide our darkling steps by some sign of life and comfort."

"We will get to the upper chamber," said the sailor, "if I can but hit upon the broken down steps: but you will find no trace of the Invisible Girl nor her light either, I warrant."

"Truly a romantic adventure of the most disagreeable kind," muttered Vernon, as he stumbled over the unequal ground: "she of the beacon-light must be both ugly and old, or she would not be so peevish and inhospitable."

With considerable difficulty, and, after divers knocks and bruises, the adventurers at length succeeded in reaching the upper story; but all was blank and bare, and they were fain to stretch themselves on the hard floor, when weariness, both of mind and body, conduced to steep their senses in sleep.

Long and sound were the slumbers of the mariners. Vernon but forgot himself for an hour; then, throwing off drowsiness, and finding his rough couch uncongenial to repose, he got up and placed himself at the hole that served for a window, for glass there was none, and there being not even a rough bench, he leant his back against the embrasure, as the only rest he could find. He had forgotten his danger, the mysterious beacon, and its invisible guardian: his thoughts were occupied on the horrors of his own fate, and the unspeakable wretchedness that sat like a night-mare on his heart.

It would require a good-sized volume to relate the causes which had changed the once happy Vernon into the most woeful mourner that ever clung to the outer trappings of grief, as slight though cherished symbols of the wretchedness within. Henry was the only child of Sir Peter Vernon, and as much spoiled by his father's idolatry as the old baronet's violent and tyrannical temper would permit. A young orphan was educated in his father's house, who in the same way was treated with generosity and kindness, and yet who lived in deep awe of Sir Peter's authority, who was a widower; and these two children were all he had to exert his power over, or to whom to extend his affection. Rosina was a cheerful-tempered girl, a little timid, and careful to avoid displeasing her protector; but so docile, so kind-hearted, and so affectionate, that she felt even less than Henry the discordant spirit of his parent. It is a tale often told; they were playmates and companions in childhood, and lovers in after days. Rosina was frightened to imagine that this secret affection, and the vows they pledged, might be disapproved of by Sir Peter. But sometimes she consoled herself by thinking that perhaps she was in reality her Henry's destined bride, brought up with him under the design of their future union; and Henry, while he felt that this was not the case, resolved to wait only until he was of age to declare and accomplish his wishes in making the sweet Rosina his wife. Meanwhile he was careful to avoid premature discovery of his intentions, so to secure his beloved girl from persecution and insult. The old gentleman was very conveniently blind; he lived always in the country, and the lovers spent their lives together, unrebuked and uncontrolled. It was enough that Rosina played on her mandoline, and sang Sir Peter to sleep every day after dinner; she was the sole female in the house above the rank of a servant, and had her own way in the disposal of her time. Even when Sir Peter frowned, her innocent caresses and sweet voice were powerful to smooth the rough current of his temper. If ever human spirit lived in an earthly paradise, Rosina did at this time: her pure love was made happy by Henry's constant presence; and the confidence they felt in each other, and the security with which they looked forward to the future, rendered their path one of roses under a cloudless sky. Sir Peter was the slight drawback that only rendered their *tête-à-tête* more delightful, and gave value to the sympathy they each bestowed on the other. All at once an ominous personage made its appearance in Vernon-Place, in the shape of a widow sister of Sir Peter, who, having succeeded in killing her husband and children with the effects of her vile temper, came, like a harpy, greedy for new prey, under her brother's roof. She too soon detected the attachment of the unsuspicious pair. She made all speed to impart her discovery to her brother, and at once to restrain and inflame his rage. Through her contrivance Henry was suddenly despatched on his travels abroad, that the coast might be clear for the persecution of Rosina; and then the richest of the lovely girl's many admirers, whom, under Sir Peter's single reign, she was allowed, nay, almost commanded, to dismiss, so desirous was he of keeping her for his own comfort, was selected, and she was ordered to marry him. The scenes of violence to which she was now exposed, the bitter taunts of the odious Mrs. Bainbridge, and the reckless fury of Sir Peter, were the more frightful and overwhelming from their novelty. To all she could only oppose a silent, tearful, but immutable steadiness of purpose: no threats, no rage could extort from her more than a touching prayer that they would not hate her, because she could not obey.

"There must be something we don't see under all this," said Mrs. Bainbridge, "take my word for it, brother,—she corresponds secretly with Henry. Let us take her down to your seat in Wales, where she will have no pensioned beggars to assist her; and we shall see if her spirit be not bent to our purpose."

Sir Peter consented, and they all three posted down to ——shire, and took up their abode in the solitary and dreary looking house before alluded to as belonging to the family. Here poor Rosina's sufferings grew intolerable:—before, surrounded by well-known scenes, and in perpetual intercourse with kind and familiar faces, she had not despaired in the end of conquering by her patience the cruelty of her persecutors;—nor had she written to Henry, for his name had not been mentioned by his relatives, nor their attachment alluded to, and she felt an instinctive wish to escape the dangers about her without his being annoyed, or the sacred secret of her love being laid bare, and wronged by the vulgar abuse of his aunt or the bitter curses of his father. But when she was taken to Wales, and made a prisoner in her apartment, when the flinty mountains about her seemed feebly to imitate the stony hearts she had to deal with, her courage began to fail. The only attendant permitted to approach her was Mrs. Bainbridge's maid; and under the tutelage of her fiend-like mistress, this woman was used as a decoy to entice the poor prisoner into confidence, and then to be betrayed. The simple, kind-hearted Rosina was a facile dupe, and at last, in the excess of her despair, wrote to Henry, and gave the letter to this woman to be forwarded. The letter in itself would have softened marble; it did not speak of their mutual vows, it but asked him to intercede with his father, that he would restore her to the kind place she had formerly held in his affections, and cease from a cruelty that would destroy her. "For I may die," wrote the hapless girl, "but marry another—never!" That single word, indeed, had sufficed to betray her secret, had it not been already discovered; as it was, it gave increased fury to Sir Peter, as his sister triumphantly pointed it out to him, for it need hardly be said that while the ink of the address was yet wet, and the seal still warm, Rosina's letter was carried to this lady. The culprit was summoned before them; what ensued none could tell; for their own sakes the cruel pair tried to palliate their part. Voices were high, and the soft murmur of Rosina's tone was lost in the howling of Sir Peter and the snarling of his sister. "Out of doors you shall go," roared the old man; "under my roof you shall not spend another night." And the words "infamous seductress," and worse, such as had never met the poor girl's ear before, were caught by listening servants; and to each angry speech of the baronet, Mrs. Bainbridge added an envenomed point worse than all.

More dead than alive, Rosina was at last dismissed. Whether guided by despair, whether she took Sir Peter's threats literally, or whether his sister's orders were more decisive, none knew, but Rosina left the house; a servant saw her cross the park, weeping, and wringing her hands as she went. What became of her none could tell; her disappearance was not disclosed to Sir Peter till the following day, and then he showed by his anxiety to trace her steps and to find her, that his words had been but idle threats. The truth was, that though Sir Peter went to frightful lengths to prevent the marriage of the heir of his house with the portionless orphan, the object of his charity, yet in his heart he loved Rosina, and half his violence to her rose from anger at himself for treating her so ill. Now remorse began to sting him, as messenger after messenger came back without tidings of his victim; he dared not confess his worst fears to himself; and when his inhuman sister, trying to harden her conscience by angry words, cried, "The vile hussy has too surely made away with herself out of revenge to us;" an oath, the most tremendous, and a look sufficient to make even her tremble, commanded her silence. Her conjecture, however, appeared too true: a dark and rushing stream that flowed at the extremity of the park had doubtless received the lovely form, and quenched the life of this unfortunate girl. Sir Peter, when his endeavours to find her proved fruitless, returned to town, haunted by the image of his victim, and forced to acknowledge in his own heart that he would willingly lay down his life, could he see her again, even though it were as the bride of his son—his son, before whose questioning he quailed like the veriest coward; for when Henry was told of the death of Rosina, he suddenly returned from abroad to ask the cause—to visit her grave, and mourn her loss in the groves and valleys which had been the scenes of their mutual happiness. He made a thousand inquiries, and an ominous silence alone replied. Growing more earnest and more anxious, at length he drew from servants and dependants, and his odious aunt herself, the whole dreadful truth. From that moment despair struck his heart, and misery named him her own. He fled from his father's presence; and the recollection that one whom he ought to revere was guilty of so dark a crime, haunted him, as of old the Eumenides tormented the souls of men given up to their torturings. His first, his only wish, was to visit Wales, and to learn if any new discovery had been made, and whether it were possible to recover the mortal remains of the lost Rosina, so to satisfy the unquiet longings of his miserable heart. On this expedition was he bound, when he made his appearance at the village before named; and now in the deserted tower, his thoughts were busy with images of despair and death, and what his beloved one had suffered before her gentle nature had been goaded to such a deed of woe.

While immersed in gloomy reverie, to which the monotonous roaring of the sea made fit accompaniment, hours flew on, and Vernon was at last aware that the light of morning was creeping from out its eastern retreat, and dawning over the wild ocean, which still broke in furious tumult on the rocky beach. His companions now roused themselves, and prepared to depart. The food they had brought with them was damaged by sea water, and their hunger, after hard labour and many hours fasting, had become ravenous. It was impossible to put to sea in their shattered boat; but there stood a fisher's cot about two miles off, in a recess in the bay, of which the promontory on which the tower stood formed one side, and to this they hastened to repair; they did not spend a second thought on the light which had saved them, nor its cause, but left the ruin in search of a more hospitable asylum. Vernon cast his eyes round as he quitted it, but no vestige of an inhabitant met his eye, and he began to persuade himself that the beacon had been a creation of fancy merely. Arriving at the cottage in question, which was inhabited by a fisherman and his family, they made an homely breakfast, and then prepared to return to the tower, to refit their boat, and if possible bring her round. Vernon accompanied them, together with their host and his son. Several questions were asked concerning the Invisible Girl and her light, each agreeing that the apparition was novel, and not one being able to give even an explanation of how the name had become affixed to the unknown cause of this singular appearance; though both of the men of the cottage affirmed that once or twice they had seen a female figure in the adjacent wood, and that now and then a stranger girl made her appearance at another cot a mile off, on the other side of the promontory, and bought bread; they suspected both these to be the same, but could not tell. The inhabitants of the cot, indeed, appeared too stupid even to feel curiosity, and had never made any attempt at discovery. The whole day was spent by the sailors in repairing the boat; and the sound of hammers, and the voices of the men at work, resounded along the coast, mingled with the dashing of the waves. This was no time to explore the ruin for one who whether human or supernatural so evidently withdrew herself from intercourse with every living being. Vernon, however, went over the tower, and searched every nook in vain; the dingy bare walls bore no token of serving as a shelter; and even a little recess in the wall of the staircase, which he had not before observed, was equally empty and desolate. Quitting the tower, he wandered in the pine wood that surrounded it, and giving up all thought of solving the mystery, was soon engrossed by thoughts that touched his heart more nearly, when suddenly there appeared on the ground at his feet the vision of a slipper. Since Cinderella so tiny a slipper had never been seen; as plain as shoe could speak, it told a tale of elegance, loveliness, and youth. Vernon picked it up; he had often admired Rosina's singularly small foot, and his first thought was a question whether this little slipper would have fitted it. It was very strange!—it must belong to the Invisible Girl. Then there was a fairy form that kindled that light, a form of such material substance, that its foot needed to be shod; and yet how shod?—with kid so fine, and of shape so exquisite, that it exactly resembled such as Rosina wore! Again the recurrence of the image of the beloved dead came forcibly across him; and a thousand home-felt associations, childish yet sweet, and lover-like though trifling, so filled Vernon's heart, that he threw himself his length on the ground, and wept more bitterly than ever the miserable fate of the sweet orphan.

In the evening the men quitted their work, and Vernon returned with them to the cot where they were to sleep, intending to pursue their voyage, weather permitting, the following morning. Vernon said nothing of his slipper, but returned with his rough associates. Often he looked back; but the tower rose darkly over the dim waves, and no light appeared. Preparations had been made in the cot for their accommodation, and the only bed in it was offered Vernon; but he refused to deprive his hostess, and spreading his cloak on a heap of dry leaves, endeavoured to give himself up to repose. He slept for some hours; and when he awoke, all was still, save that the hard breathing of the sleepers in the same room with him interrupted the silence. He rose, and going to the window, looked out over the now placid sea towards the mystic tower; the light was burning there, sending its slender rays across the waves. Congratulating himself on a circumstance he had not anticipated, Vernon softly left the cottage, and, wrapping his cloak round him, walked with a swift pace round the bay towards the tower. He reached it; still the light was burning. To enter and restore the maiden her shoe, would be but an act of courtesy; and Vernon intended to do this with such caution, as to come unaware, before its wearer could, with her accustomed arts, withdraw herself from his eyes; but, unluckily, while yet making his way up the narrow pathway, his foot dislodged a loose fragment, that fell with crash and sound down the precipice. He sprung forward, on this, to retrieve by speed the advantage he had lost by this unlucky accident. He reached the door; he entered: all was silent, but also all was dark. He paused in the room below; he felt sure that a slight sound met his ear. He ascended the steps, and entered the upper chamber; but blank obscurity met his penetrating gaze, the starless night admitted not even a twilight glimmer through the only aperture. He closed his eyes, to try, on opening them again, to be able to catch some faint, wandering ray on the visual nerve; but it was in vain. He groped round the room: he stood still, and held his breath; and then, listening intently, he felt sure that another occupied the chamber with him, and that its atmosphere was slightly agitated by another's respiration. He remembered the recess in the staircase; but, before he approached it, he spoke:—he hesitated a moment what to say. "I must believe," he said, "that misfortune alone can cause your seclusion; and if the assistance of a man—of a gentleman——"

An exclamation interrupted him; a voice from the grave spoke his name—the accents of Rosina syllabled, "Henry!—is it indeed Henry whom I hear?"

He rushed forward, directed by the sound, and clasped in his arms the living form of his own lamented girl—his own Invisible Girl he called her; for even yet, as he felt her heart beat near his, and as he entwined her waist with his arm, supporting her as she almost sank to the ground with agitation, he could not see her; and, as her sobs prevented her speech, no sense, but the instinctive one that filled his heart with tumultuous gladness, told him that the slender, wasted form he pressed so fondly was the living shadow of the Hebe beauty he had adored.

The morning saw this pair thus strangely restored to each other on the tranquil sea, sailing with a fair wind for L——, whence they were to proceed to Sir Peter's seat, which, three months before, Rosina had quitted in such agony and terror. The morning light dispelled the shadows that had veiled her, and disclosed the fair person of the Invisible Girl. Altered indeed she was by suffering and woe, but still the same sweet smile played on her lips, and the tender light of her soft blue eyes were all her own. Vernon drew out the slipper, and showed the cause that had occasioned him to resolve to discover the guardian of the mystic beacon; even now he dared not inquire how she had existed in that desolate spot, or wherefore she had so sedulously avoided observation, when the right thing to have been done was, to have sought him immediately, under whose care, protected by whose love, no danger need be feared. But Rosina shrunk from him as he spoke, and a death-like pallor came over her cheek, as she faintly whispered, "Your father's curse—your father's dreadful threats!" It appeared, indeed, that Sir Peter's violence, and the cruelty of Mrs. Bainbridge, had succeeded in impressing Rosina with wild and unvanquishable terror. She had fled from their house without plan or forethought—driven by frantic horror and overwhelming fear, she had left it with scarcely any money, and there seemed to her no possibility of either returning or proceeding onward. She had no friend except Henry in the wide world; whither could she go?—to have sought Henry would have sealed their fates to misery; for, with an oath, Sir Peter had declared he would rather see them both in their coffins than married. After wandering about, hiding by day, and only venturing forth at night, she had come to this deserted tower, which seemed a place of refuge. How she had lived since then she could hardly tell;—she had lingered in the woods by day, or slept in the vault of the tower, an asylum none were acquainted with or had discovered: by night she burned the pine-cones of the wood, and night was her dearest time; for it seemed to her as if security came with darkness. She was unaware that Sir Peter had left that part of the country, and was terrified lest her hiding-place should be revealed to him. Her only hope was that Henry would return—that Henry would never rest till he had found her. She confessed that the long interval and the approach of winter had visited her with dismay; she feared that, as her strength was failing, and her form wasting to a skeleton, that she might die, and never see her own Henry more.

An illness, indeed, in spite of all his care, followed her restoration to security and the comforts of civilized life; many months went by before the bloom revisiting her cheeks, and her limbs regaining their roundness, she resembled once more the picture drawn of her in her days of bliss, before any visitation of sorrow. It was a copy of this portrait that decorated the tower, the scene of her suffering, in which I had found shelter. Sir Peter, overjoyed to be relieved from the pangs of remorse, and delighted again to see his orphan-ward, whom he really loved, was now as eager as before he had been averse to bless her union with his son: Mrs. Bainbridge they never saw again. But each year they spent a few months in their Welch mansion, the scene of their early wedded happiness, and the spot where again poor Rosina had awoke to life and joy after her cruel persecutions.

Henry's fond care had fitted up the tower, and decorated it as I saw; and often did he come over, with his "Invisible Girl," to renew, in the very scene of its occurrence, the remembrance of all the incidents which had led to their meeting again, during the shades of night, in that sequestered ruin.

XV

The Smuggler and His Family

Whose house is some lone bark,—whose toil the sea,
Whose prey the wandering fish, an evil lot
Has chosen.—MOSCHUS*

How SWIFTLY THE sweetest flowers fade when once expanded—they but
too quickly droop upon the stalk! How do human beings pass from the
brightness and bloom of hope and youth, into the dull fruition of life,
with all its cares and woes! There is no sadder, nor more humiliating sight,
than to contrast the shews of mid-life with the promise of its dawn, and to
see the furrows and the pale hues with which the hours with busy fingers
paint the smooth brow and glowing cheek. Our low-born but most sweet
heroine was once the pride of her hamlet—the kindest, gentlest but gayest
of the village maidens. If she ever sighed, a smile followed so swift
behind, that the picture was only softened not tainted by the change. Jane
sighed, alas! because she loved;—that leveller of rank, of intellect, and
too often of moral feeling, bound her to one unworthy of her. Yet then
the youthful sailor who had engaged her affections was not destitute of
merit. If he was wild and reckless, he was generous and brave. Jane's
father opposed this union, and she submitted to his control; but when his
death left her alone in the world, and her poverty secured her few and
cold friends, she gave herself without a fear to him, whose dearest wish
was to protect, support, and render happy the sweet being who confided
her existence to his care.

These occurrences were many years old, and we draw the veil from
before her wedded life;—when the lapse of time had brought other persons, other interests on the scene. Beneath a rugged lonely crag, on the
solitary wild sea-shore, at the extreme point of Cornwall—was a rude
cot, which, somewhat sheltered from behind, was exposed to the whole
fury of the southern gales. No flower could bloom in its scant waste
garden, under the influence of the frequent spray; and the tree that rose in

* Percy Shelley's translation, published with *Alastor*, 1816 (Ed.).

203

mockery above the roof, had withered at its summit, as the roots penetrating the ungenial soil found no nourishment for the leafless boughs. The cot was thatched, and weather-beaten as it was, the strange rich colouring with which the sea and wind had painted it, made it contrast picturesquely with the white cliff and pale sands. The interior of this humble dwelling was poverty-stricken yet clean, and with some attempt at neatness. The family within sat at their frugal supper; there was besides on the scantly-covered table, a dark case bottle, frequently clutched by the master of the hut. Jane it was who sat there; her eyes having lost their lustre—her hair its golden hue—her complexion all its brightness. She was thin, faded, care-worn: yet a sweet patient smile played upon her lips, and her subdued voice possessed the same melody which had made her laugh so cheering in her happier hour. On her knee lay asleep a little cherub, but a few months old; and another child, of about three years, was greedily devouring his supper. But Jane's eyes were fixed on one some years his senior, her eldest—her darling—the only one surviving out of several born in her better days. He was about fourteen—with his mother's eyes and smile, a ruddy complexion, and such frankness on his brow, such alacrity in all his motions, as bespoke his lightsome heart and kind disposition. With louring glance—weather-worn cheeks, and an expression of mixed ferocity and endurance—sat the husband and the father, who had so ill fulfilled his part in life.

He had been bred a sailor, and on his marriage turned fisherman. Untamed passions and evil courses brought on ruin; he was forced to quit the village where he was known, and fixing himself in this desolate spot, he soon became acquainted with a desperate gang of smugglers, who persuaded him to become one of them. A remnant of shame at first induced him to conceal this new misfortune from his wife; but a pack of goods to be concealed, and a search to be evaded, forced him to disclose his secret. Since then his better feelings seemed quite to desert him, and in talk and action he assimilated himself more and more to his lawless, fierce associates. Jane's too gentle temper was incapable of coping with his rough nature, whom in spite of all she loved, even when she feared him. But far more deeply seated than the duteous, but thankless attachment she cherished as a wife, was her adoration of her son. She had been a fond daughter, and her tenderness as a mother was equally zealous and devoted. The sole reward she desired to reap for her virtues, the sole compensation for her sufferings, was to be derived from the gallant and affectionate disposition of her boy.

That he should endure the blighting ills of poverty was bad enough; that out of hearing of "village chimes," he should receive none of the benefits of civilized life—attend no school—scarce ever enter a church, and pass his days beyond the reach of public opinion and the natural restraints of society, which exert so salutary an influence over both rich and poor, was sufficing evil. That he should depend upon his parents for guidance through the tortuous paths of life, and that from her lips alone he should learn how to merit the approbation of God and man and his own conscience, were circumstances that made her pass many hours of anxious solicitude. But the reality was fraught with far greater perils.

It is no uncommon thing to find men hardening their hearts against the sense of right as regards themselves; setting the world and moral dictates at defiance, and yet painfully alive to the good name and rectitude of their children. It was this feeling that Jane had endeavoured to awaken in her husband's mind. She strove with all sweetness and gentleness to induce him to resolve that although he had been thrown by adversity on dangerous and (this she slurred over) criminal pursuits, yet that their offspring should be preserved from the hardships, the humiliations and the possible guilt attendant on a lawless mode of life. But she spoke to one formed of rugged and coarse materials—whose best virtue was a sturdy pride that made him glory in his shame. He listened with bitterness to his wife's persuasions—he swore that his son should not be brought up to despise and condemn him—and he defended with vulgar and plausible arguments his right to cheat the revenue, and to defend himself against the aggressions of its administrators.

There is no system of illegal traffic more venial in most eyes than smuggling. The laws on this score are perpetually transgressed, even by the legislators themselves—the revenue officers are held by every one in detestation, and they take a coarse pride in making themselves obnoxious. The courage, the activity, and the resource—the hardships and the dangers attendant on his pursuit, paints a smuggler in Salvator hues, and imparts a kind of heroic elevation to our idea of him. But to the anxious mother all this wore a different appearance; the unmasked truth was replete with deformity. Habits of intemperance and vice—a savage readiness to inflict injury—which though somewhat redeemed by daring to meet the same, filled the heart with such hate and violence, as was at utter war with the charity and love which distinguishes a virtuous character: an aptitude for stratagem and falsehood—which might be called resource, but which, coming in contact with the ingenuous and upright disposition of her son, she deemed frightful pollution. These were the lessons he was to learn under his father's schooling; and she reflected with agony on practises which were to cloud his fearless brow with the scowl of brutal insolence and conscious falsehood, and accustom his dear hand, which now would handle a wounded nestling with tenderness, to grasp the instruments of death, and to use them resolutely and recklessly in the pursuit of his calling.

Jane's soul was bent on rescuing her boy; while her husband, plunging deeper in the practises of his dangerous associates, grew each day more evilly inclined, and resisted still more impatiently the soft persuasions of his wife. Thus far she had concealed the real state of things from her son; and conquering, even when seeming to yield, she had hitherto prevented his father from making the fatal disclosure. She used the time thus gained by endeavouring to implant, so that they might never be uprooted, simple moral truths in his ductile and ingenuous mind. Her cares had a singular effect. Had they lived as other fishermen, Charles would have associated with companions of his own age, and become initiated in worldly practises. But the loneliness of their position and Jane's watchfulness prevented this; so that he was brought up in guarded innocence, and preserved a respect for truth and a sense of duty seldom found among the lowly bred. Still she gained another day—week—month upon her husband— still Charles's partnership in his perilous career was unasked, and his help was only afforded in their pursuit as fishermen—their ostensible mode of existence. Yet, though delayed, the awful moment for ever hovered near; the mother's soul was in tumults—should she confide in, and warn her son, and beseech him to fly, and to seek to obtain his subsistence elsewhere, before he should be forced to enter on a course of crime? The instinct of her mild soul was not to give pain—and she shrunk from the necessity of parting with her boy, and the consequent anger of her husband. She could endure much, but she had no energy to act. She was woman in every fold and corner of her too soft nature. She had stood up against her husband only through the simplicity, the singleness and charity of her character—but she felt the coward in her heart, when she thought of quitting her defensive ground, for open and aggressive resistance.

Thus the boy attained his fifteenth year, never having joined his father in any of his perilous expeditions. He looked up to him with reverence, as youth does to experience, and regarded him with filial attachment, notwithstanding his habitual roughness and occasional severity. There was a buoyancy in the youth's spirit, a fearlessness and a fortitude which the father prided himself on, as rendering him doubly fit for tasks of danger. Yet (so contradictory is human nature) in spite of pride, in spite of the bitter scorn that gnawed at his heart, when it was represented to him that his was an example to be avoided by his son, he felt a secret satisfaction in yielding to his wife's entreaties, and an unacknowledged reluctance to meet the disapproving glance of integrity and innocence. Charles adored his mother. He stored up her moral and religious lessons with pious care. To assist, to console, to caress her filled his heart with gladness—and his bright smile, elastic step, and cheering voice did console her—and spread a sun-light over her darkened life, which it was agony to imagine might ever be eclipsed.

Another year had elapsed in this way, when on a morning—a fair morning,—a light breeze just rippling the blue plains of ocean—father and son launched their fishing-boat, as usual, and put out to sea. Jane watched them while in the offing they were preparing to throw their nets; when suddenly their sail was again set, and she saw them directing their course round the promontory that shut in the little bay. The poor woman knew that the rendezvous for the smugglers lay round that point. She uttered a cry, as if her feeble voice, calling "Stop!" would be heard across the dividing waves, and she rushed to the water's edge—"He does not hear me," she cried in anguish, "he will not hear—nor the sea, nor the winds—nor God—all are deaf, and my Charles is lost for ever! What—what can it mean?"——

Her husband had returned from an expedition of peculiar length and peril but the night before, and had, kissing his wife's wan cheek—bid her "not fret, for that soon, with God's blessing, he would give up the trade, and be well to do." In the morning he had told her emphatically that he should but cast his nets and return. Had he deceived her;—or did some signal direct his movements?—It was all one.

She saw, as from a tower, the end of all—her boy the associate of vicious lawless men, exposed to hardships which the human frame could scarcely endure—painful nightwatches—apprehensions wrought to agony —and combats which, end as they would, in triumph or defeat, were attended by two-fold crime and danger. With eyes streaming with tears, she gazed upon the departing sail—the sun shone, the breeze was balmy —the waves danced and glittered beneath the bright sky, while a dark tempest loured over her foreboding soul.

Her younger son seeing her cry, immediately began an accompaniment; while Charley's dog, who was lying asleep in the sun, got up and shook himself, and stood looking as with inquiring eyes, on the disappearance of the well-known skiff; and as it was lost behind the headland, turned to his mistress with a sorrowful whine: "True, poor fellow!" said Jane, "it is evil work they are going upon." The poor animal came up to her, and licked her hand, and returned to stretch himself on the beach.

Charley's dog was an especial favourite with his mother. During an inclement winter, when wrecks were but too frequent on the coast, the fisherman and his son had put off to give their adventurous aid to the crew of a small schooner, which had struck on a sunken reef. As they approached the vessel, each vast wave threatened to overwhelm them, and as they rose and fell in the trough of the sea, it seemed as if the deck of the vessel was absolutely deserted; yet a cry was borne to them, mingled with the roar of the surges—it seemed a human cry, and Charles, though then a child, strained every little nerve to hasten to the succour of his fellow-creature in distress: it was no human being—the deck was absolutely vacant; but a dog stood on the poop, whining fearfully. The fisherman was unwilling to endanger himself to save a dog, but Charles prayed hard, and the animal seeing them near leaped into the sea; the waves dashing over him deprived him of every power of swimming, but they bore him towards Charles; he caught him up, and the half-strangled thing slowly revived when out of the water. The poor fellow seemed quite aware of his mighty debt of gratitude, and strove to pay it in love and fidelity. The first time Charles had put to sea afterwards, the dog's terror and resistance were something beyond instinct—he wailed—he pulled his new master back by his coat; and when he saw that his endeavours were vain, that his preserver was embarked, and was pushing from shore, as if resolved to share his fate, with a short sharp bark he plunged into the water and swam after them.

He was grown old now, and was usually left at home, the guard of the cottage and the playmate of the children. Still he could seldom be enticed in doors when his master was at sea; his usual post was on the beach; during calm weather he stretched his lazy length on the sands, but when the day was stormy, he perpetually watched the tumult of the waves, and his bark gave the first token of the well-known skiff having hove in sight.

The sea was tranquil, and nothing now called forth his disquietude, while Jane unable to calm her agitation, or to turn her thoughts elsewhere, stood, her eyes fixed on the point of land round which the boat had disappeared. The unclouded sun reached the zenith—Jane was obliged to occupy herself with her children—yet at every moment she was at the door of the cot, in fearful, restless expectation. The sunny summer day melting into evening,—the flow and then the ebb of the mighty flood—the light surf left glittering on the shingles—the cliff glowing with sunset hues, and her own quiet home, seeming with every other object, to repose in peace beneath the placid eye of heaven—all of beauty and of good was so much misery to Jane. The hours passed so slowly—so slowly had high water mark been gained, and then more slowly deserted; a ship or two rose on the horizon, and sunk again—the sea birds sought their nests in the rocks, but no light sail skimmed the blue surface, nor tiny hull speckled the laughing deep. Jane ascended the cliff: with her glass she visited every nook of the watery circumference; the moon rose as daylight faded, and "wove her chain upon the deep"*—her chain of light and beauty; the flickering beams sometimes presented deceptive visions to the anxious mother's eyes—her heart swelled, and then sunk within her, as hope and expectation failed.

Two endless wearying days passed thus, and a long wakeful night. She

---

* Byron, "There be none of Beauty's daughters" (Ed.).

had retired to rest again on the third, when the dog's bark roused her—she heard the splashing of the waters and steps upon the strand; soon her husband and son entered the hut: she cast a hasty inquiring glance on the first, and then fixed a long look of scrutiny on the latter. They both seemed overworn—drooping with fatigue. But little was said, except that her husband demanded supper. She placed food before them: Charles endeavoured to eat, but after a few vain efforts, he suddenly left the room. Little Tommy, who had got up to see his brother, was sent after him, and brought back word that he was gone to bed. Jane looked wistfully at her husband, but he was gloomy, and only said, "The best thing for him! We have had a hard bout of it—I shall turn in too."

Deep sleep soon came over the weary seaman; but Jane remained up, and as she listened in the stillness of night, she heard a deep sigh in her son's room: she stole in softly, and kneeling at his bedside, as he turned his open eyes away from the light, she said, "Are you ill—can I help you?"

He did not answer; and she said again—"You have not asked my blessing, Charles, to-night."

"Do not speak to me, Mother," said the lad; "I cannot speak to you, nor pray—I don't believe I ever shall again"—and then half starting from his bed as if terrified, he cried, "If I could only sleep—if I could only not see——do leave the light with me, Mother—I see something so terrible in the dark! I am afraid—I never was a coward before!"

His voice quivered; and Jane, in an agony of tears threw herself on his neck, crying—"Sinful woman that I am, I have brought you to this!"

"Then you know—Why, why did you not warn me?" Tears suffocated him as he spoke; he rested his head on her bosom, while his burthened spirit found relief in passionate weeping.

He had a direful tale to tell, which with some difficulty Jane extracted from him. She resolved to know the worst; and as he went on, her sympathy and consolation lightened the weight of his unhappiness.

It would seem that, during their last expedition, the smugglers had collected a booty of more than usual value, at less than the usual cost. This they had stowed in a cavern prepared and enlarged by them for that purpose, and had hastened to give notice of the cargo to the dealers with whom they were accustomed to traffic. They expected a golden harvest, and Jane's husband, for the first time, solaced himself with the perspective of an honester livelihood and more peaceful days. That morning he had gone to sea with a blithe heart, and looking on his son, he felt a throb of pleasure to remember that he had been brought up innocently. At that moment glancing towards the point of cliff selected by his associates for their signals, he beheld one indicative of urgent danger and pressing need of his assistance. Such are our good intentions when resting neither on principle nor truth. This man's short-lived sense of right vanished, and without another thought, save on what danger might threaten his friends, he bid Charles put the boat about, and, seizing the rudder, he steered for the place of rendezvous.

The men believed themselves to be either tracked or betrayed—at least they felt sure that they were discovered, and only not attacked on account of their numbers, and they knew that a reinforcing party had been sent for with all speed. Their immediate employment was to transfer their goods to other hiding places—to bury a part, and to hide the rest under the more desolate cliffs along the coast,—they were ready to throw it all into the sea, or destroy it in any way rather than it should fall into the hands of their enemies. Charles and his father landed, they scrambled up the rocks and entered the dark-browed cavern; its atmosphere was impregnated with the fumes of tobacco and spirits: the boy marked even in the gloom, the fierce hard faces of the men within—their garb set off by fire-arms; the bales of goods scattered about; and young, untaught, and unsuspecting as he was, the truth flashed on him at once, while the glad welcome given to "Jem Harding" revealed to him that his father was one of them.

This pen would utterly fail in its task were it to attempt to record the rough foul language of these men; their oaths, their imprecations, and their slang, in which fortunately poor Charles was no adept. His father replied in the same evil phrase, and equipped himself in all haste with arms, while one of his comrades handed a pistol to the boy, saying, "Stick this i' thy belt, youngster." Charles recoiled, and the man, with a yell of a laugh and an oath, asked if he was afraid it would bite him.

All hands now fell to work, and the day was passed almost uninterruptedly in the task of removing their goods. They knew that there were scouts about, and they adopted various expedients to mislead them. They transported a part of their ware inland, and such part as would not be injured by wet, they reserved to sink in a hole of the rocks covered at high water. Charles was obedient and worked hard among them, lending his ready aid without a murmur, so that he heard his father reproached several times for not bringing so handy a lad among them before.

Yet none of their labours was performed without danger and stratagem. At one time they discussed the eligibility of taking prisoner a man, who in the guise of a countryman was perpetually hovering about. The horrible mutterings and unintelligible language in which this discussion was carried on, hid much of their meaning from the tyro in their art; but their oaths, their dark looks, their hands frequently in gesticulation touching the weapons at their sides, awoke worse terrors in his imagination. He fancied that they meditated murder, and his blood curdled—the hair on his head seemed to stand on end, and his knees knocked together in horror. He drew a step or two nearer his father, but he was loudest in counselling the most desperate measures: the man, as if warned by instinct, appeared no more; but each time they drew near the place where he had been seen, Charles's heart beat loud, and his limbs were paralysed by fear. At another time it was necessary to mislead a person who was bent on accompanying them. Charles, as the least suspicious looking of the groupe, was to perform this task. He who in the loneliness of his home and habits of frankness with his sweet mother, had never, during his life, said the thing that was not, was now, with brazen front, boldly to assert a lie. His brow flushed, shame sat on his cheek, and his tongue refused its office. Yet he felt the necessity of fulfilling the directions given him, even for the stranger's own sake—it was done, the falsehood uttered, which appeared to him to taint his whole future life, and to render heaven itself his enemy!

All this was playing idly on the threshold of horrors. Night came on—soft balmy night, and the tranquillity of the ocean and the fair beams of the gentle moon were dressed as betrayers of their work: they were now employed in transporting several casks across a creek to a dark cleft in the rocks; two or three times had they visited it in safety—one voyage only remained, when, on nearing their destination, suddenly the sea seemed alive with boats—a file of men appeared on the cliff above—in every way they were surrounded. They threw their freight into the sea; they took to their oars; shots were fired, and a yell of voices raised that filled the very air with terror. The smugglers sought only to make good their escape; their assailants were desirous of assuring the capture of their goods, so that the struggle, though fierce, was short; and in gaining the open sea, the smugglers found that they were not pursued. At one moment—one terrible moment—a revenue officer had thrust his pistol close to Charles's breast; his father dashed it away and fired his own; the man fell heavily into the water—the boy saw the body with its distorted death-struck face float past: in a minute more the sail which his associates had contrived to set was filled by the land breeze, and they were wafted beyond the cutters of their enemies: the shouts, the voices, late so loud and dread, died away, and they found themselves free and safe in the wide and misty waters. Still the woman-taught boy fancied that the dead man floated near—his face upturned on the weltering sea. He dared not lift his gaze to the moon-lit sky, for there dwelt the Eternal One, so grievously offended. Terror had been in his heart, remorse and despair succeeded; and meanwhile he sickened to hear the imprecation and the revilings of the crew—his father loudest and fiercest among them.

All that night and the next day they did not dare approach the shore.

They had but two or three biscuits with them, which had been greedily devoured on the first sensation of hunger, and a very small portion of one had fallen to Charles's share; nor had they any thing except spirits to allay their thirst. With these some stupified themselves; others grew noisy and unruly; one man fell overboard, but the calm was such that he was easily picked up, and the accident served but to augment the loud squabbling on board. Charles turned with disgust from the maddening draughts;—sickening with hunger, and exhausted with fatigue, he stretched himself at the bottom of the boat, believing he should surely die—now crying as he thought of his dear mother—now rocked into disturbed slumbers by the waves. Towards the close of the day they drew near shore; at night-fall they landed. Charles and his father found their own skiff in the sheltered cove where they had left it, and here too they found water: a little refreshed, and yet overworn, they piloted themselves back to their well-known beach and peaceful home.

It was a difficult task for Jane to soothe and comfort her son; but by degrees his troubled thoughts grew calmer—his heavy eyes closed, and slumber crept subduingly over him. Jane watched by him and wept the while, not daring to regard the future, and seeing in the present the realization of her worst fears. Grey morning dawned: Harding awoke; he rose, and, not speaking to his wife for very shame, he went down to the beach to prepare his boat for sea. In a short time his voice was heard calling for his son. Charles had already risen, he had eaten of the breakfast set before him by his mother, but he also was silent and thoughtful. Jane's heart beat fast when she heard her husband call him; but still the lad said nothing, and walked down to the water's edge.

Soon however the unhappy woman perceived that there was strife between the father and son. Charles stood on the sands, and, unmoved in gesture, seemed with firmness but respect to assert his resolves, while Harding, with loud voice and inflamed face, poured forth a torrent of abuse; his hand too was raised, and before Jane, rushing down to stay it, could reach him, he felled his son to the earth. Charles rose again and stood as before firm and collected. Harding, not wishing to encounter his wife's reproaches, leaped alone into the boat, heaping curses on his child's head—wishing that he had suffered him to be shot, and swearing that he would himself murder him, if he found him sneaking about the house on his return—the blood fall on his head if he ever saw him more! With these last words he pushed the boat from shore, while Charles, embracing his mother, said, "Do not grieve; it must be so—I must leave you for a little time: he will be kind to you when I am gone; and soon, when I have got into a good service, I will send for you, and he too will leave this wicked trade."

"He wanted you to join them again?" asked Jane.

"Do not speak of it, Mother," said the boy; "it could not be my duty to obey him, and I would not. I will go where I can earn an honest livelihood; and we shall meet again and be happy together."

Still Charles lingered with his mother all day; and it was not until when, in the evening, a little sail in the offing seemed to betoken his father's return, that with many tears and embraces he sought her blessing; and then, his little wardrobe tied up in a handkerchief, his dog as his companion, with no weakness of purpose, though weeping still, he ascended the cliff, and took his way to a near sea-port.

He was gone—and yet the skiff did not near, and no Harding returned. Jane at first could think only of her boy—of whither he had bent his steps, and where his dear head, poor and friendless as he was, would that night find a pillow. Still as night crept on, and her husband did not come back, new fears were awakened, and on every side disasters seemed to crowd about her. She waited long; but nature was exhausted: she had slept so little the preceding nights, that at last she went to rest; and taking her youngest darling to her bosom, and giving herself to dreamy hopes, which seemed sent from heaven to console her, she sunk into a deep refreshing sleep.

When she awoke, it was with an effort that she recalled her thoughts, and became aware of her situation. Day was far advanced, yet her children slept, and all was still except the waving sea. The wind had risen, and broken up the calm which had so long brooded on the deep. The waters were now in tumult, and the high tide brought the spray to her very door. She got up and looked out—all was desert. Hers was a life of loneliness; she was at the distance of four miles from a town, and not a cottage was to be found within a considerable distance of her abode. No one ever visited her, so that now, her son away, her husband not returning, she had no one with whom to exchange conjecture, or to whom to communicate her fears. She could only watch in terror, and sadly count the hours. The little occupation her children gave her was salutary; yet it could not divest her thoughts from a dearer object.

At first her husband's protracted absence was felt as a relief by her; she dreaded to hear her angel-boy reviled, and to encounter the bad passions of this guilty man. But when three days had passed, these feelings were exchanged for a mortal inquietude. Her little stock of food had almost vanished; she was nearly destitute of money; her two children required her constant attendance, while suspense almost deprived her of every faculty, save that of listening to each sound that broke upon her frightful solitude. Still the billows warred, and broke tumultuously on the beach; and the tide rose and fell, and day was exchanged for night; but it seemed

as if never again was she to have communication with the outward world
—as if on that lonely sea-shore she was to wear her life away, in ignorance of all nearest and dearest to her.

Unable to struggle any longer with her anxiety, she at length made up
her mind to some exertion. She would walk at least to the nearest town—
perhaps her son had written to her—perhaps she should obtain some
intelligence of the party of smugglers of whom her husband was one.
Early in the morning she arose to prepare for her walk: with heaviness of
heart she endeavoured to swallow some food, but in vain—while her little
son jumped about in delight at the expected visit to the town. On a
sudden there was scratching at the door of her cot—a well-known bark;
she rushed to open it; poor Sailor the dog leaped up about her with
frantic delight—but he was alone! She ran to the beach; she called her
son's name, and he coming from behind a rock which had concealed him,
flew into her arms. At length he cried, "My Father!—is it true? I thought
he might be within—but where—I need not ask; the story I heard is true:
he is taken!"

"Taken!" exclaimed Jane.

"Dearest Mother," said Charles, terrified at what he had to reveal, "do
you not know? They were attacked again, some are prisoners, some
escaped, and some fell: I had hoped that my father might have got back
safe here."

"Gracious God!" exclaimed the unhappy woman: "My poor babes!"

"Do not be afraid, Mother!" replied her son; "at the worst I am a man
now, and can work for you: I will go to the old place; if the boat is there
I can get to —— in three or four hours, as the wind is fair, and so on to
the assize town. If he is in jail I shall soon know. I shall be back again to-
morrow, or next day at furthest."

He was running off, when he returned again: "Take care of Sailor; he
must not follow me. If you do not see me by Thursday night, go to the
post office: I will write."

He was gone; his coming had been a dream, but for the new fears he
had left behind. Some of the smugglers had fallen in the fray—she embraced her children—her *orphans*. It seemed as if it required no new
intelligence to assure her of her calamity—it was—it must be all over!

To wait—to wait! Life was one long dreary expectation. To attend to
her children; to caress Charles's dog, and to watch for his returning sail:
the sea had become calmer, and a few hours might bring him again to
her; yet he came not, and two days passed, and Thursday evening arrived,
and still no Charles! Again she had to resolve on a visit to the post office
with a yet more anxious heart. The morning came, and she was prepared
for her expedition. She ascended the cliff, and gave one last look at the
wide sea. The west wind that had reigned for many days was again rising

into tempest, and lashing the ocean to fury: the clouds fled like living things across the sky; the waters turbid and foaming, kept up an incessant roar, and the beach was covered with surf. "God grant he do not put to sea!" sighed Jane, fearing little that he would. She held her youngest child in her arms, and Tommy carrying an empty basket ran at her side. A walk of four miles was before her, for the most part over a rough and hilly road. The wind seemed a little to subside as she proceeded. Tommy was delighted with his journey, and she talked cheerily to him in spite of her despair. Her spirit bore her up; so that notwithstanding her dear burthen, she reached the town without being greatly fatigued. Her first visit was to the post office; a letter was given her, rough-looking as it was, written on coarse paper, ill folded and clumsily indited, she pressed it with transport to her lips, and hurried away to get some spot where she might read it. While her children were devouring some bread in a baker's shop, she tore it open: the words were few, and they put the seal on her worst anticipations:—

"Dearest Mother," wrote Charles—"Be comforted—it is all too late: Father is in a better place, and you must not take on. He was shot and taken, and carried to jail. I found him alive, and he gave me his blessing, which comforts me, and bid me follow good courses. Last night, dear Mother, he died, and had suffered great pain first. He will be buried to-morrow early. Dear Mother, Charles will work for you, and for Tommy and Jenny. They have been very good to me; and I have a kind friend. He has made me promise to bring you here, and given me money, and will give me work. Indeed, dear Mother, I have good news for you. You shall not live any longer in that lonesome place, but come to a pretty cottage where we shall all be together. I found the boat, and shall come back in it: expect me on Friday—so look out for me.

Your dutiful son,
CHARLES HARDING."

In tears, yet trying to resign herself, drying her eyes, and then bursting afresh into a passion of weeping, Jane began to retrace her steps homeward. The sky was overcast, and both she and her little boy grew very tired. She walked forward about two miles, and then sat down to rest. After a short time, fearful that night might overtake her, she again proceeded on her way. She had now got among the wild downs nearer home, and the wind, which had seemed lulled, rose again, tore across the open country, and swept fearfully over the exposed heath. Vast, dense masses of cloud were borne in swift career; and in a pause of the gale, another sound was heard—was it the sea?—no; a flash of lightning changed her doubts to certainty, and again the pealing thunder reverberated over her head: the rain began to fall—for a moment she thought of shelter; but the

Drawn on stone by Louis Haghe

"Struggling with wind and water, was the skiff she had so often

image of her Charles upon the stormy ocean presented itself with such terror, that though she could hardly keep her feet, she hurried on. Poor Tommy could scarce keep up with her: still as the elemental voices mingled in horrid fray, and the sea joined its hoarse roar to the thunder and the wind, he also forgot his fatigue in his fears for his brother.

O, for a sight of the dangerous ocean, of which perhaps he was already the prey! To hear her enemy's loud menaces, and yet to be blinded to their effects, gave such a sting to the miserable variety of her sorrow, that at one moment she sank on her knees, unable to pray, yet repeating with passionate cries her dear son's name. The terror of her children, who grew more and more frightened, recalled her to herself; she wiped her fast-falling tears, and went on: the way seemed endless—well did she know each turn, each change of object in her path; and yet as rain and wind, and the darkness of the storm beset her, it seemed as if each distance was doubled—as if never, never should she arrive! At length on a turn in the road, she could perceive the chimney of her cot—a few more steps, but first a strange sound was wafted to her on the blast:—was that prolonged plaintive cry human? Again it was renewed. "It is Sailor," cried her little son; and now the curtain of distance and impeding objects was withdrawn, and all was before her: the tempest-tossed and evil-boding waters, the lurid sky, and where seaward, the clouds lifted by the winds, showed beneath, the red and glaring signal of the increasing storm. Sailor was howling on the sands, and a hat borne by the breakers to the beach, was at his feet, and on the dark foaming ocean, rising and falling with the mighty waves, struggling with wind and water, was the skiff she had so often watched—now so dearly and so dangerously freighted. What hope remained?

Often the little vessel, with its one torn sail, was tossed in the yawning deep—again it rose on the edge of the waves, and then engulphed by the breaking surge, it laboured heavily amidst its howling, devouring, remorseless pursuers! The deaf billows hear not; the gloomy storm is blind; wreck and tempest have no touch of human sympathy; the driving rain falls upon the waters; the dark waves leap and dance in murderous pastime, and the thunder laughs in mockery above—it is their carnival, the carnival and masque of Death. The heartfelt prayer of the lonely one, the gushing, agonizing tears of the miserable being, who from the shore views her last hope fail—what are they to the merciless destruction which rises from its repose only to destroy!

Still the little boat made its fearful way. The sail, sole hope of the helmsman, was at one moment torn from the shrouds, and cast, shivered to rags, upon the sea; but her brave boy spread yet another, and again the keel obeyed the rudder. On she came. Breakers were ahead; but well did Charles know each hidden rock and reef on the perilous coast. The lifting clouds rose yet higher, and athwart the veil of the driving rain the clear sky was to be seen; the thunder became more faint; clouds flew wildly inland, and then a lull came—another furious blast, and then a longer pause. The sun on the ocean's verge peeped out yet more golden, and the waves seemed to obey the beaming wands of light that were stretched out over them. The boat laboured less, and there was some hope of its making a little inlet of the sea, sheltered by the cliff, where he could land. Hope now mastered fear; the tearful mother hastened to the spot: the sea here was more tranquil, and after a few moments of suspense, on going about once again, the boat got yet nearer to the wind, and entered calmer water. Yet a brief interval, and Charles, all sea-drenched and faint, yet bearing up with an unflinching spirit, was clasped in his mother's arms!

XVI

The Mortal Immortal

A TALE

JULY 16, 1833.—This is a memorable anniversary for me; on it I complete my three hundred and twenty-third year!

The Wandering Jew?—certainly not. More than eighteen centuries have passed over his head. In comparison with him, I am a very young Immortal.

Am I, then, immortal? This is a question which I have asked myself, by day and night, for now three hundred and three years, and yet cannot answer it. I detected a gray hair amidst my brown locks this very day— that surely signifies decay. Yet it may have remained concealed there for three hundred years—for some persons have become entirely white-headed before twenty years of age.

I will tell my story, and my reader shall judge for me. I will tell my story, and so contrive to pass some few hours of a long eternity, become so wearisome to me. For ever! Can it be? to live for ever! I have heard of enchantments, in which the victims were plunged into a deep sleep, to wake, after a hundred years, as fresh as ever: I have heard of the Seven Sleepers—thus to be immortal would not be so burthensome: but, oh! the weight of never-ending time—the tedious passage of the still-succeeding hours! How happy was the fabled Nourjahad!——But to my task.

All the world has heard of Cornelius Agrippa. His memory is as immortal as his arts have made me. All the world has also heard of his scholar, who, unawares, raised the foul fiend during his master's absence, and was destroyed by him. The report, true or false, of this accident, was attended with many inconveniences to the renowned philosopher. All his scholars at once deserted him—his servants disappeared. He had no one near him to put coals on his ever-burning fires while he slept, or to attend to the changeful colours of his medicines while he studied. Experiment after experiment failed, because one pair of hands was insufficient to complete them: the dark spirits laughed at him for not being able to retain a single mortal in his service.

I was then very young—very poor—and very much in love. I had been for about a year the pupil of Cornelius, though I was absent when this accident took place. On my return, my friends implored me not to return to the alchymist's abode. I trembled as I listened to the dire tale they told; I required no second warning; and when Cornelius came and offered me a purse of gold if I would remain under his roof, I felt as if Satan himself tempted me. My teeth chattered—my hair stood on end:—I ran off as fast as my trembling knees would permit.

My failing steps were directed whither for two years they had every evening been attracted,—a gently bubbling spring of pure living waters, beside which lingered a dark-haired girl, whose beaming eyes were fixed on the path I was accustomed each night to tread. I cannot remember the hour when I did not love Bertha; we had been neighbours and playmates from infancy—her parents, like mine, were of humble life, yet respectable —our attachment had been a source of pleasure to them. In an evil hour, a malignant fever carried off both her father and mother, and Bertha became an orphan. She would have found a home beneath my paternal roof, but, unfortunately, the old lady of the near castle, rich, childless, and solitary, declared her intention to adopt her. Henceforth Bertha was clad in silk—inhabited a marble palace—and was looked on as being highly favoured by fortune. But in her new situation among her new associates, Bertha remained true to the friend of her humbler days; she often visited the cottage of my father, and when forbidden to go thither, she would stray towards the neighbouring wood, and meet me beside its shady fountain.

She often declared that she owed no duty to her new protectress equal in sanctity to that which bound us. Yet still I was too poor to marry, and she grew weary of being tormented on my account. She had a haughty but an impatient spirit, and grew angry at the obstacles that prevented our union. We met now after an absence, and she had been sorely beset while I was away; she complained bitterly, and almost reproached me for being poor. I replied hastily,—

"I am honest, if I am poor!—were I not, I might soon become rich!"

This exclamation produced a thousand questions. I feared to shock her by owning the truth, but she drew it from me; and then, casting a look of disdain on me, she said—

"You pretend to love, and you fear to face the Devil for my sake!"

I protested that I had only dreaded to offend her;—while she dwelt on the magnitude of the reward that I should receive. Thus encouraged— shamed by her—led on by love and hope, laughing at my late fears, with quick steps and a light heart, I returned to accept the offers of the alchymist, and was instantly installed in my office.

A year passed away. I became possessed of no insignificant sum of money. Custom had banished my fears. In spite of the most painful vigilance, I had never detected the trace of a cloven foot; nor was the studious silence of our abode ever disturbed by demoniac howls. I still continued my stolen interviews with Bertha, and Hope dawned on me— Hope—but not perfect joy; for Bertha fancied that love and security were enemies, and her pleasure was to divide them in my bosom. Though true of heart, she was somewhat of a coquette in manner; and I was jealous as a Turk. She slighted me in a thousand ways, yet would never acknowledge herself to be in the wrong. She would drive me mad with anger, and then force me to beg her pardon. Sometimes she fancied that I was not sufficiently submissive, and then she had some story of a rival, favoured by her protectress. She was surrounded by silk-clad youths—the rich and gay—What chance had the sad-robed scholar of Cornelius compared with these?

On one occasion, the philosopher made such large demands upon my time, that I was unable to meet her as I was wont. He was engaged in some mighty work, and I was forced to remain, day and night, feeding his furnaces and watching his chemical preparations. Bertha waited for me in vain at the fountain. Her haughty spirit fired at this neglect; and when at last I stole out during the few short minutes allotted to me for slumber, and hoped to be consoled by her, she received me with disdain, dismissed me in scorn, and vowed that any man should possess her hand rather than he who could not be in two places at once for her sake. She would be revenged!—And truly she was. In my dingy retreat I heard that she had been hunting, attended by Albert Hoffer. Albert Hoffer was favoured by her protectress, and the three passed in cavalcade before my smoky window. Methought that they mentioned my name—it was followed by a laugh of derision, as her dark eyes glanced contemptuously towards my abode.

Jealousy, with all its venom, and all its misery, entered my breast. Now I shed a torrent of tears, to think that I should never call her mine; and, anon, I imprecated a thousand curses on her inconstancy. Yet, still I must stir the fires of the alchymist, still attend on the changes of his unintelligible medicines.

Cornelius had watched for three days and nights, nor closed his eyes. The progress of his alembics was slower than he expected: in spite of his anxiety, sleep weighed upon his eyelids. Again and again he threw off drowsiness with more than human energy; again and again it stole away his senses. He eyed his crucibles wistfully. "Not ready yet," he murmured;

"will another night pass before the work is accomplished? Winzy, you are vigilant—you are faithful—you have slept, my boy—you slept last night. Look at that glass vessel. The liquid it contains is of a soft rose-colour: the moment it begins to change its hue, awaken me—till then I may close my eyes. First, it will turn white, and then emit golden flashes; but wait not till then; when the rose-colour fades, rouse me." I scarcely heard the last words, muttered, as they were, in sleep. Even then he did not quite yield to nature. "Winzy, my boy," he again said, "do not touch the vessel—do not put it to your lips; it is a philter—a philter to cure love; you would not cease to love your Bertha—beware to drink!"

And he slept. His venerable head sunk on his breast, and I scarce heard his regular breathing. For a few minutes I watched the vessel—the rosy hue of the liquid remained unchanged. Then my thoughts wandered —they visited the fountain, and dwelt on a thousand charming scenes never to be renewed—never! Serpents and adders were in my heart as the word "Never!" half formed itself on my lips. False girl!—false and cruel! Never more would she smile on me as that evening she smiled on Albert. Worthless, detested woman! I would not remain unrevenged—she should see Albert expire at her feet—she should die beneath my vengeance. She had smiled in disdain and triumph—she knew my wretchedness and her power. Yet what power had she?—the power of exciting my hate—my utter scorn—my—oh, all but indifference! Could I attain that—could I regard her with careless eyes, transferring my rejected love to one fairer and more true, that were indeed a victory!

A bright flash darted before my eyes. I had forgotten the medicine of the adept; I gazed on it with wonder: flashes of admirable beauty, more bright than those which the diamond emits when the sun's rays are on it, glanced from the surface of the liquid; an odour the most fragrant and grateful stole over my sense; the vessel seemed one globe of living radiance, lovely to the eye, and most inviting to the taste. The first thought, instinctively inspired by the grosser sense, was, I will—I must drink. I raised the vessel to my lips. "It will cure me of love—of torture!" Already I had quaffed half of the most delicious liquor ever tasted by the palate of man, when the philosopher stirred. I started—I dropped the glass—the fluid flamed and glanced along the floor, while I felt Cornelius's gripe at my throat, as he shrieked aloud, "Wretch! you have destroyed the labour of my life!"

The philosopher was totally unaware that I had drunk any portion of his drug. His idea was, and I gave a tacit assent to it, that I had raised the vessel from curiosity, and that, frighted at its brightness, and the flashes of intense light it gave forth, I had let it fall. I never undeceived him. The fire of the medicine was quenched—the fragrance died away—he grew calm, as a philosopher should under the heaviest trials, and dismissed me to rest.

I will not attempt to describe the sleep of glory and bliss which bathed my soul in paradise during the remaining hours of that memorable night. Words would be faint and shallow types of my enjoyment, or of the gladness that possessed my bosom when I woke. I trod air—my thoughts were in heaven. Earth appeared heaven, and my inheritance upon it was to be one trance of delight. "This it is to be cured of love," I thought; "I will see Bertha this day, and she will find her lover cold and regardless; too happy to be disdainful, yet how utterly indifferent to her!"

The hours danced away. The philosopher, secure that he had once succeeded, and believing that he might again, began to concoct the same medicine once more. He was shut up with his books and drugs, and I had a holiday. I dressed myself with care; I looked in an old but polished shield, which served me for a mirror; methought my good looks had wonderfully improved. I hurried beyond the precincts of the town, joy in my soul, the beauty of heaven and earth around me. I turned my steps towards the castle—I could look on its lofty turrets with lightness of heart, for I was cured of love. My Bertha saw me afar off, as I came up the avenue. I know not what sudden impulse animated her bosom, but at the sight, she sprung with a light fawn-like bound down the marble steps, and was hastening towards me. But I had been perceived by another person. The old high-born hag, who called herself her protectress, and was her tyrant, had seen me, also; she hobbled, panting, up the terrace; a page, as ugly as herself, held up her train, and fanned her as she hurried along, and stopped my fair girl with a "How, now, my bold mistress? whither so fast? Back to your cage—hawks are abroad!"

Bertha clasped her hands—her eyes were still bent on my approaching figure. I saw the contest. How I abhorred the old crone who checked the kind impulses of my Bertha's softening heart. Hitherto, respect for her rank had caused me to avoid the lady of the castle; now I disdained such trivial considerations. I was cured of love, and lifted above all human fears; I hastened forwards, and soon reached the terrace. How lovely Bertha looked! her eyes flashing fire, her cheeks glowing with impatience and anger, she was a thousand times more graceful and charming than ever—I no longer loved—Oh! no, I adored—worshipped—idolized her!

She had that morning been persecuted, with more than usual vehemence, to consent to an immediate marriage with my rival. She was reproached with the encouragement that she had shown him—she was threatened with being turned out of doors with disgrace and shame. Her proud spirit rose in arms at the threat; but when she remembered the scorn that she had heaped upon me, and how, perhaps, she had thus lost one whom she now regarded as her only friend, she wept with remorse and rage. At that moment I appeared. "O, Winzy!" she exclaimed, "take me to your mother's cot; swiftly let me leave the detested luxuries and wretchedness of this noble dwelling—take me to poverty and happiness."

I clasped her in my arms with transport. The old lady was speechless with fury, and broke forth into invective only when we were far on our road to my natal cottage. My mother received the fair fugitive, escaped from a gilt cage to nature and liberty, with tenderness and joy; my father, who loved her, welcomed her heartily; it was a day of rejoicing, which did not need the addition of the celestial potion of the alchymist to steep me in delight.

Soon after this eventful day, I became the husband of Bertha. I ceased to be the scholar of Cornelius, but I continued his friend. I always felt grateful to him for having, unawares, procured me that delicious draught of a divine elixir, which, instead of curing me of love (sad cure! solitary and joyless remedy for evils which seem blessings to the memory), had inspired me with courage and resolution, thus winning for me an inestimable treasure in my Bertha.

I often called to mind that period of trance-like inebriation with wonder. The drink of Cornelius had not fulfilled the task for which he affirmed that it had been prepared, but its effects were more potent and blissful than words can express. They had faded by degrees, yet they lingered long—and painted life in hues of splendour. Bertha often wondered at my lightness of heart and unaccustomed gaiety; for, before, I had been rather serious, or even sad, in my disposition. She loved me the better for my cheerful temper, and our days were winged by joy.

Five years afterwards I was suddenly summoned to the bedside of the dying Cornelius. He had sent for me in haste, conjuring my instant presence. I found him stretched on his pallet, enfeebled even to death; all of life that yet remained animated his piercing eyes, and they were fixed on a glass vessel, full of a roseate liquid.

"Behold," he said, in a broken and inward voice, "the vanity of human wishes! a second time my hopes are about to be crowned, a second time they are destroyed. Look at that liquor—you remember five years ago I had prepared the same, with the same success;—then, as now, my thirsting lips expected to taste the immortal elixir—you dashed it from me! and at present it is too late."

He spoke with difficulty, and fell back on his pillow. I could not help saying,—

"How, revered master, can a cure for love restore you to life?"

A faint smile gleamed across his face as I listened earnestly to his scarcely intelligible answer.

"A cure for love and for all things—the Elixir of Immortality. Ah! if now I might drink, I should live for ever!"

Painted by Henry P. Briggs   *Engraved by Frederick Bacon*

BERTHA

As he spoke, a golden flash gleamed from the fluid; a well-remembered fragrance stole over the air; he raised himself, all weak as he was—strength seemed miraculously to re-enter his frame—he stretched forth his hand—a loud explosion startled me—a ray of fire shot up from the elixir, and the glass vessel which contained it was shivered to atoms! I turned my eyes towards the philosopher; he had fallen back—his eyes were glassy—his features rigid—he was dead!

But I lived, and was to live for ever! So said the unfortunate alchymist, and for a few days I believed his words. I remembered the glorious drunkenness that had followed my stolen draught. I reflected on the change I had felt in my frame—in my soul. The bounding elasticity of the one—the buoyant lightness of the other. I surveyed myself in a mirror, and could perceive no change in my features during the space of the five years which had elapsed. I remembered the radiant hues and grateful scent of that delicious beverage—worthy the gift it was capable of bestowing——I was, then, IMMORTAL!

A few days after I laughed at my credulity. The old proverb, that "a prophet is least regarded in his own country," was true with respect to me and my defunct master. I loved him as a man—I respected him as a sage—but I derided the notion that he could command the powers of darkness, and laughed at the superstitious fears with which he was regarded by the vulgar. He was a wise philosopher, but had no acquaintance with any spirits but those clad in flesh and blood. His science was simply human; and human science, I soon persuaded myself, could never conquer nature's laws so far as to imprison the soul for ever within its carnal habitation. Cornelius had brewed a soul-refreshing drink—more inebriating than wine—sweeter and more fragrant than any fruit: it possessed probably strong medicinal powers, imparting gladness to the heart and vigor to the limbs; but its effects would wear out; already were they diminished in my frame. I was a lucky fellow to have quaffed health and joyous spirits, and perhaps long life, at my master's hands; but my good fortune ended there: longevity was far different from immortality.

I continued to entertain this belief for many years. Sometimes a thought stole across me—Was the alchymist indeed deceived? But my habitual credence was, that I should meet the fate of all the children of Adam at my appointed time—a little late, but still at a natural age. Yet it was certain that I retained a wonderfully youthful look. I was laughed at for my vanity in consulting the mirror so often, but I consulted it in vain—my brow was untrenched—my cheeks—my eyes—my whole person continued as untarnished as in my twentieth year.

I was troubled. I looked at the faded beauty of Bertha—I seemed more like her son. By degrees our neighbours began to make similar observations, and I found at last that I went by the name of the Scholar bewitched. Bertha herself grew uneasy. She became jealous and peevish, and at length she began to question me. We had no children; we were all in all to each other; and though, as she grew older, her vivacious spirit became a little allied to ill-temper, and her beauty sadly diminished, I cherished her in my heart as the mistress I had idolized, the wife I had sought and won with such perfect love.

At last our situation became intolerable: Bertha was fifty—I twenty years of age. I had, in very shame, in some measure adopted the habits of a more advanced age; I no longer mingled in the dance among the young and gay, but my heart bounded along with them while I restrained my feet; and a sorry figure I cut among the Nestors of our village. But before the time I mention, things were altered—we were universally shunned; we were—at least, I was—reported to have kept up an iniquitous acquaintance with some of my former master's supposed friends. Poor Bertha was pitied, but deserted. I was regarded with horror and detestation.

What was to be done? we sat by our winter fire—poverty had made itself felt, for none would buy the produce of my farm; and often I had been forced to journey twenty miles, to some place where I was not known, to dispose of our property. It is true we had saved something for an evil day—that day was come.

We sat by our lone fireside—the old-hearted youth and his antiquated wife. Again Bertha insisted on knowing the truth; she recapitulated all she had ever heard said about me, and added her own observations. She conjured me to cast off the spell; she described how much more comely gray hairs were than my chestnut locks; she descanted on the reverence and respect due to age—how preferable to the slight regard paid to mere children: could I imagine that the despicable gifts of youth and good looks outweighed disgrace, hatred, and scorn? Nay, in the end I should be burnt as a dealer in the black art, while she, to whom I had not deigned to communicate any portion of my good fortune, might be stoned as my accomplice. At length she insinuated that I must share my secret with her, and bestow on her like benefits to those I myself enjoyed, or she would denounce me—and then she burst into tears.

Thus beset, methought it was the best way to tell the truth. I revealed it as tenderly as I could, and spoke only of a *very long life*, not of immortality—which representation, indeed, coincided best with my own ideas. When I ended, I rose and said,

"And now, my Bertha, will you denounce the lover of your youth? —You will not, I know. But it is too hard, my poor wife, that you should suffer from my ill-luck and the accursed arts of Cornelius. I will leave you—you have wealth enough, and friends will return in my absence. I will go; young as I seem, and strong as I am, I can work and gain my bread among strangers, unsuspected and unknown. I loved you in youth;

God is my witness that I would not desert you in age, but that your safety and happiness require it."

I took my cap and moved towards the door; in a moment Bertha's arms were round my neck, and her lips were pressed to mine. "No, my husband, my Winzy," she said, "you shall not go alone—take me with you; we will remove from this place, and, as you say, among strangers we shall be unsuspected and safe. I am not so very old as quite to shame you, my Winzy; and I dare say the charm will soon wear off, and, with the blessing of God, you will become more elderly-looking, as is fitting; you shall not leave me."

I returned the good soul's embrace heartily. "I will not, my Bertha; but for your sake I had not thought of such a thing. I will be your true, faithful husband while you are spared to me, and do my duty by you to the last."

The next day we prepared secretly for our emigration. We were obliged to make great pecuniary sacrifices—it could not be helped. We realised a sum sufficient, at least, to maintain us while Bertha lived; and, without saying adieu to any one, quitted our native country to take refuge in a remote part of western France.

It was a cruel thing to transport poor Bertha from her native village, and the friends of her youth, to a new country, new language, new customs. The strange secret of my destiny rendered this removal immaterial to me; but I compassionated her deeply, and was glad to perceive that she found compensation for her misfortunes in a variety of little ridiculous circumstances. Away from all tell-tale chroniclers, she sought to decrease the apparent disparity of our ages by a thousand feminine arts—rouge, youthful dress, and assumed juvenility of manner. I could not be angry— Did not I myself wear a mask? Why quarrel with hers, because it was less successful? I grieved deeply when I remembered that this was my Bertha, whom I had loved so fondly, and won with such transport—the dark-eyed, dark-haired girl, with smiles of enchanting archness and a step like a fawn—this mincing, simpering, jealous old woman. I should have revered her gray locks and withered cheeks; but thus!——It was my work, I knew; but I did not the less deplore this type of human weakness.

Her jealousy never slept. Her chief occupation was to discover that, in spite of outward appearances, I was myself growing old. I verily believe that the poor soul loved me truly in her heart, but never had woman so tormenting a mode of displaying fondness. She would discern wrinkles in my face and decrepitude in my walk, while I bounded along in youthful vigour, the youngest looking of twenty youths. I never dared address another woman: on one occasion, fancying that the belle of the village regarded me with favouring eyes, she bought me a gray wig. Her constant discourse among her acquaintances was, that though I looked so young, there was ruin at work within my frame; and she affirmed that the worst symptom about me was my apparent health. My youth was a disease, she said, and I ought at all times to prepare, if not for a sudden and awful death, at least to awake some morning white-headed, and bowed down with all the marks of advanced years. I let her talk—I often joined in her conjectures. Her warnings chimed in with my never-ceasing speculations concerning my state, and I took an earnest, though painful, interest in listening to all that her quick wit and excited imagination could say on the subject.

Why dwell on these minute circumstances? We lived on for many long years. Bertha became bed-rid and paralytic: I nursed her as a mother might a child. She grew peevish, and still harped upon one string—of how long I should survive her. It has ever been a source of consolation to me, that I performed my duty scrupulously towards her. She had been mine in youth, she was mine in age, and at last, when I heaped the sod over her corpse, I wept to feel that I had lost all that really bound me to humanity.

Since then how many have been my cares and woes, how few and empty my enjoyments! I pause here in my history—I will pursue it no further. A sailor without rudder or compass, tossed on a stormy sea—a traveller lost on a wide-spread heath, without landmark or star to guide him—such have I been: more lost, more hopeless than either. A nearing ship, a gleam from some far cot, may save them; but I have no beacon except the hope of death.

Death! mysterious, ill-visaged friend of weak humanity! Why alone of all mortals have you cast me from your sheltering fold? O, for the peace of the grave! the deep silence of the iron-bound tomb! that thought would cease to work in my brain, and my heart beat no more with emotions varied only by new forms of sadness!

Am I immortal? I return to my first question. In the first place, is it not more probable that the beverage of the alchymist was fraught rather with longevity than eternal life? Such is my hope. And then be it remembered, that I only drank *half* of the potion prepared by him. Was not the whole necessary to complete the charm? To have drained half the Elixir of Immortality is but to be half immortal—my For-ever is thus truncated and null.

But again, who shall number the years of the half of eternity? I often try to imagine by what rule the infinite may be divided. Sometimes I fancy age advancing upon me. One gray hair I have found. Fool! do I lament? Yes, the fear of age and death often creeps coldly into my heart; and the more I live, the more I dread death, even while I abhor life. Such an enigma is man—born to perish—when he wars, as I do, against the established laws of his nature.

But for this anomaly of feeling surely I might die: the medicine of the alchymist would not be proof against fire—sword—and the strangling waters. I have gazed upon the blue depths of many a placid lake, and the tumultuous rushing of many a mighty river, and have said, peace inhabits those waters; yet I have turned my steps away, to live yet another day. I have asked myself, whether suicide would be a crime in one to whom thus only the portals of the other world could be opened. I have done all, except presenting myself as a soldier or duellist, an object of destruction to my—no, *not* my fellow-mortals, and therefore I have shrunk away. They are not my fellows. The inextinguishable power of life in my frame, and their ephemeral existence, place us wide as the poles asunder. I could not raise a hand against the meanest or the most powerful among them.

Thus I have lived on for many a year—alone, and weary of myself—desirous of death, yet never dying—a mortal immortal. Neither ambition nor avarice can enter my mind, and the ardent love that gnaws at my heart, never to be returned—never to find an equal on which to expend itself—lives there only to torment me.

This very day I conceived a design by which I may end all—without self-slaughter, without making another man a Cain—an expedition, which mortal frame can never survive, even endued with the youth and strength that inhabits mine. Thus I shall put my immortality to the test, and rest for ever—or return, the wonder and benefactor of the human species.

Before I go, a miserable vanity has caused me to pen these pages. I would not die, and leave no name behind. Three centuries have passed since I quaffed the fatal beverage: another year shall not elapse before, encountering gigantic dangers—warring with the powers of frost in their home—beset by famine, toil, and tempest—I yield this body, too tenacious a cage for a soul which thirsts for freedom, to the destructive elements of air and water—or, if I survive, my name shall be recorded as one of the most famous among the sons of men; and, my task achieved, I shall adopt more resolute means, and, by scattering and annihilating the atoms that compose my frame, set at liberty the life imprisoned within, and so cruelly prevented from soaring from this dim earth to a sphere more congenial to its immortal essence.

XVII

The Trial of Love

HAVING OBTAINED leave from the Signora Priora to go out for a few hours, Angeline, who was a boarder at the convent of Sant' Anna, in the little town of Este, in Lombardy, set out on her visit. She was dressed with simplicity and taste; her faziola covered her head and shoulders; and from beneath, gleamed her large black eyes, which were singularly beautiful. And yet she was not, perhaps, strictly handsome; but, she had a brow smooth, open, and noble; a profusion of dark silken hair, and a clear, delicate, though brunette complexion. She had, too, an intelligent and thoughtful expression of countenance; her mind appeared often to commune with itself; and there was every token that she was deeply interested in, and often pleased with, the thoughts that filled it. She was of humble birth: her father had been steward to Count Moncenigo, a Venetian nobleman; her mother had been foster-mother to his only daughter. Both her parents were dead; they had left her comparatively rich; and she was a prize sought by all the young men of the class under nobility; but Angeline lived retired in her convent, and encouraged none of them.

She had not been outside its walls for many months; and she felt almost frightened as she found herself among the lanes that led beyond the town, and up the Euganean hills, to Villa Moncenigo, whither she was bending her steps. Every portion of the way was familiar to her. The Countess Moncenigo had died in childbirth of her second child, and from that time, Angeline's mother had lived at the villa. The family consisted of the Count, who was always, except during a few weeks in the autumn, at Venice, and the two children. Ludovico, the son, was early settled at Padua, for the sake of his education, and then Faustina only remained, who was five years younger than Angeline.

Faustina was the loveliest little thing in the world: unlike an Italian, she had laughing blue eyes, a brilliant complexion, and auburne hair; she had a sylph-like form, slender, round, and springy; she was very pretty, and vivacious, and self-willed, with a thousand winning ways, that rendered it delightful to yield to her. Angeline was like an elder sister: she waited on Faustina; she yielded to her in every thing; a word or smile of hers, was all-powerful. "I love her too much," she would sometimes say; "but I would endure any misery rather than see a tear in her eye." It was Angeline's character to concentrate her feelings, and to nurse them till they became passions; while excellent principles, and the sincerest piety, prevented her from being led astray by them.

Three years before, Angeline had, by the death of her mother, been left quite an orphan, and she and Faustina went to live at the convent of Sant' Anna, in the town of Este; but a year after, Faustina, then fifteen, was sent to complete her education at a very celebrated convent in Venice, whose aristocratic doors were closed against her ignoble companion. Now, at the age of seventeen, having finished her education, she returned home, and came to Villa Moncenigo with her father, to pass the months of September and October. They arrived this very night, and Angeline was on her way from her convent, to see and embrace her dearest companion.

There was something maternal in Angeline's feelings—five years makes a considerable difference at the ages of ten to fifteen, and much, at seventeen and two-and-twenty. "The dear child," thought Angeline, as she walked along, "she must be grown taller, and, I dare say, more beautiful than ever. How I long to see her, with her sweet arch smile! I wonder if she found any one at her Venetian convent to humour and spoil her, as I did here—to take the blame of her faults, and indulge her in her caprices. Ah! those days are gone!—she will be thinking now of becoming a sposa*. I wonder if she has felt any thing of love." Angeline sighed. "I shall hear all about it soon—she will tell me every thing, I am sure. —And I wish I might tell her—secrecy and mystery are so very hateful; but I must keep my vow, and in a month it will be all over—in a month I shall know my fate. In a month!—shall I see him then?—shall I ever see him again! But I will not think of that, I will only think of Faustina— sweet, beloved Faustina!"

And now Angeline was toiling up the hill side; she heard her name called; and on the terrace that overlooked the road, leaning over the balustrade, was the dear object of her thoughts—the pretty Faustina, the little fairy girl, blooming in youth, and smiling with happiness. Angeline's heart warmed to her with redoubled fondness.

Soon they were in each other's arms; and Faustina laughed, and her eyes sparkled, and she began to relate all the events of her two years' life, and showed herself as self-willed, childish, and yet as engaging and caressing as ever. Angeline listened with delight, gazed on her dimpled

---

* The name given in Italy to a betrothed girl.

cheeks, sparkling eyes, and graceful gestures, in a perfect, though silent, transport of admiration. She would have had no time to tell her own story, had she been so inclined, Faustina talked so fast.

"Do you know, Angelinetta mia," said she, "I am to become a sposa this winter?"

"And who is the Signor Sposino?"

"I don't know yet; but during next carnival he is to be found. He must be very rich and very noble, papa says; and I say he must be very young and very good-tempered, and give me my own way, as you have always done, Angelina carina."

At length Angeline rose to take leave. Faustina did not like her going —she wanted her to stay all night—she would send to the convent to get the Priora's leave; but Angeline knowing that this was not to be obtained, was resolved to go, and at last, persuaded her friend to consent to her departure. The next day, Faustina would come herself to the convent to pay her old friends a visit, and Angeline could return with her in the evening, if the Priora would allow it. When this plan had been discussed and arranged, with one more embrace, they separated; and, tripping down the road, Angeline looked up, and Faustina looked down from the terrace, and waved her hand to her and smiled. Angeline was delighted with her kindness, her loveliness, the animation and sprightliness of her manner and conversation. She thought of her, at first, to the exclusion of every other idea, till, at a turn in the road, some circumstance recalled her thoughts to herself. "O, how too happy I shall be," she thought, "if he prove true!—with Faustina and Ippolito, life will be Paradise!" And then she traced back in her faithful memory, all that had occurred during the last two years. In the briefest possible way, we must do the same.

Faustina had gone to Venice, and Angeline was left alone in her convent. Though she did not much attach herself to any one, she became intimate with Camilla della Toretta, a young lady from Bologna. Camilla's brother came to see her, and Angeline accompanied her in the parlour to receive his visit. Ippolito fell desperately in love, and Angeline was won to return his affection. All her feelings were earnest and passionate; and yet, she could regulate their effects, and her conduct was irreproachable. Ippolito, on the contrary, was fiery and impetuous: he loved ardently, and could brook no opposition to the fulfilment of his wishes. He resolved on marriage, but being noble, feared his father's disapprobation: still it was necessary to seek his consent; and the old aristocrat, full of alarm and indignation, came to Este, resolved to use every measure to separate the lovers for ever. The gentleness and goodness of Angeline softened his anger, and his son's despair moved his compassion. He disapproved of the marriage, yet he could not wonder that Ippolito desired to unite himself to so much beauty and sweetness: and then, again, he reflected, that his son was very young, and might change his mind, and reproach him for his too easy acquiescence. He therefore made a compromise; he would give his consent in one year from that time, provided the young pair would engage themselves, by the most solemn oath, not to hold any communication by speech or letter during that interval. It was understood that this was to be a year of trial; that no engagement was to be considered to subsist until its expiration; when, if they continued faithful, their constancy would meet its reward. No doubt the father supposed, and even hoped, that, during their absence, Ippolito would change his sentiments, and form a more suitable attachment.

Kneeling before the cross, the lovers engaged themselves to one year of silence and separation; Angeline, with her eyes lighted up by gratitude and hope; Ippolito, full of rage and despair at this interruption to his felicity, to which he never would have assented, had not Angeline used every persuasion, every command, to instigate him to compliance; declaring, that unless he obeyed his father, she would seclude herself in her cell, and spontaneously become a prisoner, until the termination of the prescribed period. Ippolito took the vow, therefore, and immediately after set out for Paris.

One month only was now wanting before the year should have expired; and it cannot be wondered that Angeline's thoughts wandered from her sweet Faustina, to dwell on her own fate. Joined to the vow of absence, had been a promise to keep their attachment, and all concerning it, a profound secret from every human being, during the same term. Angeline consented readily (for her friend was away) not to come back till the stipulated period; but the latter had returned, and now, the concealment weighed on Angeline's conscience: there was no help—she must keep her word.

With all these thoughts occupying her, she had reached the foot of the hill, and was ascending again the one on which the town of Este stands, when she heard a rustling in the vineyard that bordered one side of the road—footsteps—and a well-known voice speaking her name.

"Santa Vergine! Ippolito!" she exclaimed, "is this your promise?"

"And is this your reception of me?" he replied, reproachfully. "Unkind one! because I am not cold enough to stay away—because this last month was an intolerable eternity, you turn from me—you wish me gone. It is true, then, what I have heard—you love another! Ah! my journey will not be fruitless—I shall learn who he is, and revenge your falsehood."

Angeline darted a glance full of wonder and reproach; but she was silent, and continued her way. It was in her heart not to break her vow, and so to draw down the curse of heaven on their attachment. She resolved not to be induced to say another word; and, by her steady adherence to her oath, to obtain forgiveness for his infringement. She walked very quickly, feeling happy and miserable at the same time—and yet not so—happiness was the genuine, engrossing sentiment; but she feared, partly her lover's anger, and more, the dreadful consequences that might ensue from his breach of his solemn vow. Her eyes were radiant with love and joy, but her lips seemed glued together; and resolved not to speak, she drew her faziola close round her face, that he might not even see it, as she walked speedily on, her eyes fixed on the ground. Burning with rage, pouring forth torrents of reproaches, Ippolito kept close to her side—now reproaching her for infidelity—now swearing revenge—now describing and lauding his own constancy and immutable love. It was a pleasant, though a dangerous theme. Angeline was tempted a thousand times to reward him by declaring her own unaltered feelings; but she overcame the desire, and, taking her rosary in her hand, began to tell her beads. They drew near the town, and finding that she was not to be persuaded, Ippolito at length left her, with protestations that he would discover his rival, and take vengeance on him for her cruelty and indifference. Angeline entered her convent, hurried into her cell—threw herself on her knees—prayed God to forgive her lover for breaking his vow; and then, overcome with joy at the proof he had given of his constancy, and of the near prospect of their perfect happiness, her head sank on her arms, and she continued absorbed in a reverie which bore the very hues of heaven. It had been a bitter struggle to withstand his entreaties, but her doubts were dissipated, he was true, and at the appointed hour would claim her; and she who had loved through the long year with such fervent, though silent, devotion, would be rewarded! She felt secure—thankful to heaven —happy.—Poor Angeline!

The next day, Faustina came to the convent: the nuns all crowded round her. "*Quanto è bellina,*" cried one. "*E tanta carina!*" cried another. "*S' è fatta la sposina?*"—"Are you betrothed yet?" asked a third. Faustina answered with smiles and caresses, and innocent jokes and laughter. The nuns idolized her; and Angeline stood by, admiring her lovely friend, and enjoying the praises lavished on her. At length, Faustina must return; and Angeline, as anticipated, was permitted to accompany her.

"She might go to the villa with her," the Priora said, "but not stay all night—it was against the rules."

Faustina entreated, scolded, coaxed, and at length succeeded in persuading the superior to allow her friend's absence for a single night. They then commenced their return together, attended by a maid servant—a sort of old duenna. As they walked along, a cavalier passed them on horseback.

"How handsome he is!" cried Faustina: "who can he be?"

Angeline blushed deeply, for she saw that it was Ippolito. He passed on swiftly, and was soon out of sight. They were now ascending the hill, the villa almost in sight, when they were alarmed by a bellowing, a hallooing, a shrieking, and a bawling, as if a den of wild beasts, or a madhouse, or rather both together, had broken loose. Faustina turned pale; and soon her companion was equally frightened, for a buffalo, escaped from the yoke, was seen tearing down the hill, filling the air with roarings, and a whole troop of *contadini* after him, screaming and shrieking—he was exactly in the path of the friends. The old duenna cried out, "O, *Gesu Maria!*" and fell flat on the earth. Faustina uttered a piercing shriek, and caught Angeline round the waist; who threw herself before the terrified girl, resolved to suffer the danger herself, rather than it should meet her friend—the animal was close upon them. At that moment, the cavalier rode down the hill, passing the buffalo, and then, wheeling round, intrepidly confronted the wild animal. With a ferocious bellow he swerved aside, and turned down a lane that opened to the left; but the horse, frightened, reared, threw his rider, and then galloped down the hill. The cavalier lay motionless, stretched on the earth.

It was now Angeline's turn to scream; and she and Faustina both anxiously ran to their preserver. While the latter fanned him with her large green fan, which Italian ladies carry to make use of as a parasol, Angeline hurried to fetch some water. In a minute or two, colour revisited his cheeks, and he opened his eyes; he saw the beautiful Faustina, and tried to rise. Angeline at this moment arrived, and presenting the water in a bit of gourd, put it to his lips—he pressed her hand—she drew it away. By this time, old Caterina, finding all quiet, began to look about her, and seeing only the two girls hovering over a fallen man, rose and drew near.

"You are dying!" cried Faustina: "you have saved my life, and are killed yourself."

Ippolito tried to smile. "I am not dying," he said, "but I am hurt."

"Where? how?" cried Angeline. "Dear Faustina, let us send for a carriage for him, and take him to the villa."

"O! yes," said Faustina: "go, Caterina—run—tell papa what has happened—that a young cavalier has killed himself in saving my life."

"Not killed myself," interrupted Ippolito; "only broken my arm, and, I almost fear, my leg."

Angeline grew deadly pale, and sank on the ground.

"And you will die before we get help," said Faustina; "that stupid Caterina craws like a snail."

"I will go to the villa," cried Angeline, "Caterina shall stay with you and Ip——*Buon dio!* what am I saying?"

She rushed away, and left Faustina fanning her lover, who again grew very faint. The villa was soon alarmed, the Signor Conte sent off for a surgeon, and caused a mattress to be slung, with four men to carry it, and came to the assistance of Ippolito. Angeline remained in the house; she yielded at last to her agitation, and wept bitterly, from the effects of fright and grief. "O that he should break his vow thus to be punished—would that the atonement had fallen upon me!" Soon she roused herself, however, prepared the bed, sought what bandages she thought might be necessary, and by that time he had been brought in. Soon after the surgeon came; he found that the left arm was certainly broken, but the leg was only bruised: he then set the limb, bled him, and giving him a composing draught, ordered that he should be kept very quiet. Angeline watched by him all night, but he slept soundly, and was not aware of her presence. Never had she loved so much. His misfortune, which was accidental, she took as a tribute of his affection, and gazed on his handsome countenance, composed in sleep, thinking, "Heaven preserve the truest lover that ever blessed a maiden's vows!"

The next morning Ippolito woke without fever and in good spirits. The contusion on his leg was almost nothing; he wanted to rise: the surgeon visited him, and implored him to remain quiet only a day or two to prevent fever, and promised a speedy cure if he would implicitly obey his mandates. Angeline spent the day at the villa, but would not see him again. Faustina talked incessantly of his courage, his gallantry, his engaging manners. She was the heroine of the story. It was for her that the cavalier had risked his life; her he had saved. Angeline smiled a little at her egotism. "It would mortify her if I told her the truth," she thought: so she remained silent. In the evening it was necessary to return to the convent; should she go in and say adieu to Ippolito? Was it right? Was it not breaking her vow? Still how could she resist? She entered and approached him softly; he heard her step, and looked up eagerly, and then seemed a little disappointed.

"Adieu! Ippolito," said Angeline, "I must go back to my convent. If you should become worse, which heaven forbid, I will return to wait on you, nurse you, die with you; if you get well, as with God's blessing there seems every hope, in one short month, I will thank you as you deserve. Adieu! dear Ippolito."

"Adieu! dear Angeline; you mean all that is right, and your conscience approves you: do not fear for me. I feel health and strength in my frame, and I bless the inconvenience and pain I suffer since you and your sweet friend are safe. Adieu! Yet, Angeline, one word:—my father, I hear, took Camilla back to Bologna with him last year—perhaps you correspond?"

"You mistake; by the Marchese's desire, no letters have passed."

"And you have obeyed in friendship as in love—you are very good. Now I ask a promise also—will you keep one to me as well as to my father?"

"If it be nothing against our vow."

"Our vow! you little nun—are our vows so mighty?—No, nothing against our vow; only that you will not write to Camilla nor my father, nor let this accident be known to them; it would occasion anxiety to no purpose:—will you promise?"

"I will promise not to write without your permission."

"And I rely on your keeping your word as you have your vow. Adieu, Angeline. What! go without one kiss?"

She ran out of the room, not to be tempted; for compliance with this request would have been a worse infringement of her engagement than any she had yet perpetrated.

She returned to Este, anxious, yet happy; secure in her lover's faith, and praying fervently that he might speedily recover. For several days after, she regularly went to Villa Moncenigo to ask after him, and heard that he was getting progressively well, and at last she was informed that he was permitted to leave his room. Faustina told her this, her eyes sparkling with delight. She talked a great deal of her cavalier, as she called him, and her gratitude and admiration. Each day, accompanied by her father, she had visited him, and she had always some new tale to repeat of his wit, his elegance, and his agreeable compliments. Now he was able to join them in the saloon, she was doubly happy. Angeline, after receiving this information, abstained from her daily visit, since it could no longer be paid without subjecting her to the risk of encountering her lover. She sent each day, and heard of his recovery; and each day she received messages from her friend, inviting her to come. But she was firm—she felt that she was doing right; and though she feared that he was angry, she knew that in less than a fortnight, to such had the month decreased since she first saw him, she could display her real sentiments, and as he loved her, he would readily forgive. Her heart was light, or full only of gratitude and happiness.

Each day, Faustina entreated her to come, and her entreaties became more urgent, while still Angeline excused herself. One morning her young friend rushed into her cell to reproach, and question, and wonder at her absence. Angeline was obliged to promise to go; and then she asked about the cavalier, to discover how she might so time her visit, as to avoid seeing him. Faustina blushed—a charming confusion overspread her face as she cried,

"O, Angeline! it is for his sake I wish you to come."

Angeline blushed now in her turn, fearing that her secret was betrayed, and asked hastily,

"What has he said?"

"Nothing," replied her vivacious friend; "and that is why I need you. O, Angeline, yesterday, papa asked me how I liked him, and added that if his father consented, he saw no reason why we should not marry——Nor do I—and yet, does he love me? O, if he does not love me, I would not have a word said, nor his father asked—I would not marry him for the world!" and tears sprung into the sensitive girl's eyes, and she threw herself into Angeline's arms.

"Poor Faustina," thought Angeline, "are you to suffer through me?" and she caressed and kissed her with soothing fondness. Faustina continued. She felt sure, she said, that Ippolito did love her. The name fell startlingly on Angeline's ear, thus pronounced by another; and she turned pale and trembled, while she struggled not to betray herself. The tokens of love he gave were not much, yet he looked so happy when she came in, and pressed her so often to remain—and then his eyes——

"Does he ever ask anything about me?" said Angeline.

"No—why should he?" replied Faustina.

"He saved my life," the other answered, blushing.

"Did he—when?—O, I remember; I only thought of mine; to be sure, your danger was as great—nay, greater, for you threw yourself before me. My own dearest friend, I am not ungrateful, though Ippolito renders me forgetful."

All this surprised, nay, stunned Angeline. She did not doubt her lover's fidelity, but she feared for her friend's happiness, and every idea gave way to that——She promised to pay her visit, that very evening.

And now, see her again walking slowly up the hill, with a heavy heart on Faustina's account, and hoping that her love, sudden and unreturned, would not involve her future happiness. At the turn of the road near the villa, her name was called, and she looked up, and again bending from the balustrade, she saw the smiling face of her pretty friend; and Ippolito beside her. He started and drew back as he met her eyes. Angeline had come with a resolve to put him on his guard, and was reflecting how she could speak so as not to compromise her friend. It was labour lost; Ippolito was gone when she entered the saloon, and did not appear again. "He would keep his vow," thought Angeline; but she was cruelly disturbed on her friend's account, and she knew not what to do. Faustina could only talk of her cavalier. Angeline felt conscience-stricken; and totally at loss how to act. Should she reveal her situation to her friend? That, perhaps, were best, and yet she felt it most difficult of all; besides, sometimes she almost suspected that Ippolito had become unfaithful. The thought came with a spasm of agony, and went again; still it unhinged her, and she was unable to command her voice. She returned to her convent, more unquiet, more distressed than ever.

Twice she visited the villa, and still Ippolito avoided her, and Faustina's account of his behaviour to her, grew more inexplicable. Again and again, the fear that she had lost him, made her sick at heart; and again she re-assured herself that his avoidance and silence towards her resulted

Drawn by John Massey Wright   *Engraved by Charles He*

THE LETTER

from his vow, and that his mysterious conduct towards Faustina existed only in the lively girl's imagination. She meditated continually on the part she ought to take, while appetite and sleep failed her; at length she grew too ill to visit the villa, and for two days, was confined to her bed. During the feverish hours that now passed, unable to move, and miserable at the thought of Faustina's fate, she came to a resolve to write to Ippolito. He would not see her, so she had no other means of communication. Her vow forbade the act; but that was already broken in so many ways; and now she acted without a thought of self; for her dear friend's sake only. But, then, if her letter should get into the hands of others; if Ippolito meant to desert her for Faustina?—then her secret should be buried for ever in her own heart. She therefore resolved to write so that her letter would not betray her to a third person. It was a task of difficulty. At last it was accomplished.

"The signor cavaliere would excuse her, she hoped. She was—she had ever been as a mother to the Signorina Faustina—she loved her more than her life. The signor cavaliere was acting, perhaps, a thoughtless part.—Did he understand?—and though he meant nothing, the world would conjecture. All she asked was, for his permission to write to his father, that this state of mystery and uncertainty might end as speedily as possible."

She tore ten notes—was dissatisfied with this, yet sealed it, and crawling out of her bed, immediately despatched it by the post.

This decisive act calmed her mind, and her health felt the benefit. The next day, she was so well that she resolved to go up to the villa, to discover what effect her letter had created. With a beating heart she ascended the lane, and at the accustomed turn looked up. No Faustina was watching. That was not strange, since she was not expected; and yet, she knew not why, she felt miserable: tears started into her eyes. "If I could only see Ippolito for one minute—obtain the slightest explanation, all would be well!"

Thinking thus, she arrived at the villa, and entered the saloon. She heard quick steps, as of some one retreating as she came in. Faustina was seated at a table reading a letter—her cheeks flushed, her bosom heaving with agitation. Ippolito's hat and cloak were near her, and betrayed that he had just left the room in haste. She turned—she saw Angeline—her eyes flashed fire—she threw the letter she had been reading at her friend's feet; Angeline saw that it was her own.

"Take it!" said Faustina: "it is yours. Why you wrote it—what it means—I do not ask: it was at least indelicate, and, I assure you, useless —I am not one to give my heart unasked, nor to be refused when proposed by my father. Take up your letter, Angeline. O, I could not believe that you would have acted thus by me!"

Angeline stood as if listening, but she heard not a word; she was motionless—her hands clasped, her eyes swimming with tears, fixed on her letter.

"Take it up, I say," said Faustina, impatiently stamping with her little foot; "it came too late, whatever your meaning was. Ippolito has written to his father for his consent to marry me; my father has written also."

Angeline now started and gazed wildly on her friend.

"It is true! Do you doubt—shall I call Ippolito to confirm my words?"

Faustina spoke exultingly. Angeline struck—terrified—hastily took up the letter, and without a word turned away, left the saloon—the house, descended the hill, and returned to her convent. Her heart bursting, on fire, she felt as if her frame was possessed of a spirit not her own: she shed no tears, but her eyes were starting from her head—convulsive spasms shook her limbs; she rushed into her cell—threw herself on the floor, and then she could weep—and after torrents of tears, she could pray, and then—think again her dream of happiness was ended for ever, and wish for death.

The next morning, she opened her unwilling eyes to the light, and rose. It was day; and all must rise to live through the day, and she among the rest, though the sun shone not for her as before, and misery converted life into torture. Soon she was startled by the intelligence that a cavalier was in the parlour desirous of seeing her. She shrunk gloomily within herself, and refused to go down. The portress returned a quarter of an hour after. He was gone, but had written to her; and she delivered the letter. It lay on the table before Angeline—she cared not to open it—all was over, and needed not this confirmation. At length, slowly, and with an effort, she broke the seal. The date was the anniversary of the expiration of the year. Her tears burst forth; and then a cruel hope was born in her heart that all was a dream, and that now, the Trial of Love being at an end, he had written to claim her. Instigated by this deceitful suggestion, she wiped her eyes, and read these words:

"I am come to excuse myself from an act of baseness. You refuse to see me, and I write; for, unworthy as I must ever be in your eyes, I would not appear worse than I am. I received your letter in Faustina's presence —she recognized your handwriting. You know her wilfulness, her impetuosity; she took it from me, and I could not prevent her. I will say no more. You must hate me; yet rather afford me your pity, for I am miserable. My honour is now engaged; it was all done almost before I knew the danger—but there is no help—I shall know no peace till you forgive me, and yet I deserve your curse. Faustina is ignorant of our secret. Farewell."

The paper dropped from Angeline's hand.

It were vain to describe the variety of grief that the poor girl endured. Her piety, her resignation, her noble, generous nature came to her assistance, and supported her when she felt that without them, she must have died. Faustina wrote to say that she would have seen her, but that Ippolito was averse from her doing so. The answer had come from the Marchese della Toretta—a glad consent; but he was ill, and they were all going to Bologna: on their return they would meet.

This departure was some comfort to the unfortunate girl. And soon another came in the shape of a letter from Ippolito's father, full of praises for her conduct. His son had confessed all to him, he said; she was an angel—heaven would reward her, and still greater would be her recompence, if she would deign to forgive her faithless lover. Angeline found relief in answering this letter, and pouring forth a part of the weight of grief and thought that burthened her. She forgave him freely, and prayed that he and his lovely bride might enjoy every blessing.

Ippolito and Faustina were married, and spent two or three years in Paris and the south of Italy. She had been ecstatically happy at first; but soon the rough world, and her husband's light, inconstant nature inflicted a thousand wounds in her young bosom. She longed for the friendship, the kind sympathy of Angeline; to repose her head on her soft heart, and to be comforted. She proposed a visit to Venice—Ippolito consented— and they visited Este in their way. Angeline had taken the veil in the convent of Sant' Anna. She was cheerful, if not happy; she listened in astonishment to Faustina's sorrows, and strove to console her. Ippolito, also, she saw with calm and altered feelings; he was not the being her soul had loved; and if she had married him, with her deep feelings, and exalted ideas of honour, she felt that she should have been even more dissatisfied than Faustina.

The couple lived the usual life of Italian husband and wife. He was gay, inconstant, careless; she consoled herself with a cavaliere servente. Angeline, dedicated to heaven, wondered at all these things; and how any could so easily make transfer of affections, which with her, were sacred and immutable.

XVIII

The Elder Son

My father was the second son of a wealthy baronet. As he and his elder brother formed all the family of my grandfather, he inherited the whole of his mother's fortune, which was considerable, and settled on the younger children. He married a lady whom he tenderly loved; and having taken orders, and procured preferment, retired to his deanery in the north of Ireland, and there took up his abode. When I was about ten years old he lost my mother: I was their only child.

My father was something of an ascetic, if such name can be given to a rigid adherence to the precepts of morality, which arose from the excess, and not the absence of feeling. He adored my mother; he mourned for her to the verge of insanity; his grief was silent, devouring, and gloomy. He never formed another matrimonial engagement: secluding himself entirely from society, and given up to the duties of his sacred calling, he passed his days in solitude, or in works of charity among the poor.

Even now I cannot remember him without awe. He was a tall and, I thought, a venerable-looking man; for he was thin and pale, and he was partly bald. His manners were cold and reserved; he seldom spoke, and when he did it was in such measured phrase, in so calm and solemn a voice, and on such serious topics, as resembled rather oracular enunciation than familiar conversation. He never caressed me; if ever he stroked my head or drew me on his knee, I felt a mingled alarm and delight difficult to describe. Yet, strange to say, my father loved me almost to idolatry; and I knew this and repaid his affection with enthusiastic fondness, notwithstanding his reserve and my awe. He was something greater, and wiser, and better, in my eyes, than any other human being. I was the sole creature he loved; the object of all his thoughts by day and his dreams by night. Abstracted and even severe as he seemed, he has visited my bedside at night, subdued by womanly fears, and hung over me for hours, to assure himself of my life and well-being. He has watched by me in sickness night after night with unwearied assiduity. He never spoke harshly to me, and treated me at once with a distance and gentleness hard to be understood.

When I was eighteen he died. During his last illness the seal was taken from his lips, and his heart threw off that husk within which he had hitherto concealed its true nature. He died of a rapid consumption, which terminated his existence within six months of his being first taken ill. His body wasted under the effects of mortal disease; but his soul assumed new life and energy, and his temper became as soft and demonstrative as it had hitherto been repulsive and concentrated. He became my father, friend, and brother, all in one; a thousand dear relationships combined in one stronger than any. This sudden melting, this divine sensibility, which expanded at once, having been so long shut up and hid, was like a miracle. It fascinated and entranced me. I could not believe that I was about to lose him at the moment when we discovered each other's worth: I mean by that expression, as regards myself, all the happiness that he derived from the truth and vivacity of my filial affection.

It were vain to attempt to refer even to our conversations: the sublime morality he inculcated; the tenderness and charity of his expressions; the overflowing and melting eloquence with which he talked of the affections of this world, and his aspirations after a better. He died suddenly at last, as I was playing to him a simple air my mother loved. It was a moment of horror, yet of solemn and pious resignation: his soul had sought its native heaven and congenial companion—might it be blest! Yet I had lost him, and grief immeasurable was the result. The impression of the misery I suffered can never be entirely worn from my mind: I often wonder my heart did not break with the violence of my sorrow.

I had been brought up at the deanery, apart from all acquaintances. I had had a governess, a most worthy woman, who married just before my father was taken ill, and who kindly came to me when all was over, to endeavour to console the inconsolable. One of my father's objects in life had been to accumulate a fortune for me; not for the sake of placing me in the dangerous situation of an heiress, but to render me independent. It thus happened, that by his ever-lamented death I inherited considerable wealth. His own fortune, my mother's, and his savings, formed the sum of fifty thousand pounds. He left me under the guardianship of his elder brother, Sir Richard Gray, with only one restriction, that I was not to marry, even with my uncle's consent, till I was twenty-one. He wished thus to secure me freedom of choice, and time for deliberation. To this sagacious clause I owe the happiness of my life.

As soon as my health and the first agony of my grief would permit, I left the deanery. My kind governess accompanied me to Dublin, and Sir

Richard Gray came hither himself to fetch me, and to carry me to his seat in England. I was beyond measure surprised when I saw my uncle. He was a year older than my father—my venerable father—and he looked in comparison a boy. He was indeed under fifty, and had at first sight a juvenility of aspect quite astonishing. On examination, the traces of years and care became perceptible; and there was an haggardness in his face which contrasted strangely with its expression of thoughtlessness. No one could be kinder than he was to me, and yet his very kindness was revolting, from the contrast he formed with my lost parent. The world, society, and pleasure, occupied his time and thoughts. Solitude and misery were synonymous terms with him; and he called every thing solitude that did not include the idea of a crowd. He rattled away during our journey, thinking his anecdotes and good stories would enliven me. He was so sorry that it was not the season that I could go to London—he would have invited his daughter, Lady Hythe, to his seat, that he might arrange a party to enliven it for me; but she was on the continent, and his other married daughter was resident in Scotland. What was to be done? He had engagements himself during the shooting season at various gentlemen's houses; and I should be moped to death at Beech Grove. This account of the seclusion of my retreat was all my comfort. I declared that nothing should induce me to go into society for several years. He stared, and then smiled, and in his usual caressing gallant manner said, I should do as I liked; he would never contradict me in any thing: he only hoped that he should be always able to please and gratify me.

My uncle's story is soon told. He married, very early in life, a girl of inferior rank. His relations were exceedingly enraged, and discarded him. His father died; and his grandfather, fearing that he would sell his expectations and squander the whole property, offered him a large immediate income, upon condition that he would entail the estate upon his eldest son. He consented. A few years after, his grandfather died, and he came into the titles and estate. The new Lady Gray made herself many friends from the extreme propriety of her conduct. They had a large family, but lost many children; and she died in childbed of her youngest. Five only survived. The eldest son was abroad: two daughters were well married, and the youngest, a girl of only twelve years of age, lived with her governess at the family seat in Hampshire. Sir Richard talked kindly of his children, but chiefly of his eldest son, against whom therefore I conceived a prejudice; because, from his father's description, I considered him dissipated and worthless. Such, indeed, was my uncle; but I did not dislike him, for by the charm of manner he vanquished aversion, and I transferred to his favourite son the disapprobation he had at first excited. I was glad to hear that my cousin was at Vienna, and that I was not likely to see him.

We arrived at Beech Grove on the 29th August. It was a fine summer day, and the country in all its glory. The house was spacious and elegant, and situated in an extensive park, laid out with infinite taste, and kept up with extreme care. All looked so gay and smiling, so unlike the sombre scenes I had left on the shores of the dark northern ocean, that I contemplated my new abode with distaste: such is the force of habit. My uncle had expected that I should be enchanted with the novel beauty of an English park and mansion, and was disappointed at my languid praise. There were no rocks, no sea, no extensive moors. Groves of beech, a river threading verdant wooded banks, a variety of upland and valley, glade and copse, did not command my admiration; so true it is that we seldom admire that which is absolutely new. A few months totally altered this first impression. The cheerfulness of the scene imperceptibly acted on my spirits. I became reconciled to its (to a certain degree) tameness, and learnt at last to love its refined and elegant beauty.

Sir Richard talked of visiting and company. He would have called his neighbours round us, and forced me to accept invitations at the various houses where, in the shooting season, were assembled large parties of the rich and gay. I earnestly assured him that my depressed spirits and deep-rooted sorrow needed tranquillity—that the seclusion which his house promised was its principal attraction—that I was most happy to be alone. He could not believe my assertions—it hurt his feelings to leave me in this desert: he actually delayed his departure for two days, not liking to quit me. At last he went; and speedily, in the pursuit of pleasure, forgot my existence.

I was not absolutely alone in his house; my cousin Marianne inhabited it with me. She was a pretty, agreeable girl, of twelve years of age; and we got on very well together. I had recourse to her society when over-weary of thought; and she was so young that I could leave her, and betake myself to my mournful, lonely reveries, whenever I liked, without ceremony.

I had not been at Beech Grove more than a week, when late one afternoon, on returning from a drive, we distinguished lights in the dining-room. "Can it be my brother?" cried Marianne; "can Clinton have arrived!"

"I hope not," I said.

"O, do not say so," replied the little girl; "you would love Clinton; he is so lively and dear—every body loves him."

She scarce waited for the steps to be let down, but jumped from the carriage: she returned to me in a minute with an air of disappointment, "It is only my brother Vernon," she said.

"And you do not care about him?"

"O, yes," she replied, "Vernon is very good, and all that; but he is quite different from Clinton; he may stay a month in the house and I not see him twice."

The habit of solitude had rendered me a little bashful. I had dined early with my cousin, and the new-comer was at dinner. I went into the drawing-room therefore, and made her stay with me, and awaited his entrance with some alarm. He soon joined us. As he entered, I was struck with his being the handsomest man I had ever seen. His complexion was a clear olive; his eyes a dark blue; his head small and well-shaped; his figure scarcely above the middle size, but slender and elegant. I expected the courteous manners of my uncle to correspond with the grace of his appearance; but Vernon had no vivacity, no softness. His words were pregnant with meaning, and his eyes flashed fire as he spoke; but his address was abrupt, his conversation pointed and sarcastic, and a dis-agreeable ironical smile, in which he indulged, deteriorated greatly from his good looks. Still, he was very handsome, very clever, and very enter-taining.

One part of Marianne's description at least was erroneous. He spent every day and all day with us. He rode or walked with us in the morning; read to us in the evening; conversed as we worked or painted; and did all that a person most sedulous to please could do, except turning over the leaves of our music-books. He did not like music—of which my father was so passionately fond—in all else his tastes seemed mine. He gave me Italian lessons; and, except when I drove him away, was never absent from our side. Marianne declared that her brother Vernon was an altered man. I thought that I knew whence the alteration sprung.

What girl of eighteen, just emerged from solitude, could perceive the birth of love in the heart of a young, accomplished, and handsome man, and not feel her vanity gratified? My peculiar education had prevented my having any of the coquettishness of beauty or the insolence of wealth. I own I felt elated. I became of consequence in my own eyes; and my silly heart swelled with conscious triumph. Vernon grew each day more openly devoted to me, more solicitous to please, more flattering and attentive. He advanced with imperceptible steps to the desired bourne, and no impatience of temper disturbed for a moment his progress. Stealthy as a serpent, and as wily, he became necessary to my comfort; and I had compromised myself by displaying my vain triumph in my conquest, before he betrayed himself by a word.

When I found that he sought a return for his love, I was frightened. I discovered that with all his talents and agreeable qualities I scarcely liked him; and certainly could never feel a sentiment more tender than friend-ship. I reproached myself for my ingratitude—I felt ashamed of my vacillation. He saw my struggles—he was all humility—he did not deserve better—he was satisfied if I would only be a sister to him—pity him—endure his presence. I agreed, and reassumed my familiarity and good humour.

It is impossible to describe his refined artifice, or the wonderful assiduity with which he watched by his concealed net till I was completely immeshed. He contrived first that I should consent to listen to him talking of his passion;—then he excited my pity for his sufferings—he was eloquent in describing them and in exalting my merits. He asked for so little, he seemed so humble—but he was importunate, and never gave up the smallest advantage he had once gained. Forgotten by my uncle, unknown and unregarded by the rest of the world, I was delivered over to his machinations. Day after day he renewed them. He discerned and worked upon every weakness of my character. My fear to do wrong; my alarm at the idea of being the occasion of pain; my desire to preserve my integrity without a flaw—these might be termed virtues; but, distorted and exaggerated by natural conceit and youthful inexperience, they rendered me a too easy prey. At last he extracted from me a promise to marry him when I should be of age. This pledge seemed the only method left me to prove my delicacy and truth. I gave it the more readily because I admired his talents, and believed that he deserved a better wife than I, and that my want of love was a fault in me for which I ought to compensate to him. With all the rashness and inexperience of my age, I confess that I even tried to conceal my latent aversion; so that when, after having obtained my promise, he went away for a week, I willingly assented to his request that I should correspond with him, and my letters were full of affection. I found it easier to write than speak what I did not really feel, and was glad to shew my gratitude and my sense of his attachment at an easy rate. At the same time, I consented to keep our engagement secret, that thus I might have an excuse for preserving the reserve of my conduct. I took advantage of this wish on his part to insist on his leaving me for a time. I was glad when he went, yet mortified at the readiness of his obedience.

I must not be unjust. Vernon had many faults, but coldness of feeling was not among them. Vehemence and passion were his characteristics, though he could unite them to a deliberation in design, and a wiliness in execution, without example. He had determined before he saw me to win me and my fortune; but such was the violence of his disposition, that he was unavoidably caught in his own toils; and the project that was founded on self-interest ended in making him the slave of love—of a girl whom he despised. He went when I bade him eagerly; but he fulfilled his aim better by so doing. My letters were to be confirmations strong against me—in case that hereafter, as he too justly feared, I should wish to retract my vows. I heedlessly accomplished his ends, beyond his most sanguine expectations. My letters were those of a betrothed bride; and what they might want in tenderness was made up by their uncompromising acknowledgment of our relative position. Having obtained these testimonies, he returned. I was not sorry. I was too little pleased with myself to be in love with solitude. His presence kept alive the feeling of irresistible fate to which I had yielded; and his society enlivened the monotonous quiet of Beech Grove.

At length Christmas came, and my uncle returned and filled his house with visitors. Then the darker shades of Vernon's character became apparent. He was as jealous as an Italian. His disposition was sombre and averse to sociable pleasures. God knows grief sat too heavy at my heart to allow me to be very vivacious; still, I wished to please my uncle, and thought that I had no right to cloud the good humour of the company; and added to this was the elastic spirit of youth, which sprung eagerly and spontaneously from the gloom and mystery of Vernon's artifices into the more congenial atmosphere of friendly intercourse. He saw me unlike any thing he had ever seen in me before—sprightly, and ready to share the amusement of the hour. He groaned in bitterness of spirit. He reproached —reprehended—and became a very task-master. I was naturally timid and docile—in vain did my spirit revolt from his injustice: he gained and kept complete ascendency over me. Yet my soul was in arms against him even while I submitted to his control, and dislike began to develope itself in my bosom. I tasked myself severely for my ingratitude. I became in appearance kinder than ever; but every internal struggle and every outward demonstration had unfortunately one result—to alienate my affections more and more from my lover-cousin.

Our guests left us. My uncle went up to town. He told me he hoped I would accompany him there as soon as Lady Hythe returned to chaperon me. But I was more averse than ever to visiting London. Bound to Vernon by my promises, and wishing to keep my faith with him, I did not like to expose myself to the temptation of seeing others I should like better. Besides, the memory of my father was still unfaded, and I resolved not to appear in public till the year of mourning was expired. Vernon accompanied his father to town, but returned again to us almost immediately. We appeared to revert to our former mode of life; but the essence of it was changed. He was moody.—I anxious. I almost ventured to accuse him of ill-temper and tyranny, till, reading in my own heart its indifference, I was inclined to consider myself the cause of his discontent. I tried to restore his complacency by kindness, and in some degree succeeded.

One day Sir Richard suddenly appeared at Beech Grove. He seemed surprised to find Vernon, and care and even anxiety clouded his usual hilarity. He told us that he expected Clinton daily, and should, immediately on his arrival, bring him down to Hampshire.

"To celebrate my birth-day?" asked Vernon, with a sardonic smile; "I am of age on Friday."

"No," said his father; "he will not be here so soon."

"Nor I so honoured," said Vernon; "Clinton's coming of age was celebrated by tumultuous rejoicings; but he is the Elder Son."

Sir Richard gave Vernon, who spoke sneeringly, a quick glance—an indescribable expression of pain crossed his countenance.

"Have you been staying here since Christmas?" he asked at last. Vernon would have replied evasively, but Marianne said:

"O yes! he is always here now."

"You appear to have become very fond of Beech Grove of a sudden," continued his father. I felt that Sir Richard's eye was fixed on me as he spoke, and I was conscious that not only my cheeks, but my temples and neck were crimsoned with blushes. Some time after I saw my uncle in the shrubbery; he was alone, and the want of society was always so painful to him, that I thought it but a mark of duteous kindness to join him. I wondered, as I approached, to see every token of haggard care on a face usually so smiling. He saw me, and smoothed his brow; he began talking of London, of my elder cousin, of his desire that I should conquer my timidity, and consent to be presented this spring. At length he suddenly stopped short, and scrutinising me as he spoke, said:

"Pardon me, dear Ellen, if I annoy you; but I am your guardian, your second father—am I not? Do not be angry, therefore, if I ask you, are you attached to my son Vernon?"

My natural frankness prompted one reply, but a thousand feelings, inexplicable but powerful, hung on my tongue. I answered, stammering: "No—I believe so—I like him."

"But you do not love him?"

"What a question, dear uncle!" I replied, covered with confusion.

"Is it even so?" cried Sir Richard; "and is he to succeed in all?"

"You mistake," I said; for I had an horror of confessing an attachment which, after all, I did not feel, and so of making our engagement more binding. But I blushed deeply as I spoke, and my uncle looked incredulous and said:

"Yet it would make you very unhappy if he married another."

"O, no!" I cried, "he has my free leave. I should wish him joy with all my heart."

The idea—the hope that he was playing me false, and might release me from my trammels, darted through my mind with a quick thrill of delight. Sir Richard saw that I was in earnest, and his countenance cleared.

"What a strange thing is maiden coyness," he observed; "you blushed so prettily, Ellen, that I could have sworn you had given your heart to Vernon. But I see I was mistaken; I am glad of it, for he would not suit you."

No more was said, but I felt conscience-stricken and miserable. I had deceived my uncle, and yet I had not. I had declared that I did not love him to whom I had pledged my hand; and the whole was a mystery and an entanglement that degraded me in my own eyes. I longed to make a full confession; yet then all would be over—we should both be inextricably bound. As it was, some caprice might cause Vernon to transfer his affection to another, and I could give him entire freedom, without any human being knowing how foolishly I had acted.

We had no guests at dinner; Sir Richard was to leave us early the next morning. After dinner I speedily retired to the drawing-room, leaving father and son together; they remained two hours. I was on the point of withdrawing to my own room, to avoid a meeting which alarmed me, I knew not why, when they entered. It seemed as if, in the interval of my absence, they had received sudden intelligence of a dear friend's death; and yet not quite so, for though Vernon looked absorbed in thought, his gloom was strangely interspersed with glances of swelling triumph; his smiles were no longer sneers—yet they did not betray a sunshine of the heart, but rather joy on a bad victory. He looked on me askance, with a kind of greedy satisfaction, and at his father with scorn. I trembled, and turned to my uncle; but sadness and confusion marked his features—he was stamped as with disgrace, and quailed beneath my eye; though presently he rallied, drew a chair near, and was kinder than ever. He told me that he was going up to town on the morrow, and that Vernon was to accompany him; he asked me if there was any thing he could do for me, and testified his affection by a thousand little attentions. Vernon said nothing, and took leave of me so coldly, that I thought his manner implied that he expected to see me in the morning. Thinking it right to indulge him, I rose early; but he did not come down till long after Sir Richard, who thanked me for my kindness in disturbing myself on his account. They went away immediately after breakfast, and Vernon's formal adieu again struck me with wonder. Was it possible that he was indeed going to marry another? This doubt was all my comfort, for I was painfully agitated by the false position in which I had entangled myself, by the mystery that enveloped my actions, and the falsehood which my lips perpetually implied, if they did not utter.

I was habitually an early riser. On the third morning after the departure of my relations, before I rose, and while I was dressing, I thought that pebbles were thrown at my window; but my mind was too engrossed to pay attention, till at last, after my toilette had been leisurely completed, I looked from my window, and saw Vernon below, in the secluded part of the park which it overlooked. I hurried down, my heart palpitating with anxiety.

"I have been waiting for you these two hours," he said, angrily: "did you not hear my signal?"

"I know of no signal," I replied; "I am not accustomed to clandestine appointments."

"And yet you can carry on a clandestine engagement excellently well! You told Sir Richard that you did not love me—that you should be glad if I married another."

An indignant reply was bursting from my lips, but he saw the rising storm and hastened to allay it. He changed his tone at once from reproach to tender protestations.

"It broke my heart to leave you as I did," he said, "but I could do no less. Sir Richard insisted on my accompanying him—I was obliged to comply. Even now he believes me to be in town. I have travelled all night. He half suspected me, because I refused to dine with him to-day; and I was forced to promise to join him at a ball to-night. I need not be there till twelve or one, and so can stay two hours with you."

"But why this hurried journey?" I asked. "Why do you come?"

He answered by pleading the vehemence of his affection, and spoke of the risk he ran of losing me for ever. "Do you not know," he said, "that my father has set his heart upon your marrying my brother?"

"He is very good," I replied, disdainfully. "But I am not a slave, to be bought and sold. My cousin Clinton is the last person in the world whom you need fear."

"Oh, Ellen, how much do you comfort—transport me, by this generous contempt for wealth and rank! You ask why I am here—it were worth the fatigue, twice ten thousand times told, to have these assurances. I have trembled—I have feared—but you will not love this favoured of fortune—this elder son!"

I cannot describe Vernon's look as he said this. Methought envy, malice, and demoniac exultation were all mingled. He laughed aloud—I shrunk from him dismayed. He became calmer a moment after.

"My life is in your hands, Ellen," he said;—but why repeat his glossing speeches, in which deceit and truth were so kneaded into one mass, that the poison took the guise of the wholesome substance, while the whole was impregnated with destruction. I felt that I liked him less than ever; yet I yielded to his violence. I believed myself the victim of a venial but irreparable mistake of my own. I confirmed my promises, and pledged my faith most solemnly. It is true that I undeceived him as much as I could with regard to the extent of my attachment; at first he was furious at my coldness, then overwhelmed me with entreaties for forgiveness—tears even streamed from his eyes—and then again he haughtily reminded me that I forfeited every virtue of my sex, and became a monument of falsehood, if I failed him. We separated at last—I promised to write every day, and saw him ride away with a sensation as if relieved from the infliction of the torture.

A week after this scene—my spirits still depressed, and often weeping my dear father's death, which I considered the root of every evil—I was reading, or rather trying to read, in my dressing-room, but in reality brooding over my sorrows, when I heard Marianne's cheerful laugh in the shrubbery, and her voice calling me to join her. I roused myself from my sad reverie, and resolved to cast aside care and misery, while Vernon's absence afforded me a shadow of freedom; and, in fulfilment of this determination, went down to join my young light-hearted cousin. She was not alone. Clinton was with her. There was no resemblance between him and Vernon. His countenance was all sunshine; his light-blue eyes laughed in their own gladness and purity; his beaming smile, his silver-toned voice, his tall manly figure, and, above all, his open-hearted engaging manners, were all the reverse of his dark mysterious brother. I saw him, and felt that my prejudices had been ridiculous; we became intimate in a moment. I know not how it was, but we seemed like brother and sister—each feeling, each thought, being laid bare to the other. I was naturally frank, but rendered timid by education; so that it charmed me doubly when the unreserve of another invited me to indulge in the unguarded confidence of my disposition. How speedily the days now flew! they contained but one drawback, my correspondence with my cousin—not that I felt myself unfaithful towards him; my affection for my new-found relation did not disturb my conscience—that was pure, undisguised, sisterly. We had met from across the ocean of life—two beings who formed an harmonised whole; but the sympathy was too perfect, too untinged by earthly dross, to be compared with the selfish love given and exacted by Vernon. Yet I feared that his jealousy might be awakened, while I felt less inclined than ever to belie my own heart; and with aversion and hesitation penned letters containing the formula of affection and engaged vows.

Sir Richard came down to Beech Grove. He was highly pleased to see the cordial friendship that subsisted between his son and me.

"Did I not tell you that you would like him?" he said. "Every one must," I replied, "he is formed to win all hearts."

"And suits you much better than Vernon?"

I did not know what to answer; it was a tender string that he touched; but I resolved not to feel or think. Sir Richard's were all flying visits; he was to leave us in the evening. He had, during the morning, a long conversation with Clinton; and immediately after, he sought for an opportunity to talk to me.

"Ellen," he said, "I have not been a wise but I am a fond father. I have done Clinton many injuries, of which he, poor fellow, is wholly unconscious; and I have wished to compensate for all in giving him a wife worthy of him. His temper is generous; his spirit clear and noble. By my soul, I think he has every virtue under heaven; and you alone deserve him. Do not interrupt me, I beseech you; hear me this once. I confess that ever since you became my ward this has been my favourite project. There have been several obstacles; but the most serious ones seem to vanish. You have seen each other, and I flatter myself have each discovered and appreciated the good qualities of the other. Is it so, Ellen? I know not whence my fears arise, and yet they intrude themselves. I fear, while I have been endeavouring to secure my boy's happiness, I may have been adding to the ruin already heaped on his head by my means. I have talked with him to-day. He has no disguise in his nature, and he avows that he loves you. I know that this confession would come better from himself; but your fortune, your beauty, make him fear to be misinterpreted. Do not mistake—he is wholly unaware of my intention of speaking to you. I see your distress, dear Ellen; have patience but for one word more—do not trifle with Clinton's feelings, as sometimes—forgive me—it has appeared to me that you have trifled with Vernon's—do not foster hopes not to be fulfilled. Be frank, be honest, despite the bashfulness and coquetry of your sex."

After these words, fearful of having offended—overcome by more agitation than I could have imagined him capable of feeling—my uncle drew me towards him, pressed me convulsively to his bosom, and then rushed from the room.

I cannot describe the state in which he left me—a spasm of pain passed through my frame; I became sick and faint, till a flood of tears relieved my bursting heart. I wept long—I sobbed in agony—I felt the veriest wretch that ever trod the earth.

My uncle had rent the veil that concealed me from myself. I loved Clinton—he was the whole world to me—all the world of light and joy, and I had shut myself out from him for ever. And he also was my victim. I beheld his dear face beaming with hope; I heard his thrilling voice harmonised by love; and saw the fearless cordiality of his manners, which bespoke his confidence in my sympathy; while I knew that I held a poisoned dagger which I was about to plunge into his heart. Sometimes I thought to treat him coldly; sometimes—oh! I cannot tell the various imaginations that haunted me—some self-sacrificing, others wicked and false—all ended in one way. My uncle departed; we were left together, our full hearts beating to respond to each other without any division or reserve. I felt that every moment might cause Clinton to open his soul to me, and to seek in mine for a feeling too truly and too fondly alive there, but which was sinful and fatal to both. To prevent his confession, my own preceded it. I revealed to him my engagement to Vernon, and declared my resolve not to swerve from my faith. He commended me. I saw despair at losing me painted in his countenance, mingled with horror at supplanting his brother; and alarm that he, the elder born, gifted by fortune with every blessing, should be suspected of the intention of stealing the sole remaining good, which Vernon had won by his diligence, perhaps by his deserts. Forbid it, Heaven! I saw in the clear mirror of his expressive countenance the struggle of passion and principle, and the triumph of honour and virtue exalted over the truest love that ever warmed man's breast.

Our gaiety was flown; our laughter stilled. We talked sadly and seriously together, neither lamenting our fate nor acknowledging our sufferings; tamed to endurance, and consoling each other by such demonstrations of affection as were permitted to our near relationship. We read clearly in each other's hearts, and supported each other in the joint sacrifice; and this without any direct acknowledgment. Clinton talked of returning to the continent; I of my seclusion and tranquillity at Beech Grove. The time was distant—two years was an eternity at our age—before Vernon could claim my hand; and we did not advert to that fatal consummation. We gave up each other; and that single misery sufficed without a more cruel addition. I was calm, pale, and tearless. I had brought it all on myself, and must submit. I could not cast aside the younger son to select the elder; and if in my secret thoughts I cherished a hope to induce Vernon to forego his claims, that very circumstance would the more entirely divide me from Clinton. As my brother-in-law, I might see him—in some sort, our fortunes were shared; but as a rival to Vernon, a stream of blood separated us for ever.

The hours of sad sympathy which we passed were very dear to us. We knew that they were brief. Clinton had fixed the day and hour of his departure—each moment it drew nearer. We should never meet again till after my marriage; but till the hour of separation, for two short days, we were all in all to each other, despite the wall of adamant which was raised between us. We tried each to pretend to think and talk of indifferent subjects; and we *never* spoke of that nearest our hearts;—but how superfluous are words as interpreters between lovers! As we walked or rode, and spent hours in each other's society, we exchanged thoughts more intimately during long periods of absolute silence, than Vernon with his vehemence and eloquence could have conceived. Had we spoken folio volumes, we could have said no more. Our looks—the very casting down of our eyes and mutual tacit avoidance, told our resolve to fulfil our duties and to conquer our love; and yet how, by a glance or a faltering word, when the future was alluded to, did we promise never to forget, but to cherish mutual esteem and tenderness as all that was left of the paradise from which we were so ruthlessly driven! Now and then a playful expression on his part, or a blush on mine, betrayed more feeling than we considered right; the one was checked by a sigh, the other by an assumption of indifference.

It was at this time that Clinton made the sketch copied in the portrait accompanying this tale. I had been spending many hours in tears and anguish, when, resolved to overcome my weakness, and to recover an appearance of serenity before my cousin returned from his ride, I went into Marianne's school-room, and took up a book. The exhaustion of weeping had calmed me; and I thought of my kinsman—his endearing qualities, and of the tie between us, with softened feelings. As I indulged in reverie, my head resting on my hand, my book falling from my fingers, my eyes closed; and I passed from the agitated sense of life and sorrow into the balmy forgetfulness of sleep. Clinton had wished to make a portrait of me, yet had not ventured to ask me to sit—he came in at this moment; Marianne, whispering, told him not to disturb me. He took her drawing materials, and made a hasty sketch, which genius and love united to render a perfect likeness. I awoke and saw his work; it was beyond our contract; I asked him for it; he felt that I was right, and gave it. This sacrifice on his part proved that he did not palter with his sense of right. On the morrow we were to part; and he would preserve no memorial beyond a remembrance which he could not destroy.

That morrow came. Clinton asked me and his sister to walk through the park with him, to join his chariot at the further lodge. We consented; but, at the moment of going, Marianne, who knew nothing certainly, but who darkly guessed that all was not right, excused herself. I joined him alone. There was something in his person and manner that so promised protection and tenderness, that I felt it doubly hard to be torn from him. A dignified reserve, foreign to his usual nature, founded on a resolve to play only the brother's part, checked me somewhat; yet I loved him the more for it; while I would have laid down my existence so that it had only been permitted us to throw aside the mask but for one short hour, and to use the language of nature and truth. It could not be; and our conversation was upon indifferent subjects. When we approached the lodge, we found that the chariot had not come, and we retreated a little, and sat down on a turfy bank; then Clinton said a few words, the only ones that at all revealed the agitation he was enduring:—

"I have a little more experience than you, Ellen," he said; "and, besides, I am haunted by strange presentiments; we seem to know what we ought to do, and what we are to do, and act accordingly—yet life is a strange, wild thing. I wish to insure for you a friend more willing and active than Sir Richard. I have a sister to whom I am fondly attached; she is now on the continent, but I shall hasten to her, and entreat her to afford you a friendship you so richly deserve. You will love Lady Hythe for her own sake as well as for mine."

I was desirous of thanking him for this mark of kindness, but my voice failed me, and I burst into tears, overcome by the excess of anguish that deluged my heart. I tried to conceal my tears—I could not.

"Do not, Ellen, dear Ellen, I beseech you—command yourself."

Clinton spoke in a voice so broken, so full of misery, that he inspired me at once with fear and courage. The tread of a horse roused us—a horse at swift gallop. I raised my eyes, and uttered a shriek; for, reining in the animal with a sudden strong pull, Vernon halted close to us. The most violent passions convulsed his countenance. He threw himself from the horse, and, casting the bridle from him, came up. What he meant to say or do I cannot tell; perhaps to conceal the workings of his heart—and the quick departure of Clinton would have smoothed all; but I saw the barrel of a pistol peep from the pocket of his coat. I was seized with terror—I shrieked aloud. Clinton, terrified at my alarm, would have supported me, but Vernon pushed him rudely away.

"Dare not to approach or touch her, as you value your life!" he cried.

"My life! you talk idly, Vernon. I value her security—one moment of peace to her—far more."

"You confess it!" exclaimed Vernon; "and you, too, false and treacherous girl! Ha! did you think to betray me, and be unpunished? Do you think, if I so chose it, that I would not force you to look on till the blood of one of the brothers flowed at your feet? But there are other punishments in store for you."

The expressions of menace used towards myself restored my courage, and I exclaimed—"Beware that you do not break the tie that binds us—at least that bound us a moment ago—perhaps it is already broken."

"Doubtless," he cried, grinding his teeth with rage, "it is broken, and a new one created to bind you to the elder son. O, yes! you would fain cast aside the poor miserable beggar, who has vainly fawned on you, and madly loved—you would take the rich, the honourable, and honoured Sir Clinton! Base, hollow-hearted fool!"

"Vernon," said Clinton, "whatever your claims are on our cousin, I cannot stand by and see her insulted. You forget yourself."

"The forgetfulness, sir, is on your part; proud in your seniority, to rival your brother, to drive him from his all, has been a May-game for you; but know, proud fool, or villain—take which name you will—your hour is passed by—your reign at an end! Your station is a fiction, your very existence a disgrace!"

Painted by Henry Wyatt; engraved by J. Henry Robinson

ELLEN

Clinton and I both began to think that Vernon was really mad—a suspicion confirmed by his violent gestures. We looked at each other in alarm.

"Stay!" exclaimed the infuriated man, seizing my arm with a fierce grasp; while, fearful to induce Clinton's interference, I yielded. "Stay, and listen to what your lover is—or shall I wound your delicate ears? There are soft phrases and silken words to adorn that refuse of the world—a bastard!"

"Vernon, dare not!—beware, sir, and begone!"

Clinton's face crimsoned; his voice, his majestic indignation almost forced the ruffian to quail; he threw my arm from him.

"Take him, fair Ellen! it is true you take what I say—a natural son. Do you think that my information is not correct? Ask our father, for he is yours, Clinton, and our mother is the same; you are the first-born of Richard Gray and Matilda Towers; but I am the eldest son of Mr. and Mrs. Gray."

It could not have been that Vernon would have acted this cowardly and foolish part had he not been driven by a kind of madness. In truth, Sir Richard had, to quench his hopes for ever, with that carelessness of truth—his fatal propensity—affirmed that Clinton and I were acknowledged lovers; and he came goaded by worse than jealousy—by a spirit of hatred and revenge. Seeing us together, obviously engaged by the most engrossing feelings, his temper, which had been worked into fury during his journey, burst forth beyond the bounds he had prescribed for himself. I have called him a serpent, and such he was in every respect; he could crawl and coil, and hide his wily advance; but he could erect his crest, dart out his forked tongue, and infix the deadly venom, when roused as he now was. Clinton turned alternately pale and red.

"Be it as you will," he said: "my fortunes and yours are of slight moment in comparison to Ellen's safety. If there is any truth in this tale of yours, there will be time enough to discover it and to act upon it. Meanwhile, dear cousin, I see they have brought my chariot to the lodge. You cannot walk home—get into it; it will drive you to the house, and come back for me."

I looked at him inquiringly.

"Do not fear to be deserted by me," he said, "or that I shall do any thing rashly. Vernon must accompany me to town—to our father's presence, there to expiate his foul calumny, or to prove it. Be assured he shall not approach you without your leave. I will watch over him, and guard you."

Clinton spoke aloud, and Vernon became aware that he must yield to this arrangement, and satisfied that he had divided us. Clinton led me to his carriage.

"You will hear soon from some one of us, Ellen," he said; "and let me implore you to be patient—to take care of yourself—to fear nothing. I can make no remark—affirm, deny nothing now; but you shall not be kept in suspense. Promise me to be patient and calm."

"And do you," I said at last, commanding my trembling voice, "promise not to be rash; and promise not to leave England without seeing me again."

"I promise not to leave England for any time without your leave. Oh, trust me, my dear cousin, it is not in such storms as these that you shall be ashamed of me; one sentiment may subdue me, but poverty, disgrace, and every angry passion, I can master."

Vernon did not dare interrupt us. He felt that he had destroyed his carefully woven web, through his own rashness, and gnawed his lips in silent rage. I looked at him once, and turned away my eyes in contempt. I got into the chariot; it drove me to the house, and went back to take Clinton up to town. Thus we were separated, as we intended; and yet, how differently! Hope was reborn in my heart, out of the very ashes of its despair.

Two mortal days passed, and I was still in my solitude, receiving no intelligence, except, indeed, such as was contained in a letter from Vernon. In this he demanded me as a right, and fiercely insisted that I should keep my faith with him; but he did not allude to the scene in the park, nor to his strange assertions there. I threw the letter from me as unworthy of notice or thought. The third morning brought me one from my uncle. I tore it open with uncontrollable impatience: these were the contents:—

"Clinton, my dear Ellen, insists that I should join you at Beech Grove; but I cannot persuade myself to do so till I have your leave—till I have confessed my villany, and besought your forgiveness, in addition to that of my noble-hearted boy, whom I devoted to ruin before his birth, and who has pardoned me. It is a hateful subject—unfit for your ears, my gentle, virtuous girl, and I must hurry it over. When I first knew Miss Towers, I had no idea of marrying her; for she was poor and of humble birth. We loved each other, and she was willing to become mine on my own terms. Our intercourse was betrayed to her parents; and to appease them, and please Matilda, I declared that we were married. My assertion was credited; Matilda assumed my name, and all the world, all her little world, was deceived; while at the same time I declared to my father that she was merely my mistress: he did not believe me. Thus I became entangled. A little before the birth of our second boy my father died, and my grandfather offered me two thousand a-year on condition, that I would secure the whole estate to my eldest son. I loved Matilda; my fears were dissipated by my father's death, and by this acknowledgment of my union by my grandfather. I married her; and three days after Vernon's birth signed the settlement of entail. Such is my story. Lady Gray's char-

acter necessitated the concealment from every human being of the period
when the marriage was celebrated. My noble, beloved Clinton assumed
the elder son's place. I dared not reveal the truth; nay, I fancied that I
benefited him by allowing him to fill this false position till my death. He
has undeceived me; but he has not cursed me. From the moment I saw
you, I designed that you should repair my faults towards him, as you
alone could. I believed that you were formed for each other; I was not
mistaken there. I meant to acknowledge all before your marriage, but I
believed that if once your affections were engaged, you would not reject
my son from base and worldly-minded considerations. Am I not right
also in this? Meanwhile, Clinton was abroad, and I became uneasy at
observing the pains which Vernon took to ingratiate himself with you,
and the intimacy which you encouraged. I forbade him to remain with
you at Beech Grove—he defied me. Then I tried to entice him away from
you; and, as a last bribe, disclosed the secret of his birth: he, in return,
promised to leave the field open to Clinton. You know the rest. He never
meant to give you up; he was my heir, and he grasped at your fortune
besides—shall he succeed? Clinton is all kindness, and soothing angelic
goodness—but he insists on no longer filling a situation to which he has
no claim, and—is gone abroad. He fears to leave you exposed to Vernon's violence, and has made me promise to go down to Beech Grove,
and to prevent his brother from seeing you without your free and entire
consent. As I have said, I cannot prevail on myself to visit you till you
are in full possession of all the facts. Now they are in your hands. You
may expect me to-morrow. Do not fear Vernon; I will take care that he
shall not commit further outrage on you, nor injure the interest which I
fondly trust that you preserve for my godlike, my beloved Clinton."

I read and re-read this letter a thousand times; my soul was in tumults.
At first I could only think of the facts that it contained, and proudly and
joyfully determined to compensate to Clinton, as I believed I could, for
every evil; and then again I read the letter, and many parts of it filled me
with wonder and dismay. Clinton was gone abroad—against his promise
—without a word: and there was something so indelicate in the way in
which my uncle espoused his cause. It was strange—unlike any conduct I
had expected on my dear cousin's part. Of course he would write—and
yet he was gone, and no letter came! And then I dreaded to see Sir
Richard, the wrongful, penitent father: the total indifference which he
displayed to moral principle—not founded, like Vernon's, on selfishness,
but on weakness of character and natural callousness to truth, revolted
me. Where was my own dear father? He had thrown me from the sacred
shelter of his virtue into a system of dissimulation and guilt, which even
Clinton, I thought, deserting me as he did, did not redeem. I struggled
with these feelings, but their justice confounded and overcame me. Yet,

even in the midst of these disquieting reflections, a deep sense of happiness pervaded my soul. The mystery, the tyranny, which had enveloped
me, was brushed away like a spider's web. I was free—I might follow the
dictates of my feelings, and it was no longer sin to love him to whom my
heart was irrevocably given. The hours of the day flew on, while I lived as
in a dream, absorbed by wonder, hope, doubt, and joy. At length, at six
in the evening, a carriage drove up the avenue; a kind of terror at the
expectation of seeing my uncle seized me, and I retreated hastily to my
own room, gasping for breath. In a few minutes my servant tapped at my
door; she told me that it was Lady Hythe who had arrived, and delivered
me a letter. The letter was from Clinton; it was dated the same day, in
London. I pressed it passionately to my lips and heart, and devoured its
contents with eagerness. "At length, dear Ellen," he wrote, "I am satisfied; I was long uneasy on your account. I besought my father to go down
to you, yet even that did not content me—for you did not so much need
protection as sympathy and true disinterested friendship. My thoughts
turned towards my earliest and dearest friend, my sister Caroline. She
was on the continent—I set out immediately to meet her, to tell every
thing, and to ask her advice and assistance. Fortune befriended me—I
found her at Calais—she is now with you. She is my better self. Her
delicacy of character, her accurate judgment and warm heart, joined to
her position as a woman, married to the best and most generous fellow
breathing, render her the very person to whom I can intrust your happiness. I do not speak of myself—fortune cannot overcome my spirits, and
my way is clear before me. I pity my father and family; but Caroline will
explain to you better than I can my views and hopes. Adeiu, dear cousin!
Heaven bless you as you deserve! Your fortitude, I am sure, has not
deserted you; yet I am very anxious to hear that your health has not
suffered by my brother's violence. Caroline will write to me, and rejoice
me by telling me of your well-being."

I hurried down immediately to welcome Clinton's sister; and from that
moment my perplexities and sorrows vanished. Lady Hythe was a feminine likeness of Clinton; the same active kindness of heart, gentleness of
temper, and adorable frankness. We were friends and sisters on the instant, and her true affection repaid me for every suffering; none of which
I should have experienced had she been in England on my arrival. Clinton had told her of his love, but left me to reveal my own sentiments,
detailing only the artifices and jealousy of Vernon. I was without disguise,
for we were all one family, with the same objects, hopes, and pleasures.
We went up to town immediately, and there I saw Clinton, and we
exchanged our reserved, sad intercourse for a full acknowledgment of
every thought and feeling.

The only piece of prudence that Sir Richard had practised was placing

Clinton in the army, and purchasing promotion for him. He was so beloved by his fellow-officers, that on the discovery of his unfortunate birth, they all united in giving him the support of their friendship and good opinion. Clinton resolved, therefore, to enter at once on active service, and to follow up his profession with energy. Two years were to elapse before I could marry, and he expressed a wish that we should neither of us consider ourselves under any engagement. How vain are such words! Heaven designed us for each other, and the mere phrase of engagement or freedom could not affect a tie founded on affection, esteem, or, beyond this, the passion that caused us to find happiness in each other only. He went with his regiment to Ireland, and we were a good deal divided during the two years that elapsed before I was twenty-one. I continued to reside with Lady Hythe, and enjoyed with her that peace of mind which true friendship affords.

At length the day came when I completed my twenty-first year. Sir Richard had wished to be present at our nuptials, but was unable from ill health. I went to him, and saw him for the first time since the fatal discovery; for, on finding that I was happily placed with his daughter, he had carefully avoided seeing me. His character, indeed, was wholly changed. While carrying on a system of dissimulation, he had appeared gay; he was extravagant; giving up to pleasure, and spending even beyond his large income, despite the ruin in which he knew that his son would be involved on his death. He made him indeed a princely allowance, as if that was to compensate to him; while, in fact, Clinton was only thus habituated to expense. As soon as the discovery was made, Sir Richard, by one of those inconceivable changes which sometimes occur in the history of human nature, set his heart on saving a fortune for his beloved boy. He thought that I might be fickle; he feared his own death and the loss of power to benefit him. He gave up his establishment in town—he let Beech Grove—he saved every farthing that he could, and was enabled to settle twenty thousand pounds on Clinton on the day of our marriage.

I went to see him in a little lodging at Camberwell, whither he had retreated: he was emaciated and ill; his eyes brightened a little on seeing Clinton and me together.

"I would fain live a little longer," he said, "to increase my son's fortune; but God's will be done—you will make him happy, Ellen."

We were inexpressibly shocked. He had concealed his penurious style of life and declining health all this time; and nothing but his illness, and our insisting upon seeing him, caused him to betray it now. Our first care after our marriage was to oblige him to take up his abode with us; and we devoted ourselves to calming his remorse and smoothing his path to the grave. He survived only four months; but he had the comfort of knowing that Clinton was satisfied and happy; and that we both from our hearts forgave the errors which he at last expiated so dearly.

We never saw Vernon again; nor can I tell what has happened to him, except that he lives the life of the rich in England, apparently attended by prosperity. Lady Hythe stood between me and him, and screened me from his violence and reproaches. He has never married. I have never seen him since the day when, in the park at Beech Grove, he unawares conferred on me every blessing of life, by releasing me from the ties that bound me to him.

The happiness of Clinton and myself has been unclouded. I at last persuaded him to give up his profession, and we live principally abroad. Lord and Lady Hythe frequently visit us; and every event of our lives— the unimportant events of domestic life—tends to increase our prosperity, and the entire affection we cherish for each other.

XIX

The Parvenue

Why do I write my melancholy story? Is it as a lesson, to prevent any other from wishing to rise to rank superior to that in which they are born? No! miserable as I am, others might have been happy, I doubt not, in my position: the chalice has been poisoned for me alone! Am I evil-minded —am I wicked? What have been my errors, that I am now an outcast and a wretch? I will tell my story—let others judge me; my mind is bewildered, I cannot judge myself.

My father was a land steward to a wealthy nobleman. He married young, and had several children. He then lost his wife, and remained fifteen years a widower, when he married again a young girl, the daughter of a clergyman, who died, leaving a numerous offspring in extreme poverty. My maternal grandfather had been a man of sensibility and genius; my mother inherited many of his endowments. She was an earthly angel; all her works were charity, all her thoughts were love.

Within a year after her marriage, she gave birth to twins—I and my sister; soon after she fell into ill health, and from that time was always weakly. She could endure no fatigue, and seldom moved from her chair. I see her now; her white, delicate hands employed in needlework, her soft, love-lighted eyes fixed on me. I was still a child when my father fell into trouble, and we removed from the part of the country where we had hitherto lived, and went to a distant village, where we rented a cottage, with a little land adjoining. We were poor, and all the family assisted each other. My elder half-sisters were strong, industrious, rustic young women, and submitted to a life of labour with great cheerfulness. My father held the plough, my half-brothers worked in the barns; all was toil, yet all seemed enjoyment.

How happy my childhood was! Hand in hand with my dear twin sister, I plucked the spring flowers in the hedges, turned the hay in the summer meadows, shook the apples from the trees in the autumn, and at all seasons, gambolled in delicious liberty beneath the free air of Heaven; or at my mother's feet, caressed by her, I was taught the sweetest lessons of charity and love. My elder sisters were kind; we were all linked by strong affection. The delicate, fragile existence of my mother gave an interest to our monotony, while her virtues and her refinement threw a grace over our homely household.

I and my sister did not seem twins, we were so unlike. She was robust, chubby, full of life and spirits; I, tall, slim, fair, and even pale. I loved to play with her, but soon grew tired, and then I crept to my mother's side, and she sang me to sleep, and nursed me in her bosom, and looked on me with her own angelic smile. She took pains to instruct me, not in accomplishments, but in all real knowledge. She unfolded to me the wonders of the visible creation, and to each tale of bird and beast, of fiery mountain or vast river, was appended some moral, derived from her warm heart and ardent imagination. Above all, she impressed upon me the precepts of the gospel, charity to every fellow-creature, the brotherhood of mankind, the rights that every sentient creature possesses to our services alone. I was her almoner; for, poor as she was, she was the benefactress of those who were poorer. Being delicate, I helped her in her task of needlework, while my sister aided the rest in their household or rustic labours.

When I was seventeen, a miserable accident happened. A hayrick caught fire; it communicated to our outhouses, and at last to the cottage. We were roused from our beds at midnight, and escaped barely with our lives. My father bore out my mother in his arms, and then tried to save a portion of his property. The roof of the cottage fell in on him. He was dug out after an hour, scorched, maimed, crippled for life.

We were all saved, but by a miracle only was I preserved. I and my sister were awoke by cries of fire. The cottage was already enveloped in flames. Susan, with her accustomed intrepidity, rushed through the flames, and escaped; I thought only of my mother, and hurried to her room. The fire raged around me; it encircled—hemmed me in. I believed that I must die, when suddenly I felt myself seized upon and borne away. I looked on my preserver—it was Lord Reginald Desborough.

For many Sundays past, when at church, I knew that Lord Reginald's eyes were fixed on me. He had met me and Susan in our walks; he had called at our cottage. There was fascination in his eye, in his soft voice and earnest gaze, and my heart throbbed with gladness, as I thought that he surely loved me. To have been saved by him, was to make the boon of life doubly precious.

There is to me much obscurity in this part of my story. Lord Reginald loved me, it is true; why he loved me, so far as to forget pride of rank and ambition for my sake, he who afterwards showed no tendency to disregard the prejudices and habits of rank and wealth, I cannot tell; it seems strange. He had loved me before, but from the hour that he saved my life, love grew into an overpowering passion. He offered us a lodge on his estate to take refuge in; and while there, he sent us presents of game, and still more kindly, fruits and flowers to my mother, and came himself, especially when all were out except my mother and myself, and sat by us and conversed. Soon I learnt to expect the soft asking look of his eyes, and almost dared answer it. My mother once perceived these glances, and took an opportunity to appeal to Lord Reginald's good feelings, not to make me miserable for life, by implanting an attachment that could only be productive of unhappiness. His answer was to ask me in marriage.

I need not say that my mother gratefully consented—that my father, confined to his bed since the fire, thanked God with rapture; that my sisters were transported by delight: I was the least surprised then, though the most happy. Now, I wonder much, what could he see in me? So many girls of rank and fortune were prettier. I was an untaught, low-born, portionless girl. It was very strange.

Then I only thought of the happiness of marrying him, of being loved, of passing my life with him. My wedding day was fixed. Lord Reginald had neither father nor mother to interfere with his arrangements. He told no relation; he became one of our family during the interval. He saw no deficiencies in our mode of life—in my dress; he was satisfied with all; he was tender, assiduous, and kind, even to my elder sisters; he seemed to adore my mother, and became a brother to my sister Susan. She was in love, and asked him to intercede to gain her parents' consent for her choice. He did so; and though before, Lawrence Cooper, the carpenter of the place, had been disdained, supported by him, he was accepted. Lawrence Cooper was young, well-looking, well-disposed, and fondly attached to Susan.

My wedding day came. My mother kissed me fondly, my father blessed me with pride and joy, my sisters stood round, radiant with delight. There was but one drawback to the universal happiness—that immediately on my marriage, I was to go abroad.

From the church door I stepped into the carriage. Having once and again been folded in my dear mother's embrace, the wheels were in motion, and we were away. I looked out from the window; there was the dear groupe; my old father, white-headed and aged, in his large chair, my mother, smiling through her tears, with folded hands and upraised looks of gratitude, anticipating long years of happiness for her grateful Fanny; Susan and Lawrence standing side by side, unenvious of my greatness, happy in themselves; my sisters conning over with pride and joy the presents made to them, and the prosperity that flowed in from my husband's generosity. All looked happy, and it seemed as if I were the cause of all this happiness. We had been indeed saved from dreadful evils; ruin had ensued from the fire, and we had been sunk in adversity through that very event from which our good fortune took its rise. I felt proud and glad. I loved them all. I thought, I make them happy—they are prosperous through me! And my heart warmed with gratitude towards my husband at the idea.

We spent two years abroad. It was rather lonely for me, who had always been surrounded, as it were, by a populous world of my own, to find myself cast upon foreigners and strangers; the habits of the different sexes in the higher ranks so separate them from each other, that after a few months, I spent much of my time in solitude. I did not repine; I had been brought up to look upon the hard visage of life, if not unflinchingly, at least with resignation. I did not expect perfect happiness. Marriages in humble life are attended with so much care. I had none of this: my husband loved me; and though I often longed to see the dear familiar faces that thronged my childhood's home, and above all I pined for my mother's caresses and her wise maternal lessons, yet for a time I was content to think of them, and hope for a reunion, and to acquiesce in the present separation.

Still many things pained me: I had, poor myself, been brought up among the poor, and nothing, since I can remember forming an idea, so much astonished and jarred with my feelings, as the thought of how the rich could spend so much on themselves, while any one of their fellow-creatures were in destitution. I had none of the patrician charity (though such is praiseworthy), which consists in distributing thin soup and coarse flannel petticoats—a sort of instinct or sentiment of justice, the offspring of my lowly paternal hearth and my mother's enlightened piety, was deeply implanted in my mind, that all had as good a right to the comforts of life as myself, or even as my husband. My charities, they were called— they seemed to me the payment of my debts to my fellow-creatures— were abundant. Lord Reginald peremptorily checked them; but as I had a large allowance for my own expenses, I denied myself a thousand luxuries to which it appeared to me I had no right, for the sake of feeding the hungry. Nor was it only that charity impelled me, but that I could not acquire a taste for spending money on myself—I disliked the apparatus of wealth. My husband called my ideas sordid, and reproved me severely, when, instead of outshining all competitors at a fête, I appeared dowdily dressed, and declared warmly that I could not, I would not, spend twenty guineas on a gown, while I could dress so many sad faces in smiles, and bring so much joy to so many drooping hearts, by the same sum.

Was I right? I firmly believe that there is not one among the rich who will not affirm that I did wrong; that to please my husband and do honour to his rank, was my first duty. Yet, shall I confess it? even now, rendered miserable by this fault—I cannot give it that name—I can call it a misfortune—it is such to be consumed at the stake a martyr for one's faith. Do not think me presumptuous in this simile; for many years I have wasted at the slow fire of knowing that I lost my husband's affections because I performed what I believed to be a duty.

But I am not come to that yet. It was not till my return to England that the full disaster crushed me. We had often been applied to for money by my family, and Lord Reginald had acceded to nearly all their requests. When we reached London after two years' absence, my first wish was to see my dear mother. She was at Margate for her health. It was agreed that I should go there alone, and pay a short visit. Before I went, Lord Reginald told me what I did not know before, that my family had often made exorbitant demands on him, with which he was resolved not to comply. He told me that he had no wish to raise my relatives from their station in society; and that, indeed, there were only two among them whom he conceived had any claims upon me—my mother and my twin sister: that the former was incapable of any improper request, and the latter, by marrying Cooper, had fixed her own position, and could in no way be raised from the rank of her chosen husband. I agreed to much that he said. I replied that he well knew that my own taste led me to consider mediocrity the best and happiest situation; that I had no wish, and would never consent, to supply any extravagant demands on the part of persons, however dear to me, whose circumstances he had rendered easy.

Satisfied with my reply, we parted most affectionately, and I went on my way to Margate with a light and glad heart; and the cordial reception I received from my whole family collected together to receive me, was calculated to add to my satisfaction. The only drawback to my content was my mother's state; she was wasted to a shadow. They all talked and laughed around her, but it was evident to me that she had not long to live.

There was no room for me in the small furnished house in which they were all crowded, so I remained at the hotel. Early in the morning before I was up, my father visited me. He begged me to intercede with my husband; that on the strength of his support he had embarked in a speculation which required a large capital; that many families would be ruined, and himself dishonoured, if a few hundreds were not advanced. I promised to do what I could, resolving to ask my mother's advice, and make her my guide. My father kissed me with an effusion of gratitude, and left me.

I cannot enter into the whole of these sad details; all my half-brothers and sisters had married, and trusted to their success in life to Lord Reginald's assistance. Each evidently thought that they asked little in not demanding an equal share of my luxuries and fortune; but they were all in difficulty—all needed large assistance—all depended on me.

Lastly, my own sister Susan appealed to me—but hers was the most moderate request of all—she only wished for twenty pounds. I gave it her at once from my own purse.

As soon as I saw my mother I explained to her my difficulties. She told me that she expected this, and that it broke her heart: I must summon courage and resist these demands. That my father's imprudence had ruined him, and that he must encounter the evil he had brought on himself; that my numerous relatives were absolutely mad with the notion of what I ought to do for them. I listened with grief—I saw the torments in store for me—I felt my own weakness, and knew that I could not meet the rapacity of those about me with any courage or firmness. That same night my mother fell into convulsions; her life was saved with difficulty. From Susan I learned the cause of her attack. She had had a violent altercation with my father: she insisted that I should not be appealed to; while he reproached her for rendering me undutiful, and bringing ruin and disgrace on his grey hairs. When I saw my pale mother trembling, fainting, dying —when I was again and again assured that she must be my father's victim unless I yielded, what wonder that, in the agony of my distress, I wrote to my husband to implore his assistance.

O! what thick clouds now obscured my destiny! how do I remember, with a sort of thrilling horror, the boundless sea, white cliffs, and wide sands of Margate. The summer day that had welcomed my arrival changed to bleak wintry weather during this interval—while I waited with anguish for my husband's answer. Well do I remember the evening on which it came: the waves of the sea showed their white crests, no vessel ventured to meet the gale with any canvas except a topsail, the sky was bared clear by the wind, the sun was going down fiery red. I looked upon the troubled waters—I longed to be borne away upon them, away from care and misery. At this moment a servant followed me to the sands with my husband's answer, it contained a refusal. I dared not communicate it. The menaces of bankruptcy; the knowledge that he had instilled false hopes into so many; the fears of disgrace, rendered my father, always rough, absolutely ferocious. Life flickered in my dear mother's frame, it seemed on the point of expiring when she heard my father's step; if he came in with a smooth brow, her pale lips wreathed into her own sweet smile, and a delicate pink tinged her fallen cheeks; if he scowled, and his voice was high, every limb shivered, she turned her face to her pillow, while convulsive tears shook her frame, and threatened instant dissolution. My father sought me alone one day, as I was walking in melancholy guise upon the sands; he swore that he would not survive his disgrace. "And do you think, Fanny," he added, "that your mother will survive the

Drawn by Alfred Gomersal Vickers

Engraved by Robert Brandard

MARGATE

knowledge of my miserable end?" I saw the resolution of despair in his face as he spoke.—I asked the sum needed, the time when it must be given.—A thousand pounds in two days was all that was asked. I set off to London to implore my husband to give this sum.

No! no! I cannot step by step record my wretchedness—the money was given—I extorted it from Lord Reginald, though I saw his very heart closed on me as he wrote the cheque. Worse had happened since I had left him. Susan had used the twenty pounds I gave her to reach town, to throw herself at my husband's feet, and implore his compassion. Rendered absolutely insane by the idea of having a lord for a brother-in-law, Cooper had launched into a system of extravagance, incredible as it was wicked. He was many thousand pounds in debt, and when at last Lord Reginald wrote to refuse all further supply, the miserable man committed forgery. Two hundred pounds prevented exposure, and preserved him from an ignominious end. Five hundred more were advanced to send him and his wife to America, to settle there, out of the way of temptation. I parted from my dear sister. I loved her fondly; she had no part in her husband's guilt, yet she was still attached to him, and her child bound them together; they went into solitary, miserable exile. "Ah! had we remained in virtuous poverty," cried my broken-hearted sister, "I had not been forced to leave my dying mother."

The thousand pounds given to my father was but a drop of water in the ocean. Again I was appealed to; again I felt the slender thread of my mother's life depended on my getting a supply. Again, trembling and miserable, I implored the charity of my husband.

"I am content," he said, "to do what you ask, to do more than you ask; but remember the price you pay—either give up your parents and your family, whose rapacity and crimes deserve no mercy, or we part for ever. You shall have a proper allowance; you can maintain all your family on it if you please; but their names must never be mentioned to me again. Choose between us, Fanny—you never see them more, or we part for ever."

Did I do right—I cannot tell—misery is the result—misery frightful, endless, unredeemed. My mother was dearer to me than all the world— my heart revolted from my husband's selfishness. I did not reply—I rushed to my room, and that night in a sort of delirium of grief and horror, at my being asked never again to see my mother, I set out for Margate—such was my reply to my husband.

Three years have passed since then; for these three I preserved my mother, and during all this time I was grateful to Heaven for being permitted to do my duty by her, and though I wept over the alienation of my cruel husband, I did not repent. But she, my angelic support, is no more. My father survived my mother but two months; remorse for all he had done, and made me suffer, cut short his life. His family by his first wife are gathered round me, they importune, they rob, they destroy me. Last week I wrote to Lord Reginald. I communicated the death of my parents; I represented that my position was altered; that my duties did not now clash; and that if he still cared for his unhappy wife all might be well. Yesterday his answer came.—It was too late, he said;—I had myself torn asunder the ties that united us, they never could be knit together again.

By the same post came a letter from Susan. She is happy. Cooper, profiting by the frightful lesson he incurred, awakened to a manly sense of the duties of life, is thoroughly reformed. He is industrious, prosperous, and respectable. Susan asks me to join her. I am resolved to go. O! my native village, and recollections of my youth, to which I sacrificed so much, where are ye now? tainted by pestilence, envenomed by serpents' stings, I long to close my eyes on every scene I have ever viewed. Let me seek a strange land, a land where a grave will soon be opened for me. I feel that I cannot live long—I desire to die. I am told that Lord Reginald loves another, a highborn girl; that he openly curses our union as the obstacle to his happiness. The memory of this will poison the oblivion I go to seek in a distant land.—He will be free. Soon will the hand he once so fondly took in his and made his own, which, now flung away, trembles with misery as it traces these lines, moulder in its last decay.

XX

The Pilgrims

THE TWILIGHT of one of those burning days of summer whose unclouded sky seems to speak to man of happier realms, had already flung its broad shadows over the valley of Unspunnen; whilst the departing rays of a gorgeous sunset continued to glitter on the summits of the surrounding hills. Gradually, however, the glowing tints deepened; then grew darker and darker; until they finally yielded to the still more sober hues of night.

Beneath an avenue of lime trees, which, from their size and luxuriance, appeared almost coeval with the soil in which they grew, Burkhardt of Unspunnen wandered to and fro with uneasy step, as if some recent sorrow occupied his troubled mind. At times, he stood with his eyes steadfastly fixed on the earth, as if he expected to see the object of his contemplation start forth from its bosom; at other times, he would raise his eyes to the summits of the trees, whose branches, now gently agitated by the night breeze, seemed to breathe sighs of compassion in remembrance of those happy hours which had once been passed beneath their welcome shade. When, however, advancing from beneath them, he beheld the deep blue heavens with the bright host of stars, hope sprang up within him at the thoughts of that glory to which those heavens and those stars, all lovely and beauteous as they seem, are but the faint heralds; and for a time dissipated the grief which had so long weighed heavily upon his heart.

From these reflections, which, from the intensity of his feelings, shut him out, as it were, from the busy world and its many paths, he was suddenly aroused by the tones of a manly voice addressing him.

Burkhardt advancing, beheld, standing in the light of the moon, two Pilgrims, clothed in the usual coarse and sombre garb, with their broad hats drawn over their brows.

"Praise be to God!" said the Pilgrim who had just before awakened

Burkhardt's attention, and who, from his height and manner appeared to be the elder of the two. His words were echoed by a voice whose gentle and faultering accents showed the speaker to be still but of tender years.

"Whither are you going, friends? what seek you here, at this late hour?" said Burkhardt. "If you wish to rest you after your journey enter, and with God's blessing, and my hearty welcome, recruit yourselves."

"Noble sir, you have more than anticipated our petition," replied the elder Pilgrim, "our duty has led us far from our native land, being bound on a pilgrimage to fulfil the vow of a beloved parent. We have been forced during the heat of the day to climb the steep mountain paths; and the strength of my brother, whose youth but ill befits him for such fatigues, began to fail, when the sight of your castle's towers, which the moon's clear beams discovered to us, revived our hopes. We resolved to beg a night's lodging under your hospitable roof, that we might be enabled, on to-morrow's dawn, to pursue our weary way."

"Follow me, my friends," said Burkhardt, as he, with quickened step, preceded them, that he might give some orders for their entertainment. The Pilgrims rejoicing in so kind a reception, followed the knight in silence, into a high vaulted saloon; over which, the tapers, that were placed in branches against the walls, cast a solemn but pleasing light, well in accordance with the present feelings of the parties.

The knight then discerned two countenances of great beauty, the pleasing impression of which was considerably heightened by the modest yet easy manner with which the youthful pair received their host's kind attentions. Much struck with their appearance, and demeanour, Burkhardt was involuntarily led back into the train of thoughts from which their approach had aroused him; and the scenes of former days flitted before him as he recollected, that in this hall, his beloved child was ever wont to greet him with her welcome smile on his return from the battle or the chace; brief scenes of happiness, which had been followed by events that had cankered his heart, and rendered memory but an instrument of bitterness and chastisement.

Supper was soon after served, and the Pilgrims were supplied with the greatest attention, yet conversation wholly languished; for his melancholy reflections occupied Burkhardt, and respect, or perhaps a more kindly feeling, towards their host and benefactor, seemed to have sealed the lips of his youthful guests. After supper, however, a flask of the baron's old wine cheered his flagging spirits; and emboldened the elder Pilgrim to break through the spell which had chained them.

"Pardon me, noble sir," said he, "for I feel that it must seem intrusive in me to presume to seek the cause of that sorrow which thus severely oppresses you, and renders you so sad a spectator of the bounty and happiness which you liberally bestow upon others. Believe me, it is not the impulse of a mere idle curiosity that makes me express my wonder that you can thus dwell alone in this spacious and noble mansion, the prey to so deeply rooted a sorrow. Would that it were in our power, even in the slightest degree, to alleviate the cares of one who with such bounteous hand relieves the wants of his poorer brethren!"

"I thank you for your sympathy, good Pilgrim," said the old noble, "but what can it avail you to know the story of those griefs which have made this earth a desert? and which are, with rapid pace, conducting me where alone I can expect to find rest. Spare me, then, the pain of recalling scenes which I would fain bury in oblivion. As yet, you are in the spring of life, when no sad remembrance gives a discordant echo of past follies, or of joys irrecoverably lost. Seek not to darken the sunshine of your, I trust, unsullied youth, with a knowledge of those fierce, guilty beings who, in listening to the fiend-like suggestions of their passions, are led astray from the paths of rectitude; and tear asunder ties which nature, by the holiest bonds, had seemed to unite to their very souls."

Burkhardt thus sought to avoid the entreaty of the Pilgrim. But the request was still urged with such earnest though delicate persuasion, and the rich tones of the stranger's voice awoke within him so many thoughts of days long, long past, that the knight felt himself almost irresistibly impelled to unburden his long closed heart to one who seemed to enter into its feelings with a sincere cordiality.

"Your artless sympathy has won my confidence, my young friends," said he, "and you shall learn the cause of that sorrow which gnaws my heart.

"You see me now, indeed, here, lonely and forsaken, like a tree shaken by the tempest's violence. But fortune once looked upon me with her blandest smiles; and I felt myself rich in the consciousness of my prosperity, and the gifts which bounteous Heaven had bestowed. My powerful vassals made me a terror to those enemies which the protection, that I was ever ready to afford to the oppressed and helpless, brought against me. My rich and fertile possessions not only supplied my family with profusion, but enabled me, with liberal hand, to relieve the wants of the poor; and to exercise the rights of hospitality in a manner justly becoming my state and my name. But of all the gifts which Heaven had showered upon me, that which I most prized was a wife, whose virtues had made her the idol of both the rich and the poor. But she who was already an angel, and unfitted for this grosser world, was too soon, alas! claimed by her kindred spirits. One brief year alone had beheld our happiness.

"My grief and anguish were most bitter; and would soon have laid me in the same grave with her, but that she had left me a daughter, for whose dear sake I struggled earnestly against my affliction. In her were now centered all my cares, all my hopes, all my happiness. As she grew in years, so did her likeness to her sainted mother increase; and every look and gesture reminded me of my Agnes. With her mother's beauty I had, with fond presumption, dared to cherish the hope that Ida would inherit her mother's virtues.

"Greatly did I feel the sad void that my irreparable loss had occasioned me; but the very thought of marrying again would have seemed to me a profanation to the memory of my Agnes. If, however, even for a single instant I had entertained this disposition, one look at her child would have crushed it; and made me cling with still fonder hope to her, in the fond confidence that she would reward me for every sacrifice that I could make. Alas! my friends, this hope was built on an unsure foundation! and my heart is even now tortured when I think on those delusive dreams.

"Ida, with the fondest caresses, would dispel each care from my brow; in sickness and in health she watched me with the tenderest solicitude; her whole endeavour seemed to be to anticipate my wishes. But, alas! like the serpent, which only fascinates to destroy, she lavished these caresses and attentions to blind me, and wrap me in a fatal security.

"Many and deep were the affronts, revenged indeed, but not forgotten, which had long since caused (with shame, I avow it) a deadly hatred between myself and Rupert, Lord of Wädischwyl, which the slightest occasion seemed to increase to a degree of madness. As he dared no longer throw down the gauntlet, I having always in single combat come off the victor, he found means, much harder than steel or iron, to glut his revenge upon me.

"Duke Berchtold of Zähringen, one of those wealthy and powerful tyrants who are the very pests of that society of whose rights they ought to be the ready guardians, had made a sudden irruption on the peaceful inhabitants of the mountains, seizing their herds and flocks, and insulting their wives and daughters. Though possessed of great courage, yet being not much used to warfare, these unhappy men found it impossible to resist the tyrant; and hastened to intreat my instant succour. Without a moment's delay, I assembled my brave vassals, and marched against the spoiler. After a long and severe struggle, God blessed our cause; and our victory was complete.

"On the morning, that I was about to depart.on my return to my castle, one of my followers announced to me that the Duke had arrived in my camp, and wished an immediate interview with me. I instantly went forth to meet him; and Berchtold hastening towards me, with a smile, offered me his hand in token of reconciliation. I frankly accepted it; not suspecting that falsehood could lurk beneath so open and friendly an aspect.

"'My friend,' said he, 'for such I must call you; your valour in this contest having won my esteem, although I could at once convince you that I have just cause of quarrel with the insolent mountaineers. But, in spite of your victory in this unjust strife, into which doubtless you were induced to enter by the misrepresentations of those villains, yet as my nature abhors to prolong dissensions, I would willingly cease to think that we are enemies; and commence a friendship which, on my part, at least, shall not be broken. In token, therefore, that you do not mistrust a fellow soldier, return with me to my castle, that we may there drown all remembrance of our past disunion.'

"During a long time, I resisted his importunity, for I had now been more than a year absent from my home; and was doubly impatient to return, as I fondly imagined that my delay would occasion much anxiety to my daughter. But the Duke, with such apparent kindness and in such a courteous manner renewed and urged his solicitations, that I could resist no longer.

"His Highness entertained me with the greatest hospitality and unremitted attention. But I soon perceived that an *honest* man is more in his element amidst the toils of the battle, than amongst the blandishments of a court; where the lip and the gesture carry welcome, but where the heart, to which the tongue is never the herald, is corroded by the unceasing strifes of jealousy and envy. I soon too saw that my rough and undisguised manners were an occasion of much mirth to the perfumed and essenced nothings who crowded the halls of the Duke. I however stifled my resentment, when I considered that these creatures lived but in his favour; like those swarms of insects which are warmed into existence from the dunghill, by the sun's rays.

"I had remained the unwilling guest of the Duke during some days; when the arrival of a stranger of distinction was announced with much ceremony; this stranger I found to be my bitterest foe, Rupert of Wädischwyl. The Duke received him with the most marked politeness and attention; and more than once I fancied that I perceived the precedence of me was studiously given to my enemy. My frank yet haughty nature could ill brook this system of disparagement; and, besides, it seemed to me that I should but play the hypocrite if I partook of the same cup with the man for whom I entertained a deadly hatred.

"I resolved therefore to depart; and sought his Highness to bid him farewell. He appeared much distressed at my resolution; and earnestly pressed me to avow the cause of my abrupt departure. I candidly confessed that the undue favour which I thought he showed to my rival was the cause.

" 'I am hurt, deeply hurt,' said the Duke, affecting an air of great sorrow, 'that my friend, and that friend the valiant Unspunnen, should think thus unjustly, dare I add, thus meanly of me. No, I have not even in thought wronged you; and to prove my sincerity and my regard for your welfare, know that it was not chance which conducted your adversary to my court. He comes in consequence of my eager wish to reconcile two men whom I so much esteem; and whose worth and excellence place them amongst the brightest ornaments of our favoured land. Let me, therefore,' said he, taking my hand and the hand of Rupert, who had entered during our discourse, 'let me have the enviable satisfaction of reconciling two such men, and of terminating your ancient discord. You cannot refuse a request so congenial to that holy faith which we all profess. Suffer me, therefore, to be the minister of peace; and to suggest that, in token and in confirmation of an act which will draw down Heaven's blessing on us all, you will permit our holy church to unite in one, your far-famed lovely daughter, with Lord Rupert's only son; whose virtues, if reports speak truly, render him no undeserving object of her love.'

"A rage, which seemed in an instant to turn my blood into fire, and which almost choked my utterance, took possession of me.

" 'What!' exclaimed I, 'what, think you that I would thus sacrifice, *thus* cast away my precious jewel! thus debase my beloved Ida? No, by her sainted mother, I swear that rather than see her married to *his* son, I would devote her to the cloister! Nay, I would rather see her dead at my feet, than suffer her purity to be sullied by such contamination!'

" 'But for the presence of his Highness,' cried Rupert wrathfully, 'your life should instantly answer for this insult! Nathless, I will well mark you, and watch you, too, my lord; and if you escape my revenge, you are more than man.'

" 'Indeed, indeed, my Lord of Unspunnen,' said the Duke, 'you are much too rash. Your passion has clouded your reason; and, believe me, you will live to repent having so scornfully refused my friendly proposal.'

" 'You may judge me rash, my Lord Duke, and perhaps think me somewhat too bold, because I dare assert the truth, in the courts of princes. But since my tongue cannot frame itself to speak that which my heart does not dictate, and my plain but honest manner seems to displease you, I will, with your Highness' permission, withdraw to my own domain; whence I have been but too long absent.'

" 'Undoubtedly, my lord, you have my permission,' said the Duke haughtily; and at the same time turning coldly from me.

"My horse was brought, I mounted him with as much composure as I could command; and I breathed more freely as I left the castle far behind.

"During the second day's journey I arrived within a near view of my own native mountains; and I felt doubly invigorated, as their pure breezes were wafted towards me. Still the fond anxiety of a father for his beloved child, and that child his only treasure, made the way seem doubly long. But as I approached the turn of the road which is immediately in front of my castle, I almost then wished the way lengthened; for my joy, my hopes, and my apprehensions crowded upon me almost to suffocation. 'A few short minutes, however,' I thought, 'and then the truth, ill or good, will be known to me.'

"When I came in full sight of my dwelling, all seemed in peace; nought exhibited any change since I had left it. I spurred my horse on to the gate; but as I advanced, the utter stillness and desertion of all around surprised me. Not a domestic, not a peasant was to be seen in the courts; it appeared as if the inhabitants of the castle were still asleep.

" 'Merciful Heaven!' I thought, 'what can this stillness forbode! Is she, is my beloved child dead?'

"I could not summon courage to pull the bell. Thrice I attempted, yet thrice the dread of learning the awful truth prevented me. One moment, one word, even one sign, and I might be a forlorn, childless, wretched man, for ever! None but a father can feel or fully sympathize in the agony of those moments! none but a father can ever fitly describe them! My existence seemed even to depend upon the breath of the first passer by; and my eye shrank from observation lest it should encounter me.

"I was aroused from this inactive state, by my faithful dog springing towards me to welcome my return with his boisterous caresses, and deep and loud toned expressions of his joy. Then, the old porter, attracted by the noise, came to the gate which he instantly opened; but, as he was hurrying forward to meet me, I readily perceived that some sudden and painful recollection checked his eagerness. I leaped from my horse quickly, and entered the hall. All the other domestics now came forward; except my faithful steward Wilfred, he who had been always the foremost to greet his master.

" 'Where is my daughter? where is your mistress?' I eagerly exclaimed; 'let me know but that she lives. Yet stop, stop; one moment, one short moment, ere you tell me I am lost for ever!'

"The faithful Wilfred, who had now entered the hall, threw himself at my feet; and with the tears rolling down his furrowed cheeks, earnestly pressed my hand, and hesitatingly informed me that my daughter *lived*: was well, he believed, but—had quitted the castle.

" 'Now, speak more quickly, old man,' said I hastily, and passionately interrupting him: 'What is it you can mean? my daughter lives; my Ida is well, but she is *not here*. Now, have you and my vassals proved recreants, and suffered my castle in my absence to be robbed of its greatest treasure? Speak! speak plainly, I command ye!'

" 'It is with anguish, as great almost as your own can be, my beloved master, that I make known to you, the sad truth, that your daughter has quitted her father's roof to become the wife of Conrad, the son of the Lord of Wädischwyl.'

" 'The wife of Lord Rupert's son! my Ida the wife of the son of him whose very name my soul loathes!'

"My wrath now knew no bounds; the torments of hell seemed to have changed the current of my blood. In the madness of my passion I even cursed my own dear daughter! Yes, Pilgrim, I even cursed her on whom I had so fondly doted; for whose sake alone life for me had any charms. Oh! how often since have I attempted to recall that curse! and these bitter tears, which even now I cannot control, witness how severe has been my repentance of that awful and unnatural act!

"Dreadful were the imprecations which I heaped upon my enemy; and deep was the revenge I swore. I know not to what fearful length my unbridled passion would have hurried me; had I not, from its very excess, sunk senseless into the arms of my domestics. When I recovered, I found myself in my own chamber, and Wilfred seated near me. Sometime, however, elapsed before I came to a clear recollection of the past events; and when I did, it seemed as if an age of crime and misery had weighed me down, and chained my tongue. My eye involuntarily wandered to that part of the chamber where hung my daughter's portrait. But this, the faithful old man,—who had not removed it, no doubt thinking that to do so would have offended me,—had contrived to hide, by placing before it a piece of armour, which seemed as though it had accidentally fallen into that position.

"Many more days elapsed ere I was enabled to listen to the particulars of my daughter's flight; which I will, not to detain you longer with my griefs, now briefly relate.—It appeared, that urged by the fame of her beauty, and by a curiosity most natural, I confess to youth, Conrad of Wädischwyl had, for a long time sought, but sought in vain, to see my Ida. Chance, at length, however, favoured him. On her way to hear mass at our neighbouring monastery, he beheld her; and beheld her but to love. Her holy errand did not prevent him from addressing her; and well the smooth-tongued villain knew how to gain the ear of one so innocent, so unsuspicious as my Ida! Too soon, alas, did his accursed flatteries win their way to her guiltless heart.

"My child's affection for her father was unbounded; and readily would she have sacrificed her life for mine. But when love has once taken possession of the female heart, too quickly drives he thence those sterner guests, reason and duty. Suffice it therefore to say she was won; and induced to unite herself to Wädischwyl, before my return, by his crafty and insidious argument that I should be more easily persuaded to give them my pardon and my blessing, when I found that the step that she had taken was irrevocable. With almost equal art, he pleaded too that their union would doubtless heal the breach between the families of Wädischwyl and Unspunnen; and thus terminate that deadly hatred which my gentle Ida, ever the intercessor for peace, had always condemned. By this specious sophistry, my poor misguided child was prevailed upon to tear herself from the heart of a fond parent, to unite herself with an unprincipled deceiver, the son of that parent's most bitter enemy."

The pain of these recollections so overcame Burkhardt, that some time elapsed ere he could master his feelings: at length he proceeded.

"My soul seemed now to have but one feeling, *revenge*. All other passions were annihilated by this master one; and I instantly prepared myself and my vassals to chastise this worse than robber. But such satisfaction was (I now thank God) denied me; for the Duke of Zähringen soon gave me memorable cause to recollect his parting words. Having attached himself with his numerous followers to my rival's party, these powerful chiefs suddenly invaded my domain. A severe struggle against most unequal numbers ensued. But, at length, though my brave retainers would fain have prolonged the hopeless strife, resolved to stop a needless waste of blood, I left the field to my foes; and, with the remnant of my faithful soldiers, hastened, in deep mortification, to bury myself within these walls. This galling repulse prevented all possibility of reconciliation with my daughter, whom I now regarded as the cause of my disgrace: and consequently, I forbad her name even to be mentioned in my presence.

"Years rolled on: and I had no intelligence of her until I learned by a mere chance that she had with her husband quitted her native land. Altogether, more than twenty, to me long, long years, have now passed since her flight; and though, when time brought repentance, and my anger and revenge yielded to better feelings, I made every effort to gain tidings of my poor child, I have not yet been able to discover any further traces of her. The chance of so doing was indeed rendered more difficult, by the death of my faithful Wilfred, shortly after my defeat, and by the character of his successor; an individual of strict integrity, but of an austere temper and forbidding manners. Here, therefore, have I lived a widowed, childless, heart-broken old man. But I have at least learned to bow to the dispensations of an All-Wise Providence, which has in its justice stricken me, for thus remorselessly cherishing that baneful passion which Holy Law so expressly forbids. Oh! how I have yearned to see my beloved child! how I have longed to clasp her to this withered, blighted heart! With scalding tears of the bitterest repentance have I revoked those deadly curses, which, in the plenitude of my unnatural wrath, I dared to utter daily. Ceaselessly do I now weary Heaven with my prayers to obliterate all memory of those fatal imprecations; or to let them fall on my own head, and shower down only its choicest blessings on that of my beloved child! But a fear, which freezes my veins with horror, constantly haunts me lest the maledictions which I dared to utter in my moments of demoniac vindictiveness, should, in punishment for my impiety, have been fulfilled.

"Often, in my dreams, do I behold my beloved child; but her looks are always in sadness, and she ever seems mildly but most sorrowfully to upbraid me, for having so inhumanly cast her from me. Yet she must, I fear, have died long ere now; for, were she living, she would not, I think, have ceased to endeavour to regain the affections of a father who once loved her so tenderly. It is true that at first she made many efforts to obtain my forgiveness. Nay, I have subsequently learned that she even knelt at the threshold of my door, and piteously supplicated to be allowed to see me. But my commands had been so peremptory, and, as I before observed, the steward who had replaced Wilfred, was of so stern and unbending a disposition, that, just and righteous as was this her last request, it was unfeelingly denied to her. Eternal Heaven! she whom I had loved as perhaps never father loved before—she whom I had fondly watched almost hourly lest the rude breeze of winter should chill her, or the summer's heat should scorch her—she whom I had cherished in sickness through many a livelong night, with a mother's devotion, and more than a mother's solicitude, even *she*, the only child of my beloved Agnes, and the anxious object of the last moments of her life, was spurned from my door! from this door whence no want goes unrelieved, and where the very beggar finds rest! And now, when I would bless the lips that even could say to me, 'she lives,' I can no where gather the slightest tidings of my child. Ah, had I listened to the voice of reason, had I not suffered my better feelings to be mastered by the wildest, and fellest passions, I might have seen herself, and perhaps her children, happy around me, cheering the evening of my life. And when my last hour shall come, they would have closed my eyes in peace, and, in unfeigned sorrow have daily addressed to Heaven their innocent prayers for my soul's eternal rest; instead of the hirelings who will now execute the mummery of mourning, and impatiently hurry me to an unlamented, a lonely, and an unhonoured grave. To those children also, would have descended that inheritance which must at my decease fall to an utter stranger, who bears not even my name.

"You now know, Pilgrims, the cause of my grief; and I see by the tears which you have so abundantly shed, that you truly pity the forlorn being before you. Remember him and his sorrows therefore ever in your prayers; and when you kneel at the shrine to which you are bound, let not those sorrows be forgotten."

The elder Pilgrim in vain attempted to answer; the excess of his feelings overpowered his utterance. At length, throwing himself at the feet of Burkhardt, and casting off his Pilgrim's habits, he, with difficulty exclaimed,

"See here, thine Ida's son! and behold in my youthful companion, thine Ida's daughter! Yes, before you kneel the children of her whom you so much lament. We came to sue for that pardon, for that love, which we had feared would have been denied us. But, thanks be to God, who has mollified your heart, we have only to implore that you will suffer us to use our poor efforts to alleviate your sorrows; and render more bright and cheerful your declining years."

In wild and agitated surprise, Burkhardt gazed intently upon them. It seemed to him as if a beautiful vision were before him, which he feared even a breath might dispel. When, however, he became assured that he was under the influence of no delusion, the tumult of his feelings over-powered him, and he sank senselessly on the neck of the elder Pilgrim; who, with his sister's assistance, quickly raised the old man, and by their united efforts restored him, ere long, to his senses. But when Burkhardt beheld the younger Pilgrim, the very image of his lost Ida, bending over him with the most anxious and tender solicitude, he thought that death had ended all his worldly sufferings, and that Heaven had already opened to his view.

"Great God!" at length he exclaimed, "I am unworthy of these thy mercies! Grant me to receive them as I ought! I need not ask," added he, after a pause, and pressing the Pilgrims to his bosom, "for a confirmation of your statement, or of my own sensations of joy. All, all tells me that you are the children of my beloved Ida. Say, therefore, is your mother dead? or dare I hope once more to clasp her to my heart?"

The elder Pilgrim, whose name was Hermann, then stated to him, that two years had passed since his parent had breathed her last in his arms. Her latest prayer was, that Heaven would forgive her the sorrow she had caused her father, and forbear to visit her own error on her children's heads. He then added that his father had been dead many years.

"My mother," continued Hermann, drawing from his bosom a small sealed packet, "commanded me, on her death-bed, to deliver this into your own hands. 'My son,' she said, 'when I am dead, if my father still lives, cast yourself at his feet, and desist not your supplications until you have obtained from him a promise that he will read this prayer. It will acquaint him with a repentance that may incite him to recall his curse; and thus cause the earth to lie lightly on all that will shortly remain of his once loved Ida. Paint to him the hours of anguish which even your tender years have witnessed. Weary him, my son, with your entreaties; cease them not until you have wrung from him his forgiveness.'

"As you may suppose, I solemnly engaged to perform my mother's request; and as soon as our grief for the loss of so dear, so fond a parent, would permit us, my sister and myself resolved, in these pilgrim's habits,

to visit your castle; and, by gradual means, to have attempted to win your
affections, if we should have found you still relentless, and unwilling to
listen to our mother's prayer."

"Praise be to that God, my son," said Burkhardt, "at whose command
the waters spring from the barren rock, that he has bidden the streams of
love and repentance to flow once more from my once barren and flinty
heart. But let me not delay, to open this sad memorial of your mother's
griefs. I wish you, my children, to listen to it, that you may hear both her
exculpation and her wrongs."

Burkhardt hid his face in his hands, and remained for some moments
earnestly struggling with his feelings. At length, he broke the seal; and,
with a voice which at times was almost overpowered, read aloud the
contents.

"My beloved father,—if by that fond title your daughter may still
address you,—feeling that my sad days are now numbered, I make this
last effort, ere my strength shall fail me, to obtain at least your pity for
her you once so much loved; and to beseech you to recall that curse which
has weighed too heavily upon her heart. Indeed, my father, I am not quite
that guilty wretch you think me. Do not imagine, that, neglecting every tie
of duty and gratitude, I could have left the tenderest of parents to his
widowed lonely home, and have united myself with the son of his sworn
foe, had I not fondly, most ardently, hoped, nay, had cherished the idea
almost to certainty, that you would, when you found that I was a wife,
have quickly pardoned a fault, which the fears of your refusal to our
union had alone tempted me to commit. I firmly believed that my husband would then have shared with me my father's love, and have, with
his child, the pleasing task of watching over his happiness and comfort.
But never did I for an instant imagine that I was permanently wounding
the heart of that father. My youth, and the ardour of my husband's
persuasions, must plead some extenuation of my fault.

"The day that I learnt the news of your having pronounced against me
that fatal curse, and your fixed determination never more to admit me to
your presence, has been marked in characters indelible on my memory.
At that moment, it appeared as if Heaven had abandoned me, had
marked me for its reprobation as a parricide! My brain and my heart
seemed on fire, whilst my blood froze in my veins. The chillness of death
crept over every limb, and my tongue refused all utterance. I would have
wept, but the source of my tears was dried within me.

"How long I remained in this state I know not, as I at length became
insensible, and remained so for some days. On returning to a full consciousness of my wretchedness, I would instantly have rushed to your

abode, and cast myself at your feet, to wring from you, if possible, your forgiveness of my crime; but my limbs were incapable of all motion. Soon, too, I learned that the letters, which I dictated, were returned unopened; and my husband at last informed me, that all his efforts to see you had been utterly fruitless.

"Yet the moment I had gained sufficient strength, I went to the castle, but, unfortunately for me, even as I entered, I encountered a stern wretch, to whom my person was not unknown; and he instantly told me that my efforts to see his master would be useless. I used prayers and entreaties; I even knelt upon the bare ground to him. But so far from listening to me, he led me to the gate, and, in my presence, dismissed the old porter who had admitted me, and who afterwards followed my fortunes until the hour of his death. Finding that all my attempts were without hope, and that several of the old servants had been discarded on my account, with a heart completely broken, I succumbed to my fate, and abandoned all farther attempt.

"After the birth of my son (to whose fidelity and love I trust this sad memorial) my husband, who, with the tenderest solicitude, employed every means in his power to divert my melancholy, having had a valuable property in Italy bequeathed to him, prevailed upon me to repair to that favoured and beauteous country. But neither the fond attentions of my beloved Conrad, nor the bright sunshine and luxurious breezes of that region of wonders, could overcome a grief so deeply rooted as mine; and I soon found that the gay garden of Europe had less charms for me, than my own dear native land, with its dark, pine-clad mountains.

"Shortly after we had arrived at Rome, I gave birth to a daughter; an event which was only too soon followed by the death of my affectionate husband. The necessity of ceaseless attention to my infant, in some measure alleviated the intense anguish which I suffered from that most severe loss. Nevertheless, in the very depth of this sorrow which almost overcharged my heart, Heaven only knows how often, and how remorsefully, while bending over my own dear children in sickness, have I called to mind the anxious fondness with which the tenderest and best of fathers used to watch over me!

"I struggled long and painfully with my feelings, and often did I beseech God to spare my life, that I might be enabled to instruct my children in His holy love and fear, and teach them to atone for the error of their parent. My prayer has in mercy been heard; the boon I supplicated has been granted; and I trust, my beloved father, that if these children should be admitted to your affections, you will find that I have trained up two blessed intercessors for your forgiveness, when it shall have pleased Heaven to have called your daughter to her account before that dread tribunal where a sire's curse will plead so awfully against her. Recall then, oh, beloved parent! recall your dreadful malediction from your poor repentant Ida! and send your blessing as an angel of mercy to plead for her eternal rest. Farewell, my father, for ever! for ever, farewell! By the cross, whose emblem her fevered lips now press; by Him, who in his boundless mercy hung upon that cross, your daughter, your once much loved Ida, implores you, supplicates you, not to let her plead in vain!"

———

"My child, my child!" sobbed Burkhardt, as the letter dropped from his hand, "may the Father of All forgive me as freely as I from the depths of my wrung heart forgive you! Would that your remorseful father could have pressed you to his heart; with his own lips have assured you of his affection; and wiped away the tears of sorrow from your eyes! But he will cherish these beloved remembrances of you; and will more jealously guard them than his own life."

Burkhardt passed the whole of the following day in his chamber, to which the good Father Jerome alone was admitted; as the events of the preceding day rendered a long repose absolutely necessary. The following morning, however, he entered the hall, where Hermann and Ida were impatiently waiting for him. His pale countenance still exhibited deep traces of the agitation he had experienced; but having kissed his children most affectionately, he smilingly flung round Ida's neck a massive gold chain, richly wrought, with a bunch of keys appended to it.

"We must duly instal our Lady of the Castle," said he, "and invest her with her appropriate authorities.—But, hark! from the sound of the porter's horn, it seems as if our hostess would have early calls upon her hospitality. Whom have we here?" continued he, looking out up the avenue; "By St. Hubert, a gay and gallant knight is approaching, who shall be right welcome—that is, if my lady approve. Well, Willibald, what bring you? a letter from our good friend the abbot of St. Anselm. What says he?"

———

"I am sure that you will not refuse your welcome to a young knight, who is returning by your castle to his home, from the emperor's wars. He is well known to me, and I can vouch for his being a guest worthy of your hospitality, which will not be the less freely granted to him, because he does not bask in the *golden* smiles of fortune."

———

"No, no, that it shall not, my good friend; and if fortune frown upon him, he shall be doubly welcome. Conduct him hither, instantly, good Willibald."

The steward hastened to usher in the stranger, who advanced into the hall, with a modest but manly air. He was apparently about twenty-five years of age; his person was such as might well, in the dreams of a young maiden, occupy no unconspicuous place.

"Sir Knight," said Burkhardt, taking him cordially by the hand, "you are right welcome to my castle, and such poor entertainment as it can afford. We must make you forget your wounds, and the rough usage of a soldier's life. But, soft, I already neglect my duty, in not first introducing our hostess," added the aged knight, presenting Ida. "By my faith," he continued, "judging from my lady's blushing smile, you seem not to have met for the first time. Am I right in my conjecture?"

"We *have* met, sir," replied Ida, with such confusion as pleasantly implied that the meeting was not indifferently recollected, "in the parlour of the Abbess of the Ursulines, at Munich, where I have sometimes been to visit a much valued friend."

"The abbess," said the young knight, "was my cousin; and my good fortune more than once gave me the happiness of seeing in her convent this lady. But little did I expect that amongst these mountains the fickle goddess would again have so favoured a homeless wanderer."

"Well, Sir Knight," replied Burkhardt, "we trust that fortune has been equally favourable to us. And now we will make bold to ask your name; and then, without useless and tedious ceremony, on the part of ourselves and our hostess, bid you again a hearty welcome."

"My name," said the stranger, "is Walter de Blumfeldt; though humble, it has never been disgraced; and with the blessing of Heaven, I hope to hand it down as honoured as I have received it."

Weeks, months, rolled on, and Walter de Blumfeldt was still the guest of the Lord of Unspunnen; till, by his virtues, and the many excellent qualities which daily more and more developed themselves, he wound himself around Burkhardt's heart; which the chastened life of the old knight had rendered particularly susceptible of the kindlier feelings. Frequently would he now, with tears in his eyes, declare that he wished he could convince each and all with whom his former habits had caused any difference, how truly he forgave them, and desired their forgiveness.

"Would," said he one day, in allusion to this subject, "that I could have met my old enemy, the Duke of Zähringen, and with a truly heartfelt pleasure and joy have embraced him, and numbered him amongst my friends. But he is gathered to his fathers, and I know not whether he has left any one to bear his honours."

Each time that Walter had offered to depart, Burkhardt had found some excuse to detain him; for it seemed to him that in separating from his young guest, he should lose a link of that chain which good fortune had so lately woven for him. Hermann, too, loved Walter as a brother;

and Ida fain would have imagined that she loved him as a sister: but her heart more plainly told her what her colder reasoning sought to hide. Unspunnen, who had for some time perceived the growing attachment between Walter and Ida, was not displeased at the discovery, as he had long ceased to covet riches; and had learnt to prize the sterling worth of the young knight, who fully answered the high terms in which the Prior of St. Anselm always spoke of him. Walking one evening under the shade of that very avenue where he had first encountered Hermann and Ida, he perceived the latter, at some little distance, in conversation with Walter. It was evident to Burkhardt that the young knight was not addressing himself to a very unwilling ear, as Ida was totally regardless of the loud cough with which Burkhardt chose to be seized at that moment; nor did she perceive him, until he exclaimed, or rather vociferated,

"Do you know, Walter, that, under this very avenue, two pilgrims, bound to some holy shrine, once accosted me; but that, in pity to my sins and forlorn condition, they exchanged their penitential journey for an act of greater charity; and have ever since remained to extend their kind cares to an aged and helpless relative but too little worthy of their love. One, however, of these affectionate beings is now about to quit my abode, and to pass through the rest of this life's pilgrimage with a helpmate in his toilsome journey, in the person of the fair daughter of the Baron de Leichtfeldt; and thus leave his poor companion to battle the storms of the world, with only the tedious society of an old man. Say, Sir Knight, will thy valour suffer that such wrong be done; or wilt *thou* undertake to conduct this forsaken pilgrim on her way, and guide her through the chequered paths of this variable life? I see by the lowliness with which you bend, and the colour which mantles in your cheek, that I speak not to one insensible to an old man's appeal. But soft, soft, Sir Knight, my Ida is not yet canonized, and therefore cannot afford to lose a hand, which inevitably must occur, if you continue to press it with such very ardent devotion. But what says our pilgrim, does she accept of thy conduct and service, Sir Knight?"

Ida, scarcely able to support herself, threw herself on Burkhardt's neck. We will not raise the veil which covers the awful moment that renders a man, as he supposes, happy or miserable for ever. Suffice it to say, that the day which made Hermann the husband of the daughter of the Baron de Leichtfeldt, saw Ida the wife of Walter de Blumfeldt.

Six months had passed rapidly away to the happy inhabitants of Unspunnen; and Burkhardt seemed almost to have grown young again; such wonders did the tranquillity which now reigned within him perform. He was therefore one of the most active and foremost in the preparations, which were necessary, in consequence of Walter suggesting that they

Drawn by Edward Corbould   Engraved by Stodart

WALTER AND IDA

Mary Shelley: Collected Tales and Stories

should spend Ida's birth-day in a favorite retreat of his and hers. This chosen spot was a beautiful meadow, in front of which meandered a small limpid river, or rather stream; at the back was a gorgeous amphi-theatre of trees, the wide spreading branches of which cast a refreshing shade over the richly enameled grass.

In this beauteous retreat, were Burkhardt, Walter, and his Ida, passing the sultry hours of noon, with all that flow of mirth which careless hearts can alone experience; when Walter, who had been relating some of his adventures at the Court of the Emperor, and recounting the magnificence of the tournaments, turning to his bride, said;

"But what avails all that pomp, my Ida. How happy are we in this peaceful vale! we envy neither princes nor dukes their palaces, or their states. These woods, these glades, are worth all the stiffly trimmed gar-dens of the Emperor, and the great Monarch of France, to boot. What say you, my Ida, could you brook the ceremony of a court, and the pride of royalty? Methinks even the coronet of a duchess would but ill replace the wreath of blushing roses on your head."

"Gently, my good husband," replied Ida, laughing, "they say, you know, that a woman loves these vanities too dearly in her heart, ever to despise them. Then how can you expect so frail a mortal as your poor wife to hold them in contempt? Indeed, I think," added she, assuming an air of burlesque dignity, "that I should make a lofty duchess, and wear my coronet with most becoming grace. And now, by my faith, Walter, I recollect that you have this day, like a true and gallant knight, promised to grant whatever boon I shall ask. On my bended knee, therefore, I humbly sue that if you know any spell or magic wile, to make a princess or a duchess for only a single day, that you will forthwith exercise your art upon me; just in order to enable me to ascertain with how much or how little dignity I could sustain such honours. It is no very difficult matter, Sir Knight: you have only to call in the aid of Number Nip, or some such handy workman of the woods. Answer, most chivalrous hus-band, for thy disconsolate wife rises not until her prayer is granted."

"Why, Ida, you have indeed craved a rare boon," replied Walter, "and how to grant it may well puzzle my brain, till it becomes crazed with the effort. But, let me see, let me see," continued he, musingly; "I have it!—Come hither, love, here is your throne," said he, placing her on a gentle eminence richly covered with the fragrant wild thyme and the delicate harebell; "kings might now envy you the incense which is offered to you. And you, noble sir," added he, addressing Burkhardt, "must stand beside her Highness, in quality of chief counsellor. There are your attendants around you: behold that tall oak, he must be your Highness' poursuivant; and yonder slender mountain ashes, your trusty pages."

"This is but a poor fulfilment of the task you have undertaken, Sir

mummer," said Ida, with a playful, and arch affectation of disappointment.

"Have patience for a brief while, fair dame," replied Walter, laughing;
"for now must I awaken your Highness' men at arms."

Then, taking from his side, a silver horn, he loudly sounded the
melodious reveillée. As he withdrew the instrument from his lips, a
trumpet thrillingly answered to the call; and scarcely had its last notes
died away, when, from the midst of the woods, as if the very trees were
gifted with life, came forth a troop of horsemen, followed by a body of
archers on foot. They had but just entirely emerged, when numerous
peasants, both male and female, appeared in their gayest attire; and,
together with the horsemen and the archers, rapidly and picturesquely
ranged themselves in front of the astonished Ida, who had already abdi-
cated her throne, and clung to the arm of Walter. They then suddenly
divided; and twelve pages in richly emblazoned dresses advanced. After
them followed six young girls, whose forms and features the Graces might
have envied, bearing two coronets placed on embroidered cushions. In
the rear of these, supporting his steps with his abbatial staff, walked the
venerable Abbot of St. Anselm; who, with his white beard flowing almost
to his girdle, and his benign looks, that showed the pure commerce of the
soul which gave life to an eye, the brightness of which seventy years had
scarcely diminished, seemed to Ida a being of another world. The young
girls then advancing, and kneeling before Walter, and his wife, presented
the coronets.

Ida, who had remained almost breathless with wonder, could now
scarcely articulate,

"Dear, dear Walter, what is all this pomp—what does—what can it
mean?"

"Mean! my beloved," replied her husband, "did you not bid me make
you a Duchess? I have but obeyed your high commands, and I now salute
you, Duchess of Zähringen!"

The whole multitude then made the woods resound with the acclama-
tion,

"Long live the Duke, and Duchess of Zähringen!"

Walter, having for some moments, enjoyed the unutterable amazement
of the now breathless Ida, and the less evident but perhaps equally intense surprise of Burkhardt, turning to the latter, said,

"My more than father, you see in me the son of your once implacable
enemy, the Duke of Zähringen. He has been many years gathered to his
fathers; and I, as his only son, have succeeded to his title, and his large
possessions. My heart, my liberty, were entirely lost in the parlour of the
Abbess of the Ursulines. But when I learnt whose child my Ida was, and
your sad story, I resolved ere I would make her mine, to win not only her

love, but also your favour and esteem. How well I have succeeded, this little magic circle on my Ida's finger is my witness. It will add no small measure to your happiness, to know that my father had for many years repented of the wrongs which he had done you; and, as much as possible to atone for them, entrusted the education of his son to the care of this my best of friends, the Abbot of St. Anselm, that he might learn to shun the errors into which his sire had unhappily fallen. And now," continued he, advancing, and leading Ida towards the Abbot, "I have only to beg your blessing, and that this lady, whom through Heaven's goodness I glory to call my wife, be invested with those insignia of the rank which she is so fit to adorn."

Walter, or as we must now call him, the Duke of Zähringen, with Ida, then lowly knelt before the venerable Abbot; whilst the holy man, with tears in his eyes, invoked upon them the blessings of Heaven. His Highness then rising, took one of the coronets, and placing it on Ida's head, said,

"Mayst thou be as happy under this glittering coronet, as thou wert under the russet hood, in which I first beheld thee."

"God and our Lady aid me!" replied the agitated Ida; "and may He grant that I may wear it with as much humility. Yet thorns, they say, spring up beneath a crown."

"True, my beloved," said the Duke, "and they also grow beneath the peasant's homely cap. But the rich alchemy of my Ida's virtues will ever convert all thorns into the brightest jewels of her diadem."

XXI

Euphrasia

A TALE OF GREECE

Two YEARS AGO, that is at Christmas, 1836, four friends left Brighton on their way to the seat of an acquaintance, about thirty miles distant, where they intended to pass this season of festivity. Any one who was in Sussex at that time, must remember the fall of snow on Christmas eve, which transformed Brighton into a town of Siberia, and held all its sojourners prisoners. The king's courier was stopt by the drift on his way to London; no letters were sent or received for three days; the Pavilion had no guests; the horses and carriages could not make their way through the blocked-up streets; it was a strange wild sight. Still, as this party was resolved to pursue its way, four horses were harnessed to their carriage, and they set out. They arrived half way to Lewes, when the carriage became blocked up; the postilions blinded by the drift; the horses unable to move. Night was drawing in, and they saw naught but one wide expanse of snow, which was scattered in thick showers by the winds. They looked from the windows; the horses were above their knees in drift, as the postilions urged them to wade on. What made it worse was, that one of the party was a woman; a being ill suited to encounter the rude elements; whose father was overwhelmed with terror lest she should be chilled by the night air, or forced to alight and wet her feet. Her spirit was high; she had insisted on accompanying him, and wrapt in fur, had braved the season; but now he wondered at his folly in bringing her, and looked at her little foot in its satin slipper, with a sort of feeling, that if she moved from the carriage, she would be but a mouthful for the tempest, and disappear on the instant. Meanwhile darkness gathered thick around; there was no hope of moving. The father of the lady had alighted to view the scene, and then was afraid of getting into the carriage again, with a coating of snow round him, lest its thawing should give his daughter cold. She was not afraid; she was afraid of nothing; but he feared for her more than words can express. At length it was agreed that the father of the young lady and the postilions should mount the horses and make their way to Lewes, whence some sort of litter could be sent for her, and horses for the rest of the party, who remained to guard her.

They went, and those left behind continued looking wistfully on the scene, visible by its transcendent whiteness, even now that night had closed round. For a few minutes they were silent; they thought on the road the travellers had to pass; they longed for their return—a few moments seemed an age. One of the gentlemen struck his repeater; the same sound was given, as when he had struck it at the departure of his friend— a quarter past six.

"The hours will never pass!" exclaimed the anxious girl.

"O yes, they will," said the other, "I once passed a night more anxious than this promises to be, yet it had an end. It is strange that the scene I refer to should be vividly present now, being so different in scenery, in season, in personages, and in country from this."

Anxious to divert the mind of the daughter, and to lighten the slow pace of the hour, the third of this anxious party asked his young friend, Harry Valency, by name, what the events were that marked that long unforgotten night, and made him understand that he would do well to relate them, if the task were not a painful one. He understood the hint, and began. His tale was afterwards repeated to me, and, as I heard it, I wish to recount it now; yet, hearing it only at second-hand, I shall tell it lamely, and spoil the lively earnest interest he spread over every detail; while he who told it to me had but a vague recollection of dates and names of places, and even some of those of persons had entirely escaped him. However, such portion as reached me of the story, I will set down.

It was not long after the breaking out of the Greek revolution, that Harry Valency visited Greece. Many an Englishman was led thither at that time by the spirit of adventure, and many perished. Valency was not nineteen; his spirit was wild and reckless;—thought or care had never touched his brow; his heart was too light for love. Restless and energetic, he longed to try his powers, with the instinct that leads the young deer to butt against trees, or to wrestle with each other in the forest-dells. He was the only son of a widowed mother, whose life was wrapt in his, and he loved her fondly; yet left her, guided by a desire for adventure, unable to understand what anxiety and fear meant; and in his own person eager to meet even misfortune, so that it came in a guise to call forth manly and active struggles. He longed to have the pages of his young life written over by deeds that would hereafter be memories, to which he could turn with delight. The cause of Greece warmed his soul. He was in a transport of ecstacy when he touched the shores of that antique land, and looked around on mountain and mountain-stream, whose names were associated with the most heroic acts, and the most sublime poetry man ever achieved or wrote. Yes, he was now in Greece. He was about to fight in her cause against the usurping Turk. He had prepared himself by a sedulous study of Romaic; he was on his way to the seat of government, to offer his services. To proceed thither from the spot where he had disembarked, was a matter of some difficulty; the troops of the Pasha being then in possession of many of the passes. At length he heard that a band of about fifty Greek soldiers, headed by a young but brave and renowned chief, was about to pursue the same road; he asked and obtained leave to accompany them.

How delightful was the commencement of the journey! How beautiful the country!—defile and steep hill side, by which they proceeded; where the grey olive clothed the upland, or vines, embracing elms, red now with late summer tints, varied the scene. The mountain tops were bare or crowned with pines, and torrents ran down the sides and fed a stream in the dell. The air was balmy, the cicala loud and merry—to live was to be happy. Valency was mounted on a spirited horse; he made it leap and caracole. He threw a spear against a tree, and dashed after to recover it. He fired at a mark as he hurried on at full gallop; every feat was insufficient to tame his exhaustless spirits.

The Chief marked him with eyes, whose deep melancholy expression darkened as he gazed. He was known as bravest among the brave; yet gentle and kindly as a woman. He was very young, singularly handsome; his countenance was stamped with traces of intellectual refinement, while his person was tall, muscular, and strong, but so gracefully formed that every attitude reminded you of some Praxitilean shape of his own native land. Once he had been more beautiful; joy, as well as tenderness, and a soldier's ardour had lighted up his dark eye; his lip had been the home of smiles, and the thoughts, which presided in his brow, had been as clear and soft, and gladsome as that godlike brow itself. Now this was changed. Grief had become a master passion: his cheeks were sunken; his eye seemed to brood eternally over melancholy regrets; his measured harmonious voice was attuned to the utterance of no light fancy or gay sallies; he spoke only the necessary words of direction to his followers, and then silence and gloom gathered over his face. His sorrow was respected; for it was known to be well-founded, and to spring from a recent disaster. If any of his troop desired to indulge in merriment, they withdrew from his vicinity. It was strange to them to hear the light laugh of the English youth ring through the grove, and to catch the tones of his merry voice, as he sang some of their own gayest songs. The Chief gazed with interest. There was a winning frankness in the boy; he was so very young, and all he did was in graceful accordance with his age. We are alike mere youths, thought the Chief, and how different. Yet soon he may become like me. He soars like an eagle; but the eagle may be wounded, and stoop to earth; because earth contains its secret and its regret.

Suddenly Valency, who was some hundred yards in advance, was encountered by a Greek, riding at full speed towards the advancing troop.

"Back! back! silence!" the man cried. He was a scout, who had been sent on before, and now brought tidings that a troop of three or four hundred of the Turkish army was entering the defile, and would soon advance on the handful of men which Valency accompanied. The scout rode directly up to the leader, and made his report, adding,

"We have yet time. If we fall back but a quarter of a mile, there is a path I know, by which I can guide you across the mountain—on the other side we shall be safe."

A smile of scorn for a moment wreathed the lip of the Chief, at the word safety, but his face soon reassumed its usual sad composure. The troop had halted; each man bent his eye on the leader. Valency, in particular, marked the look of scorn, and felt that he would never retreat before danger.

"Comrades!" the Chief thus addressed his men, "it shall never be said that Greeks fell back to make way for the destroyers; we will betake ourselves to our old warfare. Before we entered this olive wood, we passed a thick cover; where the dark jutting mountain-side threw a deep shadow across our path; and the torrent drowned all sound of voice or hoof. There we shall find ambush; there the enemy will meet death."

He turned his horse's head, and in a few minutes reached the spot he named; the men were mostly eager for the fray—while one or two eyed the mountain side—and then the path that led to the village, which they had quitted that morning. The Chief saw their look, and he glanced also at the English youth, who had thrown himself from his horse, and was busy loading and priming his arms. The Chief rode up to him—

"You are our guest and fellow-traveller," he said, "but not our comrade in the fight. We are about to meet danger—it may be that not one of us shall escape. You have no injuries to avenge, no liberty to gain; you have friends—probably a mother—in your native land. You must not fall with us. I am going to send a message to warn the village we last passed through—do you accompany my messengers."

Valency had listened attentively at first; but as the Chief continued, his attention reverted to his task of loading his pistols. The last words called a blush into his cheek.

"You treat me as a boy," he cried; "I may be one in aspect, but you shall find me a man in heart this day. You also young, I have not deserved your scorn!"

The Chief caught the youth's flashing eye. He held out his hand to him, saying—"Forgive me."

"I will," said Valency, "on one condition; give me a post of danger—of honour. You owe it to me in reparation of the insult you offered."

"Be it so," said the Chief, "your place shall be at my side."

A few minutes more and his dispositions were made;—two of the most down-hearted of the troop were despatched to alarm the village, the rest were placed behind the rocks; beneath the bushes, wherever broken ground, or tuft of underwood, or fragment from the cliff, afforded shelter and concealment, a man was placed; while the Chief himself took his stand on an elevated platform, and, sheltered by a tree, gazed upon the road. Soon the tramp of horses, the busy sound of feet and voices were heard, overpowering the rushing of the stream; and turban and musket could be distinguished as the enemy's troop threaded the defile.

The shout of battle—the firing—the clash of weapons were over. Above the crest of the hill, whose side had afforded ambush to the Greeks, the crescent moon hung, just about to dip behind; the stars in her train burnt bright as lamps floating in the firmament; while the fire-flies flashed among the myrtle underwood and up the mountain side; and sometimes the steel of the arms strewn around, dropt from the hands of the dead, caught and reflected the flashes of the celestial or earthly stars. The ground was strewn with the slain. Such of the enemy as had cut their way through, were already far—the sound of their horses' hoofs had died away. The Greeks who had fled across the mountain had reached a spot of safety—none lay there but the silent dead—cold as the moon-beam that rested on their pale faces for a moment, and then passed off, leaving them in shadow and death. All were still and motionless—some lay on the hill side, among the underwood—some on the open road—horses and men had fallen, pell mell—none moved—none breathed.

Yet there was a sigh—it was lost in the murmur of the stream; a groan succeeded, and then a voice feeble and broken—"My mother, my poor mother!"—the pale lips that spoke these words could form no other, a gush of tears followed. The cry seemed to awake another form from among the dead. One of the prostrate bodies raised itself slowly and painfully on its arm, the eyes were filmy, the countenance white from approaching death, the voice was hollow, yet firm, that said—"Who speaks?—who lives?—who weeps?"

The question struck shame to the wounded man; he checked his overflow of passionate sobbings. The other spoke again—"It was not the voice of a Greek—yet I thought I had saved that gallant boy—the ball meant for him is now in my side.—Speak again, young Englishman—on whom do you call?"

"On her who will weep my death too bitterly—on my mother," replied Valency, and tears would follow the loved name.

"Art thou wounded to death?" asked the Chief.

"Thus unaided I must die," he replied, "the blood gushes in torrents from a deep sabre cut—yet, could I reach those waters, I might live—I must try." And Valency rose; he staggered a few steps, and fell heavily at the feet of the Chief. He had fainted. The Greek looked on the ghastly pallor of his face; he half rose—his own wound did not bleed, but it was mortal, and a deadly sickness had gathered round his heart, and chilled his brow, which he strove to master, that he might save the English boy. The struggle brought cold drops on his brow, as he rose on his knees and stooped to raise the head of Valency; he shuddered to feel the warm moisture his hand encountered. It is his blood; his life blood he thought; and again he placed his head on the earth, and continued a moment still, summoning what vitality remained to him to animate his limbs. Then with a determined effort he rose, and staggered to the banks of the stream. He held a steel cap in his hand—and now he stooped down to fill it; but with the effort the ground slid from under him, and he fell. There was a ringing in his ears—a cold dew on his brow—his breath came thick—the cap had fallen from his hand—he was dying. The bough of a tree, shot off in the morning's mêlée, lay near;—the mind, even of a dying man, can form swift unerring combinations of thought;—it was his last chance—the bough was plunged in the waters, and he scattered the grateful reviving drops over his face—vigor returned with the act, and he could stoop and fill the cap, and drink a deep draught, which for a moment restored the vital powers. And now he carried water to Valency; he dipt the unfolded turban of a Turk in the stream, and bound the youth's wound, which was a deep sabre cut in the shoulder, that had bled copiously. Valency revived—life gathered warm in his heart—his cheeks, though still pale, lost the ashy hue of death—his limbs again seemed willing to obey his will—he sat up, but he was too weak, and his head drooped. As a mother tending her sick first-born, the Greek chief hovered over him; he brought a cloak to pillow his head; as he picked up this, he found that some careful soldier had brought a small bag at his saddle bow, in which was a loaf and a bunch or two of grapes; he gave them to the youth, who ate. Valency now recognized his saviour; at first he wondered to see him there, tending on him, apparently unhurt; but soon the Chief sank to the ground, and Valency could mark the rigidity of feature, and ghastliness of aspect, that portended death. In his turn he would have assisted his friend; but the Chief stopt him—"You die if you move," he said, "your wound will bleed afresh, and you will die, while you cannot aid me. My weakness does not arise from mere loss of blood. The messenger of death has reached a vital part—yet a little while and the soul will obey the summons. It is slow, slow is the deliverance; yet the long creeping hour will come at last, and I shall be free."

"Do not speak thus," cried Valency, "I am strong now—I will go for help."

"There is no help for me," replied the Chief, "save the death I desire. I command you, move not."

Valency had risen, but the effort was vain: his knees bent under him, his head spun round; before he could save himself, he had sunk to the ground.

"Why torture yourself," said the Chief, "a few hours and help will come: it will not injure you to pass this interval beneath this calm sky. The cowards who fled will alarm the country, by dawn succour will be here: you must wait for it. I too must wait; not for help, but for death. It is soothing, even to me, to die here beneath this sky, with the murmurs of yonder stream in my ear, the shadows of my native mountains thrown athwart. Could aught save me, it would be the balmy airs of this most blessed night; my soul feels the bliss, though my body is sick and fast stiffening in death. Such was not the hour when she died, whom soon I shall meet, my Euphrasia, my own sweet sister, in Heaven!"

It was strange, Valency said, that at such an hour, but half saved from death, and his preserver in the grim destroyer's clutches, that he should feel curiosity to know the Greek Chief's story. His youth, his surpassing beauty of person—his valour—the act, which Valency well remembered, of his springing forward so as to shield him with his own person—his last words and thoughts devoted to the soft recollection of a beloved sister,— awakened an interest beyond even the present hour, fraught as it was with the chances of life and death. He questioned the Chief; probably fever had succeeded to his previous state of weakness, imparted a deceitful strength, and even inclined him to talk; for thus dying, unaided and unsheltered, except by the starry sky, he willingly reverted to the years of his youth, and to the miserable event which a few months before had eclipsed the sun of his life, and rendered death welcome.

They—brother and sister, Constantine and Euphrasia—were the last of their race. They were orphans; their youth was passed under the guardianship of the brother by adoption of their father, whom they named father, and who loved them as his own soul. He was a glorious old man, nursed in classic lore, and more familiar with the deeds of men who had glorified his country several thousand years before, than with any more modern names. Yet all who had ever done and suffered for Greece, were embalmed in his memory and honored as martyrs in the best of causes. He had been educated in Paris, and travelled in Europe and America, and was aware of the progress made in the science of politics all over the civilized world. He felt that Greece would soon share the benefits to arise from the changes then operating, and he looked forward at no distant day to its liberation from bondage. He educated his young ward for that day. Had he believed that Greece would have continued hopelessly enslaved, he had brought him up as a scholar and a recluse: but assured of the impending struggle, he made him a warrior; he implanted a detestation of the oppressor; a yearning love for the sacred blessings of freedom, a noble desire to have his name enrolled among the deliverers of his country. The education he bestowed on Euphrasia was yet more singular. He knew that though liberty must be bought and maintained by the sword, yet that its dearest blessings must be derived from civilization and knowledge, and he believed women to be the proper fosterers of these. They cannot handle a sword nor endure bodily labor for their country, but they could refine the manners, exalt the souls—impart honor, and truth, and wisdom, to their relatives and their children. Euphrasia therefore he made a scholar. By nature she was an enthusiast, and a poet. The study of the classic literature of her country corrected her taste and exalted her love of the beautiful. While a child she improvised passionate songs of liberty; and as she grew in years and loveliness, and her heart opened to tenderness, and she became aware of all the honor and happiness that a woman must derive from being held the friend of man, not his slave, she thanked God that she was a Greek and a Christian; and holding fast by the advantages which these names conferred, she looked forward eagerly to the day when Mahometanism should no longer contaminate her native land, and when her countrywomen should be awakened from ignorance and sloth in which they were plunged, and learn that their proper vocation in the creation, was that of mothers of heros and teachers of sages.

Her brother was her idol—her hope—her joy. And he who had been taught that his career must be that of deeds not words, yet was fired by her poetry and eloquence to desire glory yet more eagerly, and to devote himself yet more entirely, and with purer ardour, to the hope of one day living and dying for his country. The first sorrow the orphans knew was the death of their father of adoption. He descended to the grave, full of years and honor. Constantine was then eighteen; his fair sister had just entered her fifteenth year. Often they spent the night beside the revered tomb of their lost friend, talking of the hopes and aspirations he had implanted. The young can form such sublime, such beautiful dreams. No disappointment, no evil, no bad passion shadows their glorious visions; to dare and do greatly for Greece was the ambition of Constantine. To cheer and watch over her brother, to regulate his wilder and more untaught soul, to paint in celestial colors the bourne he tended towards by action, were Euphrasia's tasks.

"There is a heaven," said the dying man, as he told his tale; "there is a paradise for those who die in the just cause. I know not what joys are there prepared for the blest; but they cannot transcend those that were mine, as I listened to my own sweet sister, and felt my heart swell with patriotism and fond warm affection."

At length there was a stir through the land, and Constantine made a journey of some distance, to confer with the capitani of the mountains, and to prepare for the outbreak of the revolution. The moment came, sooner even than he expected. As an eagle chained when the iron links drop from him, and with clang of wing and bright undazzled eye he soars to heaven, so did Constantine feel when freedom to Greece became the war cry. He was still among the mountains, when first the echoes of his native valleys repeated that animating—that sacred word; instead of returning as he intended to his Athenian home, he was hurried off to Western Greece, and became involved in a series of warlike movements, the promised success of which filled him with transport.

Suddenly a pause came in the delirium of joy which possessed his soul. He received not the accustomed letters from his sister—missives which had been to him angelic messengers, teaching him patience with the unworthy—hope in disappointment—security in final triumph. Those dear letters ceased; and he thought he saw in the countenances of his friends around a concealed knowledge of evil. He questioned them: their answers were evasive. At the same time, they endeavoured to fill his mind with the details of some anticipated exploit, in which his presence and co-operation was necessary. Day after day passed; he could not leave his post without injury to his cause, without even the taint of dishonor. He belonged to a band of Albanians, by whom he had been received as a brother, and he could not desert them in the hour of danger. But the suspense grew too terrible; and at length, finding that there was an interval of a few days which he might call his own, he left the camp, resting neither day nor night; dismounting from one horse only to bestride another, in forty-eight hours he was in Athens, before his vacant desecrated home. The tale of horror was soon told. Athens was still in the hands of the Turks; the sister of a rebel had become the prey of the oppressor. She had none to guard her. Her matchless beauty had been seen and marked by the son of the Pasha; she had for the last two months inhabited his harem.

"Despair is a cold dark feeling," said the dying warrior; "if I may name that despair which had a hope—a certainty—an aim. Had Euphrasia died I had wept. Now my eyes were horn—my heart stone. I was silent. I neither expressed resentment nor revenge. I concealed myself by day; at night, I wandered round the tyrant's dwelling. It was a pleasure-palace, one of the most luxurious that adorned the enemies of our beloved Athens. At this time it was carefully guarded; my character was known and Euphrasia's worth, and the oppressor feared the result of his deed. Still, under shadow of darkness I drew near. I marked the position of the women's apartments—I learned the number—the length of the watch—the orders they received, and then I returned to the camp. I revealed my project to a few select spirits. They were fired by my wrongs, and eager to deliver my Euphrasia."——

Constantine broke off—a spasm of pain shook his body. After this had passed he lay motionless for a few minutes; then, starting up, as fever and delirium, excited by the exertion of speaking, increased by the agonies of recollection, at last fully possessed him. "What is this," he cried; "fire! Yes, the palace burns. Do you not hear the roaring of the flames, and thunder too—the artillery of heaven levelled against the unblest. Ha! a shot—he falls—they are driven back—now fling the torches—the wood crackles—there, there are the women's rooms—ha! poor victims, lo! you shudder and fly! Fear not; give me only my Euphrasia!—my own Euphrasia! No disguise can hide thee, dressed as a Turkish bride crowned with flowers, thy lovely face, the seat of unutterable woe, still, my sweet sister, even in this smoke and tumult of this house, thou art the angel of my life. Spring into my arms, poor frightened bird, cling to me—it is herself—her voice—her fair arms are round my neck—what ruin—what flame—what choking smoke—what driving storm, can stay me. Soft! the burning breach is passed—there are steps—gently—dear one, I am firm —fear not!—what eye glares?—fear not, Euphrasia, he is dead—the miserable retainers of the tyrant fell beneath our onset—ha! a shot— gracious Panagia, is this thy protection!" Thus did he continue to rave— the onset—the burning of the palace—the deliverance of his sister, all seemed to pass again vividly as if in present action. His eyes glared—he tossed up his arms—he shouted as if calling his followers around him— and then, in tones of heartfelt tenderness, he addressed the fair burthen he fancied that he bore—till, with a shriek, he cried again, "A shot!" and sank to the ground as if his heartstrings had broken.

An interval of calm succeeded; he was exhausted; his voice was broken.

"What have I told thee," he continued, feebly; "I have said how a mere handful of men attacked the palace, and drove back the guards—how we strove in vain to make good our entrance—fresh troops were on their way—there was no alternative; we fired the palace. Deep in the seclusion of the harem the women had retreated, a herd of frightened deer. One alone stood erect. Her eyes bent on the intruders—a dagger in her hand —majestic and fearless, her face was marked with traces of passed suffering, but at the moment, the stern resolution her soft features expressed, was more than human. The moment she saw me, all was changed; the angel alone beamed in her countenance. Her dagger fell from her hand— she was in my arms—I bore her from the burning roof—the rest you know; have I not said it? Some miscreant, who survived the slaughter, and yet lay as dead on the earth, aimed a deadly shot. She did not shriek.

Drawn by Edward Corbould   Engraved by J. Henry Robinson

CONSTANTINE AND EUPHRASIA

At first she clung closer to my neck, and then I felt her frame shiver in my arms and her hold relax. I trusted that fear alone moved her; but she knew not fear—it was death. Horses had been prepared, and were waiting; a few hours more and I hoped to be on our way to the west, to that portion of Greece that was free. But I felt her head fall on my shoulder. I heard her whisper, 'I die, my brother! carry me to our father's tomb.'

"My soul yearned to comply with her request; but it was impossible. The city was alarmed; troops gathering from all quarters. Our safety lay in flight, for still I thought that her wound was not mortal. I bore her to the spot where we had left our horses. Here two or three of my comrades speedily joined me; they had rescued the women of the harem from the flames; but the various sounds denoting the advance of the Turkish soldiery, caused them to hurry from the scene. I leapt on my horse, and placed my sweet sister before me, and we fled amain through desert streets, I well knew how to choose, and along the lanes of the suburbs into the open country, where deviating from the high road, along which I directed my companions to proceed in all haste—alone with my beloved burthen, I sought a solitary unsuspected spot among the neighbouring hills. The storm which had ceased for a time, now broke afresh; the deafening thunder drowned every other sound, while the frequent glare of the lightning showed us our path; my horse did not quail before it. Euphrasia still lay clinging to me; no complaint escaped her; a few words of fondness, of encouragement, of pious resignation, she now and then breathed forth. I knew not she was dying; till at last entering a retired valley, where an olive wood afforded shelter, and still better the portico of a fallen ancient temple, I dismounted and bore her to the marble steps, on which I placed her. Then indeed I felt how near the beloved one was to death, from which I could not save her. The lightning showed me her face; pale as the marble which pillowed it. Her dress was dabbled in warm blood, which soon stained the stones on which she lay. I took her hand, it was deathly cold. I raised her from the marble; I pillowed her cheek upon my heart. I repressed my despair, or rather my despair in that hour was mild and soft as herself. There was no help—no hope. The life blood oozed fast from her side; scarce could she raise her heavy eye-lids to look on me; her voice could no longer articulate my name. The burthen of her fair limbs grew heavier and more chill; soon it was a corse only that I held. When I knew that her sufferings were over, I raised her once more in my arms, and once more I placed her before me on my horse, and betook me to my journey, alone, though still I bore her form in my arms. The storm was over now, and the moon bright above. Earth glittered under the rays, and a soft breeze swept by, as if heaven itself became clear and peaceful to receive her stainless soul, and present it to its Maker. By morning's dawn, I stopt at a convent gate, and rang. To the holy maidens within I consigned my own fair Euphrasia. I kissed but once again her dear brow, which spoke of peace in death; and then saw her placed upon a bier, and was away, back to my camp, to live and die for Greece."

He grew more silent, as he became weaker. Now and then he spoke a few words to record some other of Euphrasia's perfections, or to repeat some of her dying words; to speak of her magnanimity, her genius, her love, and his own wish to die.

"I might have lived," he said, "till her image had faded in my mind, or been mingled with less holy memories. I die young, all her own. Those whom the gods favor, all die young."

His voice grew more feeble after this; he complained of cold. Valency continued, "I contrived to rise, and crawl about, and to collect a capote or two, and a pelisse from among the slain, with some of which I covered him; and then I drew one over myself, for the air grew chill, as midnight had passed away and the morning hour drew near. The warmth which the coverings imparted, calmed the aching of my wound, and, strange to say, I felt slumber creep over me. I tried to watch and wake. At first the stars above, and the dark forms of the mountains mingled with my dreamy feelings; but soon I lost all sense of where I was, and what I had suffered, and slept peacefully and long.

"The morning sun-beams, as creeping down the hill side, they at last fell upon my face, awoke me. At first I had forgotten all thought of the events of the passed night, and my first impulse was to spring up, crying aloud, where am I? but the stiffness of my limbs and their weakness, soon revealed the truth. Gladly I now welcomed the sound of voices, and marked the approach of a number of peasants along the ravine. Hitherto, strange to say, I had thought only of myself; but with the ideas of succour, came the recollection of my companion, and the tale of the previous night. I glanced eagerly to where he lay; his posture disclosed his state; he was still, and stiff, and dead. Yet his countenance was calm and beautiful. He had died in the dear hope of meeting his sister, and her image had shed peace over the last moment of life.

"I am ashamed to revert to myself. The death of Constantine is the true end of my tale. My wound was a severe one. I was forced to leave Greece, and for some months remained between life and death in Cefalonia, till a good constitution saved me, when at once I returned to England."

XXII

The Heir of Mondolfo

IN THE BEAUTIFUL and wild country near Sorrento in the kingdom of Naples, at the time that it was governed by monarchs of the house of Anjou, there lived a territorial noble whose wealth and power overbalanced that of the neighbouring nobles. His castle, itself a stronghold, was built on a rocky eminence toppling over the blue and lovely Mediterranean. The hills around were covered with ilex forests or subdued to the culture of the olive and vine. Under the sun no spot could be found more favoured by Nature.

If at eventide you had passed on the placid wave beneath the castellated rock that bore the name of Mondolfo, you would have imagined that all happiness and bliss must reside within its walls, which, thus nestled in beauty, overlooked a scene of such surpassing loveliness. Yet if by chance you saw its lord issue from the portal, you shrunk from his frowning brow, you wondered at what could impress on his worn cheek the combat of passions. More piteous sight was it to behold his gentle lady, who, the slave of his unbridled temper, the patient sufferer of many wrongs, seemed on the point of entering upon that only repose "where the wicked cease from troubling and the weary are at rest."* The Prince Mondolfo had been united early in life to a princess of the royal family of Sicily. She died on giving birth to a son. Many years afterwards, after a journey to the northern Italian states, he returned to his castle married. The speech of his bride declared her to be a Florentine. The current tale was that he married her for love, and then hated her as the hindrance of his ambitious views. She bore all for the sake of her only child—a child born to its father's hate; a boy of gallant spirit, brave even to wildness. As he grew up, he saw with anger the treatment his mother received from the haughty prince. He dared come forward her defender; he dared oppose his boyish courage to his father's rage. The result was natural; he

* Job 3:17.

became the object of his father's dislike. Indignity was heaped on him; the vassals were taught to disobey him, the menials to scorn him, his very brother to despise him as of inferior blood and birth. Yet the blood of Mondolfo was his; and though tempered by the gentle Isabel's more kindly tide, it boiled at the injustice to which he was a victim. A thousand times he poured forth the overflowings of his injured spirit in eloquent complaints to his mother. As her health decayed, he nurtured the project, in case of her death, of flying his paternal castle and becoming a wanderer, a soldier of fortune. He was now thirteen. The Lady Isabel, soon with a mother's penetration, discovered his secret, and on her deathbed made him swear not to quit his father's protection until he should have attained the age of twenty. Her heart bled for the wretchedness that she foresaw would be his lot, but she looked forward with still greater horror to the picture her active fancy drew of her son at an early age, wandering forth in despair alone and helpless, suffering all the extremities of famine and wretchedness—or almost worse, yielding to the temptations that in such a situation would be held out to him. She extracted this vow, and died satisfied that he would keep it. Of all the world, she alone knew the worth of her Ludovico—had penetrated beneath the rough surface and become acquainted with the rich store of virtue and affectionate feeling that lay like unmined ore in his sensitive heart.

Fernando hated his son. From his earliest boyhood he had felt the sentiment of aversion, which, far from endeavouring to quell, he allowed to take deep root until Ludovico's most innocent action became a crime; and a system of denial and resistance was introduced, that called forth all of sinister that there was in the youth's character, and engendered an active spirit of detestation in his father's mind. Thus Ludovico grew hated and hating; brought together through their common situation, the father and son, lord and vassal, oppressor and oppressed, the one was continually ready to exert his power of inflicting evil—the other perpetually on the alert to resist even the shadow of tyranny.

After the death of his mother, Ludovico's character greatly changed: the smile that as the sun had then often irradiated his countenance now never shone; suspicion, irritability, and dogged resolution, seemed his master feelings. He dared his father to the worst, endured that worst, and, prevented from flying by his sacred observance to his vow, nurtured all angry and even revengeful feelings till the cup of wrath seemed ready to overflow. He was loved by none: his good qualities expired or slept as if they would never more awaken.

His father intended him for the Church, and Ludovico until he was sixteen wore the priestly garb. That period past, he cast it aside and appeared habited as a cavalier of those days, and in short words told his parent that he refused to comply with his wishes, that he should dedicate himself to arms and enterprize. All that followed this declaration— menace, imprisonment, and even ignominy—he bore; but he continued firm, and the haughty Fernando was obliged to submit his towering will to the firmer will of a stripling. And now for the first time, while rage seemed to burst his heart, he felt to its highest degree the sentiment of hatred; he expressed this passion; words of contempt and boundless detestation were heaped upon Ludovico's head; the boy replied, and the bystanders feared that a personal encounter would ensue. Once, Fernando put his hand on his sword, and the unarmed Ludovico drew in and collected himself as if ready to spring and seize the arm that might be uplifted against him. Fernando saw and dreaded the mad ferocity his son's eye expressed. In all personal encounter of this kind, the victory rests not with the strong but the most fearless. Fernando was not ready to stake his life or even with his own hand to shed his son's blood; Ludovico, not as aggressor but in self-defence, was careless of the consequences of an attack. He would resist to the death, and this dauntless feeling gave him an ascendency his father felt and could not forgive.

From this time Fernando's conduct towards his son changed—he no longer punished, imprisoned, or menaced him. This was usage for a boy, but the prince felt that they were man to man and acted accordingly. He was the gainer by the change: for he soon acquired all the ascendency that experience, craft, and a court education must naturally give him over an hot-headed youth, who, nerved to resist all personal violence, neither saw nor understood a more covert mode of proceeding. Fernando hoped to drive his son to desperation. He set spies over him, paid the tempters that were to lead him to crime, and, by a continual system of restraint and miserable thwarting, hoped to reduce him to such despair that he would take refuge in any line of conduct that promised freedom from so irksome and degrading a slavery. His observance of his vow saved the youth; and this steadiness of purpose gave him time to read and understand the motives of the tempters. He saw his father's master hand in all, and his heart sickened at the discovery.

He had reached his eighteenth year. The treatment he had endured and the constant exertion of fortitude and resolution had already given him the appearance of manhood. He was tall, well-made, and athletic. His person and demeanour were more energetic than graceful, and his manners were haughty and reserved. He had few accomplishments, for his father had been at no pains in his education; feats of horsemanship and arms made up the whole catalogue. He hated books as being a part of a priest's insignia: he was averse to all occupation that brought bodily repose with it. His complexion was dark—hardship had rendered it even sallow; his eyes, once soft, now glared with fierceness; his lips, formed to express tenderness, were now habitually curled in contempt; his dark hair, clustering in thick curls round his throat, completed the wild but grand and interesting appearance of his person.

It was winter, and the pleasures of the chase began. Every morning the huntsmen assembled to attack the wild boars or stags, which the dogs might rouse in the fastnesses of the Apennines. This was the only pleasure that Ludovico ever enjoyed. During these pursuits he felt himself free. Mounted on a noble horse which he urged to its full speed, his blood danced in his veins and his eyes shone with rapture as he cast his eagle glance to heaven; with a smile of ineffable disdain, he passed his false friends or open tormentors and gained a solitary precedency in the pursuit.

The plain at the foot of Vesuvius and its neighbouring hills were stript bare by winter; the full streams rushed impetuously from the hills, and their roar mingled with the baying of the dogs and the cries of the hunters. (The sea, dark under a lowering sky, made a melancholy dirge as its waves broke on the shore.) Vesuvius groaned heavily, and the birds answered it by wailing shrieks; a heavy sirocco hung upon the atmosphere, rendering it damp and cold. This wind seems at once to excite and depress the human mind—it excites it to thought, but colours these thoughts as it does the sky with black. Ludovico felt this, but he tried to surmount the natural feelings with which the ungenial air filled him.

The temperature of the air changed as the day advanced; the clouded sky spent itself in snow which fell in abundance; it then became clear, and a sharp frost succeeded. The aspect of earth was changed. Snow covered the ground and lay on the leafless trees, sparkling, white, and untrod. Early in the morning a stag had been roused, and, as he was coursed along the plain skirting the hills, the hunters went at speed. All day the chase endured. At length the stag, who from the beginning had directed his course towards the hills, began to ascend them, and with various windings and evolutions almost put the hounds to fault. Day was near its close when Ludovico alone followed the stag as it made for the edge of a kind of platform of the mountain, which, isthmus-like, was connected with the hill by a small tongue of land, and on three sides was precipitous to the plain below. Ludovico balanced his spear; and his dogs drew in, expecting that the despairing animal would there turn to bay. He made one bound which conducted him to the very brow of the precipice —another—and he was seen no more. He sprung downwards, expecting more pity from the rocks beneath than from his human adversary. Ludovico was fatigued by his chase and angry at the escape of his prey; he sprung from his horse, tied him to a tree, and sought a path by which he might safely descend to the plain. Snow covered and hid the ground, obliterating the usual traces that the flocks or herds might have left as they descended from their pastures on the hills to the hamlets beneath.

But Ludovico had passed his boyhood among mountains: while his hunting spear found sure rest on the ground, he did not fear; or while a twig afforded him sufficient support as he held it, he did not doubt to secure his passage. But the descent was precipitous, and necessary caution obliged him to be long. The sun approached the horizon, and the glow of its departure was veiled by swift-rising clouds, which the wind blew upwards from the sea—a cold wind, which whirled the snow from its resting place and shook it from the trees. Ludovico at length arrived at the foot of the precipice. The snow reflected and increased the twilight, and he saw four deep marks that must have been made by the deer. The precipice was high above, and its escape appeared a miracle. It must have escaped, but those were the only marks it had left. Around lay a forest of ilex beset by thick and entangled underwood, and it seemed impossible that any animal so large as the stag in pursuit could have broken its way through the apparently impenetrable barrier it opposed. The desire to find his quarry became almost a passion in the heart of Ludovico; he walked round to seek for an opening, and at last found a narrow pathway through the forest, and some few marks seemed to indicate that the stag might have sought for refuge up the glen. With a swiftness characteristic even of his prey, Ludovico rushed up the pathway, and thought not of how far he ran, until breathless he stopped before a cottage that opposed itself to his further progress. He stopped and looked around. There was something singularly mournful in the scene. It was not dark, but the shades of evening seemed to descend from the vast woof of cloud that climbed the sky from the west. The black and shining leaves of the ilex and those of the laurel and myrtle underwood were strongly contrasted with the white snow that lay upon them. A breeze passed among the boughs, and scattered the drift that fell in flakes, and disturbed at fits the silence around; or, again, a bird twittered or flew with melancholy flap of wing beneath the trees to its nest in some hollow trunk. The house seemed desolate: its windows were glassless, and small heaps of snow lay upon the sills; there was no print of footing on the equal surface of the path that led right up to the door. Yet, a little smoke now and then struggled upwards from its chimney; and on paying fixed attention, Prince Ludovico thought he heard a voice. He called but received no answer; he put his hand on the latch, it yielded, and he entered. On the floor strewn with leaves lay a person sick and dying—for though there was a slight motion in the eyes that shewed that life had not yet deserted his throne, the paleness of the visage was that of death only. It was an aged woman, and her white hairs shewed that she descended to no untimely grave. But a figure knelt beside her, which might have been mistaken for the angel of heaven waiting to receive and guide the departing soul to eternal rest, but for the sharp agony that was stamped on the features, and the glazed but earnest gaze of her eye. She was very young and beautiful as the star of evening. She had apparently despoiled herself to bestow warmth on her dying friend, for her arms and neck were bare but for the quantity of dark and flowing hair that clustered on her shoulders. She was absorbed in one feeling, that of watching the change in the sick person. Her cheeks, even her lips, were pale; her eyes seemed to gaze as if her whole life reigned in their single perception. She did not hear Ludovico enter, or at least she made no sign that indicated that she was conscious of it. The sick person murmured, and she bent her head down to catch the sounds. She replied in an accent of despair: "I can get no more leaves, for the snow is on the ground; nor have I any other earthly thing to place over you." "Is she cold?" said Ludovico, creeping near and bending down beside the afflicted girl. "Oh, very cold," she replied, "and there is no help."

Ludovico had gone to the chase in a silken mantle lined with the choicest furs. He had thrown it off and left it with his horse that it might not impede his descent. He hastened from the cottage, he ran down the lane, and, following the marks of his footsteps, he arrived where his steed awaited him. He did not again descend by the same path. Reflecting that it might be necessary for him to seek assistance for the dying woman, he led his horse down the hill by a circuitous path; and although he did this with all possible speed, night closed in, and the glare of the snow alone permitted him to see the path that he desired to follow. When he arrived at the lane, he saw that the cottage, before so dark, was illuminated; and as he approached he heard the solemn hymn of death, as it was chaunted by the priests who filled it. The change had taken place, the soul had left its mortal mansion, and the deserted ruin was attended with more solemnity than had been paid to the mortal struggle. Amidst the crowd of priests, Ludovico entered unperceived, and he looked round for the lovely female he had left. She sat retired from the priests, on a heap of leaves in a corner of the cottage. Her clasped hands lay on her knees, her head was bent downwards, and every now and then she wiped away her fast-falling tears with her hair. Ludovico threw his cloak over her. She looked up and drew the covering round her, more to hide her person than for the sake of warmth; and then again turning away, was absorbed in her melancholy thoughts.

Ludovico gazed on her in pity. For the first time since his mother's death, tears filled his eyes, and his softened countenance beamed with tender sympathy. He said nothing, but he continued to look on as a wish arose in his mind, that he might wipe the tears that one by one fell from the shrouded eyes of the unfortunate girl. As he was thus engaged, he heard his name called by one of the attendants of the castle; and throwing the few pieces of gold he possessed into the lap of the sufferer, he suddenly left the cottage, mounted his horse, and, joining the servant who had been in search of him, rode rapidly towards his home.

As Ludovico rode along, and the first emotions of pity having as it were ceased to throb in his mind, these feelings merged into the strain of thought in which he habitually indulged and turned its course to something new. "I call myself wretched," he cried, "I, the well-clad and fed; and this lovely peasant girl, half famished, parts with her necessary clothing to cover the dying limbs of her only friend. I also have lost my only friend, and that is my true misfortune, the cause of all my real misery— sycophants would assume that name, spies and traitors usurp that office. I have cast those aside—shaken them from me as yon bough shakes to earth its encumbrance of snow, not so cold as their iced hearts. But I am alone—solitude gnaws my heart and makes me savage—miserable— worthless."

Yet, although he thought in this manner, the heart of Ludovico was softened by what he had seen, and milder feelings pressed upon him. He had felt sympathy for one who needed it, he had conferred a benefit on the necessitous, tenderness moulded his lips to a smile, and the pride of utility gave dignity to the fire of his eye. The people about him saw the change, and, not meeting with the usual disdain of his manner, they also became softened; and the alteration apparent in his character seemed ready to effect as great a metamorphosis in his external situation. But the time was not come when this change would become permanent.

On the day that succeeded to this hunt, Prince Fernando removed to Naples and commanded his son to accompany him. The residence at Naples was peculiarly irksome to Ludovico. In the country, he enjoyed comparative freedom; satisfied that he was in the castle, his father sometimes forgot him for days together; but it was otherwise here. Fearful that he should form friends and connexions, and knowing that his commanding figure and peculiar manners excited attention and often curiosity, he kept him ever in sight; or if he left him for a moment, he first made himself sure of the people around him, and left such of his own confidants whose very presence was venom to the eye of Ludovico. Add to which, Prince Mondolfo delighted to insult and browbeat his son in public; and aware of his deficiency in the more elegant accomplishments, he exposed him even to the derision of his friends.

They remained two months at Naples and then returned to Mondolfo. It was spring; the air was genial and spirit-stirring. The white blossoms of the almond trees and the pink ones of the peach just began to be contrasted with the green leaves that shot forth among them. Ludovico felt little of the exhilarating effects of spring. Wounded in his heart's core, he asked Nature why she painted a sepulchre; he asked the airs why they fanned the sorrowful and dead. He wandered forth to solitude. He rambled down the path that led to the sea; he sat on the beach watching the monotonous flow of the waves; they danced and sparkled; his gloomy thoughts refused to imbibe cheerfulness from wave or sun.

A form passed near him—a peasant girl who balanced a pitcher, urn-shaped, upon her head. She was meanly clad, but she attracted Ludovico's regard; and when having approached the fountain, she took her pitcher and turned to fill it, he recognized the cottager of the foregoing winter. She knew him also, and, leaving her occupation she approached him and kissed his hand with that irresistible grace that southern climes seem to instil into the meanest of its children. At first she hesitated and began to thank him in broken accents; but words came as she spoke, and Ludovico listened to her eloquent thanks—the first he had heard addressed to him from any human being. A smile of pleasure stole over his face—a smile whose beauty sunk deep in the gazer's heart. In a minute they were seated on the bank beside the fountain, and Viola told her story—of her poverty-stricken youth—her orphan lot—the death of her last friend; and it was now only the benign climate which in diminishing human wants made her appear less wretched than then. She was alone in the world—living in that desolate cottage, providing for her daily fare with difficulty. Her pale cheek, the sickly languor that pervaded her manner, gave evidence to the truth of her words, but she did not weep; she spoke words of good heart, and it was only when she alluded to the benefaction of Ludovico that her soft dark eyes swam with tears.

The youth visited her cottage the next day. He rode up the lane, now grass-grown and scented by violets which Viola was gathering from the banks. She presented her nosegay to him. They entered the cottage together—it was dilapidated and miserable. A few flowers placed in a broken vase was a type only of poor Viola herself—a lovely blossom in the midst of utter poverty; and the rose tree that shaded the window could only tell that sweet Italy, even in the midst of wretchedness, spares her natural wealth to adorn her children. Ludovico made Viola sit down on a bench by the window and stood opposite to her, her flowers in his hand, listening. She did not talk of her poverty, and it would be difficult to recount what was said. She seemed happy, and smiled and spoke with a gleeful voice which softened the heart of her friend, so that he almost wept with pity and admiration. After this, day by day Ludovico visited the cottage and bestowed all his time on Viola. He came and talked with her, gathered violets with her, consoled and advised her, and became happy. The idea that he was of use to a single human being instilled joy into his heart; and yet he was wholly unconscious how entirely he was necessary to the happiness of his protégée. He felt happy beside her; he was delighted to bestow benefits on her and to see her profit by them; but he did not think of love, and his mind, unawakened to passion, reposed from its long pain without a thought for the future. It was not so with the peasant girl. She could not see his eyes bent in gentleness on her—his mouth lighted by its tender smile—or listen to his voice as he bade her trust in him, for that he would be father, brother, all to her, without deeply, passionately loving him. He became the sun of her day, the breath of her life—her hope, joy, and sole possession. She watched for his coming, she watched him as he went, and for a long time she was happy. She would not repine. What though he replied to her earnest love with calm affection only—she was a peasant, he a noble—and she could claim and expect no more. He was a god; she might adore him; and it were blasphemy to hope for more than a benign acceptation of her worship.

Prince Mondolfo was soon made aware of Ludovico's visits to the cottage of the forest, and he did not doubt that Viola had become the mistress of his son. Yet he did not endeavour to interrupt this connexion or put any bar to his visits. Ludovico indeed enjoyed more liberty than ever, and his cruel father confined himself alone to the restricting him more than ever in money. His policy was apparent: Ludovico had resisted every temptation of gambling and other modes of expence thrown in his way. Fernando had long wished to bring his son to a painful sense of his poverty and dependence, and to oblige him to seek the necessary funds in such a career as would necessitate his desertion of the paternal roof. He had wound many snares around the boy, and all were snapped by his firm but almost unconscious resistance; but now without seeking, without expectation, the occasion came of itself which would lead him to require far more than his father had at any time allowed him; and now that allowance was restricted; yet Ludovico did not murmur, and until now he had enough.

For a long time Fernando abstained from all allusion to the connexion of his son; but one evening at a banquet, gaiety overcame his caution— gaiety which ever led him to sport with his son's feelings and to excite a pain that might repress the smile that his new state of mind caused to make frequent visits to his countenance. "Here," cried Fernando as he filled a goblet—"here, Ludovico, is to the health of your violet girl"— and he concluded his speech with some indecorous allusion that suffused Ludovico's cheek with red. Without replying he arose to depart. "And whither are you going, sir?" cried his father. "Take yon cup and answer my pledge, for by Bacchus none that sits at my table shall pass it uncourteously by."

Ludovico, still standing, filled his cup and raised it as he was about to speak and retort to his father's speech; but the memory of his words and the innocence of Viola pressed upon him and filled his heart almost to bursting. He put down his cup, pushed aside the people who sought to detain him, and left the castle. Soon the laughter of the revellers was no more heard by him, though it had loudly rung and was echoed through the lofty halls. The words of Fernando awakened a strange spirit in Ludovico. "Viola, can she love me? do I love her?" The last question was quickly answered. Passion, suddenly awake, made every artery tingle by its thrilling presence. His cheeks burned as his heart danced with strange exultation as he hastened towards the cottage, unheeding all but the universe of sensation that dwelt within him. He reached its door—blank and dark the walls rose before him, and the boughs of the wood waved and sighed over him. Until now he had felt impatience alone—the sickness of fear, fear of finding a cold return to his passion's feeling, now entered his heart; and retreating a little from the cottage, he sat on a bank, hid his face in his hands, while passionate tears gushed from his eyes and trickled from between his fingers. Viola opened the door of her cottage; Ludovico had failed in his daily visit, and she was unhappy. She looked on the sky—the sun had set, and Hesperus glowed in the west. The dark ilex trees made a deep shade which was broken by innumerable fireflies which flashed—now low on the ground, discovering the flowers as they slept hushed and closed in night; now high among the branches; and their light was reflected by the shining leaves of ilex and laurel. Viola's wandering eye unconsciously selected one and followed it as it flew, and ever and anon it cast aside its veil of darkness and spread a wide pallor around its own form. At length it nestled itself in a bower of green leaves, formed by a clump of united laurels and myrtles; and there it stayed flashing its beautiful light, which, coming from among the boughs, seemed as if the brightest star of the heavens had wandered from its course, and, trembling at its temerity, sat panting on its earthly perch. Ludovico sat near the laurel—Viola saw him—her breath came quick— she spoke not but stept lightly to him—and looked with such mazed ecstasy of thought that she felt, nay almost heard, her heartbeat with her emotion. At length she spoke—she uttered his name, and he looked up on her gentle face, her beaming eyes, and sylph-like form bent over him. He forgot his fears, and his hopes were soon confirmed. For the first time, he pressed the trembling lips of Viola and then tore himself away to think with rapture and wonder on all that had taken place.

Ludovico ever acted with energy and promptness. He returned only to plan with Viola the moment when they might be united. A small chapel amid the Apennines, sequestered and unknown, was selected and a priest easily procured from a neighbouring convent and easily bribed to silence. Ludovico led back his bride to her cottage in the forest, and there she continued to reside. For worlds he would not have had her change her habitation. All his wealth was expended in decorating her habitation, and his little wealth only sufficed to render it tolerable. But they were happy.

The small circlet of earth's expanse that held in his Viola was the universe to her husband; and his heart and imagination widened and filled it, until it encompassed all of beautiful and was inhabited by all of excellent this world contains. She sang to him; he listened, and the notes built around him a magic bower of delight. He trod the soil of paradise, and its winds fed his mind to intoxication. The inhabitants of Mondolfo could not recognize the haughty, resentful Ludovico in the benign and gentle husband of Viola. His father's taunts were unheeded, for he did not hear them. He no longer trod the earth, but angel-like, sustained by the wings of love, skimmed over it so that he felt not its inequalities or was touched by its rude obstacles. And Viola, with deep gratitude and passionate tenderness, repaid his love. She thought of him only, lived for him, and with unwearied attention kept alive in his mind the first dream of passion.

Thus nearly two years passed, and a lovely child appeared to bind the lovers with closer ties and to fill their humble roof with smiles and joy. Ludovico seldom went to Mondolfo; and his father, still continuing his ancient policy and glad that, in his attachment to a peasant girl, he had relieved his mind from the fear of brilliant connexions and able friends, even dispensed with his attendance when he visited Naples. Fernando did not suspect that his son had married this low-born favourite; if he had, his aversion would not have withheld him from resisting so degrading an alliance; and while his blood flowed in Ludovico's veins, he would never have avowed offspring who were contaminated by a peasant's less highly sprung tide.

Ludovico had nearly completed his twentieth year when his elder brother died. Prince Mondolfo at that time had spent four months at Naples, endeavouring to bring to a conclusion a treaty of marriage he had entered into between his heir and the daughter of a noble Neapolitan house, when this death overthrew his hopes, and he retired in grief and mourning to his castle. A few weeks of sorrow and reason restored him to himself. He had loved even this favoured eldest son more as the heir of his name and fortunes than as his child; and the web destroyed that he had woven for him, he quickly began another.

Ludovico was summoned to his father's presence. Old habit yet rendered such a summons momentous; but the youth with a proud smile threw off these boyish cares and stood with gentle dignity before his altered parent.

"Ludovico," said the prince, "four years ago, you refused to take a priest's vows, and then you excited my utmost resentment; now I thank you for that resistance."

A slight feeling of suspicion crossed Ludovico's mind—that his father was about to cajole him for some evil purpose. Two years before, he would have acted on such a thought, but the habit of happiness made him unsuspicious. He bent his head silently.

"Ludovico," continued his father, while pride and a wish to conciliate disturbed his mind and even his countenance, "my son, I have used you hardly; but that time is now passed."

Ludovico gently replied: "My father, I did not deserve your ill-treatment; I hope that I shall merit your kindness when I know——"

"Yes, yes," interrupted Fernando uneasily, "you do not understand, you desire to know why—in short, you, Ludovico, are now all my hope —Olimpio is dead—the house of Mondolfo has no support but you."

"Pardon me," replied the youth, "Mondolfo is in no danger; you, my lord, are fully able to support and even augment its present dignity."

"You do not understand—Mondolfo has no support but you. I am old, I feel my age, and these grey hairs announce it to me too glaringly. There is no collateral branch, and my hopes must rest in your children."

"My child, my lord," replied Ludovico. "I have only one, and if the poor little boy——"

"What folly is this?" cried Fernando impatiently. "I speak of your marriage and not——"

"My lord, my wife is ever ready to pay her duteous respects to you."

"Your wife—Ludovico—but you speak without thought—how? who?"

"The violet girl, my lord."

A tempest had crossed the countenance of Fernando. That his son, unknown to him, should have made an unworthy alliance convulsed every fibre of his frame, and the lowering of his brows and impatient gesture told the intolerable anguish of such a thought. The last words of Ludovico restored him. It was not his wife that he thus named—he felt assured that it was not. He smiled, somewhat ghastly, yet still it was a smile of satisfaction. "Yes," he replied, "I understand, but you task my patience. You should not trifle with such a subject or with me; I talk of your marriage. Now that Olimpio is dead and you are, in his place, heir of Mondolfo, you may in his stead conclude the advantageous, nay, even princely alliance, I was forming for him."

Ludovico replied with earnestness: "You are pleased to misunderstand me. I am already married. Two years ago, while I was still the despised, insulted Ludovico, I formed this connexion, and it will be my pride to shew the world how, in all but birth, my peasant wife is able to fulfil the duties of her distinguished situation."

Fernando was accustomed to command himself. He felt as if stabbed by a poignard, but he paused till calm and voice returned, and then he said:

"You have a child?"

"An heir, my lord," replied Ludovico, smiling—for his father's mildness deceived him—"a lovely, healthy boy."

"They live near here?"

"I can bring them to Mondolfo in an hour's space. Their cottage is in the forest, about a quarter of a mile east of the convent of Santa Chiara."

"Enough, Ludovico—you have communicated strange tidings, and I must consider of them. I will see you again this evening."

Ludovico bowed and disappeared. He hastened to his cottage and related all that he remembered or understood of this scene, and bade Viola prepare to come to the castle at an instant's notice. Viola trembled. It struck her that all was not so fair as Ludovico represented; but she hid her fears and even smiled as her husband with a kiss hailed his boy as heir of Mondolfo.

Fernando had commanded both look and voice while his son was within hearing. He had gone to the window of his chamber, and stood steadily gazing on the drawbridge until Ludovico crossed it and disappeared. Then, unrestrained, he strode up and down his apartment, while the roof rang with his impetuous tread. He uttered cries and curses, and struck his head with his clenched fist. It was long ere he could think; he felt only—and feeling was torture. The tempest at length subsided, and he threw himself in his chair. His contracted brows and frequently constricted lips shew how entirely he was absorbed in consideration. All at first was one frightful whirl; by degrees the motion was appeased; his thoughts flowed with greater calmness; they subsided into one channel whose course he warily traced until he thought that he saw the result.

Hours passed during this contemplation. When he arose from his chair as one who had slept and dreamt uneasily, his brows became by degrees smooth; he stretched out his arm and, spreading his hand, cried: "So it is, and I have vanquished him!" Evening came, and Ludovico was announced. Fernando feared his son. He had ever dreaded his determinate and fearless mode of action. He dreaded to encounter his passions with his own, and he felt in the clash that his was not the master passion. So subduing all of hate, revenge, and wrath, he received him with a smile. Ludovico smiled also. Yet there was no similarity in their look: one was a smile of frankness, joy, and affection—the other, the curled grimace of smothered malice. Fernando said: "My son, you have entered lightly into a marriage as if it were a child's game; but where principalities and noble blood are at stake, the loss or gain is too momentous to be trifled with. Silence, Ludovico; listen to me, I entreat. You have made a strange marriage with a peasant, which, though I may acknowledge, I cannot approve; which must be displeasing to your sovereign, derogatory to all who claim alliance with the house of Mondolfo." Cold dew stood on the forehead of Fernando as he spoke; he paused, recovered his self-command, and continued: "It will be difficult to reconcile these discordant interests, and a moment of rashness might cause us to lose our station, fortune, every thing. Your interests are in my hands. I will be careful of them. I trust, before the expiration of a very few months, the future Princess Mondolfo will be received at the court of Naples with due honour and respect. But you must leave it to me; you must not move in this affair; you must promise that you will not, until I permit, mention your marriage to any one, or acknowledge it if you are taxed with it."

Ludovico, after a moment's hesitation, replied: "I promise that for the space of six months I will not mention my marriage to any. I will not be guilty of falsehood, but for that time I will not affirm it or bring it forward in any manner so as to annoy you."

Fernando again paused; but prudence conquered, and he said no more. He entered on other topics with his son; they supped together, and the mind of Ludovico, now attuned to affection, received all the marks of love from his father with gratitude and joy.

A week passed thus in calm. Ludovico and Viola were perfectly happy. Ludovico only wished to draw his wife from obscurity, from that sensation of honest pride which makes us desire to declare to the whole world the excellence of a beloved object. Viola shrunk from such an exhibition; she loved her humble cottage—humble still, though adorned with all that taste and love could bestow on it. The trees bent over its low roof and shaded its windows, which were filled with flowering shrubs; its floor shone with marble; and vases of antique shape and exquisite beauty stood in the niches of the room. Every part was consecrated by the memory of their first meeting and their loves—the walk of snow and violets; the forest of ilex with its underwood of myrtle and its population of fireflies; the birds; the wild and shy animals that sometimes came in sight and, seen, retreated; the changes of the seasons and of the hues of Nature influenced by them; the alterations of the sky; the walk of the moon and the moving of the stars—all were dear, known, and commented on by this pair, who saw the love their own hearts felt reflected in the whole scene around. And their child, their noisy but speechless companion—whose smiles won kisses, and whose bright form seemed as if sent from heaven to reward their constant affection.

A week passed, and Fernando and Ludovico were riding together when the prince said: "Tomorrow early, my son, you must go to Naples. It is time that you should shew yourself there as my heir and the best representative of a princely house. The sooner you do this, the quicker will arrive the period for which no doubt you long, when the unknown Princess Mondolfo will be acknowledged by all. I cannot accompany. In fact, circumstances which you may guess make me desire that you should appear at first without me. You will be distinguished by your sovereign, courted by all; and you will remember your promise as the best means of accomplishing your object. In a very few days I will join you."

Ludovico readily consented to this arrangement and went the same evening to take leave of Viola. She was seated beneath the laurel tree where first they had made their mutual vows; her child was in her arms, gazing with wonder and laughter on the light of the flies. Two years had passed. It was summer again, and as the beams from their eyes met and mingled, they each drank in the joyous certainty that they were as still as dear to one another as when he, weeping from intense emotion, sat under that tree. He told her of his visit to Naples, and a cloud passed over her countenance; but she dismissed it; she would not fear. Yet again and again, a thrilling sense of coming evil made her heart beat, and each time was resisted with greater difficulty. As night came on, she carried her sleeping child into the cottage, and placed him on his bed, and then walked up and down the pathway of the forest with Ludovico until the moment of his departure should arrive, for the heat of the weather rendered it necessary that he should travel by night. Again the fear of danger crossed her, and again she with a smile shook off the thought; but when he turned to give her his parting embrace, it returned with full force on her. Weeping bitterly, she clung to him and entreated him not to go. Startled by her earnestness, he eagerly sought an explanation, but the only explanation she could give excited a gentle smile as he caressed her and bade her be calm; and then pointing to the crescent moon that gleamed through the trees and chequered the ground with their moving shades, he told her that he would be with her ere its full, and with one more embrace left her weeping. And thus it is. A strange prophetic sense often creeps about, and the spirit of Cassandra inhabits many a hapless human heart and utters from many lips unheeded foretellings of evils that are to be. The hearers heed them not; the speaker hardly gives them credit; and the evil comes which, if it could have been avoided, no Cassandra could have foretold. For if that spirit were not a sure harbinger, so would it not exist; nor could these half-revealings have place if the to-come did not fulfil and make out the sketch.

Viola beheld him depart with hopeless sorrow and then turned to console herself beside the couch of her child. Yet, gazing on him, her fears came thicker; and in a transport of terror, she rushed from the cottage, ran along the pathway calling on Ludovico's name: sometimes listening if she might hear the tread of his horse, and then again shrieking aloud for him to return. But he was far out of hearing, and she returned again to her cot and, lying down beside her child, clasping his little hand in hers, at length slept peacefully.

Her sleep was light and short. She arose before the sun, and hardly had he begun to cast long shadows on the ground than, attiring herself in her veil, she was about to go with her infant to the neighbouring chapel of Santa Chiara, when she heard the trampling of horses come up the pathway. Her heart beat quick—and still quicker when she saw a stranger enter her cottage. His form was commanding, and age, which had grizzled his hair, had not tempered the fire of his eye or marred the majesty of his carriage; but every lineament was impressed by pride and even cruelty. Self-will and scorn were even more apparent. He was somewhat like what Ludovico had been, and so like what he then was, that Viola did not doubt that his father stood before her. She tried to collect her courage, but the surprize, his haughty mien, and, above all, the sound of many horses and the voices of men who had remained outside the cottage so disturbed and distracted her, that her heart for a moment failed her, and she leant trembling and ashy white against the wall, straining her child to her heart with convulsive energy. Fernando spoke——

"You are Viola Arnaldi, and you call yourself, I believe, the wife of Ludovico Mondolfo?"

"I am so"—her lips formed themselves to these words, but the sound died away.

Fernando continued: "I am Prince Mondolfo, father of the rash boy who has entered into this illegal and foolish contract. When I heard of it, my plan was easily formed, and it is now about to be put into execution. I could easily have done so without coming to you, without enduring the scene which I suppose I shall endure; but benevolence has prompted me to the line of conduct I adopt, and I hope that I shall not repent it."

Fernando paused; Viola had heard little of what he had said. She was employed in collecting her scattered spirits, in bidding her heart be still, and arming herself with the pride and courage of innocence and helplessness. Every word he spoke was thus of use to her, as it gave her time to recollect herself. She only bowed her head as he paused, and he continued.

"While Ludovico was a younger son and did not seek to obtrude his misalliance into notice, I was content that he should enjoy what he termed happiness unmolested; but circumstances have changed. He has become the heir of Mondolfo and must support that family and title by a suitable marriage. Your dream has passed. I mean you no ill. You will be conducted hence with your child, placed on board a vessel, and taken to a town of Spain. You will receive a yearly stipend; and as long as you seek no communication with Ludovico or endeavour to leave the asylum provided for you, you are safe. But the slightest movement, the merest yearning for a station you may never fill, shall draw upon you and that boy the vengeance of one whose menaces are but as the uplifted arm—the blow quickly follows."

The excess of danger that menaced the unprotected Viola gave her courage. She replied: "I am alone and feeble; you are strong and have ruffians waiting on you to execute such crimes as your imagination suggests. I care not for Mondolfo—nor the title, nor the possession—but I will never, oh never, never! renounce my Ludovico—never do aught to derogate from our plighted faith. Torn from him, I will seek him, though it be barefoot and a-hungered, through the wide world. He is mine by that love he has pleased to conceive for me; I am his by the sentiment of devotion and eternal attachment that now animates my voice. Tear us asunder, yet we shall meet again; and unless you put the grave between us, you cannot separate us."

Fernando smiled in scorn. "And that boy," he said, pointing to it, "will you lead him, innocent lamb, a sacrifice to the altar of your love, and plant the knife yourself in the victim's heart?"

Again the lips of Viola became pale, as she clasped her boy and exclaimed in almost inarticulate accents—"There is a God in Heaven!"

Fernando left the cottage, and it was soon filled by men. One threw a cloak over Viola and her boy, and, dragging her from the cottage, placed her in a kind of litter, and the cavalcade proceeded silently. Viola had uttered one shriek when she beheld her enemies; but knowing their power and her impotence, she stifled all further cries. When in the litter, she strove in vain to disengage herself from the cloak that enveloped her, and then tried to hush her child who, frightened at his strange situation, uttered piercing cries. At length he slept; and Viola, darkling and fearful with nothing to sustain her spirit or hopes, felt her courage vanish; and she wept long with despair and misery. She thought of Ludovico and what his grief would be, and her tears were redoubled. There was no hope, for her enemy was relentless, her child torn from her, a cloister her prison. Such were the images constantly before her; they subdued her courage and filled her with terror and dismay.

The cavalcade entered the town of Salerno, and the roar of the sea announced to poor Viola that they were on its shores. "O bitter waves," she cried, "my tears are as bitter as ye, and they will soon mingle." Her conductors now entered a building; it was a watch tower, at some distance from the town, on the sea-beach. They lifted Viola from the litter and then led her to one of the dreary apartments of the tower. The window, which was not far from the ground, was grated with iron; it bore the appearance of a guard room. The chief of her conductors addressed her, courteously asked her to excuse the rough lodging: the wind was contrary, he said, but change was expected; and the next day he hoped that they would be able to embark. He pointed to the destined vessel in the offing. Viola, excited to hope by his mildness, began to entreat his compassion, but he immediately left her. Soon after, another man brought in food with a flask of wine and a jug of water. He also retired. Her massive door was locked. The sound of the retreating footsteps died away.

Viola did not despair; she felt, however, that it would need all her courage to extricate herself from her prison. She ate a part of the food which had been provided, drank some water, and then, a little refreshed, she spread the cloak her conductors had left on the floor, placed her child on it to play, and then stationed herself at the window to see if any might pass whom she might address; and if he were not able to assist her in any other way, he might at least bear a message to Ludovico, that her fate might not be veiled in the fearful mystery that threatened it; but probably the way past her window was guarded, for no one drew near. As she looked, however, and once advanced her head to gaze more earnestly, it struck her that her person would pass between the iron grates of her window. It was not high from the ground; the cloak, fastened to one of the staunchions, promised a safe descent. She did not dare make the essay. Nay, she was so fearful that she might be watched and that, if she were seen near the window, her jailers might be struck with the same idea, that she retreated to the further end of the room and sat looking at the bars with fluctuating hope and fear, that now dyed her cheeks with crimson and again made them pale—as when Ludovico had first seen her.

Her boy passed his time in alternate play and sleep. The ocean still roared, and the dark clouds brought up by the sirocco blackened the sky and hastened the coming evening. Hour after hour passed; she heard no clock; there was no sun to mark the time; but by degrees her room grew dark, and at last the Ave Maria tolled, heard by fits between the howling of the wind and the dashing of the waves. She knelt and put up a fervent prayer to the Madonna, protector of innocence—a prayer for her and her boy, no less innocent than the Mother and Divine Child to whom she made her orisons. Yet still she paused. Drawing near the window, she listened for the sounds of any human being. These died away, for with darkness came rain that poured in torrents, accompanied by thunder and lightning that drove every creature to shelter. Viola shuddered. Could she expose her child during such a night? Yet again she gathered courage. It only made her meditate on some plan by which she might get the cloak as a shelter for her boy after it had served for their descent. She tried the bars and found that with some difficulty she could pass; and gazing downwards from the outside, a flash of lightning discovered the ground not far below. Again she recommended herself to divine protection; again she called upon and blessed her Ludovico; and then, not fearless but determined, she began her operations. She fastened the cloak by means of her long veil which, hanging to the ground, was tied by a slipknot and would give way when pulled. She took her child in her arms and, having got without the bars, bound him with her sash and to her waist; and then without accident she reached the ground. Having then secured the cloak and enveloped herself and her child in its dark and ample folds, she paused breathlessly to listen. Nature was awake with its loudest voice. The sea roared, and the incessant flashes of lightning that discovered solitude around her were followed by such deafening peals as almost made her fear. She crossed the field and kept the sight of the white sea-foam to her right hand, knowing that thus she proceeded in an opposite direction from Mondolfo. She walked as fast as her burthen permitted her, keeping the beaten road, for the darkness made her fear to deviate. The rain ceased, and she walked on until, her limbs sinking under her, she was fain to rest, and refreshed herself with the bread she had brought with her from prison. Action and success had inspired her with unusual energy. She would not fear—she believed herself free and secure. She wept, but it was with the overflowing emotion that found no other expression. She doubted not that she should rejoin Ludovico. Seated thus in the dark night, having for hours been the sport of the elements, which now for an instant paused in their fury—seated on a stone by the road's side, a wide, dreary, unknown country about her, her helpless child in her arms, herself having just finished eating the only food she possessed—she felt triumph and joy and love descend into her heart, prophetic of future reunion with her beloved.

It was summer, and the air consequently warm. Her cloak had protected her from the wet, so her limbs were free and unnumbed. At the first ray of dawn she arose, and at the nearest pathway she struck out of the road and took her course nearer the bordering Apennines. From Salerno as far south as the eye can reach, a low plain stretched itself along the sea-side, and the hills at about the distance of ten miles bound it in. These mountains are high and singularly beautiful in their shape; their crags point to heaven, and streams flow down their sides and water the plain below. After several hours walking, Viola reached a pine forest which descended from the heights and stretched itself in the plain. She sought its friendly shelter with joy; and penetrating its depth until she saw trees only on all sides of her, she again reposed. The sirocco had been dissipated by the thunderstorm; and the sun, vanquishing the clouds that at first veiled its splendour, glowed forth in the clear majesty of noon. Southern-born, Viola did not fear the heat. She collected pinenuts, she contrived to make a fire, and ate them with appetite; and then seeking a covert, she lay down and slept, her boy in her arms, thanking heaven and the Virgin for her escape. When she awoke, the triumph of her heart had somewhat died away. She felt the solitude, she felt her helplessness, she feared pursuers; yet she dashed away her tears; and then reflecting that she was still too near Salerno, the sun being now at the sea's verge, she arose and pursued her way through the intricacies of the wood. She got to the edge of it, so far as to be able to direct her steps by the neighbouring sea. Torrents intercepted her path, and one rapid river seemed to impede it altogether; but going somewhat lower down, she found a bridge; and then approaching still nearer to the sea, she passed through a wide and desolate kind of pasture country, which seemed to afford neither shelter nor sustenance to any human being. Night closed in, and she was fearful to pursue her way; but seeing some buildings dimly in the distance, she directed her steps that way, hoping to discover a hamlet where she might get shelter and such assistance as would enable her to retrace her steps and reach Naples without being discovered by her powerful enemy. She kept these high buildings before her, which appeared like vast cathedrals, but that they were untopped by any dome or spire; and she wondered much what they could be, when suddenly they seemed to disappear. She would have thought some rising ground had intercepted them, but all before her was plain. She paused, and at length resolved to wait for dawn. All day she had seen no human being; twice or thrice she had heard the bark of a dog, and once the whistle of a shepherd, but she saw no one. Desolation was around her; this indeed had lulled her to security at first. Where no men were, there was no danger for her. But at length the strange solitude became painful—she longed to see a cottage or to find some peasant, however uncouth, who might answer her queries and provide for her wants. She had viewed with surprize the buildings which had been as beacons to her. She did not wish to enter a large town, and she wondered how one could exist in such a desert; but she had left the wood far behind her, and she required food. Night passed, balmy and sweet night; the breezes fanned her; the glowing atmosphere encompassed her; the fireflies flitted round her; bats wheeled about in the air; and the heavy-winged owl hooted anigh, while the beetles' constant hum filled the air. She lay on the ground, her babe pillowed on her arm, looking upon the starry heavens. Many thoughts crowded upon her—the thought of Ludovico, of her reunion with him, of joy after sorrow; and she forgot that she was alone, half-famished, encompassed by enemies in a desart plain of Calabria—she slept.

She awoke not until the sun had risen high—it had risen above the temples of Paestum, and the columns threw short shadows on the ground. They were near her, unseen during night, and were now revealed as the edifices that had attracted her the evening before. They stood on a rugged plain, despoiled of all roof, their columns and cornices encompassing a space of high and weed-grown grass. The deep blue sky canopied them and filled them with light and cheerfulness. Viola looked on them with wonder and reverence. They were temples to some god who still seemed to deify them with his presence: he clothed them still with beauty; and what was called their ruin might, in its picturesque wildness and sublime loveliness, be more adapted to his nature than when, roofed and gilt, they stood in pristine strength; and the silent worship of air and happy animals might be more suited to him than the concourse of the busy and heartless. The most benevolent of spirits seemed to inhabit these desart, weed-grown areas. The spirit of beauty flitted between their columns embrowned by time, painted with strange colours, and rained a genial atmosphere on the deserted altar. Awe and devotion filled the heart of the lonely Viola. She raised her eyes and heart to heaven in thanksgiving and prayer—not that her lips formed words or her thoughts suggested connected sentences, but the feeling of worship and gratitude animated her; and as the sunlight streamed through the succession of columns, so did joy, dove-shaped, fall on her and illumine her soul.

With such devotion, as seldom before she had visited a saint-dedicated church, she ascended the broken and crude steps of the larger temple and entered the plot that it enclosed. An inner circuit of smaller columns enclosed an inner area; she entered that and, sitting on a huge fragment of the broken cornice that had fallen to the ground, she silently waited, as if some oracle would visit her sense and guide her.

Thus sitting, she heard the near bark of a dog—followed by the bleating of sheep—and she saw a little flock spread itself in the field adjoining the further temple. They were shepherded by a girl clothed in rags, but the season required little covering; and these poor people, moneyless and possessing only what their soil gives them, are in the articles of clothing poor even to nakedness. In inclement weather, they wrapt rudely formed clothes of undressed sheepskin around them; during the heats of summer, they do little more than throw aside these useless garments. The shepherd girl was probably about fifteen years of age; a large black straw hat shaded her head from the intense rays of the sun; her feet and legs were bare; and her petticoat tucked up, Diana-like, above one knee, gave a picturesque appearance to her rags which, bound at her waist by a girdle, might have been the costume of a Greek maiden. Rags have even a costume of their own, as fine in their way, in their contrast of rich colours and the uncouth boldness of their drapery, as kingly robes. Viola approached the shepherdess and quietly entered into conversation with her, without making any appeal to her charity or feelings. She asked the name of the place where she was; and her boy, awake and joyous, soon attracted attention. The shepherd girl was pretty and, above all, good-natured; she caressed the child, seemed delighted to have found a companion for her solitude, and, when Viola said that she was hungry, unloaded her scrip of roasted pinenuts, boiled chesnuts, and coarse bread. Viola ate with joy and gratitude. They remained together all day; the sun went down, the glowing light of its setting faded, and the shepherdess would have taken Viola home with her. But she dreaded a human dwelling, still fearing that wherever there appeared a possibility of shelter, there her pursuers would seek her. She gave a few small silver pieces, part of what she had about her when seized, to her new friend; and bidding her bring sufficient food for the next day, entreated her not to mention her adventure to any one. The girl promised and, with the assistance of her dog, drove her flock towards their fold. Viola passed the night within the area of the larger temple.

Not doubting the success of his plan, on the very evening that followed its execution Prince Mondolfo had gone to Naples. He found his son at the Moldolfo palace. Despising the state of a court, and careless of the gaieties around him, Ludovico longed to return to the cottage of Viola. So after the expiration of two days, he told his father that he should ride over to Mondolfo and return the following morning. The conscious Fernando did not oppose him, but two hours after his departure he followed him and arrived at the castle just after Ludovico, leaving his attendants there, quitted it to proceed alone to his cottage. The first person Prince Mondolfo saw was the chief of the company who had had the charge of Viola. His story was soon told: the unfavourable wind, her imprisonment in a room barricadoed with the utmost strength, her incomprehensible escape, and the vain efforts that had subsequently been made to find her. Fernando listened as if in a dream. Convinced of the truth, he saw no clue to guide him, no hope of recovering possession of his prisoner. He foamed with rage and then endeavoured to suppress as useless the towering passion. He overwhelmed the bearer of the news with execrations; sent out parties of men in pursuit in all directions, promising every reward and urging the utmost secrecy; and then, left alone, paced his chamber in fury and dismay. His solitude was of no long duration. Ludovico burst into his room, his countenance lighted up with rage. "Murderer," he cried, "where is my Viola?" Fernando remained speechless. "Answer," said Ludovico. "Speak with those lips that pronounced her death sentence—or raise against me that hand from which her blood is scarcely washed. Oh, my Viola!—thou and my angel child—descend with all thy sweetness into my heart, that this hand write not parricide on my brow!"

Fernando attempted to speak. "No," shrieked the miserable Ludovico, "I will not listen to her murderer!—yet, is she dead? I kneel—I call you father, I appeal to that savage heart, I take in peace that hand that often struck me and now has dealt the deathblow. Tell me—oh tell me, does she yet live?"

Fernando seized on this interval of calm to relate his story. He told the simple truth; but could such a tale gain belief? It reawakened the wildest rage in poor Ludovico's heart. He doubted not that she was murdered; and after every expression of despair and hatred, he bade his father seek his heir amid the clods of the earth, for that such he should soon become, and rushed from his presence.

He wandered to the cottage; he searched the country round; he heard the tale of those who had witnessed any part of the carrying off of his Viola; he went to Salerno; he heard the tale there told with the most determined incredulity. It was the tale, he doubted not, that his father forged to free himself from accusation and to throw an impenetrable veil over the destruction of Viola. His quick imagination made out for itself the scene of her death. The very house in which she had been confined had at the other extremity of it a tower jutting out over the sea; a river flowed at its base, making its confluence with the ocean, deep and dark. He was convinced that the fatal scene had been acted there. He mounted the tower: the higher room was windowless, the iron grates of the windows had for some cause been recently taken out. He was persuaded that Viola and her child had been thrown from that window into the deep and gurgling waters below.

He resolved to die. In those days of simple Catholic faith, suicide was considered with horror; but there were other means almost as sure. He would go a pilgrim to the Holy Land, and fight and die beneath the walls of Jerusalem. Rash and energetic, his purpose was no sooner formed, than he hastened to put it in execution. He procured a pilgrim's weeds at Salerno; and at midnight, advising none of his intention, he left this city and proceeded southwards. Alternate rage and grief swelled his heart; rage at length died away. She whose murderer he execrated was an angel in heaven, an angel looking down on him; and he in the Holy Land would win his right to join her. Tender grief dimmed his eyes. The world's great theatre closed before him—of all its trappings, his pilgrim's cloak was alone gorgeous, his pilgrim's staff the only sceptre—they were the symbols and signs of the power he possessed beyond the earth, and the pledges of his union with Viola. He bent his steps towards Brundusium. He walked on fast as if he grudged all space and time that lay between him and his goal. Dawn awakened the earth, and he proceeded on his way. The sun of noon darted its rays upon him, but his march was uninterrupted. He entered a pine wood, and, following the track of flocks, he heard the murmurs of a fountain. Oppressed by thirst, he hastened towards it. The water welled up from the ground and filled a natural basin; flowers grew on its banks and looked upon the waters—unreflected, for the stream paused not, but whirled round and round, spending its superabundance in a small rivulet that, dancing over stones and glancing the sun, went on its way to *its* eternity—the sea. The trees had retreated from the fountain and formed a circle about it; the grass was green and fresh, starred with summer flowers. At one extremity was a silent pool that formed a strange contrast with the fountain—that, ever in motion, shewed no shape and reflected only the colour of the objects around it; the pool reflected the scene with greater distinctness and beauty than its real existence. The trees stood distinct, the ambient air between, all grouped and pictured with the hand of a divine artist. Ludovico drank from the fount and then approached the pool. He looked with half-wonder on the scene depicted there. A bird now flitted across in the air, and its form, feathers, and motion, were shewn in the waters. An ass came from among the trees, where in vain it sought herbage and came to graze near these waters; Ludovico saw it depicted therein and then looked on the living animal—almost appearing less real, less living than its semblance in the stream. Under the trees, from whence the ass had come, lay some one on the ground, enveloped in a mantle, sleeping. Ludovico looked carelessly, till he hardly at first knew why his curiosity was roused; then an eager thought which he deemed madness, yet resolved to gratify. Rapidly he approached the sleeper, knelt down, drew aside the cloak, and saw Viola—her child within her arms, the warm breath issuing from her parted lips, her love-beaming eyes hardly veiled by the transparent lids which soon were lifted up.

Ludovico and Viola, each too happy to feel the earth they trod, returned to their cottage—their cottage dearer than any palace—and yet, only half believing the excess of their own joy, by turns they wept and gazed on each other and their child, holding each other's hands as if grasping reality and fearful it would vanish.

Prince Mondolfo heard of their arrival. He had long suffered keenly from the fear of losing his son. The dread of finding himself childless, heirless, had tamed him. He feared the world's censure, his sovereign's displeasure, perhaps worse accusation and punishment. He yielded to fate. Not daring to appear before his intended victims, he sent his confessor to mediate for their forgiveness and to entreat them to take up their abode at Mondolfo. At first, little credit was given to these offers. They loved their cottage and had small inclination to risk happiness, liberty, and life for worthless luxury. The prince by patience and perseverance at length convinced them. Time softened painful recollections; they paid him the duty of children; and cherished and honoured in his old age, while he caressed his lovely grandchild, he did not repine that the violet girl should be the mother of the Heir of Mondolfo.

XXIII

Valerius

THE REANIMATED ROMAN

ABOUT ELEVEN O'CLOCK before noon in the month of September, two strangers landed in the little bay formed by the extreme point of Cape Miseno and the promontory of Bauli. The sky was of a deep serene blue, and the sea reflected its depth back with a darker tint. Through the clear water you saw the seaweed of various and beautiful colours as it grew on the remnants of the palaces of the Romans now buried under the waters. The sun shone bright causing an intolerable heat. The strangers on landing immediately sought a shady place where they might refresh themselves and remain until the sun should begin to descend towards the horizon. They sought the Elysian fields, and, winding among the poplars and mulberry trees festooned by the grapes which hung in rich and ripe clusters, they seated themselves under the shade of the tombs beside the Mare Morto.

One of these strangers was an Englishman of rank, as could easily be perceived by his noble carriage and manners full of dignity and freedom. His companion—I can compare him to nothing that now exists—his appearance resembled that of the statue of Marcus Aurelius in the Square of the Capitol at Rome. Placid and commanding, his features were Roman; except for his dress you would have imagined him to be a statue of one of the Romans animated with life. He wore the dress now common all over Europe, but it appeared unsuited to him and even as if he were unused to it. As soon as they were seated he began to speak thus:—

"I have promised to relate to you, my friend, what were my sensations on my revival, and how the appearance of this world—fallen from what it once was—struck me when the light of the sun revisited my eyes after it had deserted them many hundred years. And how can I choose a better place for this relation. This is the spot which was chosen by our antient and venerable religion, as that which best represented the idea oracles had given or diviners received of the seats of the happy after death. These are the tombs of Romans. This place is much changed by the sacriligious hand of man since those times, but still it bears the name of the Elysian fields. Avernus is but a short distance from us, and this sea which we perceive is the blue Mediterranean, unchanged while all else bears the marks of servitude and degradation.

"Pardon me—you are an Englishman, and they say you are free in your country—a country unknown when I lived—but the wretched Italians, who usurp the soil once trod by heroes, fill me with bitter disdain. Dare they usurp the name of Romans—dare they imagine that they descend from the Lords and Governors of the world? They forget that, when the republic died, every antient Roman family became by degrees extinct and that their followers might usurp the name, but were not and are not Romans.

"When I lived before, it was in the time of Cicero and of Cato. My rank was neither the highest nor the lowest in Rome: I was a Roman knight. I did not live to see my country enslaved by Caesar, who during my life was distinguished only by the debauchery of his manners. I died when I was nearly forty-five, defending my country against Catiline. At that time, the good men of Rome lamented bitterly the decline of morals in the city—Marius and Sulla had already taught us some of the miseries of tyranny, and I was accustomed to lament the day when the Senate appeared an assembly of demigods. But what men lived at that time?— The republic set gloriously as the sun of a bright and summer day. How could I despair of my country while such men as Cicero, Cato, Lucullus, and many others whom I knew as full of virtue and wisdom—who were my intimate and dearest friends—still existed.

"I need not trouble you with the history of my life—in modern times, domestic circumstances appear to be that part of a man's history most worth enquiring into. In Rome, the history of an individual was that of his country. We lived in the Forum and in the Senate House. My family had suffered by the civil wars: my father had been slain by Marius; and my uncle, who took care of me during my infancy, was proscribed by Sulla and murdered by his emissaries. My fortune was considerably diminished by these domestic misfortunes, but I lived frugally and filled with honour some of the highest offices of state—I was once consul.

"Nor will I now relate what would greatly interest you—all that I know concerning those great men with whose actions, even at this distance of time, you are intimately acquainted. These topics have formed and will form an inexhaustible source of conversation during the time we remain together, but at present I have promised to relate what I felt and saw when I revisited, now three years ago, this fallen Italy.

"As I approached Rome, I became agitated by a thousand emotions. I refused to see any thing or to speak to any body. Mute in a corner of the carriage, I hoarded my thoughts: sometimes thinking my companion unworthy my attention; at others still obstinately clinging, as a mother would to the memory of her lost child, to my loved country and doubting all that I had heard, all that these priests had told me. I believed in a conspiracy formed against me. I refused to speak to those we met on the road, lest their altered dialect should crush my last hope. I would visit no scenery. The eternal city survived in all its glory. It could not die—yet, still if it were dead, I would be silent till among the ruins of its Forum I should pour forth my last lament—and my words should awaken the dead to listen to me. 'Cicero—Cato—Pompey—were ye indeed dead— all trace of your path worn out. Still do ye haunt the Forum—awake— arise—welcome me!'

"The priest in vain endeavoured to draw me from my reverie. My countenance was impressed by sorrow, but I answered not. At length he exclaimed, 'Behold the Tiber!' Lovely river! Still and for ever dost thou roll on thy eternal waters; thy waves glitter in the sun or are shadowed by the thunder cloud; thy name acted as a spell. Tears gushed from my eyes. I alighted from the carriage. I hastened to the banks and kneeling down I offered up to thee, sacred names of Jupiter and Pallas, vows which made my lips quiver and the light almost pass from my eyes: 'O Jupiter—Jupiter of the Capitol—thou who has beheld so many triumphs, still may thy temples exist, still may the victims be led to thy altars!—Minerva protect thy Rome.' In that moment of agonized prayer, the fate of my country seemed yet undecided—the sword was still suspended. Alas, I could not believe that all that is great and good had departed.

"In vain, my companion tried to tear me away from the banks of the divine river. I remained seated immovably by it; my eyes did not wander on the surrounding scenery that had changed, but they were fixed on the waters or raised to the blue bright sky above. 'These—these, at least are the same—ever, ever the same!' were the only words I uttered when, from time to time, the fall of my country with the fierce agony of fire rushed across my mind. The priest tried to soothe me—I was silent. At length, the strength of passion overcame me, and after many hours of insane contest I suffered myself to be led to the carriage and, drawing up the blinds, abandoned myself to a reverie whose bitterness was only diminished by my lost strength.

"It was night when we entered Rome. 'Tomorrow,' said my companion, 'we will visit the Forum.' I assented. I did not wish him to accompany me, and therefore retired early without disclosing my intentions. But as soon as I found myself free from importunity, I demanded a guide and hastened to visit the scene of all human greatness. The moon had risen and cast a bright light over the city of Rome—if I may call that Rome which in no way resembled the Queen of Nations as I remembered her. We passed along the Corso, and I saw several magnificent obelisks, which seemed to tell me that the glory of my country had not passed away. I paused beside the Column of Antoninus, which sunk deep in the ground and, surrounded by the remains of forty columns, impressed the idea of decay upon my mind. My heart beat with fear and indignation as I approached the Forum by ways unknown to me. And the spell broke as I beheld the shattered columns and ruined temples of the Campo Vaccino —by that disgraceful name must now be designated the Roman Forum. I gazed round, but nothing there is as it was—I saw ruins of temples built after my time. The Coliseum was a stranger to me, and it appeared as if the altered state of these magnificent ruins suddenly quenched the enthusiasm of indignation which had before possessed my heart. I had never dared present to myself the image of the Roman Forum, degraded and debased; but a vague idea floated in my mind of broken columns, such as I remembered of the fallen images of the gods still left to decay in a spot where I had formerly worshipped them; but all was changed, and even the columns that remain of the temple erected by Camillus lost their identity surrounded by new candidates for immortality. I turned calmly to my guide and enquired, 'These are the ruins of the Roman Forum, and what is that immense building, whose shadow in the moonshine seems to bespeak something wonderful and magnificent, which I see at the end of the avenue of trees?'—'This is the Coliseum.'—'And what is Coliseum?' —'Do you not know? It is the renowned Circus built by Vespasian, Emperor of Rome.'—'Emperor of Rome, was he? Well, let us visit it.' We entered the Coliseum, that noble relict of imperial greatness— imperial it is true, but Roman. And that enthusiasm, which the broken columns of the Forum had extinguished, this wonderful pile again awakened. The moon shone through the broken arches and shed a glory around the fallen walls, crowned as they are by weeds and brambles. I looked around, and a holy awe seized me. I felt as if having deserted the Campo Vaccino, this had become the haunt of my noble compatriots. The seal of Eternity was on this building, and my heart heaved with the overpowering sensations under which it laboured. I said not a word.

"Alas! Alas! Such is the image of Rome fallen, torn, degraded by a hateful superstition; yet still commanding love—honour; and still awakening in the imaginations of men all that can purify and ennoble the mind. The Coliseum is the Type of Rome. Its arches—its marbles—its noble aspect which must inspire all with awe, which, in the mind of man, is akin to adoration—its wonderful, its inexpressible beauty—all tell of its greatness. Its fallen walls—its weed-covered buttresses—and more than all, the insulting images with which it is filled tell its fall.

"I dismissed my guide. I would never quit the Coliseum; this should be my abode during my second residence on earth. I visited every part of it. From its height, I beheld Rome sleeping under the cold rays of the moon: the dome of St. Peter's and the various other domes and spires which make a second city, the habitations of gods above the habitations of men; the arch of Constantine at my feet; the Tiber and the great change in the situation of the city of modern times; all caught my attention, but they only awakened a vague and transitory interest. The Coliseum was to me henceforth the world, my eternal habitation. It is true that curiosity and importunity have dragged me from it now—but my absence will be short, and my heart is still there. I shall return. And in those hallowed precincts, I shall pour forth, before I die, my last awakening call to Romans and to Liberty.

"It is true that I was now convinced that Rome had fallen, that her consuls and triumphs were at an end, the temples of her Capitol destroyed. But the Coliseum had softened those sentiments whose energy must otherwise have destroyed me. Anger, despair, all human passion died within me. I devoted myself, a pilgrim for some years, to a world in whose shews I am a careless spectator. If Rome be dead, I fly from her remains, loathsome as those of human life. It is in the Coliseum alone that I recognise the grandeur of my country—that is the only worthy asylum for an antient Roman.

"Yet suddenly, the feeling so dreadful to the human mind, the feeling of utter solitude, operated a new change on my heart. I remembered as it were but of yesterday all the shews which antient Rome had presented. Seated under one of the arches of the building and hiding my face in my hands, I revived in my imagination the memory of what I had left, when I last lost the light of day. I had left the consuls in the full enjoyment of power. Some years before, the empire, torn by Marius and Sulla and unsupported by the virtue of any, seemed tottering on the edge of subjection. But during my life, a new spirit had arisen: men were again vivified by the sacred flame that burnt in the souls of Camillus and Fabricius, and I gloried with an excessive joy to be the friend of Cicero, Cato, and Lucullus; the younger men, the sons of my friends, Brutus, Cassius, were rising with the promise of equal virtue. When I died, I was possessed by the strong persuasion that, since philosophy and letters were now joined to a virtue unparalleled upon earth, Rome was approaching that perfection from which there was no fall; and that, although men still feared, it was a wholesome fear which awoke them to action and the better secured the triumph of Good.

"When I awoke, Rome was no longer. That light, which I had hailed as the forerunner of perfection, became the torches that added splendour to her funeral—and those men, whose souls were as the temples of perfection, were the victims sacrificed at her funeral pyre. Oh, never had a nation such a death, and her murderers celebrated such games round her tomb, as destroyed nearly half the world. They were not the combats of gladiators and beasts—but the fierce strife of contending passions, the war of millions.

"But that is now all over. The exultation of the tyrant has faded. The monument of Rome, so splendid through the course of ages and adorned by the spoils of kingdoms, is now degraded in the dust. Some scattered columns and arches live to tell her site, but her people are dead. The strangers that possess her have lost all the characteristics of Romans; they have fallen off from her holy religion. Modern Rome is the Capital of Christianity, and that title is that which is crown and top of my despair.

"But human language sinks under the endeavour to describe the tremendous change operated in the world, it is true, by the slow flow of many ages, but which appeared to me in my singular situation as the work of a few days. I cannot recollect the agony of those moments—without shuddering. It was not a train of bitter thought; it was not a despair that ate into the nerves but shewed no outward sign; it was not the first pang of grief for the loss of those we love. It was a fierce fire that enveloped forests and cities in its flame; it was a tremendous avalanche that bore down with it trees and rocks and turned the course of rivers; it was an earthquake that shakes the sea and overturns mountains and threatens to shew to the eyes of man the mysteries of the internal earth. Oh, it was more than all these! More than any words can express or any image pourtray!"

The Stranger paused in his narration, and a long silence ensued. His eyes were fixed on the dead waters before him, and his companion gazed on him with wonder and emotion. A breeze slightly passed over the sea and rippled it; its rustling was heard among the trees. The smallest change awakened the Roman from his reverie, and he continued.

"A year has passed since I stood for the first time within the Coliseum. The rich dark weeds seemed blacker under the moon's rays, and the fallen arches reared themselves in stillness and beauty. The air was silent: it was the dead of night, and no sound reached me from the city—but by degrees the moon sunk, and daylight dawned. The sounds of human life began, and my own thoughts, which during the night were conversant only with memories, now turned their courses to the mean and debased reality. I considered my present situation, for I wished to form some plan for my future life. I greatly disliked the priest, my companion. During my very short residence since my return to earth, I had conceived a great aversion to the class of men to which he belonged. I disliked the Catholic superstition and wished to have no commerce with its ministers and servants. The jewels and money which I had were sufficient for my maintenance, and I wished to cast off the subjection which his presence seemed to put me under. But although in my native Rome, I was in a strange city with unknown customs. I hardly understood their language, and the recollections of my former life would only cast me into ridiculous mistakes. It was then that a kind deity interfered and, sending my good genius to watch over me, extricated me from my difficulties.

"The old priest, when the next morning he found I had disappeared, sent the guide, who had conducted me the preceding night, to bring me back and himself commenced a round of visits to publish the curiosity which he had under his keeping. Among others, he visited Lord Harley who had long been resident at Rome and to whom he was perfectly well known. You know Lord Harley and his family. I need not, therefore, describe them to you—and you who know her character can easily imagine the interest and curiosity with which the old priest's account inspired his young wife. She ordered her carriage and, taking the priest with her, hastened to his hotel to see me. I had not returned—the guide who had been to seek me informed her that I refused to quit the Coliseum. She left the priest at the inn and, accompanied only by her little son, came to my retreat.

"I was seated under the ruined arches of the south side when I saw her approach, leading her child by the hand. She sat down beside me, and after a pause of a few seconds she addressed me in Italian. 'Forgive me if I interrupt you. I have seen Padre Giuseppe and know who you are. You are unhappy and are cast upon our modern world without friends or connections. Will you allow me to offer you my friendship?'—I was thrown into confusion by this speech, addressed to me by a beautiful girl perfectly a stranger to me, and paused before I could answer so kind but so uncommon an offer; she continued—'Consider me, I entreat you, as an old acquaintance—not a modern Italian, for indeed I am not one, but as one of those many strangers which your antient city drew to gaze on her. I come from a distant country and am, therefore, unknowing in your language and laws. You shall teach me to know all that was great and worthy in your days, and I will teach you the manners and customs of ours.'

"She talked to me thus and won me over by her sweet smiles and soft eloquence to confide myself entirely to her. 'You shall consider me as your daughter,' said she, 'if a Scotch girl may pretend to that honour. I come from that *Ultima Thule* discovered by Caesar, but unknown in your days. I am married to an Englishman a good deal older than I am, but who takes a pleasure in cultivating my mind. Come with me to our house; you will be cherished and honoured there, and we will try to soften the pangs which the fallen state of your country must inflict upon you.'

"I followed her to her house and from that day began that friendship which is the only hope and comfort of my life. If on my return to earth my affections had never been awakened, I should not have lived long. But Isabell has softened my despair and nursed with angelic affection every wound of my heart. I cannot tell you how much I love her—how dear the sound of her voice is to me. Cicero did not love his Tullia as I do this divine creature. You cannot know half her virtues or half her wisdom. She is so frank-hearted, and yet so tender, that she wins my soul and binds it up in hers in a manner that I never experienced in my former life. She is Country, Friends—all, all, that I had lost is she to me.

"And now I have performed my promise in relating to you my first sensations upon awakening into life. I need not make a formal narration of what I have learnt since. In our proposed journey we shall have frequent opportunities of conversing and arguing. You have won me to a wish to see your country, and tomorrow we embark. I quit Rome—the Coliseum and Isabell—such is my restless nature. I want before I again die to examine the boasted improvements of modern times and to judge if, after the great fluctuation in human affairs, man is nearer perfection than in my days."

The sun had far descended when these friends rose and returned to the boat. As they rowed back to Naples, the sun set, leaving a rich orange tint in the sky which burned upon the waters, while Cape Miseno and the islands were marked by a black outline in the horizon. The moon rose on the other side of the bay and contrasted her silver light with the glowing colours of the Italian sunset. Night advanced, and the lights of the fisher boats glimmered across the sea, while one or two large ships seemed to pass like enormous shadows between the gazers and the moon. The brilliant spectacle of sunset and the soft light of the moon invited to reverie and forbade words to disturb the magic of the scene. The old Roman perhaps thought of the days he had formerly spent at Baiae, when the eternal sun had set as it now did, and he lived in other days with other men.

[The story ends at this point, but another and fragmentary version, told from Isabell Harley's point of view, follows in the manuscript.]

When I had drawn my singular friend from his solitude at the Coliseum, I, with the consent of Lord Harley, installed him in a room of our house. At first, he shunned all society and laboured under so great a depression of spirits that his health became affected. I found that I must make it my task to interest his feelings and to endeavour by what ever means to draw him from the apathy under which he was sunk. He appeared to regard every thing around him as a spectacle in which he had no concern. He was indeed a being cut off from our world; the links that had bound him to it had been snapped many ages before; and, unless I could succeed in joining at least one of them again, he would soon perish. I wished to engage him to visit some of those mighty ruins which tell of the antient greatness of Rome. I hesitated some time in my choice; the most majestic buildings had been built after his time, but I thought that their being situated in places familiar to his memory would give them that interest which otherwise, as unknown to him, they would want. I myself delighted to visit the baths of Antoninus, whose vast heaps of shattered walls and towers, clothed with ivy and the loveliest weeds, appear more like the natural scenery of a mountain than any thing formed of human hands. To these noble ruins I determined to conduct him.

I visited him, therefore, one day; and leading the conversation to his former life and death, I said to him: "You were happy in dying before the fall of your country and in not witnessing its degradation under the Emperors. These Emperors, who succeeded to the power and glory of the republic, enjoyed an extent of dominion and a revenue unknown in times before or after. Wild and tremendous were the deeds and errors of the omnipotent men. Their enemy could not fly from them. They trampled at will on the necks of millions. Few used their dominion for uses of beneficence, but many, even of the most wicked, spent it for the purposes of magnificence. They have left wonderful monuments behind, and I cannot regard these wonders as the acts of imperial greatness. They are the effects, although executed by unmeet hands, of republican virtue and power. When I visit them, I admire them as planned and modified by Camillus, by Fabricius, by the Scipios; and I regard Caracalla and Nero and even the more virtuous of the tribe, Titus and Adrian, as the mere workmen. When I visit the Coliseum, I do not think of Vespasian who built it or of the blood of gladiators and beasts which contaminated it, but I worship the spirit of antient Rome and of those noble heroes, who delivered their country from barbarians and who have enlightened the whole world by their miraculous virtue. I have heard you express a dislike of viewing the works of the oppressors of Rome, but visit them with me in this spirit, and you will find them strike you with that awe and reverence which power, acquired and accompanied by vice, can never give."

He suffered himself to be persuaded, and we passed under the Capitol and at the back of Mount Palatine on our way to the baths. The principal site of antient Rome is deserted, and we visit the Forum and the most populous of the hills of Rome through grassy lanes and across fields where few people ever come. This is fortunate; the ruins would lose half their beauty if surrounded by modern buildings, and we have only to regret that the Capitol has not been neglected as Mount Palatine and

Mount Caelius are. I cannot tell what the feelings of Valerius were: his emotions were strong, but he was silent, but for ever cast his eyes up to the sky; and once he said, "I like to look at the heavens, and only at them, for they are not changed." We entered the baths, and after visiting all the apartments, we ascended the shattered staircase and passed over the immense arches and the walls, which, when you are on them, appear like fields and glens and sloping hills. We were surrounded by fragrant weeds, and their height on each side of the path deceives you and adds still greater apparent extent to the ruins on which we walked. Sometimes, the top of some buttress is spread out into a field enamelled by the most beautiful flowers. And now winding about a difficult path, we reached the top of a turret and saw all Rome with the windings of the Tiber at but a short distance from us. This is of all others the place I delight most in Rome to visit: it joins the beauty and fragrance of Nature to the sublimest idea of human power; and when so united, they have an interest and feeling that sinks deep into my heart.

We seated ourselves on this pinnacle, and I sought in the eyes of my companion for an expression of wonder and delight with which mine were glistening. His were filled with tears. "You bring me here," he said, "to view the works of the Romans, and I behold nothing but destruction. What crowds of beautiful temples are fallen to the dust. My eyes wander over the seven hills, and all their glories are faded. When the columns of its Forum were broken, what could survive in Rome. The Capitol, less happy than most of the other hills who have returned to the solitude of Nature, is defiled by modern buildings. And these ruins—they are grand, but how miserable a tale do they tell. These baths did not exist in my time. They existed in all their magnificence some hundred years after I had forgotten the world. But now their roofs have fallen; their pavements have disappeared; they are grass-grown, weed-grown, shattered yet still standing; and such is the immortality of Rome. The walls of Rome still stand, and they describe an immense circuit; the modern city is filled with the ruins of the antient. Strangers flock to it and wonder at the immensity of the remains. But to me it all appears void. The antient temples where I worshipped Quirinus and the protectors of what I then called the immortal city—alas, why do I wake to be undeceived."

"You dwell," I replied, "on the most mournful ideas. Rome is fallen, but she is still venerated. It is to me a singular and even a beautiful sight to see the care and pains with which her degenerate children preserve her reliques. Every one visits her with enthusiasm and quits her with bitter regret. All appears consecrated within her walls. When a stranger resides within their bounds, he feels as if he inhabited a sacred temple—sacred although defiled; and indignation and pity mingling with his admiration, he feels such sensations that soften his heart and can never even in age and affliction be forgotten. It seems to me that, if I were overtaken by the greatest misfortunes, I should be half consoled by the recollection of having dwelt in Rome. If a man of the age of Pericles were to revive in Athens, how much more reason would he have to lament over her fall, than you over the age and decay of Rome."

As I wished to interest the feelings of Valerius and not so much to shew him all the remains of his country as to awaken in him by their sight a sentiment that he was still in some degree linked to the world, I chose as much as I could the most perfect and the most picturesque. He had not yet seen the Pantheon. I would not take him to it in the day, for I knew that its conversion to a Catholic Church, although it had probably preserved it, would be highly disgusting to him. I chose the time when the moon was yet in her encrease and when in her height she would shine over the open roof of the temple. One evening about seven o'clock, without telling him where we were going, I took him out with me. We passed round the building to a back door—it was opened, and a man lighted us down a pair of narrow dirty stairs: as we descended I said to him, "You are now going to see a temple built shortly after your time and dedicated to all the gods." He probably expected to see a ruin, but lo! we entered the most beautiful temple yet existing in the world. The bright moon shone directly over the aperture at top and lighted up the dome and the pavement—some bright stars twinkled by her side. The columns shone dimly around. The spirit of beauty seemed to shed her rays over her favoured offspring and to penetrate every thing—even the human mind—with a soft, still yet bright glory. In contemplating this scene, human admiration was unmingled with the deep feeling that it inspired— one seemed to enjoy the present god. If the work was human, the glory came from Nature; and Nature poured forth all her loveliness above this divine temple. The deep sky, the bright moon, and the twinkling stars were spread over it, and their light and beauty penetrated it. Why cannot human language express human thoughts? And how is it that there is a feeling inspired by the excess of beauty, which laps the heart in a gentle but eager flame, which may inspire virtue and love, but the feeling is far too intense for expression? We were both silent. We walked round the temple, and then we seated ourselves on the steps of an altar and remained a long time in contemplation. It is at such a time when one feels the existence of that Pantheic Love with which Nature is penetrated— and when a strong sympathy with beauty, if such an expression may be allowed, is the only feeling which animates the soul. At length, as we rose to depart, Valerius said, "Why do they tell me that all is changed; does not this temple to our gods exist?" I know not why—I ought not to have done it, for by the action I poisoned a moment of pure happiness—but I carelessly pointed to a cross that stood on the altar before which a solitary lamp burned. The cross did not alter my feelings, but those of my companion were embittered. The apple so fair to look at had turned to brackish dust. The cross told to him of change so great, so intolerable, that that one circumstance destroyed all that had arisen of love and pleasure in his heart. I tried in vain to bring him back to the deep feeling of beauty and of sacred awe with which he had been lately inspired. The spell was snapped. The moon-enlightened dome, the glittering pavement, the dim rows of lovely columns, the deep sky had lost to him their holiness. He hastened to quit the temple.

It was my first care to awaken in him a desire to know what of great and good had existed in his country after his death. He knew nothing of Virgil, Horace, Ovid, or Lucan—of Livy, Tacitus, or Seneca. You will have frequent opportunities of conversing with him, and he can tell you, much better than I can do, what the feelings were which this lecture excited in his mind. We used to visit an obscure nook of the Coliseum, where we scrambled with difficulty, and few would be inclined to follow us; or, on the walls of the baths of Caracalla or more frequently at the foot of the tomb of Cestius, that lovely spot where death appears to enjoy sunshine and the blue depth of the deep sky from which it is every where else shut out, we read together, and we discussed on what we read—our discussions were eternal. The brilliant sun of Rome shone upon us, and the air and all the scene were invested by happiness and beauty. My heart was cheerful, and it was my constant endeavour to awaken similar feelings in the bosom of my companion. We read the Georgics here, and I felt a degree of happiness in reading them that I could not have believed that words had it in their power to bestow. It was an intoxicating pleasure, which this fine climate and the sunny beautiful poetry which it inspires can give and which in a clouded atmosphere I am convinced I never should have felt. After reading, we visited some one of the galleries of Rome—Lord Harley's studious hours were then over, and he always accompanied us. The sight of the exquisite statues and paintings in Rome continued and often heightened this feeling of enjoyment. Did Valerius sympathize with me? Alas! no. There was a melancholy tint cast over all his thoughts; there was a sadness of demeanour, which the sun of Rome and the verses of Virgil could not dissipate. He felt deeply, but little joy mingled with his sentiments. With my other feelings towards him, I had joined to them an inexplicable one that my companion was not a being of the earth. I often paused anxiously to know whether he respired the air, as I did, or if his form cast a shadow at his feet. His semblance was that of life, yet he belonged to the dead. I did not feel fear or terror; I loved and revered him. I was warmly interested in his happiness, but there was mingled with these commoner sensations an awe—I cannot call it dread, yet it had something slightly allied to that repulsive feeling—a sentiment for which I can find no name, which mingled with all my thoughts and strangely characterised all my intercourse with him. Often when borne on in discourse by my thoughts, I encountered the glance of his bright yet placid eye; although it beamed only in sympathy, yet it checked me. If he put his hand upon mine, I did not shudder, but, as it were, my thoughts paused in their course and my heart heaved with something of an involuntary uneasiness until it was removed. Yet this was all very slight; I hardly noticed it, and it could not diminish my love and interest for him; perhaps if I would own all the truth, my affection was encreased by it; and not by endeavour but spontaneously I strove to repay by interest and intellectual sympathy the earthly barrier there seemed placed between us.

XXIV

An Eighteenth-Century Tale

A FRAGMENT

IN THE SUMMER of the year 17–, a lady who resided in a delightful house in Buckinghamshire assembled together a party whose sole object was to amuse themselves and to enjoy the short season of heat as pleasantly as they could. The house of this lady was situated on the river Thames, half way between Marlow and Henley. The country surrounding it was delightful: the river glided among grassy slopes, and its banks were sometimes shaded by beech woods and sometimes open to the full glare of the sun whose heat is seldom felt intolerable in England. Near her house, several beautiful islands were formed in the river, covered with willows, poplars, and elms. The trees of these islands united their branches with those of the firm land and formed a green archway which numerous birds delighted to frequent. The visitors found a thousand delightful ways of passing their time; they walked or rowed about the river; their conversation seldom languished. Many of them had been travellers, and they compared the scenes of their native country to those which they had visited; and if the latter did not gain in the comparison, it ought at least to have been satisfied by the preference it always obtained over all others when the merits of each came to be discussed as a perpetual residence.

One day, after passing the morning on the water and after having refreshed themselves under the shade of a great oak which grew on the banks of the river, the conversation fell on the strange events that had occurred in the life of a lady, one of their company; and they all entreated her—if the remembrance would not distress her—to relate those events which, although a part of them was known to almost all the company, none were fully and distinctly acquainted with. "I consent to what you ask," replied the lady, "if in return you will each relate what has passed particularly worthy of notice in each of your lives." "Indeed," replied another, "your proposition is a fair one, but it requires consideration. Let each individual examine for a moment his past life and determine how he chooses to make us all his confessors."—"You misunderstand me," replied the first lady; "I do not demand that you should make any confessions, but merely relate those events which have taken place that have reference to yourselves—not telling all the truth if you have any thing you wish to conceal (and who has not), but promising not to falsify any thing."—"And what are those to do who have nothing to tell?"—"Their history may be short, but every one can say something; and many who may at first think that they have nothing to relate will find, when they have once begun, that the subject is a richer one than they expected." The party soon consented and begged the lady who was to speak first to take upon herself the arrangement of her plan. She said—"I will commence that I may set a good example, and then you may each follow in order as you sit—and if today is not long enough, which I believe it will not be for us all to speak, we can choose a grassy spot like this tomorrow and the next day, and I think that you will find that my plan will give a zest to our little excursions. I will begin: so sit round me in a half circle, and give me your attention until I weary you; and then bid me break off, and another shall speak who will try to have better success.

"That my story may have a suitable commencement, I will inform you, what perhaps you know already, that my name is Maria Graham. My maiden name was Langley. My father and mother died before I was ten years old, so that I only remember the latter and that I wept when I lost her. I was left to the care of an aunt who had a tender affection for me—she had never been married, and as she has passed her thirtieth year it appeared unlikely that she ever would. I was brought up by her with the greatest care—we lived in the country, but she had herself been very well educated, and she spared no pains in teaching me the rudiments of all the fashionable . . ."

XXV

The Pole

It was in the early part of the month of February of the year 1831, near the close of day, that a travelling caleche, coming from Rome, was seen approaching, at full gallop, towards Mola di Gaeta. The road leading to the inn is rocky and narrow; on one side is an orange grove, extending to the sea; on the other an old Roman wall, overgrown by blossoming shrubs, enormous aloes, floating tangles of vines, and a thousand species of parasite plants peculiar to the South. Scarcely had the caleche entered this defile, when the careless postilion drove one of the wheels over a protruding ledge of rock, and overturned it; and in the next moment, a crowd of people came running to the spot. Not one of them, however, thought of relieving the traveller within the fallen vehicle; but, with violent gestures and loud outcries, began to examine what damage the caleche had sustained, and what profit they might derive from it. The wheelwright declared every wheel was shattered; the carpenter that the shafts were splintered; whilst the blacksmith, passing and repassing under the carriage, tugged at every clamp and screw and nail, with all the violence necessary to ensure himself a handsome job. The traveller it contained having quietly disengaged himself from various cloaks, books, and maps, now slowly descended, and for a moment the busy crowd forgot their restlessness, to gaze with admiration upon the noble figure of the stranger. He seemed to be scarcely two-and-twenty. In stature he was sufficiently tall to give an idea of superiority to his fellow mortals; and his form was moulded in such perfect proportions, that it presented a rare combination of youthful lightness and manly strength. His countenance, had you taken from it its deep thoughtfulness and its expression of calm intrepid bravery, might have belonged to the most lovely woman, so transparently blooming was his complexion, so regular his features, so blond and luxuriant his hair. Of all those present, he seemed the least concerned at the accident; he neither looked at the caleche, nor paid any

347

attention to the offers of service that were screamed from a dozen mouths; but, drawing out his watch, asked his servant if the carriage was broken.

"Pann,* the shafts are snapt, two of the springs are injured, and the linch-pin has flown."

"How long will it take to repair them?"

"Twenty-four hours."

"It is now four o'clock. See that every thing be in order again by to-morrow's daybreak."

"Pann, with these lazy Italians, I fear it will be impossible * * *."

"Ja pozwalam,"† replied the traveller, coldly, but decidedly. "Pay double—triple—what you will, but let all be ready for the hour I have mentioned."

Without another word, he walked towards the inn, followed by the crowd, teazing for alms. A few seconds ago they had all been active and healthy beings, so full of employment they could not afford to mend his caleche unless tempted by some extraordinary reward: now the men declared themselves cripples and invalids, the children were orphans, the women helpless widows, and they would all die of hunger if his Eccellenza did not bestow a few *grani*. "What a tedious race!" exclaimed the traveller, casting a handful of coins upon the ground, which caused a general scramble, and enabled him to proceed unmolested. At the inn new torments awaited him; a fresh crowd, composed of the landlord, the landlady, and their waiters and hostlers, gathered round, and assailed him with innumerable questions. The landlord hoped none of his limbs were broken, and begged him to consider himself master of the house; the waiters desired to know at what hour he would sup, what fare he chose, how long he intended to stay, where he came from, whither he was going; and the landlady led him, ostentatiously, through all the rooms of the inn, expatiating endlessly upon the peculiar and indescribable advantages of each. Ineffably weary of their officiousness, the traveller at last traversed a long and spacious hall, and took refuge in a balcony that looked upon the bay of Gaeta.

The inn is built upon the site of Cicero's Villa. Beneath the balcony, and on each side, along the whole curve of the bay, stretched a thick grove of orange-trees, which sloped down to the very verge of the Mediterranean. Balls of golden fruit, and blossoms faint with odour, and fair as stars, studded this amphitheatre of dark foliage; and at its extremity the liquid light of the waves pierced the glossy leaves, mingling their blue splendour with earth's green paradise. Every rock and mountain glowed

* My Lord, in Polish.
† I will it, in Polish.

with a purple hue, so intense and soft, they resembled violet vapours
dissolving into the pale radiance of the evening sky. Far away in the deep
broad flood of the ocean, rose the two mountain islands of Ischia and
Procida, between which Vesuvius thrust in his jagged form, and his floating banner of snow-white smoke. The solitary heaven was without sun or
moon, without a star or cloud, but smiled in that tender vestal light which
speaks of eternal, immutable peace.

It would be difficult to define the feelings of the traveller as he gazed
on this scene: his countenance, uplifted to heaven, was animated with a
profound and impassioned melancholy, with an expression of an earnest
and fervid pleading against some vast and inevitable wrong. He was
thinking probably of his country; and whilst he contrasted its ruined
villages and devastated fields with the splendour and glow of the fair land
before him, was breathing inwardly a passionate appeal against that blind
and cruel destiny which had consigned Poland to the desolating influence
of Russian despotism. His reverie was interrupted by the sound of a
female voice singing in Polish among the orange-trees at his feet. The
singer was invisible; but the sweetness of her voice, and the singular
reference of the words (the following prose translation conveys their
meaning) to the thoughts of his own mind, filled the traveller with surprise:—

"When thou gazest upon the azure heaven, so mighty in its calm, do
not say, O bright enchantment, hast thou no pity, that thou dawnest thus
in unattainable loveliness upon my world-wearied eyes.

"When the southern wind softly breathes, do not say reproachfully, thy
cradle is the ether of the morning sun, thou drinkest the odorous essence
of myrtle and lemon blossoms; thou should'st bear upon thy wings all
sweet emotions, all soft desires; why bringest thou then no healing to the
anguish I endure?

"Neither in the dark hour, when thou thinkest upon thy country and
thy friends, say not with grief, They are lost! They are not! Say rather
with joy, They were illustrious! and it is bliss to know that they have
been!"

It were wise in me to obey thy lesson, sweet songstress, thought the
traveller; and, revolving in his mind the singularity of the serenade, he
continued to gaze upon the trees below: there was no rustling amid their
branches, no sound which told a human being was concealed beneath
their foliage; nothing was heard beyond the almost imperceptible breath-
ings of the evening air. Did such things exist any where but in the imagination of the poet? He could almost have believed that the spirit of that
divine scene had assumed a human voice and human words, to soothe his
melancholy, so floating and airy had been the strain, so deep the silence
that succeeded it. One moment more, and there arose from the same spot

cries for help uttered in Italian, and shrieks of distress so piercing, they made the traveller fly with the speed of lightning through the great hall, down the staircase into the garden. The first object that met his eyes was the figure of a girl about sixteen, her one arm tightly embracing the stem of a tree, her other angrily repelling a young man who was endeavouring to drag her away. "I will not go with you—I love you no longer, Giorgio —and go with you, I will not," shrieked the girl, in tones of mingled violence and fear. "You must—you shall," retorted her aggressor, in a voice of thunder. "I have found you again, and I won't be duped by your fooleries, Marietta. . . . . . . And who are you, and who begged you to interfere?" added he, turning fiercely upon the traveller, whose strong grasp had torn him from Marietta. "An officer, as it should seem by your dress;—be pleased to know that I am also an officer, and risk my displeasure no further."

"No officer would ill-treat a defenceless girl," the Pole replied, with quiet contempt.

At this taunt Giorgio quivered with rage. His features, handsome and regular as those of Italians generally are, became quite distorted. His hands with convulsive movements sought about his breast for the dagger that was concealed there, his dark flashing eyes fixed intently at the same time upon his adversary, as if he hoped the fiendish spirit that burned within them might previously annihilate him.

"Be on your guard—he is a perfect wretch," cried Marietta, rushing towards her protector.

The arrival of several servants from the inn dispelled all idea of present danger: they dragged off Giorgio, telling him that, although the girl was his sister, he had no right to separate her from the *corps d'opéra*, with whom she was travelling through Gaeta.

"*E vero, è verissimo,*" cried Marietta with joyful triumph. "What is it to him if I like my liberty, and prefer wandering about, singing here and there, to being his unhappy par—"

"Marietta! beware! dare not to speak ill of me!" screamed the retiring Giorgio, looking back over his shoulder, and accompanying his words with a look of such frightful menace, as completely subdued his sister.

She watched in anxious silence till he had disappeared, and then, with affectionate humility and a graceful quickness that allowed not of its prevention, knelt lightly down, and pressed the stranger's hand to her lips. "You have more than repaid me for the song I sang to you," she said, rising and leading the way to the inn, "and, if you like it, I will sing others to you whilst you sup."

"Are you a Pole?" enquired the traveller. "A fine demand! how can I be a Pole? Did you not say yourself there was no longer any such country as Poland?"

"I? not that I recollect."

"If you did not say it, confess at least that you thought it. The Poles are all become Russians, and for nothing in the world, Signor, would I be a Russian. Why in all their language they have no word that expresses *honour*.* No! rather than be a Russian, much as I hate it, I would go with Giorgio."

"Are you an Italian?"

"No—not exactly."

"What are you, then?"

"Um! I am what I am, who can be more? But, Signor, one thing I must beg of you, do not ask me any questions about myself, nor any about Giorgio. I will sing to you, talk to you, wait upon you—any thing of that kind you please, but I will not answer questions on those subjects."

Seating herself upon a stool, in a dark corner of the traveller's apartment, as far removed as possible from him, and all other interruptions, Marietta passed the evening in playing on her guitar and singing. She was a most accomplished singer, possessing and managing all the intricacies of the art, with perfect ease, but this scarcely excited admiration in comparison with the natural beauty of her voice. There was a profound melancholy in its intense sweetness, that dissolved the soul of the traveller in grief. All that was dear to him in the memory of the past, the joys of home, and childhood, the tenderness and truth of his first friendships, the glow of patriotism; every cherished hour, every endeared spot, all that he had loved, and all that he had lost upon earth, seemed again to live and again to fade, as he listened to her strains. Without paying any attention to him, and apparently without any effort to herself, she breathed forth melody after melody for her own pleasure, like some lone nightingale, that, in a home of green leaves, sings to cheer its solitude with sweet sounds. Her countenance and figure would have been beautiful, had they been more fully developed. They resembled those sketches of a great artist in which there are only a few lightly-traced lines, but those are so full of spirit and meaning, that you easily imagine what a masterpiece it would have been when finished.

The first visit of our traveller, on arriving, next day, at Naples, was to the Princess Dashkhoff. She was a Russian lady, whose high birth, immense wealth, and talents for intrigue, had procured for her the intimacy of half the crowned heads of Europe, and had made her all powerful at the Court of St. Petersburgh. Detesting the cold barbarism of her native country, she had established herself at Naples, in a splendid mansion, near the Strada Nuova; and affecting an extravagant admiration for Italy, by her munificent patronage of the arts and artists, and by perpetual

---

* This is true. The Russian language is without that word.

exhibitions of her own skill, in drawing and singing, dancing and acting, had obtained the name of the Corinna of the North. Her *salon* was the evening resort of the wise, the idle, the witty, and the dissipated. Not to know Corinna, was to be yourself unknown; and not to frequent her *conversazioni* was, as far as society was concerned, to be banished from all that was fashionable or delightful in Naples.

It was the hour of evening reception. The Pole burned with impatience to speak to the Princess, for on her influence, at Petersburgh, depended the fate of a brother, the only being in existence he now cared for. A splendid suite of apartments, blazing with lights, crowded with company, and furnished with the munificence of an Eastern haram, lay open before him; without allowing himself to be announced he entered them. When an highly imaginative mind is absorbed by some master feeling, all opposing contrasts, all glowing extremes, serve but to add depth and intensity to that feeling. The festal scene of marble columns garlanded by roses, the walls of Venetian mirror, reflecting the light of innumerable tapers, and the forms of lovely women and gay youths floating in the mazy dance, seemed to him deceitful shows that veiled some frightful sorrow; and with eager rapid steps, as if borne along by the impulse of his own thoughts, he hurried past them. Scarcely knowing how he had arrived there, he at length found himself standing beside the Princess, in a marble colonnade, open above to the moonlight and the stars of heaven, and admitting at its sides the odorous air and blossoming almond-trees of the adjacent garden.

"Ladislas!" exclaimed the lady, starting, "is it possible—to see you here almost exceeds belief."

After remaining some moments in deep silence, collecting and arranging his thoughts, the Pole replied. A conversation ensued, in so low a voice as to be only audible to themselves; from their attitudes and gestures it might be inferred that Ladislas was relating some tale of deep anguish, mixed with solemn and impressive adjurations to which the Princess listened with a consenting tranquillizing sympathy.

They issued from the recess, walked up the colonnade, and entered a small temple that terminated it. From the centre of its airy dome hung a lighted alabaster lamp of a boat-like shape, beneath which a youthful female was seated alone sketching a range of moonlight hills that appeared between the columns. "Idalie," said the Princess, "I have brought you a new subject for your pencil,—and such a subject, my love—one whose fame has already made him dear to your imagination; no less a person than the hero of Ostralenka,* the Vistula, and the Belvedere.† So call up

---

* At Ostralenka, the Russian and Polish armies were in sight of one another. The destruction of the Poles seemed inevitable; not expecting the attack, their lines were not formed, and the Russians were triple in number, and advancing in the most per-

one of those brightest, happiest moods of your genius, in which all succeeds to you, and enrich my album with his likeness," spreading it before her.

It is difficult to refuse any request to a person who has just granted us an important favour. Ladislas suffered himself to be seated, and as soon as the Princess had quitted them, the gloom which had shadowed his brow at the names of Ostralenka, the Vistula, and the Belvedere, vanished. The surpassing beauty of the young artist would have changed the heaviest penance into a pleasure. She was lovely as one of Raphael's Madonnas; and, like them, there was a silent beauty in her presence that struck the most superficial beholder with astonishment and satisfaction. Her hair, of a golden and burnished brown (the colour of the autumnal foliage illuminated by the setting sun), fell in gauzy wavings round her face, throat and shoulders. Her small clear forehead, gleaming with gentle thought; her curved, soft, and rosy lips; the delicate moulding of the lower part of the face, expressing purity and integrity of nature, were all perfectly Grecian. Her hazel eyes, with their arched lids and dark arrowy lashes, pierced the soul with their full and thrilling softness. She was clad in long and graceful drapery, white as snow; but, pure as this garment was, it seemed a rude disguise to the resplendent softness of the limbs it enfolded. The delicate light that gleamed from the alabaster lamp above them, was a faint simile of the ineffable spirit of love that burned within Idalie's fair transparent frame; and the one trembling shining star of evening that palpitates responsively to happy lovers, never seemed more divine or more beloved than she did to Ladislas, as she sat there, now fixing a timid but attentive gaze upon his countenance, and then dropping it upon the paper before her. And not alone for Ladislas, was this hour the dawn of passionate love. The same spell was felt in the heart of Idalie, veiling the world and lifting her spirit into vast and immeasurable regions of unexplored delight. One moment their eyes met and glanced upon each other, the look of exalted, of eternal love, mute, blessed, and inexpressible. Their lids fell and were raised no more. Rapture thrilled their breasts and swelled their full hearts, a rapture felt but not seen; for

---

fect order. In this emergency, three hundred students from the University of Warsaw drew hastily up in a body, and, devoting themselves willingly to death, marched forward to meet the onset of the enemy. They were headed by a young man who distinguished himself by the most exalted courage, and was the only one of their numbers who escaped. He stationed his band in a small wood that lay directly in the path of the Russians, and checked their progress for the space of three hours. Every tree of that wood now waves above a patriot's grave. In the meantime the Polish army formed, bore down, and gained a most brilliant victory.

† The palace at Warsaw, in which the attempt to assassinate the Grand Duke Constantine was made by a party of young men.

motionless, and in deep silence, as if every outward faculty were absorbed in reverence, they continued, each inwardly knowing, hearing, seeing nothing but the divine influence and attraction of the other.

I know not if the portrait was finished. I believe it was not. Noiselessly Idalie arose and departed to seek the Princess, and Ladislas followed. "Who is that lovely being?" enquired an English traveller sometime afterward, pointing out Idalie from a group of ladies. "A Polish girl—a protégée of mine," was the reply of the Princess; "a daughter of one of Kosciusko's unfortunate followers, who died here poor and unknown. She has a great genius for drawing and painting, but she is so different in her nature from the generality of people, that I am afraid she will never get on in the world. All the family are wild and strange. There is a brother, who they say is a complete ruffian; brave as a Pole and unprincipled as an Italian; a villain quite varnished in picturesque, like one of your Lord Byron's corsairs and giaours. Then there is a younger sister; the most uncontrollable little creature, who chose to pretend my house was insupportable, and ran away into Calabria or Campagna, and set up as a *prima donna*. But these, to be sure, are the children of a second wife, an Italian; and Idalie, I must confess, has none of their lawlessness, but is remarkably gentle and steady."

Disgusted with this heartless conversation, which disturbed his mood of ecstacy, Ladislas hastily quitted the Dashkhoff palace, and entered the Villa Reale, whose embowering trees promised solitude. Not one straggler of the many gay crowds that frequent this luxurious garden from morning till midnight was now to be seen. With its straight walks buried in gloom and shadow; its stone fonts of sleeping water; its marble statues, its heaven-pointing obelisks, and the tingling silence of its midnight air, it was holy and calm as a deserted oratory, when the last strain of the vesper hymn has died away, the last taper has ceased to burn, the last censer has been flung, and both priests and worshippers have departed. Ladislas cast himself upon a stone-seat in the ilex-grove that skirts the margin of the bay. "I dreamt not of love," he exclaimed, "I sought her not! I had renounced life and all its train of raptures, hopes, and joys. Cold, and void of every wish, the shadow of death lay upon my heart; suddenly she stood before me, lovely as an angel that heralds departed spirits to the kingdom of eternal bliss. Fearless, but mild, she poured the magic of her gaze upon my soul. I speak the word of the hour. She shall be mine—or I will die!"

Reclining in the ilex-grove, Ladislas passed the remaining hours of that too-short night, entranced in bliss, as if the bright form of his beloved were still shining beside him. Gradually, every beauty of the wondrous and far-famed Bay of Naples impressed itself upon his attention. The broad and beamless moon sinking behind the tall elms of Posillipo—the broken star-light on the surface of the waves—their rippling sound as they broke at his feet—Sorrento's purple promontory, and the gentle wind that blew from it—the solitary grandeur of Capri's mountain-island, rising out of the middle of the bay, a colossal sphinx guarding two baths of azure light—Vesuvius breathing its smoke, and flame, and sparks, into the cloudless ether—all became mingled in inexplicable harmony with his new-born passion, and were indelibly associated with his recollection of that night.

The next morning Idalie was sketching in the Villa Reale. She had seated herself on the outside of a shady alley. Two persons passed behind her, and the childish, petulant voice of one of them drew her attention. That voice, so sweet even in its impatience, certainly belonged to her fugitive sister. "It is she!" exclaimed Idalie, gliding swift as thought between the trees, and folding the speaker to her bosom. "Marietta,—my dear little Marietta! at last you are come back again. *Cattivella!* now promise to stay with me. You know not how miserable I have been about you."

"No! I cannot promise any thing of the kind," replied Marietta, playing with the ribbons of her guitar. "I choose to have my liberty."

Idalie's arms sunk, and her eyes were cast upon the ground when she heard the cold and decided tone in which this refusal was pronounced. On raising the latter, they glanced upon the companion of her sister, and were filled with unconquerable emotion at discovering Ladislas, the elected of her heart.

"I met your sister here a few minutes ago," explained he, partaking her feelings; "and having been so fortunate the other day as to render her a slight service——"

"Oh, yes," interrupted Marietta; "I sung for him a whole evening at Gaeta. It was a curious adventure. His carriage was overturned close to the inn. I had arrived there half an hour before, and was walking in an orange-grove near the spot, and saw the accident happen, and heard him speak in Polish to his servant. My heart beat with joy to behold one belonging to that heroic nation. He looked wondrous melancholy: I thought it must be about his country, so I crept as softly as a mouse among the trees under his balcony, and sung him a salve-song in Polish. I *improvised* it on the spur of the moment. I do not very well recollect it, but it was about azure heavens, southern winds, myrtle and lemon blossoms, and the illustrious unfortunate; and it ought to have pleased him. Just as I had finished, out starts our blessed brother, Giorgio, from the inn, and began one of his most terrific bothers. Imagine how frightened I was, for I thought he was gone to Sicily with his regiment. However, they got him away, and I followed this stranger into his room, and sang to him the rest of the evening. All my best songs, the *Mio ben quando verrà, Nina pazza per Amore,* the *All' armi* of Generali, the *Dolce cara patria,* from Tancredi, the *Deh calma* from Otello,—all my whole stock, I assure you." Thus rattled on Marietta; and then, as if her quick eye had already discovered the secret of their attachment, she added, with an arch smile, "but don't be frightened, Idalie, though his eyes filled with tears whilst I sung, as yours often do, not a word of praise did the Sarmatian bestow on me."

"Then return and live with me, dear Marietta, and I will praise you as much, and more than you desire."

"*Santa Maria del Piè di Grotta!* What a tiresome person you are, Idalie. When you have got an idea into your head, an earthquake would not get it out again. Have I not told you that I will not. If you knew the motive, you would approve my resolution. I said I liked my liberty, and so forth, but that was not the reason of my flight. I do not choose to have any thing to do with Giorgio and the Princess; for, believe me, dearest Idalie, disgraceful as my present mode of life seems to you, it is innocence itself compared with the crimes they were leading me into."

"Some suspicion of this did once cross my mind," her sister replied with a sigh, "but I rejected it as too horrible. Dear child, think no more about them. Do you not know that I have left the Princess's house, and am living by myself in a little pavilion far up on the Strada Nuova. There you need not fear their molestations."

"Is not Giorgio, then, with you?"

"No, I have not seen him for some time. I doubt if he be in Naples."

"So, Messer Giorgio, you have deceived me again. But I might have known that, for he never speaks a word of truth. Be assured, however, he is in Naples, for I caught a glimpse of him this morning, mounting the hill that leads to the barracks at Pizzofalcone, and he is as intimate with the Princess as ever, though she pretends to disown him. As for me, I am engaged at San Carlos; the writing is signed and sealed, and cannot be broken without forfeiting a heavy sum of money; otherwise I should be happy to live peacefully with you; for you know not, Idalie, all I have had to suffer; how sad and ill-treated I have been! how often pinched with want and hunger; and worse than that, when Giorgio takes it into his head to pursue me, and plants himself in the pit, fixing his horrible looks upon me as I sing! how many times I have rushed out of the theatre, and spent the nights in the great wide Maremma, beset by robbers, buffaloes, and wild boars, till I was almost mad with fear and bewilderment. There is a curse upon our family, I think. Did not our father once live in a splendid castle of his own, with an hundred retainers to wait upon him; and do you remember the miserable garret in which he died? But I cannot stay any longer. I am wanted at the rehearsal: so, farewell, dearest Idalie. Be you at least happy, and leave me to fulfil the evil destiny that hangs over our race."

"No! No!" exclaimed Ladislas, "that must not be—the writing must be cancelled,"—and then, with the affection and unreserve of a brother, he entered into their sentiments; with sweet and persuasive arguments overcame their scruples of receiving a pecuniary obligation from him, and finally, taking Marietta by the hand, led her away to San Carlos, in order to cancel her engagement.

And in another hour it was cancelled. Marietta was once more free and joyful; and, affectionate as old friends, the three met again in the little pavilion, which was Idalie's home. It stood alone in a myrtle wood on the last of the green promontories, which form the Strada Nuova, and separate the Bay of Naples from the Bay of Baia,—a lonely hermitage secluded from the noise and turmoil of the city, whose only visitors were the faint winds of morning and evening, the smiles of the fair Italian heaven, its wandering clouds, and, perchance, a solitary bird. From every part of the building you could see the Baian Ocean sparkling breathlessly beneath the sun; through the windows and the columns of the portico you beheld the mountains of the distant coast shining on, hour after hour, like amethysts in a thrilling vapour of purple transparent light, so ardent yet halcyon, so bright and unreal, a poet would have chosen it to emblem the radiant atmosphere that glows around Elysian isles of eternal peace and joy. Marietta soon left the building to join some fisher boys who were dancing the tarantella upon the beach below. Idalie took her drawing, which was her daily employment, and furnished her the means of subsistence, and Ladislas sat by her side. There was no sound of rolling carriages, no tramp of men and horse, no distant singing, no one speaking near; the wind awoke no rustling amid the leaves of the myrtle wood, and the wave died without a murmur on the shore. Ladislas' deep but melodious voice alone broke the crystal silence of the noon-day air. Italy was around him, robed in two splendours of blue and green; but he was an exile, and the recollections of his native land thronged into his memory, and oppressed him with their numbers and their life. During the three months it had taken him to effect his escape from Warsaw to Naples, his lips had been closed in silence, whilst his mind had been wrapt in the gloom of the dreadful images that haunted it. In Idalie's countenance there was that expression of innocence and sublimity of soul, of purity and strength, that excited the warmest admiration, and inspired sudden and deep confidence. She looked like some supernatural being that walks through the world, untouched by its corruptions; like one that unconsciously, yet with delight, confers pleasure and peace; and Ladislas felt that, in speaking to her of the dark sorrows of his country, they would lose their mortal weight and be resolved into beauty, by her sympathy. In glowing terms he described the heroic struggle of Poland for liberty; the triumph and exultation that had filled every bosom during the few months they were free; the hardships and privations they had endured, the deeds of daring bravery of the men, the heroism it had awakened in the women; and then its fall—the return of the Russians; the horrible character of Russian despotism, its sternness and deceit, its pride and selfish ignorance: the loss of public and private integrity, the disbelief of good, the blighted, hopeless, joyless life endured by those whom it crushes beneath its servitude.

Thus passed the hours of the forenoon. Then Ladislas fixing his eyes upon the coast of Baia, and expressing at the same time his impatience to visit that ancient resort of heroes and of emperors, Idalie led the way by a small path down the hill to the beach. There they found a skiff dancing idly to and fro upon the waves, and, unmooring it from its rocky haven, embarked in it. It had been sweet to mark the passage of that light bark freighted with these happy lovers, when borne by its sails it swept through the little ocean-channel that lies between the beaked promontories of the mainland and the closing cliffs of the island of Nisida; and when with gentler motion it glided into the open expanse of the bay of Baia, and cut its way through the translucent water, above the ruins of temples and palaces overgrown by sea-weed, on which the rays of the sun were playing, creating a thousand rainbow hues, that varied with every wave that flowed over them. In all that plane of blue light it was the only moving thing; and as if it had been the child of the ocean that bore it, and the sun that looked down on it, it sped gaily along in their smiles past the fortress where Brutus and Cassius sought shelter after the death of Cæsar; past the temples of Jupiter and Neptune; by the ruins of that castle in which three Romans once portioned out the world between them, to the Cumaean hill that enshadows the beloved Linternum of Scipio Africanus, and in which he died. The whole of this coast is a paradise of natural beauty, investing with its own loveliness the time-eaten wrecks with which it is strewn; the mouldering past is mingled with the vivid present; ruin and grey annihilation are decked in eternal spring. The woody windings of the shore reveal, in their deep recesses, the gleaming marble fragments of the abodes of ancient heroes: the verdurous hues of the promontories mingle with the upright columns of shattered temples, or clothe, with nature's voluptuous bloom, the pale funereal urns of departed gods; whilst the foliage and the inland fountains, and the breaking waves upon the shore, were murmuring around their woven minstrelsy of love and joy. Earth, sea, and sky, blazed like three gods, with tranquil but animated loveliness; with a splendour that did not dazzle—with a richness that could not satiate. The air on that beautiful warm coast was as a field of fragrance; the refreshing sea-breeze seemed to blow from Paradise, quickening their senses, and bringing to them the odour of a thousand unknown blossoms. "What world is this?" exclaimed Ladislas, in a tone of rapture that nearly answered its own question. "I could imagine I had entered an enchanted garden; four heavens surround me; the one above; the pure element beneath me with its waves that shine and tremble as stars; the adorned earth that hangs over it; and the heaven of delight they create within my breast. Morning is here a rose, day a tulip, night a lily; evening is, like morning, again a rose, and life seems a choral-hymn of beautiful and glowing sentiments, that I go singing to myself as I wander along this perpetual path of flowers."

It was night ere they again reached the pavilion. It stood dark and deserted in the clear moonshine; the door was locked; the windows and their outer shutters had been closed from within, so securely as to deny all admittance, unless by breaking them open, which the solid nature of the shutters rendered almost impossible. After calling and knocking repeatedly without obtaining any answer, it became evident that Marietta had quitted the dwelling. In the first moment of surprise which this occurrence occasioned, they had not observed a written sheet of paper, of a large size, which lay unfolded and placed directly before the door, as if to attract attention. Idalie took it up and read the following lines, traced by Marietta.

"Oh, Idalie! what a fiendish thing is life. But a few hours ago, how calm and secure we were in happiness—now danger and perhaps destruction is our portion. One chance yet remains, the moment you get this, persuade—not only persuade—but compel that adorable stranger to fly instantly from Naples. He is not safe here an instant longer. Do not doubt what I say, or his life may be the forfeit. How can I impress this on your mind. I would not willingly betray any one, but how else can I save him? Giorgio has been here. Oh! the frightful violence of that man. He raved like an insane person, and let fall such dark and bloody hints as opened worlds of horror to me. I am gone to discover what I can. I know his haunts, and his associates, and shall soon find out if there be any truth in what he threatens. I could not await your return, neither dare I leave the pavilion open. Who knows if, in the interval between my departure and your return, an assassin might not conceal himself within; and your first welcome be, to see the stranger fall lifeless at your feet. His every step is watched by spies armed for his destruction. I know not what to do—and yet it seems to me that my going may possibly avert the catastrophe. —MARIETTA."

Ladislas listened to these lines unmoved; but the effect they produced on Idalie was dreadful. She gave implicit credence to them, and every word sounded as a knell. She lost all presence of mind; every reflection that might have taught her to avert the stroke she so much dreaded, was swallowed up in anguish, as if the deed that was to be consummated were already done. What task can be more difficult than to describe the overwhelming agony which heavy and unexpected misery produces. To have lived the day that Idalie had just lived—a day in which all the beauty of existence had been unveiled to its very depths; to have dreamt as she had done, a dream of love that steeped her soul in divine, and almost uncommunicable joy; and now to sink from this pinnacle of happiness into a black and lampless cavern, the habitation of death, whose spectral form and chilling spirit was felt through all the air! This is but a feeble metaphor of the sudden transition from rapture to misery, which Idalie experienced. She looked upon Ladislas, and beheld him bright and full of life; the roseate hues of health upon his cheek, his eyes beaming with peaceful joy, his noble countenance varying not in the least from that imperturbable and godlike self-possession which was its habitual expression. And as her imagination made present to her the fatal moment, when beneath the dagger of the assassin this adored being should sink bleeding, wounded, and then be ever lost in death, her blood rushed to her heart, a deadly pause ensued, from which she awoke in a bewildering mist of horror. The still air and quite moonshine to her seemed brooding mischief; a thousand shadows that proceeded from no one, but were the creatures of her distressed brain, flitted around, and filled the empty space of the portico. Poor Idalie! an eternity of bliss would have been dearly bought at the price of that moment's overwhelming anguish! Ladislas beheld her excess of emotion with pain, in which, however, all was not pain, for it was blended with that triumphant exultation, that a lover ever feels when he for the first time becomes assured that he is beloved by the object of his love with an affection tender and intense as his own.

As soon as Idalie recovered some presence of mind, with passionate supplications she entreated Ladislas to leave her, to fly this solitary spot, and to seek safety amid the crowded streets of Naples. He would not hear of this; he gently remonstrated with her upon the unreasonableness of her terrors, urging how little probable it was that his passing *rencontre* with Giorgio at Gaeta could have awakened in him such a deadly spirit of revenge as Marietta represented. He viewed the whole thing lightly, attributing it either to the vivacity of Marietta's imagination, which had made her attach a monstrous import to some angry expressions of her brother, or looking upon it as some merry device which she had contrived, in order to frighten them; and tranquillized Idalie, by assurances that they would shortly see her wild sister return laughing, and full of glee at the success of her plot. In this expectation two hours passed away, but still no Marietta appeared, and it had grown too late to seek another shelter, without exposing Idalie to the slander of evil-minded people.

They passed the rest of the night therefore in the portico, Idalie some-times pale and breathless, with recurring fears, and sometimes calm and happy, as Ladislas poured forth his tale of passionate love. His feelings on the contrary were pure and unalloyed. Where Idalie was, there was the whole universe to him; where she was not, there was only a formless void. He had an insatiable thirst for her presence, which only grew intenser with the enjoyment of its own desire; and he blessed the fortunate occur-rence that prolonged his bliss during hours which otherwise would have been spent pining in absence from her. No other considerations intruded. Blessings kindled within his eyes as he gazed upon that lovely coun-tenance and faultless form, and angels might have envied the happiness he felt.

Morning came, bright and serene; the sun arose, the ocean and the mountains again resumed their magic splendour; the myrtle-woods and every minuter bloom of the garden shone out beneath the sun, and the whole earth was a happy form made perfect by the power of light. They recollected that they had promised to join the Princess Dashkhoff, and a large party of her friends, at eight o'clock, in an excursion to Pæstum. The point of meeting was the shore of the Villa Reale, where the numer-ous guests were to embark in a steamer which had been engaged for the occasion. In Idalie's present homeless and uncertain condition, this plan offered some advantages. It would enable them to pass the day in each other's society under the auspices of the Princess, and it was to be hoped that on their return the mystery of Marietta's disappearance would be unravelled, and Idalie find her home once more open to her. They had scarcely settled to go, ere one of those horse calessini which ply in the streets of Naples, was seen coming towards them. Its driver, a ragged boy, sat on the shaft, singing as he drove; another urchin, all in tatters, stood as lacquey behind, and between them sat Marietta; the paleness of fear was on her cheeks, and her eyes had the staggered affrighted look of one who has gazed upon some appalling horror. She hastily descended, and bade the calessino retire to some distance, and await further orders. "Why is he yet here?" said she to her sister. "You foolish blind Idalie, why did you not mind my letter—too proud I suppose to obey any but yourself; but mark, you would not hear my warnings—we shall lose him, and you will feel them in your heart's core." She then, with all the violent gesticulation of an Italian, threw herself at the feet of Ladislas, and with a countenance that expressed her own full conviction in what she said, besought him to fly instantly, not only from Naples, but from Italy, for his life would never be safe in that land of assassins and traitors. With entreaties almost as violent as her own, Ladislas and Idalie urged her to explain, but this only threw her into a new frenzy; she wept and tore her hair; she declared the peril was too urgent to admit of explanation,—

every moment was precious—another's hour's stay in Naples would be his death.

The situation of Ladislas was a curious one. He had served in the Russian campaigns against Persia and Turkey, and had been there daily exposed to the chances of destruction; in the late struggle between Poland and Russia, he had performed actions of such determined and daring bravery as had made his name a glory to his countrymen, and a terror to their enemies. In all these exploits he had devoted himself so unreservedly to death, that his escape was considered as a miraculous interposition of heaven. It was not to be expected that this Mars in a human form, this Achilles who had braved death in a thousand shapes, should now consent to fly before the uplifted finger and visionary warnings of a dreamsick girl, for such Marietta appeared to him to be. He pitied her sufferings, endeavoured to soothe her, but asserted he had seen no reason that could induce him to quit Naples.

A full quarter of an hour elapsed before an explanation could be wrung from Marietta. The chaos that reigned in her mind may easily be imagined. She had become possessed of a secret which involved the life of two persons. Ladislas refused to save himself unless she revealed what might place her brother's life in jeopardy. Whichever way she looked, destruction closed the view. Nature had bestowed on her a heart exquisitely alive to the sufferings of others; a mind quick in perceiving the nicest lines of moral rectitude, and strenuous in endeavouring to act up to its perceptions. Any deviations in her conduct from these principles had been the work of a fate that, strong and fierce as a tempest, had bent down her weak youth like a reed beneath its force. She had once loved Giorgio; he had played with and caressed her in infancy—with the fond patronage of an elder brother had procured her the only indulgences her orphaned childhood had ever known. Fraternal love called loudly on her not to endanger his life; gratitude as loudly called on her not to allow her benefactor to become his victim. This last idea was too horrible to be endured. The present moment is ever all-powerful with the young, and Marietta related what she knew.

Well might the poor child be wild and disordered. She had passed the night in the catacombs of San Gennaro, under Capo di Monte. In these subterranean galleries were held the nightly meetings of the band of desperate *bravi* of whom Giorgio was in secret the chief. The entrance to the catacombs is in a deserted vineyard, and is overgrown by huge aloes: rooted in stones and sharp rocks, they lift their thorny leaves above the opening, and conceal it effectually. A solitary fig-tree that grows near renders the spot easily recognisable by those already acquainted with the secret. The catacombs themselves are wide winding caves, the burial-place of the dead of past ages. Piles of human bones, white and bleached by time, are heaped along the rocky sides of these caverns. In one of these walks, whilst they were friends, Giorgio had shown the place to Marietta. In those days he feared not to entrust his mysterious way of life to her; for although in all common concerns she was wild and untractable, yet in all that touched the interests of those few whom she loved, Marietta was silent and reserved as Epicharis herself. The menaces Giorgio let fall in his visit on the preceding forenoon had excited her highest alarm, and she determined, at any risk, to learn the extent of the danger that hung over the stranger. After waiting in vain for Idalie's return till the close of evening, she had hastened to Capo di Monte, entered the catacombs alone, and, concealed behind a pile of bones, had awaited the arrival of the confederates. They assembled at midnight. Their first subject of consultation was the stranger. Giorgio acquainted them with his history, which he told them had been communicated to him that very morning, by a Russian lady of high consequence, who had likewise charged him with the business he had to unfold to them. He described Ladislas as a fugitive, unprotected by any government; he bore about his person certain papers which had been found in the palace of Warsaw, and were the confidential communications of the Russian Autocrat to his brother the Viceroy of Poland, and were of such a nature as to rouse all Europe in arms against their writer. These papers had been entrusted to Ladislas, whose intention was to proceed to Paris, and publish them there. Private business, however, of the greatest importance, had forced him to visit Naples before going to Paris. The Russian government had traced him to Naples, and had empowered a certain Russian lady to take any step, or go any lengths, in order to obtain these papers from Ladislas. This lady had made Giorgio her emissary; her name he carefully concealed, but Marietta averred, from his description, that it could be no other than the Princess Dashkhoff. After much consulting among the band, the assassination of the Pole had been decided upon. This seemed to be the only sure method, for he carried the papers ever about his person, was distinguished for his bravery, and if openly attacked would resist to the last. Giorgio was no stickler in the means he employed, and told his companions he had the less reason to be so in this case, as he had received assurances from the highest quarter, that his crime should go unpunished, and the reward be enormous. Ladislas was almost unknown in Naples; the government would not interest itself for a fugitive, without passport, country or name; and what friends had he here, to inquire into the circumstances of his destruction, or to interest themselves to avenge it?

Such was Marietta's tale, and Ladislas instantly acknowledged the necessity of flight. He was too well acquainted with the perfidy and barbarism of the Russians, to doubt that even a lady of a rank so distinguished as the Princess Dashkhoff, might be induced to undertake as foul a task as that attributed to her by Marietta. The worldly and artificial manners of this lady, in an Italian or a French-woman, would only have resulted from habits of intrigue; but a Russian, unaccustomed to look on human life as sacred, taught by the government of her own country that cruelty and treachery are venial offences, wholly destitute of a sense of honour, concealed, under such an exterior, vices the most odious, and a callousness to guilt unknown in more civilised lands. Ladislas knew this; and he knew that the badness of the Neapolitan government afforded scope for crime, which could not exist elsewhere; and he felt that on every account it were better to withdraw himself immediately from the scene of danger.

While musing on these things, Idalie's beseeching eyes were eloquent in imploring him to fly. He consented; but a condition was annexed to his consent, that Idalie should share his flight. He urged his suit with fervour. It were easy for them on a very brief notice to seek the young lady's confessor, induce him to bestow on them the nuptial benediction, and thus to sanctify their departure together. Marietta seconded the young lover's entreaties, and Idalie, blushing and confused, could only reply,— "My accompanying you could only increase your danger, and facilitate the bravo's means of tracing you. How could I get a passport? How leave this place?" "I have a plan for all," replied Ladislas; and he then related that the Sully steam-packet lay in the harbour of Naples, ready to sail on the shortest notice; he would engage that for their conveyance, and so speedily bid adieu to the shores of Naples, and all its perils. "But that boat," exclaimed Idalie, "that steam-packet is the very one engaged by the Princess for our excursion to Pæstum, this morning." This, for a time, seemed to disarrange their schemes, but they considered that no danger could happen to Ladislas while one of a party of pleasure with the Princess, who from this act of his would be quite unsuspicious of his intended departure. At night, upon their return from Pæstum, when the rest of the party should have disembarked at Naples, Ladislas and Idalie would remain on board, and the vessel immediately commence its voyage for France. This plan thus assumed a very feasible appearance, while Ladislas, in accents of fond reproach, asked Idalie wherefore she refused to share his fortunes, and accompany him in his journey; and Marietta, clapping her hands exclaimed, "She consents! she consents! Do not ask any more, she has already yielded. We will all return to Naples. Ladislas shall proceed immediately to seek out the captain of the Sully, and arrange all with him; while, without loss of time, we will proceed to the convent of Father Basil, and get every thing ready by the time Ladislas shall join us, which must be with as much speed as he can contrive." Idalie silently acquiesced in this arrangement, and Ladislas kissed her hand with warm and overflowing gratitude. They now contrived to stow themselves in the little calessino, and as they proceeded on their way, Ladislas said: "We seem to have forgotten the future destiny of our dear Marietta, all this time. The friendless condition in which we shall leave her fills me with anxiety. She is the preserver of my life, and we are both under the deepest obligations to her. What shall you do, Marietta, when we are gone?" "Fear not for me," exclaimed the wild girl, "it is necessary I should remain behind to arrange those things which Idalie's sudden departure will leave in sad disorder; but you will see me soon in Paris, for how can I exist apart from my sister?"

When near to Naples, Ladislas alighted from the calessino, and directed his steps towards the port, while the fair girls proceeded on their way to the convent. What the bashful conscious Idalie would have done without her sister's help, it is difficult to guess. Marietta busied herself about all; won over the priest to the sudden marriage, contrived to put up articles of dress for the fair bride's journey, and thinking of every thing, with far more watchfulness and care than if her own fate had depended on the passing hour, seemed the guardian angel of the lovers. Ladislas arrived at the convent; he had been successful with the master of the steam-packet, and all was prepared. Marietta heard this from his own lips, and carried the happy news to Idalie. He did not see her till they met at the altar, where, kneeling before the venerable priest, they were united for ever. And now time, as it sped on, gave them no moment to indulge their various and overpowering feelings. Idalie embraced her sister again and again, and entreating her to join them speedily in Paris, made her promise to write, and then, escorted by her husband, proceeded to the Sully, on board of which most of the party were already assembled.

The smoke lifted its stream of dishevelled tresses to the wind, which was right aft; the engine began to work, and the wheels to run their round. The blue wave was disturbed in its tranquil water, and cast back again in sheeted spray on its brother wave. Farewell to Naples! That Elysian city, as the poet justly calls it; that favourite of sea, and land, and sky. The hills that surround it smooth their rugged summits, and descend into gentle slopes, and opening defiles, to receive its buildings and habitations. Temples, domes, and marble palaces, are ranged round the crescent form of the bay, and above them arise dark masses, and wooded clefts, and fair gardens, whose trees are ever vernal. Before it the mighty sea binds its wild streams, and smoothes them into gentlest waves, as they kiss the silver, pebbly shore, and linger with dulcet murmur around the deep-based promontories. The heaven—who has not heard of an Italian heaven?—one intense diffusion, one serene omnipresence, for ever smiling in inextinguishable beauty above the boundless sea, and for ever bending in azure mirth over the flowing outlines of the distant mountains.

The steam-boat proceeded on its equal and swift course along the shores, each varying in beauty, and redolent with sweets. They first passed Castel-a-Mare, and then the abrupt promontories on which Sorrento and ancient Amalfi are situated. The sublimity and intense loveliness of the scene wrapt in delight each bosom, not inaccessible to pure and lofty emotions. The hills, covered with ilex, dark laurel, and bright-leaved myrtle, were mirrored in the pellucid waves, which the lower branches caressed and kissed as the winds waved them. Behind arose other hills, also covered with wood; and, more distant, forming the grand back-ground, was sketched the huge ridge of lofty Apennines, which extends even to the foot of Italy. Still proceeding on their way to Pæstum, they exchanged the rocky beach for a low and dreary shore. The dusky mountains retired inland, and leaving a waste, the abode of mal'aria, and the haunt of robbers, the landscape assumed a gloomy magnificence, in place of the romantic and picturesque loveliness which had before charmed their eyes. Ladislas leaned from the side of the vessel, and gazed upon the beauty of nature with sentiments too disturbed for happiness. He was annoyed by the unpropitious presence of the idle and the gay. He saw Idalie in the midst of them, and did not even wish to join her while thus situated. He shrank into himself, and tried, forgetting the immediate discomforts of his position, to think only of that paradise into which love had led him, to compensate for his patriotic sorrows. He strove patiently to endure the tedious hours of this never-ending day, during which he must play a false part, and see his bride engaged by others. While his attention was thus occupied, the voice of the Princess Dashkhoff startled him, and looking up, he wondered how a face that seemed so bland, and a voice that spoke so fair, could hide so much wickedness and deceit. As the hours passed on, his situation became irksome in the extreme. Once or twice he drew near Idalie, and tried to disengage her from the crowd; but each time he saw the Princess watching him stealthily, while his young bride, with feminine prudence, avoided every opportunity of conversing apart with him. Ladislas could ill endure this. He began to fancy that he had a thousand things to say, and that their mutual safety depended on his being able to communicate them to her. He wrote a few lines hastily on the back of a letter, with a pencil, conjuring her to find some means of affording him a few minutes' conversation, and telling her that if this could not be done before, he should take occasion, while the rest of the company were otherwise occupied, to steal from them that evening to the larger temple, and there to await her joining him, for that every thing depended on his being able to speak to her. He scarcely knew what he meant as he wrote this; but driven by contradiction and impatience, and desirous of learning exactly how she meant to conduct herself on the Princess's disembarking at Naples, it seemed to him of the last importance that his request should be complied with. He was folding the paper, when the Princess was at his side, and addressed him. "A sonnet, Count Ladislas; surely a poetic imagination inspires you; may I not see it?" And she held out her hand. Taken unaware, Ladislas darted at her a look of indignation and horror, which made her step back trembling and in surprise. Was she discovered? The idea was fraught with terror. His revenge would surely be as fierce as the wrongs he suffered might well inspire. But Ladislas, perceiving the indiscretion of his conduct, masked his sensations with a smile, and replied,—"They are words of a Polish song, which I wish Idalie to translate for the amusement of your friends;" and stepping forward he gave Idalie the paper, and made his request. All pressed to know what the song was. Idalie glanced at the writing, and changing colour, was scarcely able to command her voice to make such an excuse as the imprudence of her husband rendered necessary. She said that it required time and thought, and that she could not at the moment comply; then crushing the paper between her trembling fingers, began confusedly to talk of something else. The company interchanged smiles, but even the Princess only suspected some loverlike compliment to her protégée. "Nay," she said, "we must at least know the subject of these verses: what is it? tell us, I entreat you." "Treachery," said Ladislas, unable to control his feelings. The Princess became ashy-pale; all her self-possession fled, and she turned from the searching glance of the Pole with a sickness of heart which almost punished her for her crimes.

They were now drawing near their destination. Idalie, grasping the paper, longed to read it before they should reach the shore. She tried to recede from the party, and Ladislas, watching her movements, in order to facilitate her designs entered into conversation with the Princess. He had effectually roused her fears and her curiosity, and she eagerly seized the opportunity which he offered her of conversing with him, endeavouring to find out whether he indeed suspected any thing, or whether her own guilty conscience suggested the alarm with which his strange expression had filled her. Ladislas thus contrived to engross her entire attention, and led her insensibly towards the stern of the vessel; and as they leant over its side, and gazed on the waters beneath, Idalie was effectually relieved from all observation. She now disengaged herself from the rest of the party, and walking forward, read the lines pencilled by Ladislas. Then terrified by the secret they contained, and unaccustomed to bear the weight of concealment—she tore the paper, as if fearful that its contents might be guessed, and was about to throw the fragments into the sea, when gazing cautiously round, she perceived the position of the Princess and Ladislas, and was aware that the lady's quick eye would soon discern the floating scraps, as the boat passed on. Idalie feared the least shadow of danger, so she retreated from the vessel's side, but still anxious to get rid of the perilous papers, she determined to throw them into the hold. She approached it, and looked down. Had the form of a serpent met her eye, she had not been more horror-struck; a shriek hovered on her lips, but with a strong effort she repressed it, and, staggering on, leant against the mast, trembling and aghast. She could not be deceived; it was Giorgio's dark and scowling eye that she had encountered; his sinister countenance, upturned, could not be mistaken. Was danger, then, so near, so pressing, or so inevitable? How could she convey the fatal intelligence to her husband, and put him on his guard? She remembered his written request, with which she had previously determined in prudence not to comply. But it would now afford her an opportunity, should no other offer, of informing him of the unexpected messmate which the crew had on board.

Thus perfidy, dark hate, and trembling fear, possessed the hearts of these human beings, who, had a cursory observer seen them as they glided over that sea of beauty, beneath the azure heaven, along that enchanted shore, attended by every luxury, waited on by every obvious blessing of life—he would have imagined that they had been selected from the world for the enjoyment of perfect happiness. But sunny sky and laughing ocean appeared to Idalie only as the haunt and resort of tigers and serpents; a dark mist seemed to blot the splendour of the sky, as the guilty souls of her fellow-creatures cast their deforming shadows over its brightness.

They had now arrived close on the low shore, and horses and two or three light open carriages were at the water's edge to convey them to the temples. They landed. Ladislas presented himself to hand Idalie across the plank from the vessel to the beach. "Yes?"—he asked her, in a voice of entreaty, as he pressed her hand. She softly returned the pressure, and the word "Beware," trembled on her lips, when the young Englishman who had before admired her, and had endeavoured to engross her attention the whole day, was again at her side, to tell her that the Princess was waiting for her in her carriage, and entreated her not to delay.

The party proceeded to where those glorious relics stand, between the mountains and the sea, rising like exhalations from the waste and barren soil, alone on the wide and dusky shore. A few sheep grazed at the base of the columns, and two or three wild-eyed men, clothed in garments of undressed sheep-skin, loitered about. Exclamations of wonder and delight burst from all, while Ladislas, stealing away to the more distant one, gladly escaped from the impertinent intrusion of the crowd, to indulge in lonely reverie among these ruins. "What is man in his highest glory?" he thought. "Had we burst the bonds of Poland; and had she, in her freedom, emulated the magical achievements of Greece; nevertheless, when time, with insidious serpent windings, had dragged its length through a few more centuries, the monuments we had erected would have fallen like these, and our monuments, a new Pæstum, have existed merely to excite the idiot wonder and frivolous curiosity of fools!"

Ladislas was certainly in no good humour while he thus vented his spleen; but was annoyed by two circumstances, sufficient to irritate a young philosopher: he beheld a scene, whose majestic beauty filled his soul with sensibility and awe, in the midst of a crowd of pretenders, more intent on the prospect of their pic-nic dinner, than on regarding the glories of art; and he saw his bride, surrounded by strangers, engrossed by their conversation and flattery, and unable to interchange one word or look of confidence with him. He sighed for the hours passed under the portico of Idalie's solitary pavilion, and the near prospect of their voyage did not reconcile him to the present; for his soul was disturbed by the necessity of interchanging courtesies with his enemy, and haunted by images of treacherous attempts, from which his valour could not protect him.

It had been arranged that the party should dine at the archbishop's palace, and not embark again until ten o'clock, when the moon would rise. After a couple of hours spent among the ruins, the servants informed them that their repast was ready; it was now nearly six o'clock, and after they had dined, more than two hours must elapse before they could depart. Night had gathered round the landscape, and its darkness did not invite even the most romantic to wander again among the ruins: the Princess, eager to provide for the amusement of her guests, contrived to discover a violin, a flute, and a pipe, and with the assistance of this music, which in the hands of Italian rustics was as true to time and expression as if Wieprecht himself had presided, they commenced dancing. Idalie's hand was sought by the Englishman; she looked round the room, Ladislas was not there; he had doubtless repaired to the temples to wait for her, and ignorant of the presence of Giorgio, wholly unsuspicious, and off his guard, to what dangers might he not be exposed? Her blood ran cold at the thought; she decidedly refused to dance, and perceiving the Princess whirling round in a waltz at a distant part of the room, she dispatched her officious admirer on some feigned errand for refreshment, and hastily quitting the house, hurried along over the grass towards the temples. When she had first emerged into the night, the scene seemed wrapped in impenetrable darkness, but the stars shed their faint rays, and in a few moments she began to distinguish objects, and as she drew near the temple, she saw a man's form moving slowly among the columns: she did not doubt that it was her husband, wrapped in his cloak, awaiting her. She was hurrying towards him, when, leaning against one of the pillars, she saw Ladislas himself, and the other, at the same moment, exchanging his stealthy pace for a tiger-like spring. She saw a dagger flashing in his hand; she darted forward to arrest his arm, and the blow descended on her; with a faint shriek, she fell on the earth, when Ladislas turned and closed with the assassin; a mortal struggle ensued; already had Ladislas wrested the poignard from his grasp, when the villain drew another knife. Ladislas warded off the unexpected blow aimed at him with this, and plunged his own stiletto in the bravo's breast; he fell to earth with a heavy groan, and then the silence of the tomb rested on the scene; the white robe of Idalie, who lay fainting on the ground, directed Ladislas to her side. He raised her up in speechless agony—as he beheld the blood which stained her dress; but by this time she had recovered from her swoon; she assured him her wound was slight, that it was nothing; but again sank into his arms insensible. In a moment his plan was formed; ever eager and impetuous, he executed it ere any second thought could change it. He had before resolved not to rejoin the party in the archbishop's palace, but after his interview with Idalie, to hasten on board the steam-boat; he had therefore ordered his horse to be saddled, had led it to the temple, and fastened it to one of the columns. He lifted the senseless Idalie carefully in his arms, mounted his horse, and turning his steps from the lighted and noisy palace, wound his way to the lonely shore, where he found the captain and his crew already preparing for their homeward voyage. With their help Idalie was taken on board, and Ladislas gave orders for the instant heaving of the anchor, and their immediate departure. The captain asked for the rest of the company. "They return by land," said Ladislas. As he spoke the words he felt a slight sensation of remorse, remembering the difficulty they would have to get there; and how, during the darkness of night, they might fear to proceed on their journey on a tract of country haunted by banditti; but the senseless and pale form of Idalie dissipated these thoughts: to arrive at Naples, to procure assistance for her, and then if, as he hoped, her wound was slight, to continue their voyage before the Princess Dashkhoff's return, were motives too paramount to allow him to hesitate. The captain of the Sully asked no more questions; the anchor was weighed, the wheels set in motion, and a silver light in the east announced the rising of the moon, as they stood off from the shore, and made their swift way back to Naples. They had not gone far, before the care of Ladislas revived his fair bride. Her wound was in her arm, and had merely grazed the skin. Terror for her husband, horror for the mortal strife which had endangered his life, had caused her to faint, more than pain or loss of blood. She bound up her own arm; and then, as there appeared no necessity for medical aid, Ladislas revoked his orders for returning to Naples, but stretching out at once to sea, they began their voyage to Marseilles.

Meanwhile, during a pause in the dance, the absence of Ladislas and Idalie was observed by the feasters in the archbishop's palace. It excited some few sarcasms, which as it continued, grew more bitter. The Princess Dashkhoff joined in these, and yet she could not repress the disquietude of her heart. Had Ladislas alone been absent, her knowledge of the presence of Giorgio, and his designs, had sufficiently explained its cause, and its duration, to her; but that Idalie also should not be found might bring a witness to the crime committed, and discover her own guilty share in the deed of blood perpetrated at her instigation. At length the rising of the moon announced the hour when they were to repair to the shore. The horses and carriages were brought to the door, and then it was found that the steed of Ladislas was missing. "But the Signora Idalie, has she not provided herself with a palfry?" asked the Englishman, sneering. They were now about to mount, when it was proposed to take a last look of the temples by moonlight. The Princess opposed this, but vainly; her conscience made her voice faint, and took from her the usual decision of her manner; so she walked on silently, half fearful that her foot might strike against some object of terror, and at every word spoken by the party, anticipating an exclamation of horror; the fitful moonbeams seemed to disclose here and there ghastly countenances and mangled limbs, and the dew of night appeared to her excited imagination as the slippery moisture of the life-blood of her victim.

They had scarcely entered the temple, when a peasant rushed in with the news that the steam-boat was gone:—he brought back Ladislas' horse, who had put the bridle into the man's hands on embarking; and the fellow declared that the fainting Idalie was his companion. Terror at the prospect of their dark ride, indignation at the selfish proceeding of the lovers, raised every voice against them; and the Princess, whom conscience had before made the most silent, hearing that the Pole was alive and safe, was now loudest and most bitter in her remarks. As they were thus all gathered together in dismay, debating what was to be done, and the Princess Dashkhoff in no gentle terms railing at the impropriety and ingratitude of Idalie's behaviour, and declaring that Poles alone could conduct themselves with such mingled deceit and baseness, a figure all bloody arose from the ground at her feet, and as the moon cast its pale rays on his yet paler countenance, she recognised Giorgio: the ladies shrieked, the men rushed towards him, while the Princess, desiring the earth to open and swallow her, stood transfixed as by a spell, gazing on the dying man in terror and despair. "He has escaped, Lady," said Giorgio, "Ladislas has escaped your plots, and I am become their victim:" he fell as he spoke these words, and when the Englishman drew near to raise, and if possible assist him, he found that life had entirely flown.

Thus ended the adventures of the Pole at Naples. The Countess returned in her caleche alone, for none would bear her company; the next day she left Naples, and was on her way to Russia, where her crime was unknown, except to those who had been accomplices in it. Marietta spread the intelligence of her sister's marriage, and thus entirely cleared Idalie's fair fame; and quitting Italy soon after, joined the happy Ladislas and his bride at Paris.

The arrangement of these notes is as follows:

1. *Critical Remarks*—interpretive and evaluative judgments on each story. To shorten citations, *MSL* is used for *The Letters of Mary W. Shelley*, 2 vols., ed. Frederick L. Jones (Norman: University of Oklahoma Press, 1944); and *MSJ*, for *Mary Shelley's Journal*, ed. Frederick L. Jones (Norman: University of Oklahoma Press, 1947).

2. *Manuscript*—identification of extant manuscript and its location.

3. *Bibliography*—listing of the story's first and subsequent printings. *Tales and Stories* (1891; rpt. 1975) designates *Tales and Stories by Mary Wollstonecraft Shelley*—Now First Collected, with an Introduction by Richard Garnett (London: William Paterson & Co., 1891); and the reprint of this volume, with a new introduction by Joanna Russ (Boston: Gregg Press, 1975). Bracketed information following the other entries identifies the name under which the story was published and, where applicable, the accompanying plate and the different title as listed in the Table of Contents.

4. *Copy-text*—identification of basis of text in this edition.

5. *Textual Notes*—listing of editorial emendations to copy-text, which are keyed to page and line numbers in this edition. For the twenty-two stories based on previously printed texts, all emendations are recorded. Their number is minimal, because the text has not been modernized but rather corrected according to nineteenth-century standards: e.g., a misused colon *within* a series has been changed to a semicolon; and quotation marks are supplied where forgotten, deleted if mistakenly present, or reduced from double to single where warranted. Nineteenth-century spellings and forms (e.g., "groupe," "pourtray," "scirocco," "to-day," "to-morrow," and "villanous") have been retained, and emendations have been made only for obvious errors ("palor" to "pallor" or "Panargia" to "Panagia"), for uncommon spellings having no contemporary (late eighteenth- or early nineteenth-century) sanction in the *Oxford English Dictionary*, and for one of two different spellings within the same story (e.g., "tript" to "tripped" or "heaven" to "Heaven," with the more modern or more frequent spelling preferred in these cases). However, each story is given its own integrity, and no attempt has been made to regularize spellings among the stories: hence the reader may encounter "wo" or "shew" in one story and "woe" or "show" in another.

Fair-copy MSS are extant for six of the twenty-two stories based on previously published texts: "The Dream," "The Brother and Sister," "The Mortal Immortal," "The Trial of Love," "The Parvenue," and "Euphrasia." The MSS of "The Brother and Sister" and "The Mortal Immortal" bear postmarks and addresses and were actually folded and posted to the editor of *The Keepsake*. All six of these MSS, to varying degrees, bear evidence (e.g., ink fingerprints from the compositor, typesetting symbols such as the double underline for the title to be set in caps, repagination of MS pages in accordance with the position of the story among the other MSS sent to the printer, marginal computations of the number of words in a story) that suggests they were used as the printer's copy-texts. Yet because Mary Shelley revised these stories in proof, the first printed text, rather than the MS in these cases, has been selected as copy-text for this edition. Minor differences between copy-text and MS (e.g., in diction, syntax, and punctuation—see other examples in Introduction to this edition) are not recorded in the textual notes. However, readings from these MSS are recorded when editorial emendations have been made to the copy-texts; and when, in the case of "The Dream," "The Brother and Sister," and "The Parvenue," the MS differs substantially from the copy-text.

The MS itself is used as copy-text for three stories: "The Heir of Mondolfo"; "Valerius: The Reanimated Roman"; and "An Eighteenth-Century Tale: A Fragment." The edited texts for these stories reproduce the paragraphing of the MSS, and, where possible (in accordance with the practices in the other stories), the diction, spelling, syntax, and punctuation of the MSS. The textual notes record all MS readings where words have been added, deleted, or changed; where spelling changes involve changes in meaning (e.g., "an" to "and" or "past" to "passed"); or where spelling has been made consistent within a story (e.g., "stopt" to "stopped" when both spellings are used in the same MS). However, the editor has silently corrected other spelling errors (e.g., "delighful" to "delightful"), and he has silently supplied, changed, and regularized punctuation and capitals.

I. A TALE OF THE PASSIONS

"A Tale of the Passions," which appeared in January 1823 in No. 2 of *The Liberal* (the literary journal begun by Percy Shelley, Lord Byron, and Leigh Hunt), was Mary Shelley's first published work after her husband's death on 8 July 1822. But the story was probably finished prior to that time: the MS, not located by the present editor, was described by Elizabeth Nitchie as bearing an endorsement by Shelley (*Mary Shelley: Author of "Frankenstein"* [New Brunswick: Rutgers University Press, 1953], p. 156*n*); Despina's idealization of death and the dead Manfred recalls stanzas from Percy Shelley's *Adonais* (1821), an elegy on John Keats; and the conflict between Guelphs and Ghibellines was also used in *Valperga*, a novel that Mary Shelley wrote from 1820 until early 1822. While extensively researching medieval Italian history for the circumstances of this novel, she apparently became interested in the youthful Corradino (Conradin), whose life ended in 1268 in the manner the story records. By November 1822, Mary submitted the MS of "A Tale of the Passions" to Leigh Hunt for transmittal to England, and he judged it "a very good" story (see Payson G. Gates, "A Leigh Hunt–Byron Letter," *Keats–Shelley Journal* 2 [1953]: 16). Of special note are the sketch of Monna Gegia, the realistic dialogue, and the concentrated action of most of the narrative within a period less than twenty-four hours (a concentration lacking in some of the more diffusely plotted *Keepsake* stories). But as a reviewer in Leigh Hunt's *Examiner* for 29 December 1822 explained, "the catastrophe might have been managed more felicitously" (quoted by William H. Marshall, *Byron, Shelley, Hunt, and "The Liberal"* [Philadelphia: University of Pennsylvania Press, 1960], p. 149). For Mary Shelley's authorship of this tale and other essays in *The Liberal*, see Marshall, passim; and Charles W. Dilke, " 'The Liberal,' " *Notes and Queries*, Ser. 8, 4 (1893): 10.

1) "A Tale of the Passions," *The Liberal: Verse and Prose from the South*, No. 2 [January 1823], pp. 289–325. [Published anonymously.]

2) "A Tale of the Passions," *The Weekly Entertainer; and West of England Miscellany*, n.s. 7 (1823): 57–60, 65–68, 81–83, 137–40, 148–51. [Published anonymously.]

3) "A Tale of the Passions, or The Death of Despina," *The Romancist, and Novelist's Library: The Best Works of the Best Authors*, I (London: J. Clements, 1839), 14–16. ["Mrs. Shelley."]

4) "A Tale of the Passions; or, The Death of Despina," *Tales and Stories* (1891; rpt. 1975), pp. 112–47.

[Copy-text: *Liberal*: L.]

2:27	*coloratio*] *calrasio* L
2:41	*Carroccio*] *Carrocio* L
3:12	beaten;] beaten: L
3:41	has] have L
7:6	soul. The] soul, the L
8:40	authoritative] authorative L
9:30	stopped] stopt L
10:2	Gegia.] Gezia. L
10:18	*Governo;*] *Governo;* L
10:42	Palace of Government.] palace of government. L
12:10	cannot] can not L
17:17	Cincolo] Cinculo L
17:28	*Governo:*] *Governo:* L
18:7	dei Elisei] de' Elisei L
18:21	Lisa] Lissa L
18:28	de' Giudi] de Giudi L
19:1–2	de' Bosticchi] de Bosticchi L
21:9	foster-father] foster father L
22:5	Astura,] Asturi, L
22:11	Tagliacozzo,] Taglicozzo, L

II. RECOLLECTIONS OF ITALY

In a letter to Leigh Hunt, Mary Shelley recorded on 5 October 1823 that she was "now busy writing an article" for the *London Magazine* (MSL, I: 272), where "Recollections of Italy" was published in the January 1824 issue. In this narrative essay, the author fused together a number of elements from her own and her husband's previous writings and experiences: the introductory description of the Thames is taken in part from her "Eighteenth-Century Tale: A Fragment" (see p. 345 of this edition); the six-line quotation that is footnoted as "Spenser's Ruins of Rome" is to be found in Mary's journal entry for 5 March 1819 (see *MSJ*, p. 117); Edmund Malville presents the author's own recollections of Italy; Malville's excursion from Pisa to Vico Pisano on 15 September 18– reproduces the Shelleys' trip to the same place with Edward and Jane Williams on 15 September 1821 (see *MSJ*, p. 160); Malville's " 'best, and now lost friend' " was actually Percy Shelley; and this friend's eloquent description of the scenery on the return to Pisa reproduces with but slight variation Percy Shelley's MS prose fragment, which was later published by Richard Garnett, ed., *Relics of Shelley* (London: Edward Moxon & Co., 1862), pp. 89–90.

1) "Recollections of Italy," *London Magazine* 9 (January 1824): 21–26. [Published anonymously.]

[Copy-text: *London Magazine*: LM.]
24:6   nor] or LM
25:25   fleckered] flequered LM
26:21   'Ca Stali!'] "Cast Ali!" LM
26:34   'a . . . name,'] "a . . . name," LM
26:35   'painted . . . world—'] "painted . . . world—" LM
27:5   watery] watry LM
29:13   'Felicissima . . . Signoria;'] "Felicissima . . . Signoria;" LM
30:3   de Noce,] de 'Noce, LM
31:4   boat in a] boat under a LM

III. THE BRIDE OF MODERN ITALY

"The Bride of Modern Italy" resembles "The False Rhyme" in its sharp delineation of character, economical yet precise description, and unity of plot. In this case, however, Mary Shelley's inspiration came from her own experience, for Clorinda was modeled on Emilia Viviani, whom Mary met in December 1820 and described as a "beautiful girl wearing out the best years of her life in an odious convent" (*MSL*, I: 124) while awaiting her marriage, which was being arranged by her parents. But Emilia first enthralled Percy Shelley and became the subject of his "Italian Platonics" and of his poem *Epipsychidion* (1821). A year later, in March 1822, after Emilia had been married off, Mary Shelley dismissed the whole episode with a sardonically applied nursery rhyme (see *MSL*, I: 161); and sometime before 1824, when "The Bride of Modern Italy" was published anonymously in *London Magazine*, she gently satirized Emilia as Clorinda, using among other biographical facts what Claire Clairmont recorded in her journal for 23 July 1821: "Emilia says that she prays always to a Saint, and every time she changes her lover, she changes her Saint, adopting the one of her lover" (*The Journals of Claire Clairmont*, ed. Marion Kingston Stocking [Cambridge: Harvard University Press, 1968], p. 243). For further analysis of the biographical antecedents in this story (including Percy Shelley portrayed as the English painter Marcott Alleyn), see Elizabeth Nitchie, *Mary Shelley: Author of "Frankenstein"* (New Brunswick: Rutgers University Press, 1953), pp. 64–66, 132–34. For Mary's authorship of this story, see the attribution in Beddoes' April 1824 letter to Thomas Forbes Kelsall, *The Works of Thomas Lovell Beddoes*, ed. H. W. Donner (London: Oxford University Press, 1935), p. 586.

1) "The Bride of Modern Italy," *London Magazine* 9 (April 1824): 357–63. [Published anonymously.]

[Copy-text: *London Magazine*: LM.]
33:1   come,"] come;" LM
34:43   which] them LM
35:1   face;] face: LM
37:4   tripped] tript LM
38:13   Mallecho;] Malecho; LM
38:37   S——,] S.——, LM
39:2   ——."] ——". LM

40:1   'Not . . . forced,'] "Not . . . forced," LM
40:1–6   'beware . . . avail.'] "beware . . . avail." LM
40:23   *corrèdo*] *corrado* LM
41:34   once; he] once he LM

IV. ROGER DODSWORTH: THE REANIMATED ENGLISHMAN

On 28 June 1826, the *Journal du Commerce de Lyon* reported the story of Roger Dodsworth's reanimation; and from 4 until 9 July 1826, no less than six British newspapers translated and published the same report. For the next four months, various newspapers and magazines delighted their readers by perpetuating this cryogenic hoax. Among the many discussing it were Thomas Moore, Joseph Jekyll, William Cobbett, Samuel Rogers, Theodore Hook, and even Roger Dodsworth himself. But most of Mary Shelley's contemporaries did not know of her interest in Dodsworth: she finished her narrative essay by September or October 1826 and submitted it to the *New Monthly Magazine*; but it was not published until 1863, when Cyrus Redding (working editor of the *NMM* in the 1820s) printed it for the first time in a volume of his reminiscences. Here republished for the first time in over a hundred years, this narrative confirms Mary's interest in reanimated men (see her story on Valerius) and demonstrates that she had a greater sense of humor than her modern critics allow. For more on this subject, see Charles E. Robinson, "Mary Shelley and the Roger Dodsworth Hoax," *Keats–Shelley Journal* 24 (1975): 20–28.

1) An untitled narrative essay, in Cyrus Redding, *Yesterday and To-day* (London: T. Cautley Newby, Publisher, 1863), II: 150–65. ["Mrs. Shelley."]

[Copy-text: *Yesterday and To-day*: YT.]
43:3   Mount] mount YT
43:19   elegiac,] elegaic, YT
44:17   seizing] siezing YT
46:5   governors look] governorslook YT
47:10   patrimony (the] patrimony, (the YT
50:17   1826; Aged 209.] 18;— Aged 107. YT
50:21   showed] shewed YT

V. THE SISTERS OF ALBANO

"The Sisters of Albano," perhaps the first story that Mary Shelley prepared specifically for *The Keepsake*, manifests the deficiencies of some of the narratives included in the English Annuals: a thin plot; an explicit moral lesson that is not always integrated with the plot; and a narrative that is but tangentially related to the accompanying plate. Here Mary Shelley artificially constructs an introductory frame to describe the Turner plate and moralizes in the words of the Countess Atanasia, the second narrator, that the "mingling of love with crime is a dread conjunction." Unwittingly, however, the Countess embodies in her story a more sophisticated moral, that of "No Greater Love"—Maria's Christ-like self-sacrifice for her sister Anina.

1) "The Sisters of Albano," *The Keepsake for MDCCCXXIX*, ed. Frederic Mansel Reynolds (London: Hurst, Chance, and Co. [1828], pp. 80–100. ["the Author of Frankenstein"; with plate entitled "Lake Albano," drawn by J. M. W. Turner and engraved by Robt Wallis.]

2) "The Sisters of Albano," *Friendship's Offering: A Christmas, New Year, and*

Birthday Present, for MDCCCXLVII (Boston: Phillips and Sampson, 1847), pp. 134–58. ["the Author of Frankenstein."]

3) "The Sisters of Albano," *Tales and Stories* (1891; rpt. 1975), pp. 1–19.

4) "The Sisters of Albano," *The Masterpiece Library of Short Stories,* ed. J. A. Hammerton (London: The Educational Book Company, n.d.), VII: 154–67. ["Mary Wollstonecraft Shelley."]

[Copy-text: *Keepsake* for 1829: K.]
51:4   vines;] vines: K
51:6   aziola] aziolo K
54:8   fireflies] fire-flies K
54:23   saints;] saints: K
55:29   *ladri*] *laddri* K
56:18   *tabarro*] *tabaro* K
58:37   *podere;*] *podere;* K
63:28   Countess] countess K

VI. FERDINANDO EBOLI: A TALE

With references to Napoleon, Murat (brother-in-law of Napoleon and King of Naples from 1808 to 1815), and other contemporaries, "Ferdinando Eboli" seems to justify the narrator's contention that this "strange and wonderful" story was "gathered from eye-witnesses." Although the ostensibly unique frustrations of Count Eboli have antecedents in Gothic romances where heroes are assailed by villainous twins or diabolical doppelgängers, it is possible that Mary Shelley herself heard this tale while living in Naples from November 1818 through February 1819. If the tale offers more "truth" than "fiction," that would explain away the narrator's hurrying over and omission of certain details as well as the lack of poetic or fictional justice at the end, when the villainous brother Ludovico experiences such an incredibly spontaneous reformation.

1) "Ferdinando Eboli: A Tale," *The Keepsake for MDCCCXXIX,* ed. Frederic Mansel Reynolds (London: Hurst, Chance, and Co. [1828]), pp. 195–218. ["the Author of Frankenstein"; with plate entitled "Adelinda" [*sic*], drawn by A. E. Chalon and engraved by C. Heath; Table of Contents lists "Ferdinando Eboli."]

2) "Ferdinando Eboli," *Friendship's Offering: A Christmas, New Year, and Birthday Present for MDCCCXLV* (Boston: Lewis and Sampson, 1845), pp. 183–212. ["the Author of Frankenstein."]

3) "Ferdinando Eboli," *The Keepsake: A Gift for the Holidays* (New York: John C. Riker, 1854), pp. 188–214. ["the Author of Frankenstein."]

4) "Ferdinando Eboli," *Tales and Stories* (1891; rpt. 1975), pp. 20–41.

[Copy-text: *Keepsake* for 1829: K; K employs the names "Ferdinando Eboli" and, with two exceptions, "Ferdinand"; emendations for the exceptions are noted below.]
69:6   Ferdinand] Ferdinando K
72:11   surprise.] surprise; K
74:33   Adalinda,] Adalina, K
78:9   exchanging] exhanging K
78:36   Ferdinand] Ferdinando K

VII. THE MOURNER

"The Mourner" contains many of Mary Shelley's stock fictional elements: a hero patterned on her husband, Shelley (in this case, Horace Neville also went to Eton and

Oxford); an orphaned heroine who intensely loved her father, became a parricide, and wished to be a suicide; a death at sea; a plot determined by uncertainty and mystery; a broken leg suffered by a fall from a horse; and a colossal coincidence by which the lives of Horace Neville and Lewis Elmore were joined by their common affection for Ellen Burnet/Clarice Eversham. The narrative lacks the intense character study of such stories as "The Brother and Sister," but it is unified by Neville's point of view—save for the description of Virginia Water by an introductory narrator. One suspects that these extensive descriptive passages were inserted because the editor, and perhaps Mary Shelley, wished to flatter the artist, J. M. W. Turner.

1) "The Mourner," *The Keepsake for MDCCCXXX*, ed. Frederic Mansel Reynolds (London: Hurst, Chance, and Co. [1829]), pp. 71–97. ["the Author of 'Frankenstein' "; with two plates entitled "Virginia Water," drawn by J. M. W. Turner and engraved by R. Wallis; Table of Contents lists "The Mourner, a Tale."]
2) "The Mourner," *Tales and Stories* (1891; rpt. 1975), pp. 83–107.

[Copy-text: *Keepsake* for 1830: K.]
83:30 well-wooded, well-watered] well wooded, well watered K
85:35 away.—] away."— K
88:24 woeful] woful K
89:16 woe,] wo, K
94:17 self-possession,] self possession, K
95:35 to] o K

VIII. THE EVIL EYE

"The Evil Eye," with its Albanian setting and unfamiliar detail, is unlike most of Mary Shelley's stories, but it has antecedents in other Eastern narratives published by her contemporaries: e.g., Byron's *Childe Harold* II (1812), Thomas Hope's *Anastasius* (1819), and Prosper Mérimée's *La Guzla* (1827)—all of which Mary Shelley read and admired. But the last of these three appears to have provided the inspiration for "The Evil Eye," for she reviewed *La Guzla* by January 1829, ten months before her Albanian story appeared in *The Keepsake*. In her review article ("Illyrian Poems —Feudal Scenes," *Westminster Review* 10 [January 1829]: 71–81), Mary explained that *La Guzla* "imports to be a translation of a collection of Illyrian national poems" and that Mérimée, "by a strong effort of the imagination, . . . writes as if the mountains of Illyria had been the home of his childhood." Within the next few months, Mary herself made a "strong effort" to write a detailed account of the relationship between an Albanian Klepht and a Corinthian adventurer. That "The Evil Eye" was influenced by Mérimée's work is further suggested by Mary's translation of three of the poems in *La Guzla* in her review: one of these, "The Flame of Perrussich," deals with the oath of friendship between "Pobratimi"; another, with the "superstition attached to an evil eye." For a reprint of this review article, see *"Appendix B"* in A. W. Raitt, *Prosper Mérimée* (New York: Charles Scribner's Sons, 1970), pp. 375–82.

1) "The Evil Eye," *The Keepsake for MDCCCXXX*, ed. Frederic Mansel Reynolds (London: Hurst, Chance, and Co. [1829]), pp. 150–75. ["the Author of Frankenstein"; with plate entitled "Zella," drawn by H. Corbould and engraved by Charles Heath; Table of Contents lists "The Evil Eye, a Tale."]
2) "The Evil Eye," *Tales and Stories* (1891; rpt. 1975), pp. 42–65.

[Copy-text: *Keepsake* for 1830: K.]

100:10	Tepellenè,] Terpellène, K
101:23	sacoleva,] sacovela, K; *in all subsequent references,* sacovela *has been emended to* sacoleva
102:25	owe.] owe K
103:37	Aegina.] Egina. K
105:1	Panagia] Panargia K
105:7	abode.] abode K
105:29	Aegina:] Egina: K
105:41	or] nor K
106:3	was: the] was: The K
106:19	haggard,] hagard, K
106:38	Protoklepht;] Proto-Klepht; K
108:4	Gulf of Aegina,] gulf of Egina, K
110:2	Moirae,] Morai, K
110:34	Tepellenè,] Terpellenè, K
111:9	Klepht] klepht K
111:14	Panagia,] Panargia, K
111:24	Panagia] Panargia K
112:10–11	Tepellenè,] Terpellenè, K
112:20	Klepht,] klepht, K
112:36	Klephts] klephts K
113:2	Klepht] klepht K
113:13	Dodona's] Dordona's K
115:15	Klepht] klepht K

IX. THE FALSE RHYME

This sixteenth-century anecdotal tale, which was reprinted at least three times within a year after its publication in 1829, shows Mary Shelley at her best. Despite or perhaps because of its brevity, "The False Rhyme" successfully coordinates action and theme; and its engraved plate, which the author economically yet precisely describes, is well-served by the narrative.

1) "The False Rhyme," *The Keepsake for MDCCCXXX*, ed. Frederic Mansel Reynolds (London: Hurst, Chance, and Co. [1829]), pp. 265–68. ["the Author of 'Frankenstein' "; with plate entitled "Francis the First & His Sister," painted by R. P. Bonington and engraved by Charles Heath; Table of Contents lists "The false Rhyme, a Tale."]

2) "The False Rhyme," *The Athenaeum*, No. 107 (11 November 1829), pp. 702–03.

3) "The False Rhyme," *The Polar Star of Entertainment and Popular Science, and Universal Repertorium of General Literature* 2 (1830): 171–72. ["the Author of 'Frankenstein.' "]

4) "The False Rhyme," *The Casket, Flowers of Literature, Wit & Sentiment*, No. 5 (May 1830), pp. 203–04. ["the Author of Frankenstein."]

5) "The False Rhyme," *The American Keepsake: A Christmas and New-Year's Offering, 1835* (New York: J. C. Riker, n.d.), pp. 133–38. ["the Author of 'Frankenstein.' "]

6) "The False Rhyme," *The Masterpiece Library of Short Stories*, ed. J. A. Hammerton (London: The Educational Book Company, n.d.), VII: 168–70. ["Mary Wollstonecraft Shelley."]

7) "The False Rhyme," *Tales and Stories* (1891; rpt. 1975), pp. 108–11.
8) "The False Rhyme," *The Golden Book Magazine* 13, No. 75 (March 1931): 68. ["Mary W. Shelley."]

[Copy-text: *Keepsake* for 1830: K.]
117:22   lèse] lêse K
119:4   fie'?] fie?' K
119:35   queen] Queen K
119:39   queen;] Queen; K
120:24   queen.] Queen. K
120:28   false-speaking window,] false speaking-window, K

X. TRANSFORMATION

Mary Shelley had employed a diabolical doppelgänger or second self as early as *Frankenstein*, but "Transformation" has more immediate antecedents in Byron's drama, *The Deformed Transformed*, transcribed by Mary Shelley in 1822–23 and published in 1824. In Byron's drama, the hunchbacked Arnold receives a new body from a diabolical Stranger, who then assumes the old and deformed body of the hero and follows him as his shadow or second self. Although Byron's drama is incomplete, its conclusion is recorded in the so-called "Unwritten Drama of Lord Byron," where the hero kills himself by killing his double. In "Transformation," Mary Shelley reverses some of Byron's incidents: Guido exchanges his handsome body for that of the deformed dwarf, and the vague resolution to the catastrophe is far from tragic. Because of the happy ending, Guido as narrator suggests that his diabolical double, who externalized Guido's "fiendly pride," may have been an angelic agent. Because of this circumstance, "Transformation" shares an additional resemblance to Poe's doppelgänger tale, "William Wilson," which also owes its inspiration to Byron's "Unwritten Drama," what was actually a sketch of the unfinished *Deformed Transformed*. For more on Byron's drama and the literary history of this tradition, see Charles E. Robinson, "The Devil as Doppelgänger in *The Deformed Transformed*: The Sources and Meaning of Byron's Unfinished Drama," *Bulletin of the New York Public Library* 74 (1970): 177–202.

1) "Transformation," *The Keepsake for MDCCCXXXI*, ed. Frederic Mansel Reynolds (London: Hurst, Chance, and Co. [1830]), pp. 18–39. ["the Author of 'Frankenstein'"; with plate entitled "Juliet," painted by Miss Sharpe and engraved by J. C. Edwards; Table of Contents lists "Transformation, a Tale."]
2) "Transformation," *The Spirit of the Annuals, for MDCCCXXXI* (Philadelphia: E. Littell, 1831), pp. 294–317. ["the Author of 'Frankenstein.'"]
3) "Transformation," *The Tale Book*, Second Series (Paris: Baudry's European Library, 1835), pp. 32–51. ["Mrs. Shelley."]
4) "Transformation," *The International Monthly Magazine of Literature, Science, and Art* 3 (April 1851): 70–77. ["the Late Mrs. Shelley."]
5) "Transformation," *Tales and Stories* (1891; rpt. 1975), pp. 165–85.
6) "Transformation," *The Gentlewomen of Evil: An Anthology of Rare Supernatural Stories from the Pens of Victorian Ladies*, selected and introduced by Peter Haining (New York: Taplinger Publishing Company, 1967), pp. 15–31. ["Mary Shelley."]
7) "The Transformation," *Masters of Horror*, ed. Alden H. Norton (New York: A Berkley Medallion Book, 1968), pp. 68–87. ["Mary W. Shelley."]

8) "The Transformation," *The Nightmare Reader*, ed. Peter Haining (New York: Doubleday & Company, 1973), pp. 13–31. ["Mary Shelley."]

[Copy-text: *Keepsake* for 1831: K.]
123:10   were] was K
132:36   upraised] praised K

XI. THE SWISS PEASANT

Although this story might be dismissed as a sentimental "tale of soul-subduing joys and heart-consuming woes," which is enclosed in an artificial and incomplete frame and which is too frequently punctuated with the narrator's confessions of incompetence, "The Swiss Peasant" offers, or at least attempts, a structural unity. Ashburn offers the Wordsworthian thesis that the "veriest weather-worn cabin is a study for colouring, and the meanest peasant will offer all the acts of a drama in the apparently dull routine of his humble life." The first-person narrator ostensibly concedes Ashburn's point and retells Fanny's "true tale," but the narrator, like the Solitary in Wordsworth's *Excursion*, is afflicted by ennui and boredom. He benefits neither from Ashburn's aesthetic nor from the themes that opposites can be fruitfully reconciled or that constancy is the reward of fortitude and patience. Like Bonnivard, the Prisoner of Chillon who desired freedom, the narrator attained solitude, the object of his desire, "with a sigh." By having the narrator disparagingly compare himself to Byron and his tale to *The Prisoner of Chillon* (written during a rainy three-day period on the shores of Lake Geneva in 1816), Mary Shelley makes evident her theme: that the genial spirits of the narrator's imagination have failed him. Like Wordsworth's Solitary and Byron's Bonnivard, the narrator finds no meaning in Nature: "the hoar side of a dark precipice . . . might as well be the turf stack or old wall that bounded Cumberland's view as he wrote the 'Wheel of Fortune.'" That Mary Shelley could attempt such a sophisticated character study and at the same time offer the readers of *The Keepsake* a tale of joy and woe manifests both her talents as an artist and the restrictions of her medium.

1) "The Swiss Peasant," *The Keepsake for MDCCCXXXI*, ed. Frederic Mansel Reynolds (London: Hurst, Chance, and Co. [1830]), pp. 121–46. ["the Author of 'Frankenstein' "; with plate entitled "The Swiss Peasant," painted by H. Howard and engraved by Charles Heath; Table of Contents lists "The Swiss Peasant, a Tale."]

2) "The Swiss Peasant," *The Tale Book*, First Series (Paris: Baudry's European Library, 1834), pp. 416–38. ["Mrs. Shelley."]

3) "The Swiss Peasant," *Friendship's Offering: A Christmas, New Year, and Birthday Present for MDCCCXLV* (Boston: Lewis and Sampson, 1845), pp. 66–99. ["the Author of 'Frankenstein.' "]

4) "The Swiss Peasant," *The Tale Book* (Königsberg: J. H. Bon, 1859), pp. 55–74. [Not seen; cited from Jean de Palacio, *Mary Shelley dans son œuvre: Contributions aux études shelleyennes* (Paris: Klincksieck, 1969), p. 674.]

5) "The Swiss Peasant," *Tales and Stories* (1891; rpt. 1975), pp. 186–209.

[Copy-text: *Keepsake* for 1831: K.]
136:14   Brunnen,] Brunen, K
137:6   Subiaco,] Soubiaco, K
137:23   Goethe.] Goëthe. K
142:23   Louis's] Louis' K
142:42   protégée] protegée K
143:27   four] for K

145:10   chalet] chalêt K
145:17   chalet] chalêt K
148:9   indeed already] indeed, already K
149:42   "Attendez-moi,"] "Attendez moi," K
150:16   chalet,] chalêt, K
151:16   Subiaco,] Soubiaco, K
152:21   Subiaco] Soubiaco K

XII. THE DREAM

With many antecedents in John Keats's *The Eve of St. Agnes*, Mary Shelley's "The Dream" has a heroine who is uncertain about human love, who is separated from her lover by a family feud, and who employs a superstitious religious ritual in order to determine the future object of her love. Like Keats's Madeline who awakes from St. Agnes's Eve to be united with the real Porphyro, Mary Shelley's Constance awakes from her night on St. Catherine's couch to choose human over divine love. "The Dream" might lack the concentered intensity and patterned imagery of Keats's poem, but it is no unworthy imitation. Mary Shelley idealized the circumstances of her story by means of Constance's internal monologue, "Do not all things love" (p. 161), which is a paraphrase of Percy Shelley's lyric "Love's Philosophy," where "All things by a law divine / In one spirit meet and mingle." Constance's initial rejection of this law of love is even more apparent in the fair-copy MS, which, like that of "The Brother and Sister," had to be changed to accommodate the plate accompanying the story. In this case, Constance originally preferred night to day and her own darkened room to the "lighter shews of nature—her darkened casements, her black hung rooms, were more in unison with her feelings than the flowering earth and laughing sky." But when faced with the plate of Constance in a bower where Gaspar is about to intrude during the late afternoon, Mary Shelley had to rewrite the scene. In so doing, she changed both character and structure: Constance, encountering Gaspar during the day in a setting reminding her of past love, seems less likely to resist Gaspar's suit than she did at night in her "black hung rooms"; and the natural beauty of the bower less effectively prepares the reader for the events on St. Catherine's couch than did the original scene, where "silence and darkness rendered the scene about [Constance] congenial" to her depressed spirits. The reader may reconstruct the MS narrative from the collation below; the present editor chose the first printing as his copy-text, but prefers the original version. Above quotations from MS are by permission of The Carl H. Pforzheimer Library.

Manuscript—"The Dream," a 25-page fair-copy holograph in the collection of The Carl H. Pforzheimer Library, New York, New York.

1) "The Dream," *The Keepsake for MDCCCXXXII*, ed. Frederic Mansel Reynolds (London: Longman, Rees, Orme, Brown, and Green [1831]), pp. 22–38. ["the Author of Frankenstein"; with plate entitled "Constance," painted by Miss L. Sharpe and engraved by Charles Heath; Table of Contents lists "The Dream, a Tale."]

2) "The Dream," *Leaflets of Memory: An Annual for MDCCCXLVI*, ed. Reynell Coates (Philadelphia: E. H. Butler & Co., 1846), pp. 197–217. ["the Author of Frankenstein."]

3) "The Dream," *Friendship's Offering: A Christmas, New-Year, and Birthday Present, for MDCCCLV* (Philadelphia: E. H. Butler & Co., 1855), pp. 306–28. ["the Author of Frankenstein."]

4) "The Dream," *Tales and Stories* (1891; rpt. 1975), pp. 66–82.

5) "The Dream," *Gothic Tales of Terror: Classic Horror Stories from Great Britain, Europe and the United States 1765–1840*, ed. Peter Haining (New York: Taplinger Publishing Company, 1972), pp. 287–300. ["Mary Wollstonecraft Shelley."]

6) "The Dream," *Gothic Tales of Terror, Volume One: Classic Horror Stories from Great Britain*, ed. Peter Haining (Baltimore: Penguin Books, 1973), pp. 327–42. ["Mary Wollstonecraft Shelley."]

[Copy-text: *Keepsake* for 1832: K; manuscript readings, designated by MS, are offered when emendations have been made to K or when MS substantially differs from K. Quotations below from MS are by permission of The Carl H. Pforzheimer Library.]

153:10   Catholics] catholics K; Catholics MS

155:11   weeping. Mistress] weeping. The gloomy winter was yielding to the sweet influence of spring—but Constance abhorred the lighter shews of nature—her darkened casements, her black hung rooms, were more in unison with her feelings than the flowering earth and laughing sky—night was dearer to her than day.—Mistress MS

155:19–   Constance had . . . ancient trees."] "And even this and life is grudged
156:40   to me," such was the hapless mourner's reverie, when she had received intimation of King Henry's visit—"I ask but to dwell in my father's halls—in the spot familiar to my infancy—To water with my frequent tears a spot ah! how hallowed to my miserable heart—and smiless and alone to wear away a life which surely will soon end. But no; I am driven to a cloister or to the altar—better wed death than any other than——"

It was the midnight of the eve of Henry's arrival—and Constance, instead of seeking her couch, was roaming through the lofty halls of her Castle—too pleased to wake and watch during night—when silence and darkness rendered the scene about her congenial to her spirit. She paced hastily the paved apartments—or she leant against the high casement and looked out upon the night—the waning moon was struggling among huge dark-winged clouds—The trees moaned and swung in the gale, which rushed and roared round the Castle walls—and then, as one thought pressed on her, the Lady sank on her knees—covered her streaming eyes with her hands, and breathed a prayer—to forget.

Was that a step? she rose—her heart beat high—all was still—then again—it must be that silly Manon, with her impertinent entreaties for her to go to rest.—But the step was not a woman's Beyond the hall in which the young Countess kept her vigils, was a suite of huge dim apartments—while another door opened on a corridor that led to the other parts of the Chateau—by the corridor her attendant would approach—but that step came from the most distant room of the suite. Fear for a moment blanched her cheek—the door that led to the apartments was half open, admitting sound—concealing all view—and now the steps which had been continuous and approaching—faltered—once the intruder seemed to turn back—now he was close to the half open door—"What can you fear Constance," said the trembling girl to herself—"while I can bear one thought, and the agony it brings, can any other ill occasion fear? Peace, my heart, return to thy accustomed woe, and be not so despicable in trifles as to leap at any new emotion.—"

Thought is swift, and as the Countess schooled herself thus—still the intruder loitered and the moon emerging from a cloud cast his shadow through the aperture of the door on to the pavement of the hall, in which

Constance stood. Now indeed she trembled, shook as an aspen in the stormy north—the Visitant threw back the door, and she would have sunk to the ground, but that she was supported by the buttress against which she leaned. Starting on beholding her, the unbidden guest at first hurried forward—then as she waved him away with her hand, he sunk on his knee saying—"Constance—hear me!"—

"No—no—" cried she, vehemently—"I must not—will not;—my vow is registered above,—begone! how came you here?"

"That needs no reply," replied her visitor, sadly. "You taught me how to enter these deserted rooms, when love was young, and you were kind."— MS

157:3–6   when evening . . . of love."] When night brought me to your feet, and while hate and vengeance was as its atmosphere to this Castle, our hearts were the shrine of love." MS

157:19–20 when daylight . . . and here,] when storms raged, and for worlds I would not have exposed your dear head to their fury, I scaled yon window—your fair hands unclasped the bars, and in innocence and joy—here, MS

157:36   Christian] christian K; Christian MS

157:38–40 the bower: . . . she gave] the room; with swift steps, she sought her apartment—she barred its door and then throwing herself upon its floor, she gave MS

158:1   Suddenly a thought] Suddenly as she lay there, a thought MS

158:2   She called] She rose and called MS

158:9   woe] wo K; woe MS

158:14   to-morrow."] tomorrow, that is this very day—for Matins is ringing even now." MS

158:18   to-morrow night] this night MS

158:22–23 worst." ¶The] worst."—— ¶And now morning peered through the casement; and with those calmer feelings which are the result of any determined plan however wild that plan be, Constance watched the dawn and offered up her orisons with all the devotion and all the earnestness, which when heavenly faith and earthly love unite, are apt to animate us in our prayers. ¶The MS

158:37   memory] night MS

159:2   countess'] countess's K; Countess's MS

159:13   gate. Henry] gate. She was dressed in deep mourning, but Henry MS

159:29   nonce,"] novice," K; nonce," MS

159:35   evening] night MS

163:24   woe] wo K; woe MS

164:23   Many a vision, she said, she] "Many a vision," she said, "she K; Many a vision, she said she MS

164:28   days—till suddenly] days, was as a mariner on a wide shoreless sea—while night and day visit him, yet shew him no port of refuge—Till suddenly MS

164:37   bones.] bones." K; bones"— MS

XIII. THE BROTHER AND SISTER: AN ITALIAN STORY

Although the casual reader might judge this story to be a pretty romance where love reconciles feuding families, "The Brother and Sister" offers a sophisticated study of a young girl's idealization of her brother. As Mary Shelley describes the relationship, Lorenzo "was a part of [Flora's] religion; reverence and love for him had been moulded into the substance of her soul from infancy. . . . her patience, her fortitude, and her obedience, were all offerings at the shrine of her beloved Lorenzo's desires." Such a reverence on Flora's part is reinforced by the religious diction employed in the story and by Flora being termed an "angel." Mary Shelley's intent is further understood by means of the fair-copy MS, in which "Angeline" served as both the title of the story and the name of the heroine; and from which several lengthy passages, emphasizing Angeline/Flora's idealization of her brother, were deleted before publication in *The Keepsake* (see textual notes below). The title and heroine's name were changed to accommodate the accompanying plate entitled "Flora," and the passages were probably deleted because of the editor's restrictions on length. But Mary Shelley seems to have regretted these alterations, for she reemphasized the angelic nature of Angeline/Flora by introducing into the story a companion named "Angeline" to assist the heroine in her "pilgrimage" to her brother. All of these alterations were made between July 1832 (when the MS was sent to Frederic Mansel Reynolds, editor of *The Keepsake*) and November 1832 (when *The Keepsake* was published). This 34-page MS lacks a final sheet that apparently was not sent to Reynolds, because in a letter to him on 2 August 1832 Mary Shelley complained that "there wanted a page of my story in the proof—I should like to have corrected that also—as it was the *last* & the most likely to be incorrect in the manuscript" (*MSL*, II: 62–63).

Manuscript—"Angeline," a 34-page fair-copy holograph in the Robert H. Taylor Collection, Princeton, New Jersey. The MS itself was folded and posted in at least three sections to the editor of *The Keepsake*: pp. 18, 26, and 34 bear the address ("F. Mansel Reynolds Esq / 48 Warren St. Fitzroy Sq / London"); p. 18 bears the London evening duty stamp of 5 July 1832; pp. 26 and 34, that of 7 July 1832.

1) "The Brother and Sister, An Italian Story," *The Keepsake for MDCCCXXXIII*, ed. Frederic Mansel Reynolds (London: Longman, Rees, Orme, Brown, Green, and Longman [1832]), pp. 105–41. ["the Author of Frankenstein"; with plate entitled "Flora," drawn by Miss L. Sharpe and engraved by F. Engleheart.]

2) "The Brother and Sister: An Italian Story," *Match-Making, and Other Tales* (Philadelphia: E. L. Carey & A. Hart, 1832), II: 179–216. ["the Author of Frankenstein."]

3) "Le Frère et la Sœur," *Le Salmigondis: Contes de toutes les couleurs* (Paris: H. Fournier Jeune, Libraire, 1832), III: 159–219. ["Mistress Shelley."]

4) "The Brother and Sister: An Italian Story," *Tales and Stories* (1891; rpt. 1975), pp. 227–61.

[Copy-text: *Keepsake* for 1833: K; manuscript readings, designated by MS, are offered when emendations have been made to K or when MS substantially differs from K.]

166:4	Capelletti] Ciapelletti K, MS
169:31	de' Tolomei] dei Tolomei K; de' Tolomei MS
170:15	Flora] Flora K; Angeline MS; *the same change from* Angeline *in* MS *to* Flora *in* K *was made in all subsequent references*
170:32–34	superhuman. ¶ Two] superhuman. It was impossible indeed to know Lorenzo and not to love him—he was spirited yet gentle. full of lofty aspiration, but devoid of envy and baser passions, he rejoiced in the excellences of his foe, as making him a worthier rival. His education he derived wholly from his own resources and there was a grace, a decision, and a majesty in all that he did, which no master could impart. Intelligent and persevering—the glassy rectitude of his mind knew no flaw,

and his courage was unflinching. These qualities, if they made no outward shew—yet were painted in the texture of his soul, and outweighed the glittering accomplishments of others, as the coloring of Guido and Raphael transcends in worth barbaric gilding. He was moreover blessed with a sanguineness of disposition which made him place strong reliance on providence and await with calm but cheerful fortitude the coming of the impending [?] hour when his fortunes should change. ¶Two MS

172:27   recognized] recognised K; recognized MS

173:27–28   vow in the interim. They had] vow until that period should have expired. He hoped to provide for her safe and honorable treatment—and he trusted to come and relieve her from any thing painful in her position before the time he fixed—after that was gone by if he came not—"But now they had MS

175:33–34   injuries. ¶The] injuries. Lorenzo was no longer the dear associate of her happy hours—he was an outcast and a wanderer upon earth. Often she figured him to herself wounded, neglected, dying; and his pale image haunting dreams, made her daily trials appear trivial in her eyes; she felt perfectly satisfied when at her frame [?] she could withdraw from every eye, and wrapping herself up in her woes, preserve sacred from observation, her sighs and tears. ¶The MS

175:36   dependants] dependents K; dependants MS

178:38–   To repay . . . of him.] She was unlike any girl the old woman had ever
179:1   known—superior to their foibles and follies, she seemed of another species, while her extreme piety excited the dame's unequivocal respect. How could Angeline be other than devout? She lived only for heaven and her brother—that dear brother, whom she could only communicate with in prayers—Where did he now now wander? This was the question for ever alive in her mind while the lapse of time made her yet more anxious for the answer still denied. Three years were flown since he had left her—and except a little gold cross, brought to her by a pilgrim for Milan, but one month after his departure, she had received no tidings of him. The five years to which he had extended her hope were not gone—but still she knew that he meditated a far more speedy return— and it was only to cheer her at the worst, that he had named so distant a period. Had he prospered in his career she felt assured that he would not have left her a day beneath the roof of their enemy. Her thoughts were wholly occupied at all times by imaginings on this subject.—To repay the kindness of her entertainers, she still devoted much time to her needle. She was working a large piece of tapestry to adorn the Countess's favorite apartment—and besides, on her own account, she was employed on alter piece she had vowed to the Madonna, on the return of her brother. This occupation but engaged half her attention, and as she plied her needle, she could give herself up to endless reverie on the subject of Lorenzo's fortunes. MS

179:11–12   absence. ¶Sometimes] absence. She pictured a thousand disasters: wounds, illness, imprisonment—far wanderings in distant and savage lands among infidels. She lived in this fanciful creation; and while these meditations exalted her to gladness or depressed her with grief—while thus her mind was conversant only with images of victorious daring, generous intrepidity and virtuous fortitude, no wonder that the beings and things around her grew trivial in her eyes, and that she rejoiced in

her seclusion, which shut out all but Nature and her own imagination.
¶Sometimes MS

179:17–18   countess, a sharp,] countess—her mind being at the Greek Emperor's
court in Constantinople, whither she had led her brother to receive,
after innumerable hardships, the reward of his glorious toils, when suddenly a sharp MS

180:3   recognized] recognised K; recognized MS

181:33–35   He . . . hands] This had at once retarded and assisted her recovery: for
while she was near he felt so tranquil in spirit, so happy beyond happiness—that his body receiving benign influence from his soul's calm—
acquired strength and health. But in her absence, his annoyance and
impatience was doubled by the consciousness, that these disturbing emotions were the swift shooting fibres of a passion, which he was resolved
should not take root within him—Irritated by the anticipation of an internal combat—and miserable at her absence, he vented his impatience
in violence towards others—till on her reappearance all disquietude again
vanished—and he wondered where his pain had flown—so impossible
was it for him to revive even the recollection in her presence. He had
returned to Sienna resolved to forget her—and the Elysium, to which
she could with a word conduct him—& which without her was for ever
shut against him. The endeavour was too much for him in his weak
state—and he came back to her, feeling assured that his life and death
were in her hands. MS

182:28–29   disgust. ¶The] disgust. Poor Angeline! She was not aware that where
she was, a Paradise bloomed for Fabian—and that where she was not,
so drear and stormy a darkness brooded—that worlds would not have
tempted him to encounter its horror. ¶The MS

184:32   despite herself,] despite of herself, K; despite herself, MS

185:14–22   Lorenzo. She . . . Here] Lorenzo. Towards evening she wandered into
the wood contiguous to the villa to take leave of a spot dear to her. Here
MS; *the character of the companion Angeline was introduced into the*
story after the MS was submitted and after the heroine's name was
changed from Angeline to Flora

185:36–42   At . . . Flora was] At this moment the chords of an harp struck her ear.
Fabian was unable to bring himself to depart on his journey without
seeing her once again. He had ridden over to the villa—and unwilling
to intrude on her sorrows, had announced his presence by those sweet
sounds, which spoke so feelingly affection and regret. She was MS

186:22   shewed] showed K; shewed MS

186:36–37   and with . . . attired] and attired MS

186:40–43   Then she . . . her pilgrimage] *not in MS*

188:8   drawn way. Yet] drawn pilgrimage, which now it seemed to her would
never end Yet MS

189:16–17   indeed Flora. ¶"These] indeed Angeline—little could he recognize his
little sister in the lovely women that knelt before him ¶"These MS

189:23–39   true thing . . . for us."] *a sheet of MS with these two and a half para-*
graphs is missing from the fair copy

189:27   town——"] town—— K

XIV. THE INVISIBLE GIRL

Unlike the narrator of "The Swiss Peasant," the first-person narrator of "The Invisible Girl" is relatively functionless. His "slender narrative" and "slight sketch" could just as effectively have been rendered from the third-person point of view, and Mary Shelley seems to use him as an excuse for a story in which little attention is given, in the narrator's own words, to "the development of situations and feelings." That lack of development is most visible when Mary Shelley apologizes for not writing "a good-sized volume to relate the causes which had changed the once happy Vernon into the most woeful mourner that ever clung to the outer trappings of grief." The good-natured reader will accept her apology and be grateful that the story is no longer than it is.

    1) "The Invisible Girl," *The Keepsake for MDCCCXXXIII*, ed. Frederic Mansel Reynolds (London: Longman, Rees, Orme, Brown, Green, and Longman [1832]), pp. 210–27. ["the Author of Frankenstein"; with plate entitled "Rosina," painted by W. Boxall and engraved by J. C. Edwards; Table of Contents lists "The Invisible Girl, a Tale."]

    2) "The Invisible Girl," *Match-Making, and Other Tales* (Philadelphia: E. L. Carey & A. Hart, 1832), II: 33–50. ["the Author of Frankenstein."]

    3) "The Invisible Girl," *The Keepsake: A Gift for the Holidays* (New York: John C. Riker, 1854), pp. 146–66. ["the Author of 'Frankenstein' "; with untitled plate (the same as in #1 above), entitled "The Invisible Girl" in List of Illustrations.]

    4) "The Invisible Girl," *Tales and Stories* (1891; rpt. 1975), pp. 210–26.

[Copy-text: *Keepsake* for 1833: K.]
195:13   woeful] woful K
196:4   *tête-à-tête*] *tête-à-tête* K
197:18 "infamous seductress,"] infamous seductress, K

XV. THE SMUGGLER AND HIS FAMILY

Jane Harding, orphaned, impoverished, and then widowed, is a typical heroine in Mary Shelley's short fiction. But because "The Smuggler and His Family" was submitted to *Original Compositions*, a volume published in 1833 "for the benefit of a family in reduced circumstances" (editor's note on dedication page), it appears that Mary Shelley was using her story to instruct the family in the disastrous effects of crime and the eventual triumph of virtuous and responsible love between mother and son. The story also has some biographical significance in that Jane Harding's maternal affection for her son Charles reproduces the author's protective love for her own son Percy Florence. Like her heroine, Mary Shelley feared that the "merciless" sea, which killed her husband, might also claim her only son.

    1) "The Smuggler and His Family," *Original Compositions in Prose and Verse, Illustrated with Lithographic Drawings; to Which Is Added Some Instrumental Music* (London: Edmund Lloyd, 1833), pp. 27–53. [Table of Contents lists "Mrs. Shelley" as author of story; with plate illuminating final scene ("Struggling with wind and water . . ."), drawn on stone by L. Haghe and used as frontispiece for *Original Compositions*.]

[Copy-text: *Original Compositions*: OC; continuous left-margin quotation marks for dialogue have been silently eliminated.]
208:9   were] was OC
214:31 post office:] Post Office: OC

XVI. THE MORTAL IMMORTAL: A TALE

The name "Winzy" might suggest that the protagonist of this story is a comic character; but the Scottish word "winze" means curse and is here used to emphasize the tragic curse of eternal life suffered by the Mortal Immortal. And by portraying Bertha as a ridiculous coquette who deserves the embarrassment she experiences, Mary Shelley insures that the reader's sympathy will be reserved for Winzy. His histrionics at the end of this first-person narrative may seem laughable, but again such action follows logically from his desire for purpose either in life or in death. As in the cases of *Frankenstein* and the less well-known tales of Valerius and Roger Dodsworth, two mortals who cheat death through their reanimation, the author uses a supernatural action as a mere device to introduce a study in character. But it is the idea of an *elixir vitae* rather than the portrayal of Winzy's loneliness which has made "The Mortal Immortal" the most frequently anthologized of Mary Shelley's stories.

Manuscript—"The Mortal Immortal: A Tale," a 36-page fair-copy holograph in the collection of The Houghton Library, Harvard University, Cambridge, Massachusetts. The MS itself was folded and posted from Harrow to the editor of *The Keepsake*: p. 35 is blank and p. 36 bears the address ("F. Mansel Reynolds Esq / 48 Warren St. / Fitzroy Sq"), the Twopenny Post receiving house stamp from Harrow, and the London main office stamp of 7 p.m., 29 July 1833.

1) "The Mortal Immortal: A Tale," *The Keepsake for MDCCCXXXIV*, ed. Frederic Mansel Reynolds (London: Longman, Rees, Orme, Brown, Green, and Longman [1833]), pp. 71–87. ["the Author of Frankenstein"; with plate entitled "Bertha," painted by H. Briggs and engraved by F. Bacon.]

2) "The Mortal Immortal," *The Casquet of Literature: Being a Selection of Prose and Poetry from the Works of the Most Admired Authors*, ed. Charles Gibbon and Mary Elizabeth Christie (London: Blackie & Son, n.d.), III: 369–75. ["Mary Wollstonecraft Shelley."] Although I have not seen it, a 1873 edition of this volume (with "The Mortal Immortal" appearing in III: 353–59) is recorded by Jean de Palacio, *Mary Shelley dans son œuvre: Contribution aux études shelleyennes* (Paris: Klincksieck, 1969), p. 675.

3) "The Mortal Immortal," *The Library of Choice Literature and Encyclopædia of Universal Authorship: The Masterpieces of the Standard Writers of All Nations and All Time*, ed. Ainsworth R. Spofford and Charles Gibbon (Philadelphia: Gebbie & Co., 1890), III: 353–59. ["Mary Wollstonecraft Shelley."]

4) "The Mortal Immortal," *Tales and Stories* (1891; rpt. 1975), pp. 148–64.

5) *The Mortal Immortal*, Issued by Mossant, Vallon & Co., n.d. ["Mary W. Shelly" (sic); the text occupies 24 pages in this unpaginated brochure owned by Sam Moskowitz and believed by him to have been published between 1880 and 1910.]

6) "The Mortal Immortal," *Great Short Stories of Detection, Mystery and Horror*, Second Series, ed. Dorothy L. Sayers (London: Victor Gollancz, 1931), pp. 1080–92. ["Mary Wollstonecraft Shelley."]

7) "The Mortal Immortal," *A Century of Thrillers: From Poe to Arlen*, with a Foreword by James Agate (London: Daily Express Publications, 1934), pp. 167–80. ["Mary Shelley."]

8) "The Mortal Immortal," *Century of Thrillers* (New York: President Press, 1937), III: 94–106. ["Mary Shelley."]

9) "The Mortal Immortal," *Masterpieces of Science Fiction*, ed. Sam Moskowitz (Cleveland, Ohio: The World Publishing Company, 1966; rpt. Westport, Connecticut: Hyperion Press, 1974), pp. 44–59. ["Mary Wollstonecraft Shelley."]

10) "Ms. Found in an Oxygen Bottle," *The Magazine of Fantasy and Science Fiction* (December 1973), pp. 88–100. ["Gary Jennings and Mary Wollstonecraft Shelley"; this story by Jennings details the further adventures of the Mortal Immortal and incorporates substantial portions of Mary Shelley's original tale.]

[Copy-text: *Keepsake* for 1834: K; manuscript readings, designated MS, are offered when emendations have been made to K.]

221:42   eyed] eyes K; eyes MS
227:25   gray] grey K; grey MS
228:42   bought] brought K; bought MS
229:20   star] stone K; star MS
230:10   place] places K; places MS

XVII. THE TRIAL OF LOVE

In "The Brother and Sister," Mary Shelley had been denied using the name of Angeline, but in "The Trial of Love" she chose it again for her "angelic" protagonist. The name is apt in that Angeline's love was both pure and constant, a love that was to be satisfied only when she dedicated herself to heaven and took "the veil in the convent of Sant' Anna." The reader should be pleased with the plotting of "The Trial of Love," which shares with "The False Rhyme" and "The Bride of Modern Italy" a unity of action within a relatively short period of time (excepting the "two or three years" used in the final two paragraphs to determine the consequences of the action); and instead of a radical alteration or reformation in character by which a happy ending is achieved, the constant Angeline, the capricious Faustina, and the inconstant Ippolito act in character throughout the narrative, the latter two receiving their just deserts in an unhappy marriage, which proves that marital love can indeed be a "trial."

Manuscript—"The Trial of Love," a 40-page fair-copy holograph in the collection of The Carl H. Pforzheimer Library, New York, New York.

1) "The Trial of Love," *The Keepsake for MDCCCXXXV*, ed. Frederic Mansel Reynolds (London: Longman, Rees, Orme, Brown, Green, and Longman [1834]), pp. 70–86. ["the Author of Frankenstein"; with plate entitled "The Letter," drawn by J. M. Wright and engraved by C. Heath.]
    2) "Angeline and Faustina; or, The Trial of Love," *The Coronet; or, Choice Gems for the Home Circle* (Philadelphia: J. B. Lippincott & Co., n.d.), pp. 157–79. [Published anonymously; with untitled plate, entitled "The Trial of Love" in List of Illustrations.]
    3) "The Trial of Love," *A Cabinet of Gems: Short Stories from the English Annuals*, ed. Bradford Allen Booth (Berkeley: University of California Press, 1938), pp. 140–58. ["Mary Shelley."]

[Copy-text: *Keepsake* for 1835: K; manuscript readings, designated by MS, are offered when emendations have been made to K. Quotations below from MS are by permission of The Carl H. Pforzheimer Library.]

232:39   years'] years K; years MS
238:41   that is] that, is K; that is MS
243:29   how any] how, any K; how any MS

XVIII. THE ELDER SON

Published in *Heath's Book of Beauty*, edited by Lady Blessington and destined for the more fashionable readers of English society, "The Elder Son" differs in certain respects from the stories written for *The Keepsake*, where supernatural events, impoverished orphans, and foreign or historical settings abound. In this story, the contemporary heroine has a dowry of £50,000, and the plot turns on the entailing of English estates to elder sons. Nevertheless, the traditional elements of Mary Shelley's short narratives are here represented: Ellen is an orphan who idealizes her father; she survives her naiivté and the machinations of her false lover, Vernon; she succeeds in marrying Clinton; and in the process, she converts her father-in-law to a more respectable life. As in many of the stories in the Annuals, the engraved plate for "The Elder Son" is artificially linked to the narrative; and in this case, Ellen the narrator directly refers the reader to "the portrait accompanying this tale."

1) "The Elder Son," *Heath's Book of Beauty*, 1835, ed. The Countess of Blessington (London: Longman, Rees, Orme, Brown, Green, and Longman [1834]), pp. 83–123. ["Mrs. Shelley"; with plate entitled "Ellen," painted by H. Wyatt and engraved by H. Robinson.]

2) "The Elder Son," *Tales and Stories* (1891; rpt. 1975), pp. 328–58.

[Copy-text: *Heath's Book of Beauty* for 1835: BB.]
261:24   uncontrollable] uncontrolable BB

XIX. THE PARVENUE

Like Winzy in "The Mortal Immortal" and the monster in *Frankenstein*, the despairing narrator of this story seeks a sympathetic judgment from the reader. But "The Parvenue" replaces the Gothic trappings of these other supernatural stories with a naturalistic description of contemporary society. Fanny, by her marriage and her principles, discovers herself alienated from the self-seeking and greedy poor as well as from the indifferent and selfish rich. And she concludes her restrained and controlled narrative by suggesting that she will soon end her life as a suicide. For a discussion of the biographical antecedents in this story, see Burton R. Pollin, "Mary Shelley as the Parvenue," *A Review of English Literature* 8, No. 3 (July 1967): 9–21. Pollin, however, mistakenly conjectured that Mary Shelley purposefully incorporated descriptions of her own trips abroad and to Margate in this narrative: according to him, Fanny's "two years abroad" with Lord Reginald was probably "more amply treated before being abridged to fit the requirements of the editor" (p. 12); and her trip to Margate "enabled the editor to commission one of the costly engravings for which the annual was famous" (p. 13). But the fair-copy MS of "The Parvenue," which Pollin did not see, invalidates his points: no additional description of Europe was offered; and Mary appears to have introduced Margate into her fair copy because she had been told that "Margate" was the title of the plate which would accompany the story. Only after seeing the plate did Mary, probably in proof, add the specific description of the "troubled waters" and the ship without "any canvas except a topsail" (see collation below).

Manuscript—"The Parvenue," a 16-page fair-copy holograph in the collection of The Houghton Library, Harvard University, Cambridge, Massachusetts.

1) "The Parvenue," *The Keepsake for MDCCCXXXVII*, ed. The Lady Emmeline Stuart Wortley (London: Longman, Rees, Orme, Brown, Green, and Longman

[1836]), pp. 209–21. ["Mrs. Shelley"; with plate entitled "Margate," drawn by A. G. Vickers and engraved by R. Brandard.]

2) "The Parvenue," *The Amaranth; or, Token of Remembrance: A Christmas and New Year's Gift for MDCCCXLVIII* (Boston: N. C. Barton, 1848), pp. 262–78. ["Mrs. Shelley."]

3) "The Parvenue," *The Remember Me; A Token of Love, for 1855* (Philadelphia: Henry F. Anners, 1854), pp. 15–31. ["Mrs. Shelley."]

4) "The Parvenue," *Tales and Stories* (1891; rpt. 1975), pp. 262–73.

5) "The Parvenue," *Great English Short Stories*, ed. Lewis Melville and Reginald Hargreaves (New York: The Viking Press, 1930), pp. 220–28. ["Mary Shelley."]

[Copy-text: *Keepsake* for 1837: K; manuscript readings, designated by MS, are offered when emendations have been made to K or when MS substantially differs from K.]

266:23	half-sisters] half sisters K; half sisters MS
266:25	half-brothers] half brothers K; half brothers MS
267:15–19	Above all . . . were poorer.] not in MS
267:16	fellow-creature,] fellow creature, K
267:43–268:1	he who . . . and wealth,] not in MS
268:28	well-disposed,] well disposed, K; well disposed MS
268:37	white-headed] white headed K; white headed MS
268:39	anticipating long . . . grateful Fanny;] not in MS
269:1	We had . . . dreadful evils;] not in MS
269:14	so] as K; so MS
269:16–17	and above . . . a time] not in MS
269:27	hearth and . . . piety, was] hearth, and . . . piety was K; hearth, was MS
270:8	acceded] acceeded K; acceded MS
270:41	half-brothers] half brothers K; half brothers MS
271:24–32	The summer . . . a refusal.] I paced them day after day—I waited for my husband's answer with anguish—it brought a refusal. MS
271:42	sands; he . . . his disgrace.] sands, he . . . his disgrace; K; sands he . . . his disgrace— MS
273:17	sister. I] sister, I K; sister—I MS
273:40	Heaven] heaven K; heaven MS
274:10	profiting] profitting K; profiting MS

XX. THE PILGRIMS

"The Pilgrims," like all other stories in *The Keepsake* for 1838, was published anonymously, and no external evidence presently exists by which to confirm that Mary Shelley was the author. In his advertisement, the editor of the volume noted that "nearly *all* the most eminent of its former contributors still devote their talents to its pages," and in 1891 Richard Garnett included "The Pilgrims" in his edition of Mary Shelley's stories. Although Garnett possibly had access to a letter or MS by which to determine her authorship, it is equally possible that he merely made a reasonable guess. Nevertheless, on Garnett's authority, the present editor includes "The Pilgrims" in this collection. The setting of the story is not typical, but the coincidental and elongated plot, the forlorn and orphaned protagonists, and the contrived happy ending all have antecedents in Mary Shelley's short fiction.

1) "The Pilgrims," *The Keepsake for MDCCCXXXVIII* (London: Longman, Orme, Brown, Green, and Longmans [1837]), pp. 128–55. [Published anonymously;

with plate entitled "Walter and Ida," drawn by Edward Corbould and engraved by Stodart.]

2) "The Pilgrims: A Tale of Chivalry," *The Snow-Flake: A Christmas, New-Year, and Birthday Gift, for MDCCCLII* (Philadelphia: E. H. Butler & Co., 1852), pp. 49–87. [Published anonymously.]

3) "The Pilgrims," *Tales and Stories* (1891; rpt. 1975), pp. 359–86.

[Copy-text: *Keepsake* for 1838: K.]
276:5   "If] If K
277:30   which the protection,] which, the protection K
281:22   gate] grate K
281:33   lived:] lived: K
282:43   Unspunnen;] Unsprunnen; K
286:4   Burkhardt, "at] Burkhardt," at K
289:18   wanderer."] wanderer. K

XXI. EUPHRASIA: A TALE OF GREECE

Mary Shelley frequently employed a frame tale to begin her narratives, but she did not always return the reader to the circumstances of the outer frame. Such an incongruity is most apparent in "Euphrasia: A Tale of Greece," where a Sussex snowstorm in 1836 occasions Harry Valency's tale which also contains Constantine's tale of Euphrasia (which means, ironically, "well-told"). The reader is fully informed of Euphrasia's and Constantine's deaths and of Valency's recovery, but he never learns if Valency survived the Sussex snowdrifts. Were it not for an extant fair-copy MS, the present editor might have speculated that limitations of space forced the editor of *The Keepsake* to eliminate the concluding paragraphs that explained what happened to the travellers from Brighton. Although the MS permits no such hypothesis, it does resolve the question raised, for the first-person narrator of the entire story was originally "the third of this anxious party" awaiting rescue (rather than, in the printed text, merely one who had heard the story "second-hand"—a rather feeble device designed as a further excuse for the narrator's "vague recollection of dates and names of places, and even some of those of persons"). In the MS, the original narrator in the Sussex frame had asked Valency what "the events were that marked that long, unforgotten night" and then observed: "I wish to repeat his tale—yet I shall tell it lamely, for on our arrival at Lewes that night, Valency instead of proceeding with us, for some cause I now forget continued his way to London, and we have never met since. Hearing his narration only once, on the occasion I mention, no wonder that my recollection is vague—that dates & names of places & even persons have entirely escaped me. however such portion as remains in my memory I will set down." The existence of this snow-bound auditor and narrator helps to explain but not redeem the awkward shift in point of view in the last three paragraphs of the story.

Manuscript—"Euphrasia: A Tale of Greece," a 32-page fair-copy holograph in the collection of The Houghton Library, Harvard University, Cambridge, Massachusetts.

1) "Euphrasia: A Tale of Greece," *The Keepsake for MDCCCXXXIX*, ed. Frederic Mansel Reynolds (London: Longman, Orme, Brown, Green, and Longmans [1838]), pp. 135–52. ["Mrs. Shelley"; with plate entitled "Constantine and Euphrasia," drawn by Edward Corbould and engraved by H. Robinson.]

2) "Euphrasia: A Tale of Greece," *Leaflets of Memory: An Illuminated Annual*

for MDCCCXLVII, ed. Reynell Coates (Philadelphia: E. H. Butler & Co., 1847), pp. 243–64. ["Mrs. Shelley."]

3) "The Brother: A Tale of Greece," *The Keepsake: A Gift for the Holidays* (New York: J. C. Riker, 1851), pp. 126–46. ["Mrs. Shelley"; with untitled plate (same as in #1 above), entitled "The Brother" in List of Illustrations.]

4) "Euphrasia: A Tale of Greece," *Tales and Stories* (1891; rpt. 1975), pp. 311–27. [This reprinting omits the six introductory paragraphs to the story.]

[Copy-text: *Keepsake* for 1839: K; manuscript readings, designated by MS, are offered when emendations have been made to K.]

296:2	whence] when K; when MS
296:23	lamely,] tamely, K; lamely, MS
296:26–27	*in neither K nor MS was there a line spacing between these paragraphs*
297:18	caracole.] caricole. K; caricole. MS
297:36	well-founded,] well founded, K; *the clause,* for it was known to be well-founded, and to spring from a recent disaster, *is not in MS*
298:7	was] were K; were MS
299:23	moon-beam] moon beam K; moon beam MS
300:6	pallor] palor K; pallor MS
300:19	mêlée,] melée, K; melée MS
300:30	drooped.] dropped. K; drooped; MS
302:17	loveliness,] lovliness, K; loveliness MS
302:33	revered] reverend K; revered MS
304:23	Panagia,] Panargia, K; Panargia MS
306:13	leapt] lept K; leapt MS
306:21	lightning] lightening K; lightening MS

XXII. THE HEIR OF MONDOLFO

"The Heir of Mondolfo" was not published until 1877, when it appeared in *Appletons' Journal* (New York) with the following prefatory note: "This posthumous story by Mrs. Shelley has not before appeared in print. It was found among the unpublished papers of Leigh Hunt, and is authenticated by S. R. Townshend Mayer, Esq., editor of *St. James's Magazine*, London." The MS of this story is now owned by Professor Kenneth Brooks and is presently housed in the Keats House, London; and the present editor believes that the 1877 printing was based on this MS, where, for example, "royal," "unmined," "their roar," and "kisses" (all in MS) were misprinted in 1877 as "regal," "unsunned," "there was," and "hopes"; or where infelicitous repetitions were changed (e.g., "afterwards after" in MS became "subsequently, after" in 1877). The MS itself is the combined result of at least three different periods of writing: Mary Shelley's fair-copy hand occupies all of the first three pages, the final page, and five intervening pages—in each case Ludovico is written as the hero's name; but the remainder of the MS is occupied by a larger and more hastily written hand where the hero is alternately named Lionel, Lucian, and Julian before being canceled for Ludovico. Although Mary Shelley may have intended to make a complete fair copy from this MS, she possibly submitted it in this state to Leigh Hunt for his judgment. The state of the MS, the rejected names of Lionel and Julian (with their antecedents in Percy Shelley's poetry), and the story's inordinate length (relative to the little action of the plot)—all suggest that "The Heir of Mondolfo" was written before the mid 1820s: i.e., before Mary Shelley began writing for the Annuals where restrictions of space disciplined her art to a greater extent.

Manuscript—"The Heir of Mondolfo," a 97-page holograph in the collection of Kenneth Brooks and housed in the Keats House, London.

1) "The Heir of Mondolfo," *Appletons' Journal: A Monthly Miscellany of Popular Literature*, n.s. 2 (January 1877): 12–23. ["Mary Wollstonecraft Shelley, Author of 'Frankenstein,' etc."]

2) "The Heir of Mondolfo," *Seven Masterpieces of Gothic Horror*, ed. Robert Donald Spector (New York: Bantam Books, 1963), pp. 331–61. ["Mary Shelley."]

[Copy-text: MS.]

308:18	and the weary] and weary MS
308:19	life to a] life a MS
308:23–24	of his ambitious] of ambitious MS
308:27	prince.] Count. MS
309:3	and] an MS
310:24	nor] or MS
311:12	were] was MS
312:22	stopped] stopt MS
312:26	were] was MS
312:33	and] an MS
314:43	asked Nature] asked the Nature MS
315:10–11	climes seem] climes & seem MS
315:42	to the happiness] to happiness MS
316:20	way.] was. MS
316:21	oblige him to] oblige to MS
316:23	snapped] snapt MS
317:2	rung] rang MS
317:38	and a priest] & priest MS
318:14	passed,] past MS
318:21	aversion would] aversion for would MS
319:28	ghastly,] ghasttily— MS
320:6	Santa Chiara."] St. Claire." MS; Santa Chiara *is the reading in a subsequent reference in the* MS
320:18	up and] upon & MS
320:22–23	constricted] conricted[?] MS
320:27	passed] past MS
321:15–16	and the mind] and mind MS
321:17	love from his] love his MS
321:37	passed,] past MS
322:8	passed.] past MS
323:22	put into] put it into MS
323:36	passed.] past— MS
324:41	that they would] that would MS
325:18	window, her] window that her MS
325:25	passed;] past MS
325:32	sounds] sound MS
325:32	for with] & with MS
326:7	were] was MS
326:14	with her from] with from MS
326:34	its depth] it depth MS
327:8	nor] or MS
327:33	Ludovico,] Lionel MS

328:2	called] called called MS
328:6	The most . . . inhabit] *in the* MS, The most benevolent of spirits inhabit *is written above* God indeed seemed to reign over[?], *but the latter phrase, rejected here, is not canceled*
328:33	might have been] *in the* MS, bore the happearance[?] *is written above* might have been, *but the latter phrase, retained here, is not canceled*
329:26	news] new MS
330:29	trappings,] trapping, MS
331:1	starred] stared MS

XXIII. VALERIUS: THE REANIMATED ROMAN

In this story of *sic transit gloria mundi* presented in exaggerated terms, readers of Mary Shelley will discover yet another of her narratives based on a supernatural event. Yet her interest was less on the fact of reanimation (nowhere is it explained) and more on Valerius's reactions to his new existence. As he explained to his English auditor, he chose to relate neither the history of his life nor the actions of the great men during the fall of the Roman republic; instead, he related what he "felt and saw" upon revisiting Rome nearly nineteen hundred years after his death. Mary's descriptions of the Coliseum and the Pantheon are based on her own visits to them in the spring of 1819 (e.g., on 19 March, she recorded in her journal: "Visit the Pantheon. Visit it again by moonlight, and see the yellow rays fall through the roof upon the floor of the Temple. Visit the Coliseum" [*MSJ*, p. 117]). As both Elizabeth Nitchie (ed. of Mary Shelley's *Mathilda* [Chapel Hill: University of North Carolina Press, 1959], p. 103) and Jean de Palacio (*Mary Shelley dans son œuvre: Contribution aux études shelleyennes* [Paris: Klincksieck, 1969], pp. 189n–190n) argue, this story was probably written in 1819. And by 1826, when Mary wrote her narrative essay on the reanimated Roger Dodsworth, she explained that she had "often made conjectures how such and such heroes of antiquity would act, if they were reborn in these times."

Manuscript—an untitled 62-page holograph in the collection of Lord Abinger (Microfilm reel #11, Abinger Collection, Duke University Library, Durham, North Carolina).

[Copy-text: MS.]

332:3	Miseno . . . Bauli.] Mycæne . . . Baulis. MS
332:4	its] it MS
332:7	bright causing] bright & causing MS
333:16	nor] or MS
333:21	Sulla] Scylla MS
333:34	Sulla] Scylla MS
334:24	altars!] alters! MS
334:36	insane] *conjectural reading of word written through and canceling internal in MS*
335:6	surrounded] surround MS
335:9–10	Vaccino—] Vaccina— MS
335:17	in a spot] in spot MS
335:19	lost] lossed MS
335:24	'That is the] That the MS
335:25	Vespasian,] Titus, MS; *in a subsequent reference to the builder of the Coliseum,* Titus *is canceled and replaced by* Vespasian

335:33   Vaccino,] Vacino, MS
335:42   Its fallen] It fallen MS
336:15   consuls . . . end,] cosuls & triumphs wer at at end— MS
336:29   Sulla] Scylla MS
336:42   became the] were the MS
336:43   were as] where as MS
337:18   not a train] not not a train MS
337:32   passed] past MS
337:33   the moon's rays,] its rays MS
338:3–4   in a strange] in strange MS
338:11, 13   Harley] —— MS
338:33   teach me to] teach to MS
339:13–14   shall have frequent] shall frequent MS
339:22   Miseno] Myceno MS
340:2   to it had been snapped] to to it had been snapt MS
340:4   ruins which] ruins of which MS
340:14   said to him:] said him— MS
340:41   lose] loose MS
340:42   surrounded] surround MS
341:10   buttress is] butress it is MS
341:40   resides] resided MS
342:23–34   The spirit . . . both silent.] *although uncanceled on pp. 50–52 of the MS, this passage seems intended for replacement by the following insert written on pp. 54–56:* and their polished surfaces slightly reflected the light which streamed down in the midst of them. It seemed as if the senseless stones possessed human feeling and enjoyed the the visitation of loveliness which hallowed them. There was that tranquillity in the scene which while all is silent fills the mind with busy thoughts—One feels as if one had a new life infused the limbs repose but the soul is agitated agitated even to pain while at the same time it enjoys the greatest felicity of which it is capable—The occasions are few in the course of one's life when the mind is permitted this enjoyment which leaves it languid & fainting—but here I was animated and gay he was depressed—but his sorrow in some degree modified me
342:36–39   in contemplation . . . the soul.] *this passage is conjecturally added to p. 52 of the MS from an insert written on p. 56*
343:7   snapped.] snapt MS
343:22   were] was MS
343:34   there] their MS

XXIV. AN EIGHTEENTH-CENTURY TALE: A FRAGMENT

This fragment is characteristic of Mary Shelley's use of a scenic frame by which to enclose a retrospective narrative. It was written before 1824: not only does the holograph MS share the same Abinger notebook with the story of Valerius (?1819); it also duplicates and appears to be the source of some of the introductory narrative description in the author's "Recollections of Italy," published in the *London Magazine* in January 1824. In both "Recollections" and this fragment, the author assumes an ironic preference for England over Italy. Whether the tale of Maria Graham was finished and published, I have been unable to determine.

Manuscript—an untitled and fragmentary 6-page holograph in the collection of Lord
   Abinger (Microfilm reel #11, Abinger Collection, Duke University Library, Durham, North Carolina).

[Copy-text: MS.]

345:6   grassy] glassy MS
345:26   with.] with them— MS
345:29   proposition] prosition MS
346:1   past] passed MS
346:11   begged] begging MS
346:20-29   "That my story . . .] *this last paragraph is canceled in MS*
346:29   fashionable . . ."] fashiona MS

XXV. THE POLE

"The Pole" was published under the name of "the Author of 'Frankenstein' " in both
The Court Magazine (1832) and *The English Annual* (1836), it was reprinted as
Mary Shelley's in Richard Garnett's *Tales and Stories* (1891), and it has been discussed as Mary Shelley's story in Joanna Russ's introduction to the recent reprinting
of *Tales and Stories* (1975). Despite this "evidence," however, "The Pole" was
mostly written by Claire Clairmont, as Bradford A. Booth demonstrated nearly forty
years ago ("The Pole: A Story by Clare Clairmont?" *Journal of English Literary History* 5 [1938]: 67–70). Additional proof of Claire's authorship may be found in her
MS leaflet containing a short description of the Bay of Baia that is used in "The
Pole" (see *The Journals of Claire Clairmont*, ed. Marion Kingston Stocking [Cam-
bridge: Harvard University Press, 1968], p. 438; and Stocking's unpublished doctoral
thesis, "Claire Clairmont: A Biographical and Critical Study" [Duke University,
1952], p. 264). In arguing their cases, both Booth and Stocking quote Claire's letter
of 24 March 1832 to Mary Shelley in which Claire announced she would forward
her story "about a Pole" and asked Mary to "correct it," to "write the last scene of
it," and to submit it to *The Keepsake* under the signature "Mont. Obscur." It is
impossible to determine to what extent Mary corrected and finished the story, and
the present editor prints it in this collection for purposes of availability and inclusive-
ness. Both Booth and Stocking have conjectured that Mary wrote only the final melo-
dramatic scene in which Giorgio, "a figure all bloody," exposes the deceit of Princess
Dashkhoff, but other additions or revisions may have been made, especially if Mary
made a fair copy of Claire's MS. For example, to the scene in which Idalie sketches
the portrait of Ladislas (a circumstance Claire introduced because she hoped to publish "The Pole" in *The Keepsake*, where stories were accompanied by engraved
plates), Mary Shelley probably added the two sentences: "I know not if the portrait
was finished. I believe it was not." This revision would have been necessary if the
original MS had directed the reader to an accompanying plate of Ladislas, which was
not used in *The Court Magazine*. "The Pole" was probably not submitted to *The
Keepsake*, because its editor had already accepted two of Mary Shelley's stories ("The
Brother and Sister" and "The Invisible Girl") for publication in November 1832; and
it was probably submitted elsewhere under the name of "the Author of 'Frankenstein' " in order to increase the chances for publication and, at the same time, preserve
the anonymity Claire desired.

   1) "The Pole," *The Court Magazine, and Belle Assemblée*, 1 (August and September 1832): 64–71, 129–36. ["the Author of 'Frankenstein.' "]

   2) "The Pole," *The English Annual, for MDCCCXXXVI* (London: Edward
Churton, 1836), pp. 32–74. ["the Author of 'Frankenstein.' "]

3) "The Pole," *Tales and Stories* (1891; rpt. 1975), pp. 274–310.
4) "The Pole," *A Cabinet of Gems: Short Stories from the English Annuals,* ed. Bradford Allen Booth (Berkeley: University of California Press, 1938), pp. 159–97. ["Claire Clairmont."]

[Copy-text: *Court Magazine*: CM.]

348:11	"Ja pozwalam,"] "Ya paswalam, CM
348:11	"Pay] Pay CM
349:17	orange-trees] orange trees CM
350:27	*opéra,*] *opera,* CM
350:29	*verissimo,"*] *verissimo,,"* CM
350:40	sup."] sup. CM
353:12–13	brown (the . . . sun),] brown, (the . . . sun,) CM
354:7–8	protégée] protegée CM
354:22	ecstacy,] exstacy, CM
355:1	Posillipo—] Posylippo— CM
356:8	yours] your's CM
356:22	Princess's] Princess' CM
356:27	Giorgio,] Giorgo, CM
358:30	Cumaean] Cumean CM
359:8	Morning] 'Morning CM
361:18	Pæstum.] Pœstum. CM; *in all subsequent references,* Pœstum *has been emended to* Pæstum
362:8	devoted] dovoted CM
367:19	protégée.] protegée. CM
367:30	any thing,] anything, CM
369:27	Wieprecht] Weipert CM
370:33	moon,] morn, CM
371:8	moon] morn CM
371:13	moonlight.] mornlight. CM
371:17	moonbeams] mornbeams CM
371:43	caleche] calêche CM

THE JOHNS HOPKINS UNIVERSITY PRESS

This book was composed in Linotype Fairfield text and Bernhard Cursive display type by the Maryland Linotype Composition Co., Inc., from a design by Susan Bishop. It was printed on 50-lb. Publishers Eggshell Wove and bound in Joanna Arrestox cloth by Universal Lithographers, Inc.

Library of Congress Cataloging in Publication Data

Shelley, Mary Wollstonecraft Godwin, 1797–1851.
   Collected tales and stories.

PZ3.S545Co3 [PR5397] 823'.7 75–36931
ISBN 0–8018–1706–4